# Language
# Arts
# Essentials

# Language Arts Essentials

## Gail E. Tompkins

California State University, Fresno

PEARSON

Merrill
Prentice Hall

Upper Saddle River, New Jersey
Columbus, Ohio

Library of Congress Cataloging in Publication Data

Tompkins, Gail E.
   Language arts essentials / Gail E. Tompkins.—1st ed.
      p. cm.
   Includes bibliographical references and index.
   ISBN 0-13-172006-6
   1. Language arts (Elementary)—United States. I. Title.

LB1576.L656 2006
372.6—dc22                                   2005053543

**Vice President and Executive Publisher:** Jeffery W. Johnston
**Senior Editor:** Linda Ashe Montgomery Bishop
**Senior Development Editor:** Hope Madden
**Senior Production Editor:** Mary M. Irvin
**Design Coordinator:** Diane C. Lorenzo
**Senior Editorial Assistant:** Laura Weaver
**Text Design:** Kristina Holmes
**Cover Designer:** Terry Rohrbach

**Cover Images:** Laurence Martin and
Linda Bronson
**Photo Coordinator:** Lori Whitley
**Production Manager:** Pamela D. Bennett
**Director of Marketing:** Ann Castel Davis
**Marketing Manager:** Darcy Betts Prybella
**Marketing Coordinator:** Brian Mounts

This book was set in Garamond by Carlisle Communications, Ltd. It was printed and bound by Courier Kendallville, Inc. The cover was printed by Phoenix Color Corp.

**Photo Credits:** © Jose Luis Pelaez, Inc./Corbis: 2–3; David Mager/Pearson Learning Photo Studio: 3 (bottom), 32, 80 (center), 147 (bottom); Anthony Magnacca/Merrill: 2 (top), 80 (left); Bob Daemmrich/The Image Works: 2 (center); Scott Cunningham/Merrill: 2 (left), 36, 114 (top), 146–147; Getty Images—Photodisc: 3 (top), 39 (top); Gail E. Tompkins: 11–14, 15–18, 19–22, 23–26, 114 (center), 124, 146 (center); Jonathan Nourok/PhotoEdit: 38–39; EyeWire Collection/Getty Images—Photodisc: 39 (bottom); Laura Bolesta/Merrill: 38 (top), 59 (bottom); Mary Kate Denny/PhotoEdit: 38 (center); Anne Vega/Merrill: 38 (left); © LWA-Dann Tardif/Corbis: 58–59, 81 (bottom); Patrick White/Merrill: 58 (top), 80 (left); Tom Watson/Merrill: 58 (center), 66, 80 (top); Michael Newman/PhotoEdit: 58 (left); Digital Stock: 59 (top), 115 (top); Getty Images: 81 (top); ThinkStockLLC/Index Stock Imagery, Inc.: 114–115; Pearson Learning Photo Studio: 115 (bottom); Tony Freeman PhotoEdit: 114 (left); Will Hart/PhotoEdit: 146 (top); Cynthia Cassidy/Merrill: 146 (left); Comstock: 147 (top).

**Credits: Page 5,** excerpts from *Shiloh:* Reprinted with the permission of Atheneum Books for Young Readers, an imprint of Simon & Schuster Children's Publishing Division, from SHILOH by Phyllis Reynolds Naylor. Copyright © Phyllis Reynolds Naylor. **Page 141:** Excerpts from ANASTASIA KRUPNIK by Lois Lowry. Copyright © 1979 by Lois Lowry. Reprinted by permission of Houghton Mifflin Company. All rights reserved. **Page 166:** Excerpt from AUNT FLOSSIE'S HATS (AND CRAB CAKES LATER) by Elizabeth Fitzgerald Howard. Text copyright © 1991 by Elizabeth Fitzgerald Howard. Reprinted by permission of Clarion Books, an imprint of Houghton Mifflin Company. All rights reserved. **Page 166:** Excerpt from *Sylvester and the Magic Pebble:* Reprinted with the permission of Simon & Schuster Books for Young Readers, an Imprint of Simon & Schuster Children's Publishing Division, from SYLVESTER AND THE MAGIC PEBBLE by William Steig. Copyright © 1969 William Steig.

Some content—artifacts and feature boxes—is based on content in *Language Arts: Patterns of Practice,* Sixth Edition, by Gail E. Tompkins, Copyright © 2005 by Pearson Education.

Pearson Education Ltd.
Pearson Education Singapore Pte. Ltd.
Pearson Education Canada, Ltd.
Pearson Education—Japan

Pearson Education Australia Pty. Limited
Pearson Education North Asia Ltd.
Pearson Educación de Mexico, S.A. de C.V.
Pearson Education Malaysia Pte. Ltd.

10 9 8 7 6 5 4 3 2
ISBN: 0–13–172006–6

# About the Text

Welcome to *Language Arts Essentials*! As you flip through this text, you'll see that it's different from other textbooks. At first glance, the colorful photos and graphics may catch your eye, but then I hope you'll notice the text's concise presentation of information and quick and easy resources to help you with lesson planning. I hope you will also see how this text has been developed to provide you the absolute essentials to teach the six language arts effectively. And I hope you'll be able to use this textbook as you teach to give you the confidence and tools to develop successful language arts lessons.

**What are the essentials in teaching language arts?**

There are six language arts—listening, talking, reading, writing, viewing, and visually representing. Your responsibilities as a teacher are to know what you're expected to teach about each language art, and how to teach each language art effectively.

The teachers I work with are situated in the reality of today's classrooms. To help you envision how to use the language arts strategies and resources I present in this text, I describe the work of some very fine teachers and the way they considerately meet the needs of students in their culturally and linguistically diverse classrooms. The instructional choices they make reflect federal legislation and state standards, and they are all about balance—integrating strategies to balance literacy experiences for their students. For example, in the Classroom Close-Ups at the beginning of each book part, you'll read about how kindergarten through eighth-grade teachers have mastered the integration of language arts teaching with the teaching of literacy and other curriculum needs.

**How is the text organized?**

I've divided this text into six parts:

- Teaching Language Arts Today
- Listening
- Talking
- Reading
- Writing
- Language Tools

Information about the four traditional language arts—listening, talking, reading, and writing—is presented in separate book parts. Material about the two new "visual" language arts—viewing and visually representing—is woven throughout the text. In the last book part, I present information about vocabulary, grammar, and spelling—the tools you will help your students learn how to use so they might communicate and "learn to learn" successfully.

Within each book part, there are six sections:

- **Introduction.** You'll read a brief overview introducing the big ideas about each of the language arts and its role in teaching and learning.

- **Classroom Close-Up.** You'll explore real-life classrooms where experienced teachers utilize the language arts concepts they have learned.

- **Essentials.** You'll read about the nuts and bolts of language arts practice that's supported by current and classic research.

- **Strategies.** You'll find accessible language arts strategies that are most important for your students' success in learning to communicate effectively, and most helpful for your lesson planning. Especially useful are the sample minilessons that will direct you in teaching some skills and many critical strategies.

- **Classroom Practice.** You'll discover innovative ways to teach the language arts. Specific ideas for using stories, informational books, and poetry are included. You will also find practical guidance for assessing your students' learning.

- **Review.** You'll review the big ideas presented in each book part and reflect on ways to examine your own instructional practices.

**How do you teach language arts?**

If you have been teaching for a while or even if you are new to teaching, you realize that teaching is not as simple as opening a textbook and following the directions in the teacher's guidebook. Instead, teachers use their knowledge about how children learn and about language arts content to create an instructional program that incorporates as many available and enriching resources as possible, such as high-quality children's literature. To help you plan your instructional program, be sure to examine these featured text materials:

- Coverage of *four instructional approaches* and photo essays of *authentic teacher experiences* depicted using these approaches, all located in Part 1
- Specific coverage of *language arts strategies* and how to teach them
- *Minilessons* to use when teaching specific strategies
- *Theory to Practice features* identifying critical elements of language arts practice
- *Step-by-step directions* for implementing the instructional procedures discussed in the text

- *Assessment ideas* in the *A* Is for Authentic Assessment section in each part
- Suggestions for developing *classroom inquiry projects* at the end of each book part

**What about English learners?**

Classrooms are increasingly diverse today, and many teachers are working with children who are learning to speak English at the same time they're learning to read and write. You might be surprised to learn that teachers all over the country have English learners in their classrooms. It's crucial, then, that teachers know how to scaffold English learners so they can be successful. That's why features throughout the text—Scaffolding English Learners—describe ways to teach academic English and adjust instruction to support every student's learning.

**Why cover just the essentials?**

The "essentials" format gives you the information you need in a price- and time-conscious way. Whether you are learning or reviewing language arts methods as part of a college course or you are personally revisiting the newest, most proven strategies to further your professional development, I'm confident that *Language Arts Essentials* will provide you with the needed theoretical information and teaching strategies to help you be successful.

**How does the content of *Language Arts Essentials* align with the content of *Literacy for the 21st Century, 4e*?**

I wrote this new text, *Language Arts Essentials,* immediately after completing the revision of the fourth edition of *Literacy for the 21st Century.* This put me in a unique place to carefully consider what information I could and should share in this new text to explain how the development of language arts skills and strategies complement learning to read and write—without duplicating textual information. This was a wonderful and challenging opportunity for me. It forced me to reexamine carefully everything I have learned over the years and everything I have ever written about research and practice and share it with you in new ways. This is a new book, one that I think shares my best work with you. *Language Arts Essentials* offers you critical and pivotal ideas for integrating language arts and reading instruction. I have written this book just for you. I hope you are wildly successful.

**What supplements are available with this text for course work?**

Several carefully conceived supplemental materials are available to assist you or your professor in enriching your experience with this text:

**Companion Website:** This robust online support system offers many rich and meaningful ways to deepen and expand the information presented to you in the text.

- *Chapter Objectives* provide a useful advance organizer for each chapter's online companion.

- *Meeting the standards* a three-part module delivering IRA/NCTE Standards integration through chapter correlations, immediate links to all major federal and state standards, and adaptable, standards-driven minilessons. These minilessons provide tools to take right into the classroom that align with national as well as state standards.
- *Self-Assessments* help users gauge their understanding of text concepts.
- *Web Links* provide useful connections to all standards and many other valuable online literacy sources.

**Electronic Instructor's Manual:** This useful tool for instructors provides rich instructional support:

- A test bank of multiple choice and essay tests.
- PowerPoints specifically designed for each chapter.
- Chapter-by-chapter materials, including chapter objectives, suggested readings, discussion questions, and in-class activities.

You'll find this valuable resource at *www.prenhall.com*, available to adopting professors with an access code. Simply click on the Instructor Support button and then go to the Download Supplements section. Here you will be able to log in or complete a one-time registration for a user name and password. Or enter the eIM ISBN 0131720082 in the search field.

**CD ROM:** *Writing Workshop* (ISBN 0-13-117590-4). Adopting professors can package this CD with this text, or you can order the supplement on its own. Experience the effective instruction that takes place in classroom communities by analyzing video footage of master teachers who integrate minilessons and strategy and skill development in the use of writing workshops.

**Acknowledgments**

Creating *Language Arts Essentials* has been a team project, and I am grateful to everyone on Jeff Johnston's remarkable team at Merrill who enthusiastically embraced this mission.

First, I want to thank Linda Montgomery, my acquisitions editor, for enticing me with this book venture and giving me the latitude to invent this text. Thanks, too, for ensuring that my vision of an engaging, reader-friendly text became a reality. My development editor, Hope Madden, is my taskmaster, nudging me toward impossible deadlines. All taskmasters should have your spirit! Your ability to cultivate my writing never ceases to amaze me. Thanks, too, to Laura Weaver, who's always willing to assist in so many ways.

I love the vibrant, contemporary look that design coordinator Diane Lorenzo and text and cover designer Kristina Holmes created for this book. You've surpassed my expectations! I'm indebted to production manager Pam Bennett, who worked behind the scenes to remove roadblocks and smooth the production process. My production editor, Mary Irvin, is a marvel! Thank you for cheerfully taking on this project even though the design features and text layout undoubtedly required extra effort. You've moved this book through production with your usual thoroughness and efficiency. Melissa Gruzs, my copyeditor and proofreader, has become an indispensable member of the production team. I appreciate your dogged attention to detail, and since we've been working together, you've taught me to be a more careful writer. And, I applaud senior marketing manager Darcy Betts Prybella for her brilliant marketing ideas to reach the language arts market with *Language Arts Essentials* and my other texts.

I'm privileged to work with very talented teachers. I want to express my sincere appreciation to the teachers profiled in this text: Jennifer Miller-McColm, Manuel Hernandez, Susan Zumwalt, Carol Ochs, Sandy Harris, and Mike Martinez. Thanks for welcoming me into your classrooms. I learned as I watched you and worked side-by-side with you and your stu-

dents. The students whose photos and work samples appear in this book deserve special recognition. The text seems "real" because of you.

Thanks, too, to quiltmaker Laurence Martin and artist Linda Bronson, whose dynamic work is featured on the cover and inside this text. Your talent enriches my words.

Finally, I want to acknowledge the professors who carefully reviewed my manuscript, asked thoughtful questions, and offered many useful suggestions: Debra Price, Sam Houston State University; Carolyn Jaynes, California State University, Sacramento; Bonnie Armbruster, University of Illinois, Urbana-Champaign; Cindy Wilson, Southwest Missouri State University; and Ula Manzo, California State University, Fullerton. Thank you. This text is more effective now because of your efforts.

# About the Author

I am a teacher, first and foremost. I began my career as a first-grade teacher in Virginia in the 1970s. During my first year of teaching, I used the famous "Dick and Jane" basal reading series, but soon after began using trade books to teach reading and writing. I remember one first grader who cried as the first day of school was ending. When I tried to comfort him, he sobbed accusingly, "I came to first grade to learn to read and write and you forgot to teach me." The next day, I taught that child and his classmates to read and write! We made small books about one of our classroom stuffed animals, a dog named Tom. I wrote some of the words and the students supplied the others, and I made copies of the book for each child. We practiced reading it until everyone memorized our little book about Tom. The children then took their books home to read to their parents. I've never forgotten that child's comment and what it taught me: Teachers must understand their students and meet their expectations. Every year after that, my first graders made books on the first day of school because I knew they came to first grade to learn to read and write.

My first year of teaching left me with more questions than answers, but I knew I wanted to become a better teacher. While I kept teaching, I started taking graduate courses in the evening. In time I earned a master's degree, and then a doctorate in Reading/Language Arts, both from Virginia Tech. Through my graduate studies, I learned a lot of answers, but more important, I learned to keep on asking questions.

Then I began teaching at the university level. First, I taught at Miami University in Ohio, then at the University of Oklahoma, and finally at California State University, Fresno. At these universities, I've taught preservice teachers and practicing teachers working on master's degrees, and I've directed doctoral dissertations. Throughout the years, my students taught me as much as I taught them. I'm grateful to all of them for what I've learned.

I am currently the director of the San Joaquin Valley Writing Project in Fresno, and before that, I directed the Oklahoma Writing Project. It's another way I get to teach. I nurture teachers at summer invitational institutes and in inquiry groups, and I support them as they work with partnership schools and give presentations to groups of teachers. I strongly encourage you to locate the closest National Writing Project site and participate in the activities it sponsors. It's not only the best way to learn more about teaching writing, but you'll also make friends with a group of very committed and professional teachers.

I've been writing college textbooks in the areas of reading, writing, and language arts for 20 years, and I think of the books I write as teaching, too. I'll be teaching you as you read this text. As I write a book, I try to anticipate the questions you might ask and provide that information. I also include students' samples so you can see concepts that I'm explaining, and I include lists of trade books that you can refer to as you work with students.

I'm honored to have been able to teach. I am privileged to have received several awards for my teaching. In 2000, I was awarded the prestigious Provost's Award for Excellence in teaching at California State University, Fresno. I also received the Regents' Award for Superior Teaching when I taught at the University of Oklahoma, and in 1998, I was inducted into the California Reading Association's Reading Hall of Fame.

When I'm not teaching, I like to make quilts. Piecing together a quilt is a lot like piecing together the elements of good teaching, which is why I sometimes use quilt pieces on my book covers. Right now, I'm making a quilt for my newest granddaughter, Gillian.

# Contents

1 Teaching Language Arts Today

2 Listening

# PART 3
# **58 Talking**

# PART 4
# **80 Reading**

# PART 5
# 114 Writing

5
Writing

6 Language Tools

# PART 6
## 146 Language Tools

Note: Every effort has been made to provide accurate and current Internet information in this book. However, the Internet and information posted on it are constantly changing, so it is inevitable that some of the Internet addresses listed in this textbook will change.

# 1

# Teaching Language Arts Today

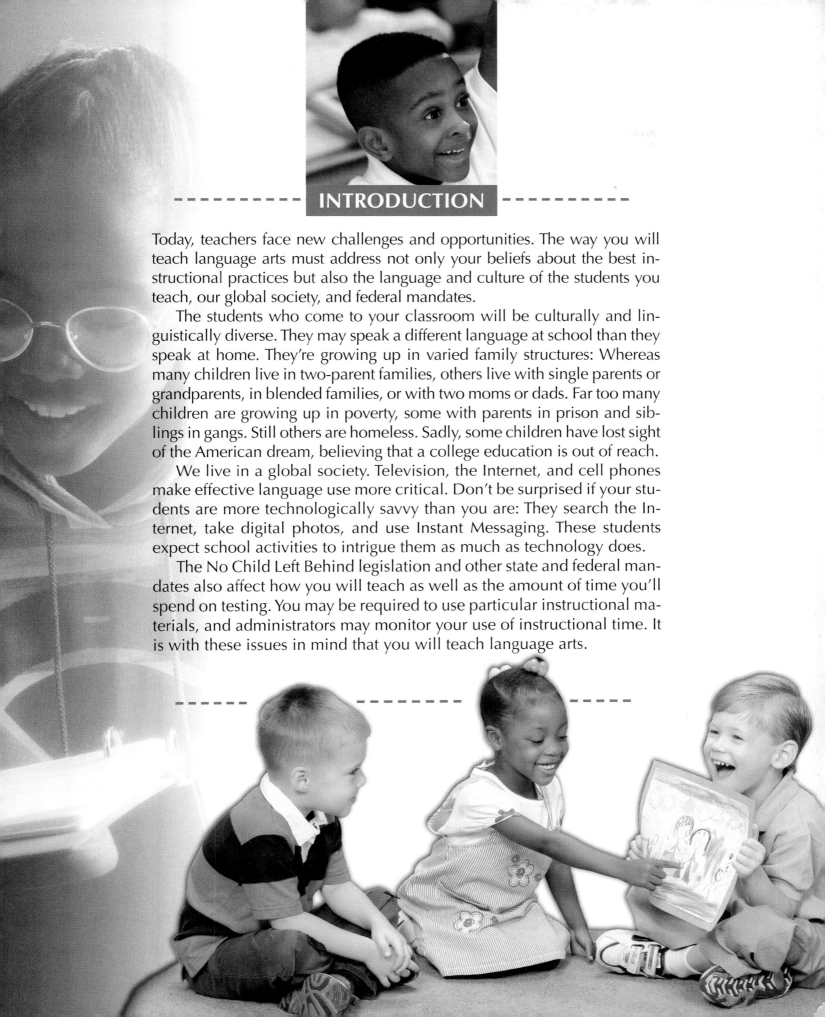

## INTRODUCTION

Today, teachers face new challenges and opportunities. The way you will teach language arts must address not only your beliefs about the best instructional practices but also the language and culture of the students you teach, our global society, and federal mandates.

The students who come to your classroom will be culturally and linguistically diverse. They may speak a different language at school than they speak at home. They're growing up in varied family structures: Whereas many children live in two-parent families, others live with single parents or grandparents, in blended families, or with two moms or dads. Far too many children are growing up in poverty, some with parents in prison and siblings in gangs. Still others are homeless. Sadly, some children have lost sight of the American dream, believing that a college education is out of reach.

We live in a global society. Television, the Internet, and cell phones make effective language use more critical. Don't be surprised if your students are more technologically savvy than you are: They search the Internet, take digital photos, and use Instant Messaging. These students expect school activities to intrigue them as much as technology does.

The No Child Left Behind legislation and other state and federal mandates also affect how you will teach as well as the amount of time you'll spend on testing. You may be required to use particular instructional materials, and administrators may monitor your use of instructional time. It is with these issues in mind that you will teach language arts.

# Classroom Close-Up

## Mrs. Miller-McColm Teaches Language Arts

Mrs. Miller-McColm teaches sixth grade in a low-income multicultural community. One way that her students show their affection for her is by calling her "Mrs. M." Most of her students speak Spanish at home and are learning English at school. Because many of them also are struggling readers and writers, Mrs. M adapts her instruction to meet these students' needs.

Mrs. M sits on her teacher's stool and picks up Natalie Babbitt's *Tuck Everlasting* (1988), the highly acclaimed story of a family who drinks from a magical spring and becomes immortal. "Yesterday, we stopped at Chapter 6," she says to her sixth graders. "Who remembers what was happening?" A sea of hands go up, and Mrs. M calls on Junior. "Winnie wanted to run away from home, but she got kidnapped by the Tucks. I don't know why, though," he says. Next, Isabel says, "I think she goes with the Tucks because she wants to. I think she wants an adventure, so she'll stay with them forever."

The students continue talking about the story for several minutes, and then Mrs. M begins reading aloud. She's a strong oral reader, and her students listen intently. After she reads the middle of page 34, she stops and asks, "Why does Mae Tuck say, 'We're not bad people, truly we're not. We had to bring you away—you'll see why in a minute—and we'll take you back just as soon as we can. Tomorrow. I promise'?"

Mrs. M asks the students to break into small groups to talk for several minutes about whether the Tucks are "bad" people for kidnapping Winnie and to speculate about why they abducted her. The students' desks are arranged in five groups, and the classmates in each group talk eagerly. After several minutes, the teacher brings the class back together to continue the discussion. "We don't think the Tucks are bad people," Noemi offers, "because bad people aren't nice, and Mae Tuck is. They must have a good reason for what they did." Donavon says, "They may be nice people, but we don't think Winnie will get free 'tomorrow.'" Iliana agrees: "Winnie won't get free until the book ends, and there are a lot of pages still to read."

After the students share their ideas, Mrs. M reads to the end of this chapter and continues reading the next chapter, where the Tucks explain to Winnie about their "changelessness" and why they abducted her. She finishes reading the last page of Chapter 7, puts the book down, and looks at the students. They look back at her, dazed; no one says a word.

To help the sixth graders sort out their ideas and feelings, Mrs. M asks them to quickwrite in their reading logs. The students write for about 5 minutes, and then they're ready to talk. Some students read their quickwrites aloud, and others just talk. Mrs. M asks, "Do you believe the Tucks? Are they telling the truth?" About half of the students think the Tucks are telling the truth; others aren't so sure. Next, she asks them to write again, this time about whether they believe the Tucks' story.

Mrs. M uses the novels she reads aloud to teach students about the structure of stories; for this book, her focus is on plot development. Yesterday, the students discovered the problem in this story—Winnie Foster is abducted by the Tucks. Mrs. M also has taught them about conflict situations. At this point in the story, the students think the conflict is between Winnie and the Tucks; later, they'll see that the conflict is within Winnie herself as she decides whether to stay with the Tucks forever.

The students create projects after reading each book. Usually they pursue different projects individually or in small groups, but after they finish reading *Tuck Everlasting*, everyone will write a persuasive essay. Mrs. M will ask students to think about the advantages and disadvantages of living forever, decide if they would want to live forever, and write persuasive essays detailing their choice.

Mrs. M spends the first hour of the language arts period teaching a literature focus unit using a book from her district's list of "core" literature selections. She reads the book aloud because about half of her students couldn't read it on their own. She already has read *Holes* (Sachar, 1998), *A Wrinkle in Time* (L'Engle, 1962), and *Julie of the Wolves* (George, 1972), and by the end of the school year, she will have read 11 or 12 novels.

Next, Mrs. M's students participate in book groups, another name for literature circles. Her students read at fourth- through eighth-grade levels, and she divides them into seven book groups according to reading level. Then students choose novels to read after their teacher gives book talks to introduce several choices for each group. Currently, students are reading these books:

*Stone Fox* (Gardiner, 1980) (level 4)
*Sarah, Plain and Tall* (MacLachlan, 1985) (level 4)

### How do teachers organize for instruction?

Teachers organize for language arts instruction in a variety of ways, often incorporating four instructional approaches—literature focus units, literature circles, reading and writing workshop, and thematic units. Some teachers also add mandated programs, such as basal readers, to their instructional plan. No matter which instructional approaches teachers use, they combine direct instruction, small-group activities, and opportunities for students to use the language arts independently in each day's plan. As you read this Classroom Close-Up, notice how Mrs. Miller-McColm incorporates all four instructional approaches in her language arts program.

*Shiloh* (Naylor, 1991) (level 5)
*Ralph the Mouse* (Cleary, 1993) (level 5)
*Maniac Magee* (Spinelli, 1990) (level 6)
*The BFG* (Dahl, 1982) (level 6)
*Harry Potter and the Goblet of Fire* (Rowling, 2002) (level 8)

Students meet with their groups to set reading schedules. They read during this period and at home and meet with Mrs. M for 20 minutes twice each week to talk about the book they're reading. They also create displays about the books on a bulletin board that is divided into eight sections. In one section, Mrs. M posts the directions for book groups, and each group takes responsibility for one of the other sections. For this round of book groups, the focus is on plot development. Each group creates a graphic display emphasizing the conflict situations in their novel.

Mrs. M meets with the group reading *Sarah, Plain and Tall*, a story about a mail-order bride in the early 1900s. She asks the students to summarize the story so far, and Gabrielle says, "A woman named Sarah is coming to stay at a farm. She might marry the dad and be a mom for the children, Anna and Caleb." "Has she arrived yet?" Mrs. M asks, and April responds, "She just arrived. She came on a train and everyone is very nervous." Then students make connections between the story and their own lives, the world around them, and other lit-

erature. Mrs. M helps them analyze the plot and identify the conflict situation, which is between Sarah and the other characters. The students decide to draw open-mind portraits of the characters to post in their section of the bulletin board. For their portraits, they will draw pictures of the characters and attach three sheets of paper behind the pictures where they will draw and write about the conflict each character feels at the beginning of the story, in the middle, and at the end.

Next, Mrs. M meets with the group reading *Shiloh*. These students have just finished reading this novel about a boy who sticks his neck out to save an abused dog. The students eagerly talk about the book, making connections to personal experiences and to other dog stories they've read. Mrs. M asks them to think more deeply about the story and rereads the last paragraph of the story aloud:

> I look at the dark closing in, sky getting more and more purple, and I'm thinking how nothing is as simple as you guess—not right or wrong, not Judd Travers, not even me or this dog I got here. But the good part is I saved Shiloh and opened my eyes some. Now that ain't bad for eleven. (p. 144)

She asks what Marty, the main character in the story, means when he says, "nothing is as simple as you guess . . . " Omar begins, "At first, Marty thought he was all good and Judd Travers was all bad,

## Other Book Sets for Literature Circles

| Reading Level | Books |
|---|---|
| 4 | Bruchac, J. (1997). *Eagle son.* New York: Dial Books.<br>Coerr, E. (1977). *Sadako and the thousand paper cranes.* New York: Putnam.<br>Dahl, R. (1980). *The twits.* New York: Puffin Books.<br>King–Smith, D. (1995). *The school mouse.* New York: Hyperion Books. |
| 5 | Creech, S. (1994). *Walk two moons.* New York: HarperCollins.<br>Paterson, K. (1996). *Jip, his story.* New York: Putnam.<br>Spinelli, J. (1996). *Crash.* New York: Knopf.<br>Taylor, M. D. (1995). *The well.* New York: Dial Books. |
| 6 | Anaya, R. (1999). *My land sings: Stories from the Rio Grande.* New York: HarperCollins.<br>Cooney, C. B. (2000). *Mummy.* New York: Scholastic.<br>Hesse, K. (1997). *Out of the dust.* New York: Scholastic.<br>Paterson, K. (1977). *Bridge to Terabithia.* New York: HarperCollins. |
| 7–8 | Barrett, T. (1999). *Anna of Byzantium.* New York: Delacorte.<br>Cormier, R. (1974). *The chocolate war.* New York: Random House.<br>Norton, M. (1980). *The borrowers.* Orlando: Harcourt Brace.<br>Taylor, M. D. (1976). *Roll of thunder, hear my cry.* New York: Viking. |

## Roles Students Assume in Literature Circles

**Director**
The director guides the group's discussion and keeps the group on task.

**Passage Master**
The passage master shares several memorable quotes with the group and explains why he or she chose each one.

**Word Wizard**
The word wizard identifies four to six important, unfamiliar words, checks their meaning in a dictionary, and shares the information about the words with group members.

**Connector**
The connector makes meaningful text-to-self, text-to-world, and text-to-text connections.

**Summarizer**
The summarizer prepares a brief summary of the reading to convey the big ideas to share with the group.

**Artist**
The artist draws a picture or diagram related to the book, and the group talks about it before the artist explains it.

but then Marty did something dishonest to get Shiloh. He didn't like doing bad things, but he did them for a good reason, so I think that's OK." The students continue talking about being responsible for their own actions, both good and bad. After the discussion ends, the teacher checks the group's section of the bulletin board, and the students make plans to finish it before the end of the week. The teacher also takes them over to the classroom library and introduces them to *Shiloh Season* (Naylor, 1996) and *Saving Shiloh* (Naylor, 1997), the second and third books in the Shiloh trilogy, and the students eagerly decide to read these two books next.

Students take a recess break, and afterward, Mrs. M teaches a word work lesson on suffixes, beginning with the word *changelessness* from *Tuck Everlasting*. She points out the two suffixes, *-less*, meaning "without," and *-ness*, meaning "state of being." The students talk about the word's meaning and how the suffixes affect the root word. Then the teacher presents a list of other words ending in *-less*, including *weightless, effortless,* and *careless*. The students talk about the meaning of each word and identify which ones can also take the suffix *-ness*, such as *weightlessness*. Then students use the last 10 minutes of the period to practice their spelling words with partners.

Mrs. M begins writing workshop with a 15-minute minilesson on a writing strategy or skill; today is the first in a series of three minilessons on writing narrative leads. She displays a chart of four techniques that writers use to hook their audience and explains each one:

- ◆ **Action.** The main character does something interesting.
- ◆ **Dialogue.** The main character says something interesting.
- ◆ **A thought or a question.** The main character shares something that he or she is thinking or asks a question.
- ◆ **A sound.** The author begins with an interesting sound related to the story.

She reads aloud the first sentence from *Chocolate Fever* (Smith, 1972), *Freaky Friday* (Rodgers, 1972), *The Sign of the Beaver* (Speare, 1983), *Stone Fox* (Gardiner, 1980), *The Breadwinner* (Ellis, 2000), and *Bridge to Terabithia* (Paterson, 1977), and the students identify the hook each author used. Tomorrow, the students will work together as a class to write sample leads using each technique, and on the third day, partners will write leads and share them with the class.

After the minilesson, the students write independently for 40 minutes. For the past month, they have been writing on self-selected topics; many are writing stories, but some students are writing poetry and informational books. Mrs. M has already announced that students should finish the pieces they are working on by Friday because beginning next week, they'll be using writing workshop time to write reports as part of their theme.

The students use the writing process when they write. Some are working independently at their desks, and others are meeting with small groups of classmates to revise their writing, conferencing with the teacher, or working with partners to proofread their writing. The four computers in the classroom are all occupied, too, as students word process their compositions and print out final copies. They place their final copies in a box on Mrs. M's desk, and she binds their compositions into books for them.

Mrs. M conferences with students as they are writing to monitor their progress, and after they turn in their final copies, she meets individually with them to assess their work. They evaluate both the quality of the composition and the student's use of the writing process. Students also reflect on their work and set goals for their next writing project.

During the last 5 minutes of writing workshop, students take turns sitting in the author's chair to read aloud their completed writings. The other students sit on the floor around the author's chair and listen attentively as their classmate reads. Ricky, who wants to be a race car driver, reads an informational book he's written about the Winston Cup Series. He's also included this year's schedule of races and a map of the United States showing where the tracks are. After he finishes reading, the students clap and then ask questions. Junior asks, "What does NASCAR stand for?" and Ricky explains that it is an acronym for the National Association for Stock Car Automobile Racing. Omar asks for more clarification about how the races are run, and Briana asks how winners of each race gain points. The students get so interested that they don't want to stop talking even though it is lunchtime!

In the afternoon, Mrs. M teaches alternating thematic units on social studies and science topics; currently, they are learning about ancient Egypt. The students are reading from a text set of books, Internet articles, and other materials and are making notes of important information about ancient Egypt in their learning logs. These logs are divided into sections on geography, culture, people and their work, government, religion, and history, and students take notes in the appropriate sections as they read. Mrs. M taught a series of minilessons on note taking at the beginning of the unit, and students have been applying what they learned as they read and take notes. For the first 30 minutes of the period, students finish reading text set materials and taking notes. As they work, the teacher circulates around the classroom for a final check that students have adequate notes in each section of their logs.

Next, Mrs. M brings the class together to talk about the reports they will write. She begins by asking them to brainstorm a list of the achievements of the ancient Egyptian civilization, including:

> the remarkable pyramids
> gods and goddesses
> how the Egyptians farmed near the Nile River
> the mummification process
> the hieroglyphic system of writing
> Egyptian women's make-up and jewelry

Then she explains that she wants students to choose one achievement that particularly interests them, continue to research it, and share what they learn in a report. They also will make an artifact to go with the report; if their topic is the Sphinx, for example, they would make a clay model of it. The students are excited; they eagerly choose topics and suggest artifacts they can make. Mrs. M distributes the rubric that students will use to self-assess their projects and that she will use to grade them, and they read it together. Then she passes around several reports and artifacts from last year; the students examine them and compare them to the rubric to better understand what their teacher wants them to do.

Over the next 3 weeks, students will create reports and artifacts, working during the writing workshop and the-

## Riley's Report on the Sphinx

### The Sphinx

The sphinx is one of the wonders of the world, and the only one still standing. It was carved from a huge piece of bedrock of the Giza plateau. So huge that the paws themselves are 50 feet long. The entire thing is a whopping 150 feet. Most people believe that it was ordered to be built by King Kafre during his reign. It lines right up with his pyramid, and the head looks a little like ancient pictures of him. Traces of paint can still be found on the head, little bits of red and yellow that show that the sphinx used to be bright and colorful. Over hundreds of years, the nose and beard have broken off. The nose was shot off by a Turkish army during a target-practice session. Recently, the sphinx has undergone a restoration put on by the Egyptians. The back paw and tail have been redone, stopping the fixing at a certain point so people could tell what part was built by ancient Egyptians and what has been redone.

In between the paws, there is something called a dream stela. There is a story from the 18 dynasty that's on this stela where Thutmosis IV fell asleep in between the front paws of the sphinx. He dreamed that the sphinx told him that if he dug the sphinx out of the sand that it was buried in at the time, then he would become king. As the story goes, he dug the carving out, and then became king. This was probably just a story made up to make Thutmosis IV out to look like he was destined for the throne, but enjoyably none the less.

I would love to be able to see the sphinx in person. After all this studying, I still believe that it would be much easier to comprehend its sheer mass in person.

matic unit periods, and Mrs. M will provide support and guidance as they work through minilessons, demonstrations, and conferences.

As you continue reading, think about how Mrs. Miller-McColm incorporates the topics being presented. Here are three questions to guide your reading:

- ◆ How did Mrs. Miller-McColm involve her students in each of the six language arts?
- ◆ What did Mrs. Miller-McColm do to meet the needs of her culturally diverse students?
- ◆ Which language arts strategies did Mrs. Miller-McColm's students show evidence of using?

## Ancient Egypt Project Rubric

REPORT

strong 5 4 3 2 1 weak — **(5)** circled

- ✓ Clear and effective communication of ideas
- ✓ Rich details and examples
- ✓ Mechanical correctness
- ✓ Bibliography with at least two references
- ✓ Rough draft with revisions and editing corrections

*Fascinating information in your report.*

VISUAL AID

5 4 3 2 1 — **(5)** circled

- ✓ Appealing
- ✓ Original
- ✓ Accurate
- ✓ Adds information to the report

*Cool PowerPoint presentation!*

ORAL PRESENTATION

5 4 3 2 1 — **(4)** circled

- ✓ Knowledgeable
- ✓ Interested in the topic
- ✓ Easy to hear and understand
- ✓ Good eye contact with the audience
- ___ Enthusiastic presentation style

*You're usually much more enthusiastic.*

SCORING

| 14–15 points | = A |
| 11–13 points | = B |
| 8–10 points | = C |
| 4–7 points | = D |
| 0–3 points | = F |

_____14_____

GRADE

(A) B C D F

# Essentials

## ESSENTIAL #1: The Six Language Arts

Traditionally, the language arts have been defined as the study of the four language processes: listening, talking, reading, and writing. Both children and adults use these four processes for communicating and learning. In 1996, however, the National Council of Teachers of English and the International Reading Association (1996) identified two new language arts—viewing and visually representing. These new language arts reflect the growing importance of nonprint texts in our global society and the need to expand children's appreciation of the power of visual ways to gather and share information (Ernst, 1993; Whitin, 1996).

The six language arts can be categorized in several ways. For example, listening and talking are oral processes, reading and writing are written processes, and viewing and visually representing are visual processes. Considered from a different viewpoint, listening, reading, and viewing are receptive in that the person doing the listening, reading, or viewing is receiving information. In contrast, talking, writing, and visually representing are productive because the person doing the talking,

### Categorizing the Language Arts

| | RECEPTIVE | PRODUCTIVE |
|---|---|---|
| **ORAL** | Listening | Talking |
| **WRITTEN** | Reading | Writing |
| **VISUAL** | Viewing | Visually Representing |

writing, or visually representing is producing information. These categorizations are important because they suggest certain implications for teaching the language arts:

- Reading and writing should be connected to enhance students' reading development.
- Students' reading development should be supported with the other two receptive language processes.
- Children should be encouraged to use talk and visually representing activities to support their writing development.
- The visual language processes should be used to support English learners' development of the oral and written language arts.

**Listening** The ability to listen effectively is essential for school success, but listening is often neglected because teachers assume that children already know how to listen. I present an alternative view in Part 2: Children need to learn to listen strategically to stories, informational books, and poetry.

**Talking** Children use talk to communicate and for learning. In Part 3, you'll read that sometimes the talk is exploratory, such as when children ask questions and share ideas about books they are reading and when they meet in writing groups to provide feedback about classmates' writing. At other times, the talk is more formal, such as when they present oral reports. Drama is an especially powerful talk application: Children understand stories better when they retell them using puppets and dramatize them.

**Reading** Reading often overshadows the other language arts and is the subject of entire books and university courses. In Part 4, the focus is on how to integrate reading with writing and the other language arts and how to use all six language arts to support students as they read stories, informational books, and poems.

**Writing** Beginning with Donald Graves's (1983, 1994) groundbreaking study of children's writing, this language art has steadily gained in importance. Today, children use the writing process to create stories, reports, and poems. In Part 5, you'll learn how to help them focus on ideas, organization, and the other qualities of good writing as they develop and refine their compositions.

**Viewing** Children are bombarded with visual media today: They watch television shows and commercials, videos, and films, explore Internet Web sites, and play computer games, and they view illustrations and advertisements when they read magazines and comics. Because visual media are so commonplace, children need to learn how to interpret and critically assess them. In addition, children use viewing when they examine illustrations in picture books, compare film versions of books with the books themselves, and read charts, tables, and diagrams in informational books.

**Visually Representing** Students draw pictures, take photos, create diagrams and graphic organizers, and produce videos to present information visually. Through these visually representing projects, students present something familiar in a new way and gain new insights through the experience (Harste, 1993). Students often create projects involving visual texts as they read literature and participate in thematic units. Instead of including separate sections on viewing and visually representing, I've woven information about these new language arts throughout the book.

**Relationships Among the Language Arts** Discussing the language arts one by one suggests a division among them, as though they could be used separately. In reality, they are used simultaneously and reciprocally: Almost any activity involves more than one of the language arts.

Researcher Walter Loban (1976) studied the language growth of 338 students from kindergarten through 12th grade to examine the differences between children who used language effectively and those who did not. Three of Loban's conclusions are especially noteworthy: First, he found positive correlations among the language arts—that is, children who were capable listeners also tended to be capable talkers, readers, and writers. Second, children with less effective oral language abilities tended to have less effective written language abilities. And third, a strong relationship existed between children's oral language ability and their overall academic ability. Loban's study of 30 years ago is still valuable today because it convincingly demonstrates strong relationships among the language processes and emphasizes the need to teach listening and talking as well as reading and writing.

## ESSENTIAL #2: The Instructional Approaches

Although teachers use a variety of instructional approaches for teaching language arts, literature focus units, literature circles, reading and writing workshop, and thematic units are four of the most effective ones. Students apply the six language arts in each of these approaches as they read and respond to literature and participate in writing activities. Teachers usually organize their daily schedule to include more than one instructional approach, as Mrs. Miller-McColm did. When teachers have limited time available, Lewin (1992) recommends alternating teacher-led literature focus units with student-selected litera-

**Learn More About Visually Representing**

Burmark, L. (2002). *Visual literacy: Learn to see, see to learn.* Alexandria, VA: Association for Supervision and Curriculum Development.

Ernst, K. (1993). *Picturing learning.* Portsmouth, NH: Heinemann.

Moline, S. (1995). *I see what you mean: Children at work with visual information.* York, ME: Stenhouse.

Rief, L. (1999). *Vision and voice: Extending the literacy spectrum.* Portsmouth, NH: Heinemann.

Whitin, P. E. (1996). *Sketching stories, stretching minds.* Portsmouth, NH: Heinemann.

ture circles or reading and writing workshop; both teacher-led and student-selected instructional approaches provide valuable language-learning opportunities. Because no one approach provides all the opportunities that students need, the logical solution is to use a combination of patterns.

**Literature Focus Units** Teachers organize literature focus units around award-winning or other high-quality trade books that are appropriate for students' interest level but too challenging for students to read independently. In the Classroom Close-Up, Mrs. Miller-McColm was teaching a literature focus unit on *Tuck Everlasting* (Babbitt, 1988). Students read the featured selection using a five-stage reading process in which they preread, read, responded, explored, and applied their reading. Because students read together as a class, they became a community of learners.

Here are the four components of literature focus units:

- **Reading.** Students read an award-winning or other high-quality book together as a class.
- **Responding.** Students write in reading logs and participate in discussions called *grand conversations* to deepen their understanding of the book.
- **Teaching Minilessons.** Teachers teach minilessons on strategies and skills and make connections to the book students are reading.
- **Creating Projects.** Students create projects, such as poems, reports, and dramatizations, to extend their reading experience.

**Literature Circles** Students read and respond to high-quality trade books in small-group literature circles (Daniels, 2002; Day, Spiegel, McLellan, & Brown, 2002). What matters most is that students are reading and discussing something that interests them and is manageable in a supportive community of learners. Even young children can participate in literature circles, and through the experience of reading and discussing books, they develop academic knowledge and social skills (Frank, Dixon, & Brandts, 2001).

Literature circles include these components:

- **Reading.** Teachers collect multiple copies of five or six books and introduce the books with a book talk. Students then sign up for the book they want to read and form small groups.
- **Responding.** Students participate in grand conversations.
- **Creating Projects.** Students prepare projects to extend their understanding of the books they have read.
- **Sharing.** Each group shares its book and the project they developed with the class.

The workshop approach emphasizes reading and writing for authentic purposes (Atwell, 1998; Cohle & Towle, 2001). Students assume responsibility for choosing books and writing topics and for monitoring their own progress. Two types of workshops are reading workshop and writing workshop.

**Reading Workshop.** Students choose books that interest them and are appropriate for their reading level and read them independently. Through reading workshop, students develop lifelong reading habits. Here are the components:

- **Reading and Responding.** Students spend 30 to 60 minutes reading books independently and participate in weekly conferences with the teacher.
- **Sharing.** For the last 15 minutes of reading workshop, the class gathers together to share books.
- **Teaching Minilessons.** The teacher spends approximately 15 minutes teaching minilessons on strategies and skills.

**Writing Workshop.** The classroom becomes a community of writers who write and share their writing, and students come to see themselves as writers (Calkins, 1994; Fletcher & Portalupi, 2001; Gillet & Beverly, 2001). These are the components of writing workshop:

- **Writing.** Students spend 30 to 45 minutes writing. They use the writing process to draft and refine their writing. Many times, they compile their final copies to make books, but they sometimes publish their writing in other ways.
- **Sharing.** Students take turns sitting in the author's chair to read their compositions aloud.
- **Teaching Minilessons.** Teachers present minilessons on writing strategies and skills.

**Thematic Units**

Teachers integrate language arts with social studies, science, and other curricular areas in these interdisciplinary units. Students use all six language arts as they investigate topics and learn big ideas (Rief, 1999). They also use the language arts at the end of the unit to demonstrate their new learning. These language arts activities take place during thematic units:

- **Reading.** Students read informational books and magazines, stories, and poems related to the unit as well as content-area textbooks. They also research topics on the Internet.
- **Keeping Learning Logs.** Students keep learning logs in which they write entries about what they are learning, record new and interesting words, make graphic organizers, and reflect on their learning.
- **Making Visual Representations.** Students create clusters, maps, time lines, Venn diagrams, data charts, and other diagrams and displays. They use these visual representations as tools to organize information and represent relationships about the topic they are studying.
- **Creating Projects.** Students create alphabet books, posters, oral reports, and other projects to apply their learning and demonstrate their new knowledge.

## Theory to Practice
### Integrating the Language Arts in a First-Grade Classroom

Mrs. Mendez integrates the six language arts as her first graders read and respond to *The Runaway Tortilla* (Kimmel, 2000), a Southwestern version of "The Gingerbread Boy" story, and other versions of the folktale.

**L**istening

The first graders actively listen as Mrs. Mendez reads aloud *The Runaway Tortilla*, joining in to repeat the familiar refrains. Children take turns holding up stuffed animals, pictures, and other props related to the story. They also listen to their teacher read aloud *The Gingerbread Boy* (Galdone, 1983), *The Gingerbread Boy* (Egielski, 2000), and *The Gingerbread Baby* (Brett, 1999).

**T**alking

The first graders talk about each story in a grand conversation, making comparisons with the other versions they've read. They also dramatize *The Runaway Tortilla*, retelling it with puppets they've made and other props that Mrs. Mendez has collected.

**R**eading

Mrs. Mendez writes the tortilla's refrain on chart paper for students to read as she reads the story aloud. They also read an easy-to-read version of "The Gingerbread Boy" story with partners.

**W**riting

Students create a class collaboration book of the story. Children each write and illustrate one page, and then the teacher assembles the pages and binds the book. Once the book is finished, Mrs. Mendez sits in the author's chair and reads it aloud. Afterward, the first graders will take turns taking the book home to share with their families.

**V**iewing

Children visit the book's interactive Web site for games and activities, information about the author and the illustrator, and links to other sites.

**V**isually Representing

The first graders make puppets of the characters that they use in retelling the story. In addition, the class creates a data chart to compare five versions of "The Gingerbread Boy" story that they've read. Across the top of the chart, they list these headings: the runaway character, the last character the runaway character meets, and the runaway character's fate. Down the side of the chart, they write the titles of each version of the story and add a small picture of the book's cover.

# Reading

The fifth graders in Mrs. Kenney's class are reading Roald Dahl's delicious fantasy, *Charlie and the Chocolate Factory* (1964). It's the story of Charlie Bucket, an honest and kind boy who finds the fifth winning Golden Ticket, which entitles him to a visit inside Willy Wonka's famous chocolate factory. Charlie and the four other winners have a wild time visiting the factory, and, in the end, Mr. Wonka gives Charlie the best present of all—his factory!

Mrs. Kenney varies the ways students read each chapter. She reads the first chapter aloud, using whole-class shared reading, and students follow along in their copies of the book. For the other chapters, students alternate reading independently, reading with a buddy, reading in small groups, and reading together as a class.

*Create your own Wonka goodie.*

# Responding

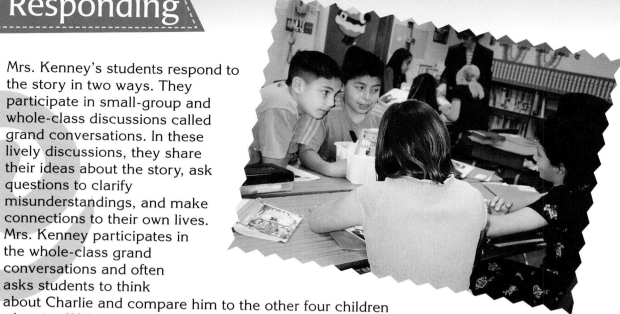

Mrs. Kenney's students respond to the story in two ways. They participate in small-group and whole-class discussions called grand conversations. In these lively discussions, they share their ideas about the story, ask questions to clarify misunderstandings, and make connections to their own lives. Mrs. Kenney participates in the whole-class grand conversations and often asks students to think about Charlie and compare him to the other four children who visit Willy Wonka's chocolate factory.

The fifth graders also write in double-entry reading logs. At the beginning of the literature focus unit, students staple together booklets of paper for their journals and divide each page into two columns. After reading each chapter, they choose a quote and write it in the left column and then write a response in the right column.

| Quote | Response |
|---|---|
| Ch. 19 Pg. 94 "The place was like a witch's kitchen!" | I chose this quote because did you know — it's a simile! |

| QUOTE | MY THOUGHTS |
|---|---|
| Ch 11 Pg 50 "You've got a Golden Ticket! You found the last Golden Ticket! Hey, what do you know?" | I feel excited and happy because Charlie never had anthing much in his life. maybe now his life will take a turn for the better. |

# Teaching Minilessons

Mrs. Kenney and her students choose important words from each chapter as they read *Charlie and the Chocolate Factory*. The words are organized by parts of speech on the word wall because Mrs. Kenney is teaching a series of minilessons about the parts of speech. The noun list includes *hooligan*, *precipice*, and *verdict*; the verb list includes *beckoned*, *revolt*, *stammer*, and *criticize*. The adjective list includes *despicable*, *scraggy*, and *repulsive*; *ravenously*, *violently*, and *frantically* are on the adverb list.

Mrs. Kenney also uses the words from the word wall as she teaches minilessons on root words and affixes to small groups of students. Students take turns choosing a word from the word wall and breaking apart the word's prefix, root, and suffix as Mrs. Kenney writes the information on the white board. Then students record the information on small, individual white boards.

In this literature focus unit, Mrs. Kenney is focusing on character. During a series of minilessons, students investigate how Roald Dahl developed Charlie's character and compare him with Willy Wonka and the other four children with winning Golden Tickets.

After studying about the characters, students create open-mind portraits of one of the characters. One student's open-mind portrait of Willy Wonka is shown here. The portrait goes on top and the page showing his thoughts goes underneath.

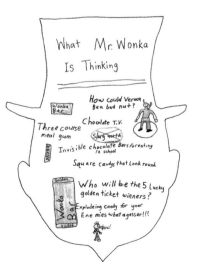

What Mr. Wonka Is Thinking

How could Veruca Bea bad nut?

Chocolate T.V.

Three course meal gum

Invisible chocolate Bars for eating in school

Square candys that look round

Who will be the 5 lucky golden ticket winners?

Exploding candy for your Enemies what a gasser!!!

# Creating Projects

Students create a variety of projects to extend the book and apply their learning. These two boys created a model of Willy Wonka's chocolate factory. Other students researched how chocolate is made and created a poster to display what they learned, wrote poems about each of the characters in *Charlie and the Chocolate Factory*, or read another of Roald Dahl's stories.

As the concluding activity, Mrs. Kenney and her students view *Willy Wonka and the Chocolate Factory*, the film version of the story starring Gene Wilder, and work in small groups to create Venn diagrams comparing the book and the film versions. One student's Venn diagram is shown here. After discussing the differences, most students agree that they preferred the book.

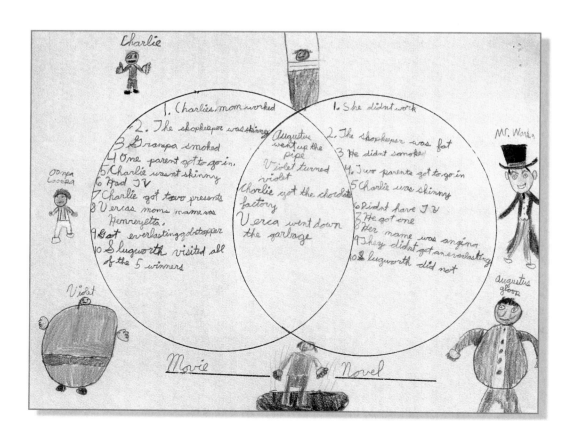

# Reading

Mrs. Goodman's eighth graders participate in literature circles. Mrs. Goodman introduces eight books written at varying levels of difficulty, and students sign up for the book they want to read. The students are currently reading these books:

- *The Outsiders* by S. E. Hinton (1967)
- *The Face on the Milk Carton* by Caroline Cooney (1990)
- *Holes* by Louis Sachar (1998)
- *I Am the Cheese* by Robert Cormier (1977)
- *To Kill a Mockingbird* by Harper Lee (1960)
- *What Jamie Saw* by Carolyn Coman (1995)

Students have set a schedule for reading their books, and they spend time reading during class and at home.

Students in each literature circle assume roles to deepen their understanding of the story and ensure the smooth functioning of their group. They rotate these roles each day so that everyone has the opportunity to experience all roles.

| ROLES IN A LITERATURE CIRCLE | |
|---|---|
| **1** Discussion Leader | This student keeps classmates focused on the big ideas in the story. |
| **2** Harmonizer | This student helps everyone stay on task and show respect to classmates. |
| **3** Wordsmith | This student identifies important words in the story and checks the meaning of words in a dictionary. |
| **4** Connector | This student connects events in the story with real-life experiences. |
| **5** Illustrator | This student draws pictures to help classmates visualize events in the story. |

# Responding

Students frequently meet in their literature circles to discuss the story they are reading, and students fulfill their roles. They talk about what is happening in the story, ask questions to clarify confusions, make connections to their own lives, and predict what will happen next. As students talk, Mrs. Goodman circulates around the classroom, joining each group for a few minutes.

Students also write in reading logs. Sometimes they write summaries and make predictions, and at other times, they write reflections and ask questions. After writing, students often divide into groups of two or three to read their entries to classmates.

### Reading Log

I am liking <u>To Kill a Mockingbird</u> a lot. But it's very different from other books I've read. Instead of describing the scenery and how the people look, it tells the history of everything. The book tells you what has happened. That makes it harder to picture what is happening but easier to make up what you want. I don't think I've ever read a description of Scout anywhere in the book. I didn't quite understand the beginning of the book because it was introducing everything really fast. But now, I'm beginning to understand what is going on.

### Reading Log

My questions are:

- Why don't Scout and Jim call their father Dad but use his real name (Atticus)?

- Why doesn't Scout play with other girls?

- What does everyone look like?

- Why doesn't anyone search for the truth about the Radleys?

# Creating Projects

Students create projects after they finish reading and discussing a story. They write poems and sequels, research a topic on the Internet, develop PowerPoint presentations, create artifacts related to the story, and design story quilts.

After students identify a project they want to develop, they meet with Mrs. Goodman and she approves their choice and helps them get started.

"When Jamie saw Van Throw Nin"

This picture is a square from a story quilt about *What Jamie Saw*, a story about child abuse. Students in the literature circle draw pictures to represent events from the book and put them together to make the quilt, which presents a strong message about the effects of child abuse.

## Sharing

Sharing is the concluding activity. Students in each literature circle share the book they have read and their project with Mrs. Goodman and the class. Sometimes students work together to give a group presentation to the class, and sometimes students develop individual presentations. The students demonstrate their understanding of the story through their presentation, and they hope to interest their classmates in choosing the book and reading the story.

Mrs. Goodman explains how students will be graded before the literature circle begins and posts the criteria in the classroom. For this literature circle, students are graded on four items; each item is worth 25 points. At the end of the literature circle, Mrs. Goodman prepares a grading sheet with the criteria, grades students' work, and assigns the grades.

**GRADING SHEET**

Name _Laura_

Book _To Kill A Mockingbird_

1. Reading Log ............................................ 20
2. Roles in the Literature Circle ............. 25
3. Working Together in a Group ........... 25
4. Project at the End ................................. 22

(92)

# Reading and Writing Workshop

## Reading & Responding

**M**rs. McClenaghan's fifth and sixth graders participate in reading workshop for an hour each morning. The students read books they have selected from the classroom library, including *A Wrinkle in Time* (L'Engle, 1962), *The Sign of the Beaver* (Speare, 1983), *Harry Potter and the Sorcerer's Stone* (Rowling, 1998), *Missing May* (Rylant, 1992), and *Tuck Everlasting* (Babbitt, 1988).

Students also respond to the books they are reading, and their response activities vary according to what Mrs. McClenaghan is teaching. This week's focus is on a reading strategy—forming interpretations. The students identify a big idea in the chapter they are reading and provide evidence from the text to support the idea on T-charts they have made.

## Conferencing

As her students read and respond, Mrs. McClenaghan moves around the classroom, stopping to conference with students. She asks students to read a short excerpt and tell about their reading experience and the reading strategies they are using. They talk about the story so Mrs. McClenaghan can monitor their comprehension and clarify any misunderstandings. She carries a clipboard with her and writes notes about each student, including what book the student is reading and the progress he or she is making.

## Reading Aloud

Mrs. McClenaghan is reading aloud *The Cay* (Taylor, 1969), a survival story about an elderly African American man and a Caucasian boy who are shipwrecked in the Caribbean and who become friends through the experience. She reads aloud a chapter or two each day, and the students talk about the story in a grand conversation. She also uses the book in the minilessons she is teaching.

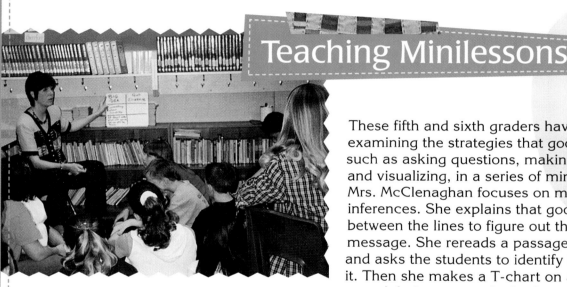

## Teaching Minilessons

These fifth and sixth graders have been examining the strategies that good readers use, such as asking questions, making connections, and visualizing, in a series of minilessons. Today, Mrs. McClenaghan focuses on making inferences. She explains that good readers read between the lines to figure out the author's message. She rereads a passage from *The Cay* and asks the students to identify the big idea in it. Then she makes a T-chart on a white board to record their answers. In the first column, she writes the big idea and in the second, a quote from the text to support the big idea. Then she reads another passage several pages later in the text, and they rephrase the big idea to clarify it and finish the chart.

| BIG Idea | Text Evidence |
|---|---|
| It's about friendship. | p. 76 I said to Timothy, "I want to be your friend." He said softly, "Young bahss, you 'ave always been my friend." |
| It doesn't matter what color you are, you can still be friends. | p. 79 "I don't like some white people my own self, but 'twould be outrageous if I didn't like any o' dem." |

## Writing

After spending 60 minutes in reading workshop, students begin writing workshop, which lasts for 45 minutes. Students usually write two- to four-page stories about events in their own lives—autobiographical incidents—during writing workshop. They work at their own pace, moving through the stages of the writing process. Most students write four or five drafts as they develop and refine the content of their writing.

### Really Hungry

One day, when it was close to dinner time, my big brother was so hungry he got there before any of us. He was waiting impatiently and when we were at the table with our food in front of us he already started devouring the vegetables and rice.

My mother looked at him, and he stopped stuffing himself. He waited very impatiently while she said grace. Mother's grace isn't short but it isn't very long either. He fidgeted and squirmed untill she finished. "You should make it shorter," he said.

He gobbled all of his rice, vegetables and chicken. We watched him in amazement. He asked for seconds and he started to swallow his food.

"Don't eat like that," snapped my mother. "Disgusting!" She bit her chicken wing and chewed.

## Responding

Students meet with classmates and with Mrs. McClenaghan several times during the writing process to revise and edit their writing. The students provide useful feedback to classmates because they have learned about the qualities of a good piece of writing and they know how to identify problem spots.

# Teaching Minilessons

In this writing minilesson, Mrs. McClenaghan shares an essay written by a student from another class. She asks the students to rate it using their district's 6-point writing rubric. They raise their hands and show with their fingers the score they would give the paper. Most students rate it a 4, and Mrs. McClenaghan agrees. They talk about the strong points in the paper and the areas that need improvement.

Then Mrs. McClenaghan reviews the asking-questions and magnifying-a-sentence revision strategies and the symbols students use to represent the two strategies. Next, students reread the essay and attach small self-stick notes to the paper with the symbols written on them to indicate revision points. Students also underline the specific sentence to which each note refers.

# Sharing

During the last 5 minutes of writing workshop, one student sits in the author's chair and shares a newly published composition. The classmates applaud and offer compliments after the student finishes reading. They are an appreciative audience because Mrs. McClenaghan and her students have developed a supportive classroom community.

# Reading

**M**s. McCloskey works with 40 kindergarten through third-grade students in their multi-age classroom. The students are engaged in a thematic unit on insects, integrating all areas of the curriculum. They participate in a variety of reading activities. They listen to Ms. McCloskey read books aloud and read along with her as she shares big books. During centers time, they reread familiar books with buddies and read independently. They also read other books at their own reading levels during guided reading.

## Learning Logs

Each day, students write entries for their learning logs at the writing center. They meet with Ms. Russell, a student teacher working in the classroom, to write about insects. Many of the students are English learners, so Ms. Russell helps them to expand their sentences and include science words in their entries. She also reviews spelling, capitalization, punctuation, and grammar skills with individual students. Then students file their papers in their learning log folders, which are kept at the writing center. At the end of the thematic unit, students compile their learning logs and decorate the covers.

This entry, titled "Wings," was written by a kindergartner who is still learning about capital letters and punctuation marks. He added the second part "because it has wings" in response to Ms. Russell's question, "How can a ladybug fly?"

Wfs

A LadeBug can fly,
BeKcse it hs wfs.

# Visual Representations

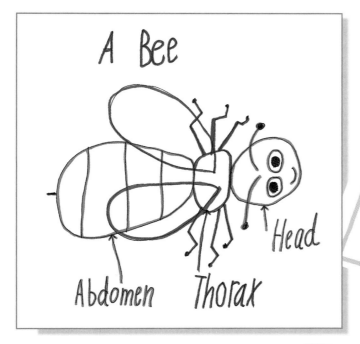

The students make diagrams, charts, and drawings to record information they are learning about insects. They learn to draw insects accurately with three body parts and six legs. They use diagrams to organize information they are learning as Ms. McCloskey reads a book or presents a demonstration. They also use attribute charts to record descriptive words as they observe insects in the "Look and Learn" science center.

# Creating Projects

The students are creating a multigenre display on insects. Each student writes a story, poem, or report for the display, which will cover an entire wall of the classroom. The students use the writing process to develop their compositions, and all students, even the kindergartners, type their final copies on the computer.

What body Parts?
thorax
head
abdomen
wings
stinger
antennae
legs
eyes

Where do they live?
colony
hive

Bees

What type of bees?
queen bee
drone bee
worker bees

What do they eat?
Pollen
nectar

### The Bees

Bees have three body parts: a thorax, an abdomen, and a head. On their body they have some little and big wings, a stinger, two antennae, six legs, and two large black eyes.

The bees live in a hive. Sometimes bees live in a group of bees, and it is called a colony. A lot of bees live in a colony and a lot of bees live in a hive.

There are three kinds of bees. There is a queen bee, a drone bee, and worker bees. The queen lays eggs on the hive and the worker bees take care of the baby bees. One of the worker bees gets pollen from the flowers. When the worker bees get pollen, they dance because they can't talk.

Bees eat pollen and nectar to make honey. When bees make honey they have to go get pollen and nectar. We need bees because bees could make honey for us. If bees is not in this state there will be no honey for us.

### Dragonfly

Dragonfly fly, fly, fly.
Dragonfly fly around the pond.
Dragonfly fly by the flower.
Dragonfly fly by me.
Dragonfly fly, fly, fly.

# Strategies

## What Is a Strategy?

We all have skills that we use automatically as well as self-regulated strategies for things that we do well—driving defensively, playing volleyball, training a new pet, or maintaining classroom discipline. Strategies are problem-solving mechanisms that involve complex thinking processes, and skills are automatic behaviors. The important difference between skills and strategies is how they are used: Skills are used unconsciously, and strategies are used deliberately (Paris, Wasik, & Turner, 1991).

When we are learning to drive a car, for example, we learn both skills and strategies. Some of the first skills we learn are how to start the engine, make left turns, and parallel park. With practice, these skills become automatic. Some of the first strategies we learn are how to pass another car and how to stay a safe distance behind the car ahead of us. At first, we have only a small repertoire of strategies, and we don't always use them effectively; that's why we take lessons from a driving instructor and have a learner's permit that requires a more experienced driver to ride along with us. These seasoned drivers teach us defensive driving strategies. We learn strategies for driving on interstate highways, on slippery roads, and at night. With practice and guidance, we become more successful drivers, able to anticipate driving problems and take defensive actions.

Children develop general learning strategies, and as they grow older, their ability to use these strategies improves (Flavell, 2001). They rehearse by repeating information over and over to remember something, for example, and to elaborate by expanding on the information presented. They also organize by grouping information into categories and monitor by regulating or keeping track of progress.

As they acquire more effective methods for learning and remembering information, children also become more aware of their own cognitive processes and better able to regulate them. Children can reflect on their strategy use and talk about themselves as readers and writers. For example, third grader Mario reports that "it's mostly after I read a book that I write" (Muhammad, 1993, p. 99), and fifth grader Hobbes reports that "the pictures in my head help me when I write stuff down 'cause then I can get ideas from my pictures" (Cleary, 1993, p. 142). Eighth grader Chandra talks about poetry: "Poetry is a fine activity, and it can get you in tune with yourself. . . . I think that my favorite person who does poetry is Maya Angelou" (Steinbergh, 1993, p. 212).

Children become more realistic about the limitations of their memories and more knowledgeable about which strategies are most effective in particular learning situations. They also become metacognitive, or increasingly aware of what they know and don't know. The term *metacognition* refers to this knowledge children acquire about their own cognitive processes and

to children's regulation of their cognitive processes to maximize learning.

## Language Arts Strategies

Children apply general learning strategies to language arts and acquire specific language arts strategies. Although there is no definitive list of strategies, researchers have identified a number of strategies that students learn to use, including activating background knowledge, blending, predicting, proofreading, and revising (Fletcher & Portalupi; 1998; Paris & Jacobs, 1984; Schmitt, 1990).

Some strategies, such as blending, are used specifically in phonemic awareness, phonics, and spelling, and many others are applied in all six language arts. Consider revising, for example. Probably the best-known application is in writing: Students revise meaning as they add, substitute, delete, and move information in their rough drafts. As students create visual representations and oral presentations, they use revising the same way writers do. Students also revise as they listen to a speaker, read a book, or view a DVD: They revise their understanding as they continue listening, reading, or viewing and get more information.

## Skills Are Important, Too!

Skills are information-processing techniques that students use automatically and unconsciously. Many language arts skills focus at the word level, but some require students to attend to larger chunks of text. For example, readers use skills such as decoding

## Twenty Language Arts Strategies

Here are 20 of the language arts strategies that children apply as they listen, talk, read, write, view, and visually represent:

- Activating Background Knowledge
- Blending
- Brainstorming
- Connecting
- Evaluating
- Identifying Big Ideas
- Identifying Root Words
- Inferencing
- Monitoring
- Noticing Nonverbal Cues
- Organizing
- Playing With Language
- Predicting
- Proofreading
- Questioning
- Revising
- Segmenting
- Setting Purposes
- Summarizing
- Visualizing

unfamiliar words, noting details, and sequencing events, and writers employ skills such as forming contractions, using punctuation marks, and capitalizing people's names.

Here are five categories of language arts skills:

- **Comprehension Skills.** Students learn to separate facts and opinions, compare and contrast, and recognize literary genres and structures.
- **Print Skills.** Students learn to sound out words, notice word families, use root words and affixes to decode and spell words, and use abbreviations.
- **Study Skills.** Students learn to skim and scan, take notes, make clusters, and preview a book before reading.
- **Language Skills.** Students learn to identify meanings of words, notice idioms, divide words into syllables, and choose synonyms.
- **Reference Skills.** Students learn to alphabetize a list of words, use a dictionary, and read and make graphs and other diagrams.

Teachers often wonder when they should teach particular skills. State and school districts have frameworks, standards, and curriculum guides that identify the skills to be taught at each grade level. These resources provide guidelines, but teachers decide which skills to teach based on their students' level of development and the activities in which their students are involved.

## What About Teaching Strategies and Skills?

Teachers use a combination of direct and indirect instruction to provide information that students need to know about skills and strategies. Direct instruction is planned. Teachers often teach minilessons, brief 10- to 30-minute lessons, in which they explicitly explain a particular strategy or skill, model its use, and provide examples and opportunities for practice. In the Classroom Close-Up, for example, Mrs. Miller-McColm presented a minilesson on writing effective leads. Indirect instruction involves taking advantage of teachable moments to reexplain a strategy or skill to a student or clarify a misconception. Both types of instruction are necessary in order to meet students' needs.

Teachers plan strategy and skill instruction that grows out of language arts activities using a whole-part-whole sequence: The language arts activity is the first *whole*, the minilesson is the *part*, and having students apply what they are learning in other language arts activities is the second *whole*. This instructional sequence is recommended to ensure that the instruction is meaningful and that students learn to use the strategies and skills independently (Mazzoni & Gambrell, 2003).

The goal of instruction is for students to be able to use the strategies and skills that they've learned independently. Dorn and Soffos (2001) have identified four behaviors that teachers use as part of both direct and indirect instruction to develop self-regulated learners:

- **Modeling.** Teachers demonstrate how to use strategies and skills for language arts activities. When teachers read books aloud to students, for instance, they model expressive reading as well as predicting, inferencing, connecting, and other strategies.
- **Coaching.** Teachers direct students' attention and encourage their active engagement in activities. Teachers serve as coaches as they provide information and guide students' attention during minilessons.
- **Scaffolding.** Teachers adjust the support they provide according to students' needs. When students participate in interactive writing activities, for example, teachers use scaffolding as they assist students in writing letters and words.
- **Fading.** Teachers relinquish control as students become more capable of using a strategy or performing an activity. When students participate in writing workshop, for instance, teachers fade as they allow students to move through the stages of the writing process at their own speed.

It's not enough to simply explain strategies and skills or remind students to use them. Teachers must actively engage students, encourage and scaffold them while they are learning, and then gradually withdraw their support if they want their students to learn to use strategies and skills independently.

## MINILESSONS

**1 Introduce the topic**
Teachers introduce the strategy or skill by naming it and making a connection between the topic and activities going on in the classroom.

**2 Share examples**
Teachers show how to use the topic with examples from students' writing or from children's books.

**3 Provide information**
Teachers provide information explaining and demonstrating the strategy or skill.

**4 Supervise practice**
Students practice using the strategy or skill with teacher supervision.

**5 Assess learning**
Teachers monitor students' progress and evaluate their use of newly learned strategies or skills.

# Classroom Practice

## What's the Relationship Between Language and Learning?

Language facilitates learning. Through interactions with adults and collaboration with classmates, children learn things they could not accomplish on their own. Adults guide and support children as they move from their current level of knowledge toward a more advanced level. Russian psychologist Lev Vygotsky (1978) described these two levels as (1) the actual developmental level, the level at which children can perform a task independently, and (2) the level of potential development, the level at which children can perform a task with assistance. Children can typically do more difficult things in collaboration than they can on their own, which is why teachers are important models for their students and why children often work with partners and in small groups.

A child's "zone of proximal development" (Vygotsky, 1978) is the range of tasks that the child can perform with guidance from others but cannot yet perform independently. Vygotsky believed that children learn best when what they are attempting to learn is within this zone. He felt that children learn little by performing tasks they can already do independently—tasks at their actual developmental level—or by attempting tasks that are too difficult or beyond their zone of proximal development.

Vygotsky (1986) and Jerome Bruner (1986) both used the term *scaffolding* as a metaphor to describe adults' contributions to children's learning. Scaffolds are support mechanisms that teachers, parents, and others provide to help children successfully perform a task within their zone of proximal development. Teachers serve as scaffolds when they model or demonstrate a procedure, guide children through a task, ask questions, break complex tasks into smaller steps, and supply pieces of information. As children gain knowledge and experience about how to perform a task, teachers gradually withdraw their support so that children make the transition from social interaction to internalized, independent functioning.

The teacher's role in scaffolding or guiding students' learning within the zone of proximal development has three components, according to Dixon-Krauss (1996):

1. **Social Interaction.** Teachers support children's learning through talk.
2. **Students' Needs.** Teachers provide support based on feedback from the children as they are engaged in the learning task.
3. **Variable Support.** Teachers vary the amount of support they provide according to children's needs.

Teachers provide scaffolds that are responsive to English learners' language and learning tasks. In this text, you'll often see scaffolding boxes that delineate specific ways that teachers provide scaffolds to ensure all students' success.

## The Goal of Language Arts Instruction

The goal of language arts instruction is for students to develop communicative competence, the ability to use language appropriately in a variety of social contexts (Hymes, 1972). Students use these four language systems as they develop communicative competence:

- Phonological, or sound, system
- Semantic, or meaning, system
- Syntactic, or grammar, system
- Pragmatic, or social use, system

No matter whether students are listening, talking, reading, writing, viewing, or visually representing, they use these systems to communicate and learn.

Communicative competence is context specific. That means that students may participate effectively in classroom conversations but not know how to give a more formal oral presentation. Similarly, students may know how to read informational books but not how to write a report to share information. At each grade level, teachers expand students' abilities to use the six language arts meaningfully in new contexts.

Through language arts instruction, students acquire the characteristics of competent language users. They become more aware of language units (such as phonemes, root words, and homophones) and genres, more strategic and more creative in their use of language, better able to use language as a tool for learning, and more reflective in their interpretations.

## The Language Systems

| Phonological System | Semantic System |
|---|---|
| The sound system of English has 44 sounds that students use to decode words when reading and spell words when writing. | The key component of the meaning system is vocabulary. Students learn new words and new meanings for familiar words. |

| Syntactic System | Pragmatic System |
|---|---|
| The grammar system regulates how words are combined into sentences and how affixes are added to words. Students learn these rules as they study grammar and vocabulary. | This system deals with the social and cultural aspects of language use. Students vary how they speak and write according to their purpose and their audience. |

# Scaffolding English Learners

## Ways to Scaffold English Learners

- Build students' background knowledge using artifacts, videos, photos and maps, and picture books.
- Highlight important words on word walls and add illustrations to help students identify words.
- Have students work in small groups or with partners.
- Demonstrate how to do projects, and show samples so students will understand what they are expected to do.
- Read aloud to students every day.
- Have students each share an idea at the end of a grand conversation or state a fact they have learned at the end of an instructional conversation.
- Have students dramatize vocabulary words they are learning, stories they have read, historical events they are studying, and other topics to enhance their learning.
- Use interactive writing to teach writing strategies and skills.
- Make graphic organizers and other diagrams to structure what students are learning.
- Have students share ideas with a partner as a rehearsal before sharing with the whole class.

## Characteristics of Competent Language Users

The National Council of Teachers of English (1996) has identified these seven characteristics of competent language users.

**Personal Expression**
Students use language to express themselves, make connections between their own experiences and their social world, choose books they want to read and topics they want to write about, and create a personal voice.

**Aesthetic Appreciation**
Students use language aesthetically—for pleasure—to read literature, talk with others, and enrich their lives.

**Collaborative Exploration**
Students use language as a learning tool as they investigate topics and issues in collaboration with classmates.

**Strategic Language Use**
Students use strategies as they create and share meaning through language.

**Creative Communication**
Students use text forms and genres creatively as they express ideas through language.

**Reflective Interpretation**
Students use language to organize and evaluate learning experiences, question personal and social values, and think critically.

**Thoughtful Application**
Students use language to solve problems, persuade, and take action.

**The Teacher's Role**

Teachers vary in how they believe they can best assist students in developing communicative competence. Very broadly, teachers can be described as having a teacher-centered or a child-centered approach, and the classroom practices they use reflect their belief systems (Squires & Bliss, 2004). In a teacher-centered approach, teachers orchestrate the life of the classroom. For instance, they choose many of the books that students read, ask many questions to direct discussions, and manage students' use of the writing process. Literature focus units are an example of a more teacher-centered approach. In contrast, in a child-centered approach, students assume more responsibility for their own learning. For example, they make choices, do more of the talking in discussions, engage in inquiry, and work collaboratively with classmates. Literature circles and reading and writing workshop are examples of more child-centered approaches. No matter which of the approaches teachers use, however, they are helping their students develop communicative competence when students are using the six language arts for authentic purposes.

**The Impact of Mandated Programs**

In recent years, state and federal mandates have increasingly dictated which instructional approaches and materials teachers use in teaching language arts and developing students' communicative competence. Those that are grounded in scientific evidence are endorsed (Lyon & Chhabra, 2004). The most far-reaching initiative is George W. Bush's No Child Left Behind (NCLB) Act of 2001, which was designed to close the achievement gap between White, affluent students and other students. This initiative, based on the report of the National Reading Panel (2000), has mandated an increased emphasis on teaching basic skills and holds schools accountable for students' performance. Schools are now required to administer standardized tests each year to students in grades 3–8 to monitor their progress.

The NCLB Act affects every school in the United States. All schools set annual achievement goals, and those that meet their goals are labeled "schools of choice." If schools do not make adequate yearly progress for 2 consecutive years, they are required to implement special programs to improve test scores, and parents may transfer their children to higher-achieving schools.

The NCLB initiative's emphasis on basic skills has narrowed the goal of language arts instruction in many schools to having students meet grade-level standards on standardized achievement tests; to meet that goal, teachers are increasingly being required to use scripted basal reading programs under the mistaken assumption that they were recommended by the National Reading Panel (Shanahan, 2003).

Because of the NCLB Act, state-designed lists of grade-level standards or competencies, and other mandated programs, teachers feel a loss of professional autonomy in determining what and how to teach. There is increased pressure from parents, administrators, and politicians for teachers to "teach to the test" rather than to develop children's communicative competence by engaging their students in meaningful language arts activities. Some teachers have embraced the new instructional programs, and others have quietly resisted them and continued to use child-centered approaches as often as they could. Still others are actively resisting the imposition of these programs because they reject the conformity and loss of teacher control inherent in new state and federal mandates (Garan, 2004; Novinger & Compton-Lilly, 2005).

Teachers, administrators, and parents can point to both positive and negative outcomes of these state and federal mandates (Valencia & Villarreal, 2003). Some teachers feel more confident about their teaching ability now because they are being told how to teach language arts, and in many schools, students' test scores are rising. At the same time, however, other teachers are discouraged and frustrated because they are not allowed to use the instructional approaches that have been effective for them in the past. Some of their students continue to fail because they cannot do work at their grade level, and they also are concerned about the amount of time diverted from instruction for testing. In some schools, testing takes more than one month of the school year. In addition, some parents have expressed concern that their children have developed test anxiety and are preoccupied with the "high-stakes" tests they must pass each spring.

## STUDENTS TODAY: Culturally and Linguistically Diverse

The United States is a culturally pluralistic society, and our ethnic, racial, and socioeconomic diversity is reflected in our classrooms. Today, nearly a third of us classify ourselves as non-European Americans (Wright, 2004). The percentage of

### Learn More About the NCLB Act

Coles, G. (2003). *Reading the naked truth: Literacy, legislation, and lies.* Portsmouth, NH: Heinemann.

Garan, E. (2004). *In defense of our children: When politics, profit, and education collide.* Portsmouth, NH: Heinemann.

International Reading Association. (2001). *Evidence-based reading instruction: Putting the National Reading Panel report into practice.* Newark, DE: Author.

Meier, D., & Wood, G. (2004). *Many children left behind: How the No Child Left Behind Act is damaging our children and our schools.* Boston: Beacon Press.

Popham, W. J. (2004). *America's "failing" schools: How parents and teachers can cope with No Child Left Behind.* London: Falmer Press.

culturally diverse children is even higher: In California, 51% of school-age children belong to ethnic minority groups, and in New York state, 40% do. Given current birthrates and immigration patterns, it has been estimated that within a few years, Hispanic American and Asian American populations will have grown by more than 20%, and the African American population will have grown by 12%. These changing demographic realities are having a significant impact on kindergarten through eighth-grade classrooms, as more and more students come from linguistically and culturally diverse backgrounds.

Because the United States is a nation of immigrants, dealing with cultural diversity is not a new responsibility for public schools; however, the magnitude of diversity is much greater now. In the past, the United States was viewed as a melting pot in which language and cultural differences would be assimilated or combined to form a new, truly American culture. What actually happened, though, was that the European American culture remained dominant.

## How to Prepare Students for High-Stakes Testing

Because of the importance of high-stakes tests in making educational decisions about students, it's essential that teachers prepare students to take standardized achievement tests by teaching them how to read and answer test items and having them take practice tests to hone their test-taking strategies (McCabe, 2003). Here are eight suggestions:

- Teach test-taking strategies by modeling how to read, think about, and answer test items.
- Design practice tests with the same types of items used on the tests students will take.
- Use easy-to-read reading materials for practice tests so students can focus on practicing test-taking strategies.
- Include a combination of unrelated narrative and expository passages on the tests.
- Have students take practice tests on a regular schedule.
- Begin with untimed tests and move to timed tests as students gain experience with test-taking strategies.
- Simulate testing conditions in the classroom, or take students to where the test will be administered for the practice sessions.
- Graph students' results on practice tests so they can see their progress.

## Multicultural Books

### Stories

Argueta, J. (2003). *Xochitl and the flowers.* San Francisco: Children's Book Press. (P)

Cheng, A. (2004). *Honeysuckle house.* Front Street. (M)

Choi, Y. (2001). *The name jar.* New York: Knopf. (P)

English, K. (2004). *Hot day on Abbott Avenue.* New York: Clarion Books. (P)

Herrera, J. F. (2003). *Super cilantro girl.* San Francisco: Children's Book Press. (P–M)

Jiménez, F. (1997). *The circuit.* Albuquerque: University of New Mexico Press. (U)

Pak, S. (2003). *Sumi's first day of school ever.* New York: Viking. (P)

Ryan, P. M. (2000). *Esperanza rising.* New York: Scholastic. (M)

Shea, P. D. (2003). *Tangled threads: A Hmong girl's story.* New York: Clarion Books. (M–U)

Soto, G. (1993). *Too many tamales.* New York: Putnam. (P)

Woodson, J. (2003). *Locomotion.* New York: Putnam. (M–U)

### Informational Books

Ancona, G. (1993). *Powwow.* Orlando: Harcourt Brace. (M)

Freedman, R. (2004). *The voice that challenged a nation: Marian Anderson and the struggle for equal rights.* New York: Clarion Books. (U)

King Farris, C. (2003). *My brother Martin: A sister remembers growing up with the Rev. Dr. Martin Luther King Jr.* New York: Simon & Schuster. (P–M)

Krull, K. (2003). *Harvesting hope: The story of Cesar Chavez.* San Diego: Harcourt Brace. (P–M)

Medearis, A. S. (2003). *Our people.* New York: McGraw-Hill. (P–M)

Robinson, S. (2004). *Promises to keep: How Jackie Robinson changed America.* New York: Scholastic. (M–U)

Wolf, B. (2003). *Coming to America: A Muslim family's story.* New York: Lee & Low. (P–M)

### Poems

Crews, N. (2004). *The neighborhood Mother Goose.* New York: Greenwillow. (P)

Medina, J. (2004). *The dream on Blanca's wall: Poems in English and Spanish.* Honesdale, PA: Wordsong/Boyds Mills Press. (M–U)

Soto, G. (1992). *Neighborhood odes.* Orlando: Harcourt Brace. (M–U)

---

P = primary grades (K–2); M = middle grades (3–5); U = upper grades (6–8)

---

The concept of cultural pluralism has replaced the ideas of assimilation. Cultural pluralism respects people's right to retain their cultural identity within American society, recognizing that each culture contributes to and enriches the total society. This concept is an outgrowth of the Civil Rights movement of the 1960s. All ethnic cultures have been inspired and empowered by the Civil Rights movement, too (Banks, 2001).

Children of diverse cultures come to school with a broad range of language and literacy experiences, although their experiences may be different than those of European American children (Samway & McKeon, 1999; Wink, 2000). They have learned to communicate in at least one language, and if they don't speak English, they want to learn English in order to make friends, learn, and communicate just like their classmates.

Cultural and linguistic diversity is not a problem to overcome; rather, it provides an opportunity to enhance and enrich the learning of all students (Gibbons, 2002; Wink, 2000). Teachers must be prepared to work with this ever-growing population because they are likely to have students in their classrooms from a variety of cultural groups. In addition, even if all the students in their classroom are from one cultural group, teachers still need to incorporate a multicultural perspective into their curriculum to prepare their students to interact effectively in the increasingly multicultural American society.

**Multicultural Books** Multicultural stories, informational books, and poetry can introduce cultures, traditions, and the universality of life experiences to all students (Yokota, 1993). When students read books such as *The Name Jar* (Choi, 2001), *Super Cilantro Girl* (Herrera, 2003), and *Locomotion* (Woodson, 2003), they step into the lives of other children and adolescents. For culturally diverse students, the familiar experiences in these books and characters who look like them and have names like them make them feel valued and respected.

> "Cultural and linguistic diversity is not a problem to overcome; rather, it provides an opportunity to enhance and enrich the learning of all students."

Rasinski and Padak (1990) identified four ways to incorporate multicultural literature into the language arts program. The approaches are based on Banks's (1994) multicultural curriculum model and differ in the extent to which multicultural issues become a central part of the curriculum.

**The Contributions Approach.** This approach focuses on lessons taught in connection with a holiday or another special occasion. The purpose of the activities is to familiarize students with holidays, specific customs, or the contributions of important people, but they do not teach cultural values or challenge students to reexamine their beliefs. A single lesson, for example, might focus on reading *Seven Candles for Kwanzaa* (Pinkney, 1993), a story about Kwanzaa, an African American holiday celebrated from December 16 to January 1. This approach is an easy way to include a multicultural component in the curriculum, but students gain through it only a superficial understanding of cultural diversity.

**The Additive Approach.** Lessons using multicultural literature are added to the existing curriculum in this approach. In a genre unit on folktales, for instance, *Mufaro's Beautiful Daughters: An African Tale* (Steptoe, 1987), *Yeh Shen: A Cinderella Story From China* (Louie, 1982), and *The Persian Cinderella* (Climo, 1999) might be added as multicultural versions of the Cinderella story. Or, for a literature focus unit, a middle-grade teacher might choose to read a multicultural chapter book such as *Esperanza Rising* (Ryan, 2000), the story of a remarkable girl and her mother who leave their comfortable life in Mexico to become migrant laborers in California; teachers choose to feature this book because it is a powerful, well-written story, one that their students will enjoy. This approach is similar to the contributions approach because the curriculum remains anchored in the European-American perspective. Information about cultural diversity is added to the curriculum, but not woven through it.

**The Transformation Approach.** Literature focus units and thematic units are modified in this approach to promote the study of historical events and contemporary issues from the viewpoint of culturally diverse groups. Primary-grade students, for instance, might read *A Chair for My Mother* (Williams, 1982) and *Too Many Tamales* (Soto, 1993) as part of a unit on families, and then talk about the common features of families from diverse cultural groups. Or, during a thematic unit on World War II, upper-grade students might read novels and informational books to learn about the Japanese American viewpoint on the war and their unjust internment. These literature experiences and related response activities allow students to see the interconnectedness of various ethnic groups within American society and the ways that diverse cultural groups have shaped American history.

**The Social Action Approach.** Students study important social issues and take action to solve problems during thematic units. They read culturally conscious literature to gain an "inside" view on social issues. For example, students might study immigration and begin by reading to learn about modern-day

refugees who risk their lives coming to the United States. Afterward, they can talk about their own attitudes toward immigrant groups and research how and when their families came to the United States. The question "Who belongs here?" might direct their study and lead them to find ways to encourage tolerance and assist with refugee programs in their community. In this approach, students read, do research, think deeply about social issues, and apply what they are learning in their own communities.

**How Do Teachers Differentiate Instruction?**
Teachers know that their students vary—their interests and motivation, their background knowledge and prior experiences, and their language proficiency—so it's important to allow for these individual differences as they plan for instruction. According to Carol Ann Tomlinson (2001), differentiated instruction "means 'shaking up' what goes on in the classroom so that students have multiple options for taking information, making sense of ideas, and expressing what they learn" (p. 1). Differentiating instruction is especially important for struggling students who haven't been successful and for very capable students who aren't challenged by grade-level assignments.

Teachers differentiate instruction in these ways as they implement instructional approaches in their classrooms:

♦ **Offer choices.** Teachers offer choices when students select books to read in literature circles and in reading workshop, and students often choose their writing topics and genres during writing workshop. Students also make choices about the projects they create during literature focus units, literature circles, and thematic units.

♦ **Organize students into small groups.** Teachers group students flexibly for literature circles, guided reading groups, writing groups, and other instructional activities. Students also work in small groups to develop projects and to write reports and other compositions.

♦ **Use all six language arts.** Teachers provide opportunities for students to develop expertise in all six language arts, not just reading and writing. During literature focus units, for example, students often use viewing and visually representing to support reading and writing. Because many students are better able to understand and express themselves through the oral and visual language arts than through the written language arts, using all six language arts scaffolds their learning. Other students who are capable readers and writers may have less expertise in the other language arts and need to develop those abilities, too.

♦ **Preteach and reteach.** Teachers scaffold struggling students by bringing them together to introduce a lesson, build

**Learn More About Critical Literacy**

Heffernan, L. (2004). *Critical literacy and writer's workshop.* Newark, DE: International Reading Association.

Lewison, M., Flint, A. S., & Van Sluys, K. (2002). Taking on critical literacy: The journey of newcomers and novices. *Language Arts, 79,* 382–392.

McLaughlin, M., & DeVoogd, G. L. (2004). *Critical literacy: Enhancing students' comprehension of text.* New York: Scholastic.

Vasquez, V. (2003). *Getting beyond 'I like the book': Creating space for critical literacy in K–6 classrooms.* Newark, DE: International Reading Association.

background knowledge, and introduce important vocabulary before teaching the lesson to the class and then meet with them a second time to review the lesson after teaching it. With this extra support, many English learners and other struggling students are able to learn as successfully as their classmates.

♦ **Incorporate projects.** Students create projects as a culminating activity for literature focus units, literature circles, and thematic units to explore topics that interest them, use the language arts for meaningful purposes, and demonstrate their learning in authentic ways.

When teachers consider the needs of their students and plan instruction that incorporates these four ways to differentiate instruction, students are more likely to be successful.

# CRITICAL LITERACY: Using Language for Social Action

Critical literacy is a theory of language use that explores how language works in society. Friere and Macedo (1987) describe critical literacy as learning how to "read the word and the world" (p. 32). In addition to using the language arts to communicate, solve problems, and persuade people, students can use them to analyze their social worlds to raise their consciousness of oppression and power and to give voice to the ways their lives are socially, culturally, and politically mediated (Dyson, 2001).

Henry Giroux (1988) challenges teachers not to accept the status quo, but to take control of their own teaching and consider the impact of what they do in the classroom. For example, which books do you choose for literature focus units and literature circles? Do they reflect diverse voices and viewpoints? Do they examine historical and contemporary social issues? Books are available today that present tough social issues, such as *Smoky Night* (Bunting, 1994), a story set during the 1992 Los Angeles riots; *Click, Clack, Moo: Cows That Type* (Cronin, 2000), the story of farmyard animals who go on strike; *Witness* (Hesse, 2001), a story told from multiple viewpoints about the effects of the Ku Klux Klan in a town; and *Homeless Bird* (Whelan, 2000), the story of an Indian girl who has no future when she is widowed soon after her marriage. Books such as these present controversial topics that students can think about and question (Foss, 2002; Lewison, Flint, & Van Sluys, 2002). In fact, teachers report that their students are often more engaged in reading stories like these than other books (Leland, Harste, & Huber, 2005).

Ciardiello (2004) identified these five practices that teachers use to encourage students to examine "the democratic vision of justice and fair play for all people" (pp. 138–139) as they think about books they are reading and topics they are learning:

- **Multiple Viewpoints.** Students examine what they are reading or learning from multiple viewpoints to understand other perspectives.
- **Authentic Voices.** Students, especially those who have been marginalized or excluded, find their authentic voice so that they can express themselves freely.
- **Self-Identity.** Students consider the effects of prejudice on self-identity and help classmates from cultural groups who have suffered discrimination regain their identity.
- **Social Barriers.** Students examine how social barriers exclude people on the basis of race, gender, and ethnicity.
- **Civic Service.** Students respond to "the call to service" (p. 144) by participating in school and community service programs.

Teachers can address these practices as students discuss books they are reading and in activities during thematic units.

Critical literacy also plays a role in writing. Heffernan (2004) found that he could move his students from writing about stereotypical and gender-biased topics to writing passionately about social issues in their own lives. You might ask yourself whether your students' writing reflects social issues or perpetuates stereotypes.

## A Is for Authentic Assessment

Authentic assessment is the best way to examine and document students' language learning because it resembles real language use (Valencia, Hiebert, & Afflerbach, 1994). A test on spelling words, for example, won't assess students' ability to spell words correctly in their own writing; tests evaluate students' ability to memorize the spelling of a particular set of words. Even though most teachers administer weekly spelling texts, they recognize their limitations. So, when they want to determine whether students remember how to spell words they've studied in their own writing and how students attempt to spell unfamiliar words, teachers examine their writing.

To authentically assess students' learning, teachers must examine both the processes students use as they listen, talk, read, write, view, and visually represent and the artifacts or products they create, such as projects and reading logs. Students also participate in assessing their own learning. Authentic assessment has these purposes:

- Document milestones in students' language development
- Identify students' strengths in order to plan for instruction
- Examine students' language arts projects
- Learn more about how students become strategic language learners

Through this kind of assessment, teachers learn about their students, about themselves as teachers, and about the impact of the instructional program; and when students self-assess their learning, they learn about themselves as learners and also about their own learning. Ultimately, teachers want their students to learn to self-regulate their learning and accept responsibility for it.

**Helping Students Take Charge of Their own Learning**

Students can learn to take charge of their own learning instead of turning to the teacher for feedback, and when they use self-assessment, their achievement increases, too (Johnston, 2005). Sometimes asking "How's it going?" is all that's necessary to get students thinking about what they are doing, what's going well, or why they're having a problem. Teachers can ask other questions, too, including:

- What were you thinking as you were doing this activity?
- Which language arts strategies are you using?
- What was the hardest thing about this activity?
- What have you learned about yourself as a reader or writer?
- What do you want to learn next?

Asking students about their own language processes helps them become more aware of what they are doing, and that, in turn, increases their ability to use self-assessment.

Once you start listening to students talking about what they're doing, you'll realize they know a great deal about their own language use. They can talk how they vary the way they listen to stories and informational books or why they think one composition is better than another. They can explain the strategies they use to spell multisyllabic words or why the poems they write evoke powerful images.

To ensure that students learn to self-assess their language arts activities, teachers need to model self-assessment procedures and teach students how to talk about their thoughts. Students need to know about language arts concepts and related terminology—the language arts strategies, the stages of the writing process, the elements of story structure, the qualities of good writing, and the poetic devices, for example. They also need opportunities to work collaboratively in small groups, respond to literature, participate in grand conversations, and use writing rubrics in order to reflect on their use.

## Guidelines for Authentic Assessment

- Choose an appropriate assessment tool.
- Use a variety of assessment tools.
- Use the results of assessment to inform your teaching.
- Focus on what students can do, not on what they can't do.
- Examine both the language processes students use and the products they create.
- Assess students' learning in a variety of contexts.
- Make time to observe and conference with individual students.
- Teach students to self-assess their learning.

With the current emphasis on accountability, it's important to understand the differences between authentic assessment and tests. Consider the often-confused terms *assessment* and *evaluation:* Assessment is diagnostic and ongoing. Teachers use assessment tools to plan instruction and monitor student progress. In contrast, evaluation is used to judge students' learning (Cobb, 2003). It often involves testing, using teacher-made tests, unit tests that accompany textbooks, or end-of-year standardized achievement tests. Teachers use evaluation after instruction to assign grades and at the end of the year to determine if students have met grade-level standards and should progress to the next grade level.

Authentic assessment tools and tests provide different kinds of information. Authentic assessment gives a more complete picture of what students know about language arts and the strategies and skills they can use, whereas tests judge student performance against a grade-level standard (Wilson, Martens, & Arya, 2005). A child who scores 95% on a unit test is judged to have learned more than a child who scores a 70% on the same test, but it's usually not clear exactly what the student knows or which strategies and skills he or she has learned to use.

Most teachers are required to administer tests that accompany textbook programs as well as end-of-year standardized achievement tests to show students' growth and demonstrate accountability. Even with this emphasis on testing, it's important that teachers continue to use authentic assessment to inform their instruction and monitor student learning.

# Review

## The Big Ideas

The goal of language arts instruction is to develop students' communicative competence, their ability to use the six language arts effectively. To accomplish this goal, teachers organize instruction using literature focus units, literature circles, reading and writing workshop, and thematic units as well as other approaches.

These big ideas were presented in Part 1:

- Teachers understand the relationships among the language arts, using listening and viewing to support students' reading development and talking and visually representing to support students' writing development.
- Teachers organize effective instruction through a combination of instructional approaches, including literature focus units, literature circles, reading and writing workshop, and thematic units.
- Teachers present minilessons to teach strategies and skills.
- Teachers use scaffolding to support their students' learning and especially to meet the needs of culturally and linguistically diverse students.
- Teachers apply critical literacy theory to create ways for students to use their language arts competencies for social justice.
- Teachers use authentic assessment methods to monitor students' language arts development and document their accomplishments.

## Classroom Inquiry

You can learn a great deal about how to teach language arts by reading this text, but you can learn even more by examining how the concepts you've read about are implemented in real classrooms. To assist you, I offer some directions for classroom inquiry. If you're a preservice teacher, you may want to observe in a classroom you're visiting, and if you're a practicing teacher, you can examine what's happening in your own classroom (Stewart, 2003).

A classroom inquiry project involves five steps. To begin, identify a question to study; a list of possible topics and questions related to the information presented in Part 1 is listed here. Second, collect data to use in answering your question. You can observe your students and make anecdotal notes; you might focus on one student or on a small group of students. Or, you might videotape a lesson and view it to study your instructional practices. You can also interview your students to learn more about their perspectives, or collect their writing samples to examine. Next, analyze the data you've collected, looking for patterns. It might be necessary to refocus your study and collect additional data, if what you've collected doesn't answer your question. Fourth, report your findings. If you're a preservice teacher, share what you've learned with your professor and classmates, and if you're an inservice teacher, share your results with your colleagues and administrators. Finally, apply what you've learned to improve your teaching.

**The Six Language Arts** Researchers recommend that teachers infuse all six language arts into their instructional programs so that students develop communicative competence. To explore what your students know about the language arts and

### Learn More About Classroom Inquiry

Arhar, J. M., Holly, M. L., & Kasten, W. C. (2000). *Action research for teachers: Traveling the yellow brick road.* Upper Saddle River, NJ: Merrill/Prentice Hall.

Hubbard, R. S., & Power, B. M. (2003). *The art of classroom inquiry: A handbook for teacher researchers.* Portsmouth, NH: Heinemann.

Johnson, A. P. (2004). *A short guide to action research* (2nd ed.). Boston: Allyn & Bacon.

MacLean, M. S., & Mohr, M. M. (1999). *Teacher-researchers at work.* Berkeley, CA: National Writing Project.

Mohr, M. M., Rogers, C., Sanford, B., Nocerino, M. A., MacLean, M. S., & Clawson, S. (2004). *Teacher research for better schools.* Berkeley, CA: National Writing Project.

the ones they use confidently, consider these questions:

- Which language arts do I teach during a typical week?
- Which language arts do my students use?
- How can I incorporate the language arts I teach less often or those that my students rarely use?
- Which language arts do my students want to learn more about?

**Language Arts Strategies** Students who have developed a repertoire of strategies use the language arts more effectively. To think about what your students know about strategies and how they use them, ask yourself these questions:

- Which strategies have I taught?
- How do I teach a strategy?
- How do my students demonstrate their ability to use strategies?
- What do my students understand about strategies?

**Multicultural Perspective** It's crucial that you incorporate a multicultural perspective into your classroom to prepare your students to interact effectively in American society today. To examine how you deal with cultural and linguistic diversity, ask yourself these questions:

- How are my attitudes about linguistic and cultural diversity reflected in my classroom?
- How often do my students read multicultural literature?
- How central do I make multicultural literature in my language arts program?
- What kinds of support do I provide for English learners?

# 2

# Listening

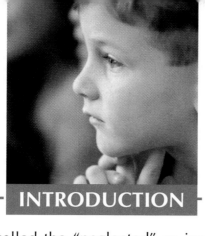

## INTRODUCTION

Listening has been called the "neglected" or ignored language art for more than 50 years because it is rarely taught in kindergarten through eighth-grade classrooms (Pinnell & Jaggar, 2003). Students are admonished to listen, but few teachers teach students how to improve their listening strategies. Teachers usually assume that children come to school already knowing how to listen. Also, some teachers feel that it is more important to spend the limited instructional time available on reading and writing instruction. Despite these concerns about teaching listening, most teachers agree that students need to know how to listen because it is the most used language art (Opitz & Zbaracki, 2004).

Listening is the first language process that children acquire, and it provides the basis for the other language arts (Lundsteen, 1979). Infants use listening to begin the process of learning to comprehend and produce language. From the beginning of their lives, children listen to sounds in their immediate environment, attend to speech sounds, and construct their knowledge of oral language. Listening also is important in learning to read. Children are introduced to written language by listening to stories that parents and other caregivers read to them. When children are read to, they begin to see the connection between what they hear and what they see on the printed page and to gain an understanding of stories. The processes of reading, viewing, and listening and the strategies used during these three processes are similar in many ways.

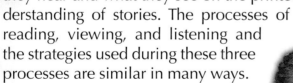

# Classroom Close-Up

## Second Graders Listen to Cook-a-Doodle-Doo!

The second graders in Mr. Hernandez's classroom are involved in a monthlong study of folktales, and this week, they're comparing several versions of "The Little Red Hen" and reading related books. On Monday, Mr. Hernandez read aloud Paul Galdone's *Little Red Hen* (1985), and the students reread it with buddies the next day. Next, he read aloud Margot Zemach's *The Little Red Hen: An Old Story* (1983), and the second graders compared it to Galdone's version. On Wednesday and Thursday, the students read "The Little Red Hen" in their basal reading textbooks and compared this version with the others.

Parent volunteers came into the classroom on Wednesday to make bread with the students. The second graders learned how to read a recipe and use measuring cups and other cooking tools as they made the bread. They baked the bread in the school kitchen, and what the students especially enjoyed was eating their freshly baked bread—still warm from the oven—dripping with butter and jam.

The nest day, Mr. Hernandez read aloud *Bread, Bread, Bread* (Morris, 1989), an informational book about the kinds of bread that people eat around the world, and parents brought in different kinds of bread for the students to sample, including tortillas, rye bread, croissants, bagels, Jewish matzoh, blueberry muffins, Indian chapatty, and biscuits. As they sampled the breads, the students took turns talking about the kinds of bread their families eat.

Today, the students are sitting on a carpet as Mr. Hernandez prepares to read aloud *Cook-a-Doodle-Doo!* (Stevens & Crummel, 1999), the story of the Little Red Hen's great-grandson, Big Brown Rooster, who manages to bake a strawberry shortcake with the help of three friends—Turtle, Iguana, and Pig. The teacher sets out a story box of objects related to the story: a chef's hat, a flour sifter, an egg beater, a plastic strawberry, an oven mitt, a shortcake pan, a timer, a pastry blender, and measuring cups and spoons. The students identify the objects, and Mr. Hernandez prepares a word card for each one so that students can later practice matching objects and word cards at a center. Almost immediately, Mikey guesses, "I know what the story is about! Little Red Hen is going to cook something, but it isn't bread. Um . . . Maybe it is strawberry jam to put on the bread."

"That's a good prediction, Mikey, but let me get one more clue for this story box," Mr. Hernandez says, as he reaches over to a nearby rack of puppets. He selects a rooster puppet and adds it to the box. He looks at the students expectantly, and Mallory asks, "Is that a hen?" "No, it isn't," Mr. Hernandez replies. Again he waits, until Cristina offers, "I think it's a rooster." "You're right! A rooster is a male chicken, and a hen is a female chicken," he explains. Then Mikey revises his prediction, "Now I know! It's a story about a rooster who cooks strawberries."

Mr. Hernandez shows the cover of *Cook-a-Doodle-Doo!* and reads the title. At first, the students laugh at the title, and several of them repeat it aloud. "What does the title make you think of?" Mr. Hernandez asks. Jesus jumps up and imitates a rooster: "Cock-a-doodle-doo! Cock-a-doodle-doo!" The students compare the sound a rooster makes to the book's title and conclude that the rooster in this book is going to do some cooking.

The teacher draws the students' attention back to the cover of the book and asks, "What do you think the rooster is going to cook?" Lacey and Connor both answer "strawberry pancakes," and the class agrees. Mr. Hernandez asks if anyone has ever tasted strawberry shortcake, but no one has. He explains what it is and tells the class it's his favorite dessert. Then he looks back at the cover, and says, "I keep looking at this picture, and it looks just like strawberry shortcake."

As Mr. Hernandez get ready to begin reading, he says, "I hope you'll enjoy this story because it's really funny, and I want you to think about how the story compares to *The Little Red Hen*." He reads the first two pages of the story that introduce the Little Red Hen's great-grandson, Big Brown Rooster, who is the main character in the story. The students point out the similarity between Little Red Hen and Big Brown Rooster's names: They are each three words long, they each have a size word, a color word, and an animal name, and words are in the same order in each name.

Mr. Hernandez continues reading, and the students learn that Rooster does plan to make strawberry shortcake—their teacher's favorite dessert. "What's shortcake?" Larry asks. "Is it

### Should teachers encourage discussion as they read a story aloud or postpone it until afterward?

Teachers often ask students to listen quietly while they read a story aloud and then encourage them to talk about it afterward, sharing ideas, clarifying confusions, and making connections to deepen their understanding. Other teachers, however, invite students to become actively involved in the story as they are reading it aloud. These teachers stop reading periodically to pose questions to stimulate discussion and ask students to make predictions. As you read this Classroom Close-Up, notice which approach Mr. Hernandez uses and think about how he uses discussion to support his second graders' comprehension.

the opposite of tall cake?" Everyone laughs, including Mr. Hernandez. He explains that shortcake is flatter than cake, like a biscuit. Mikey asks, "Is it like a brownie? Brownies are flatter than chocolate cake." "That's a good comparison," Mr. Hernandez says. Sammy offers: "A tortilla is flatter than a piece of bread." "Good! That's another good comparison," the teacher responds. "All this talk about food is making me hungry."

"Look at this," Mr. Hernandez says as he points to the cookbook that Big Brown Rooster is holding in the illustration. "That's Little Red Hen's cookbook—*The Joy of Cooking Alone*," he laughs. "My wife's favorite cookbook is called *The Joy of Cooking*," he explains. "I wonder why the word *alone* has been added to the title of her cookbook." "That's because no one would help her make bread," Mallory explains.

The teacher continues reading the story aloud. He turns the page and shows students the illustration, a picture of Big Brown Rooster talking to a dog, a cat, and a goose, and the students, remembering the events from "The Little Red Hen," spontaneously call out to Rooster, "No, don't ask them. They won't help you!" Big Brown Rooster does ask the three animals to help him, and as the students predicted, they refuse. As Mr. Hernandez reads the "Not I" refrain, the students join in. Sondra comments on the similarities to "The Little Red Hen" story: "There's a dog, a cat, and a goose like in the other story, and they won't listen to the Big Brown Rooster either." Then the students predict that Big Brown Rooster, like Little Red Hen, will have to cook alone.

On the next several pages, the students learn that three other animals—Turtle, who can read recipes, Iguana, who can get "stuff," and Pig, who is a tasting expert—offer to help. The students get excited. "I think this story is going to be different. It's better," Cristina comments. Mr. Hernandez wonders aloud if these three animals will be good helpers, and the students agree that they will be.

The rooster calls the four of them a "team" on the next page, and Mr. Hernandez asks, "What is a team?" The students mention basketball teams and name their favorite teams, so the teacher rephrases his question: "What makes a group of basketball players a team? What do they do when they are a team?" Students respond that players work together to make a score and win a game. "So, what kind of team are the rooster, the turtle, the iguana, and the pig?" Connor explains, "They are a cooking team. I predict they will work together to cook strawberry shortcake." Then Raymond adds, "And Mr. Hernandez is the captain of the team!"

Mr. Hernandez continues reading, as Turtle reads the recipe and Iguana collects the needed ingredients for strawberry shortcake. In the story, Iguana doesn't know the difference between a flower and flour, and because the students seem confused, too, the teacher explains the homophones. Iguana doesn't know about cooking tools and procedures either; he wants to use a ruler instead of a measuring cup to measure flour and he looks for teaspoons in a teapot, for example. Because the students recently used measuring cups and spoons when they baked bread, they are more knowledgeable than Iguana; Sammy says, "That iguana is silly. He's not very smart either." On the next page, Iguana misunderstands "stick of butter." He breaks a stick from a tree branch, and Lacey calls out, "No, Iguana, that's the wrong kind of stick."

As each ingredient is added, Pig offers to taste the batter, but Big Brown Rooster replies "not yet." Mr. Hernandez pauses after he reads this and reflects, "Pig seems very eager to taste the shortcake batter. I wonder how long he'll wait patiently for his turn to taste." "Maybe Big Brown Rooster should give him something else to do," Sondra offers. "I'd tell him to go in the living room and watch a video because that's what my mama tells my brother," says Connor. Mr. Hernandez continues reading, and in the story, Pig is getting more desperate to taste the batter. Jesus calls out, "Oh no! Now Pig really, really wants to taste it. Something bad is going to happen." Everyone agrees.

## How do children respond to stories?

Children make different types of responses as they talk about stories. Sipe (2002) identified these five types, and Mr. Hernandez's second graders made responses representing each type:

**Dramatizing**
Children spontaneously act out the story in both nonverbal and verbal ways. Mr. Hernandez's second graders, for example, dramatized cutting strawberries and beating cream as he read aloud.

**Talking Back**
Children talk back to the characters, giving them advice or criticizing and complimenting them. At the beginning of the story, for example, Mr. Hernandez's students tell Rooster not to ask the cat, the dog, and the goose for help, and later in the story, they tell Iguana that he has the wrong kind of stick.

**Critiquing/Controlling**
Children suggest alternative plots, characters, or settings to personalize the story. For example, several of Mr. Hernandez's students suggest ways that Rooster could handle Pig more effectively.

**Inserting**
Children insert themselves or their friends into the story. One of Mr. Hernandez's students, for example, inserts Mr. Hernandez into the story and says that he is the team captain.

**Taking Over**
Children take over the text and manipulate it to express their own creativity; these responses are usually humorous and provide an opportunity for children to show off. For example, after Mr. Hernandez's students suggest several possible endings for the story after the pig eats the first strawberry shortcake, Larry gets a big laugh when he suggests a different ending using words from "The Gingerbread Man."

Children make these types of responses when teachers encourage their active participation in the story, but the tricky part is to balance the time spent reading and talking.

The teacher reads that the characters finish mixing the ingredients and put the batter in the oven to bake. "Wow! I'm surprised that Pig is being so good," Mallory offers. "I thought he'd gobble up all the shortcake from the mixing bowl." The other students agree. "So, now you think the shortcake is going to turn out right?" Mr. Hernandez asks. Most of the students think that it will, but Jesus and Mikey predict trouble ahead.

Mr. Hernandez continues reading: The characters cut the strawberries in half and make whipped cream while the shortcake is in the oven. As the teacher reads, some of the students spontaneously pretend to cut strawberries or use the egg beater to whip the cream—they dramatize cooking activities.

The next several pages tell how Rooster takes the shortcake out of the oven, lets it cool, and slices it in half, and assembles the layers of shortcake with cake, whipped cream, and strawberries. Mikey notices that Pig smells the shortcake when it comes out of the oven and really wants to taste it. "I still think that Pig is bad news," he says.

Finally the strawberry shortcake is ready to eat, and Rooster says, "If Great-Granny could see me now!" Mr. Hernandez asks what the sentence means. Connor answers, "Rooster wants her to know he is a good cook, too!" Lacey suggests, "Rooster is really proud of himself." Raymond says, "I think Rooster wants Little Red Hen to know that he has a team to help him cook."

Mr. Hernandez turns the page, and the students gasp: The illustration shows the strawberry shortcake falling off the plate as Iguana carries it to the table. "Oh no, it's ruined!" Mallory says. "They can't eat it because it's on the floor." "Pig can! Yes, Pig can! Now it really is his turn!" Mikey says gleefully. Jesus cheers.

"What about the other animals?" Mr. Hernandez asks. "Won't they get to eat strawberry shortcake?" At first, the students guess that they won't, and then Jacob offers, "Well, they could go to the store and buy more food and make another strawberry shortcake." Most of the students agree that Jacob has a good idea, but Larry disagrees, "No way. 'Snip, snap, snout. This story's told out,' said Pig." Both the teacher and the students laugh as Larry suggests an alternative ending using the final words from the "The Gingerbread Man" story they read several weeks before.

Mr. Hernandez reads the last few pages in the book, and the students learn that the animals do make another delicious strawberry shortcake for everyone to eat. The students are satisfied with how the story turned out. "I'm really glad everyone got to eat some strawberry shortcake," Cristina says. "It's a really good story," Sammy

reflects, "because it's funny and serious, too." "What's funny in the story?" the teacher asks. The students say that Iguana is the funniest character, and the funniest part is when the shortcake falls on the floor and Pig gobbles it up. Then Mr. Hernandez asks, "What's serious in the story?" The students recognize the authors' message and identify it as the serious part of the book. They say the book's message is that a job is easier to do when you work together as a team. "I'm glad Rooster had a team," said Sondra. "What about us?" Mr. Hernandez asks, "Do we have a team?" Mikey says, "I never really thought of it before, but I guess our class is a team." Mr. Hernandez responds, "What do you think makes us a team?" "We help each other learn and do our work," Larry answers. The other students agree.

Finally, Mr Hernandez shows the students the last page of the book with Little Red Hen's recipe for strawberry shortcake, and he surprises them by announcing that he brought in the ingredients and that they will make strawberry shortcake after lunch.

The students regularly make charts using a combination of drawing and writing in their reading logs to help them remember an important idea about each story they read or listen to read aloud. After reading *Cook-a-Doodle-Doo!*, they make charts about how the characters in the story were a team. Mr. Hernandez helps the students brainstorm a list of words they might want to use on their charts and writes the words on the chalkboard so that they can spell them correctly. The words they brainstorm include: *team, Big Brown Rooster, Turtle,*

## One Student's Chart About the Team

We are a Team!

| Rooster | Iguana | Turtle | Pig |
|---------|--------|--------|-----|
| I need a Team. | I can get stuf! | I can read the reicpe! | I am the Taster! I like to et. |

*Iguana, Pig, Little Red Hen, strawberry shortcake, helper, recipe,* and *taster.*

As you continue reading Part 2, think about how Mr. Hernandez applies the topics being presented. Here are three questions to guide your reading:

- ◆ How did Mr. Hernandez involve students in the read-aloud?
- ◆ Which types of listening did Mr. Hernandez's students use?
- ◆ Which listening strategies did the second graders demonstrate as they listened to the story?

# Essentials

## ESSENTIAL #1: The Listening Process

Listening is elusive; in fact, teachers often don't know whether listening has occurred until they ask students to apply what they have listened to through discussions, projects, and other assignments. Even then, there is no guarantee that the students' responses indicate that they have listened, because they may have known the material before listening or may have learned it from someone else at about the same time.

Listening, like the other language arts, involves a process. It is more than just hearing, even though we often use the terms *hearing* and *listening* synonymously (Lundsteen, 1979). Actually, hearing is only one step; the crucial part is comprehending what was heard.

The listening process has three steps: receiving, attending, and assigning meaning (Wolvin & Coakley, 1995). In the first step, listeners receive the aural stimuli or the combined aural and visual stimuli presented by the speaker. Next, listeners focus on important stimuli while ignoring other, distracting stimuli. Because so many stimuli surround students in the classroom, they must attend to the speaker's message, focusing on the most important information in that message. In the third step, listeners comprehend or assign meaning to the speaker's message. Responding to the message is not considered part of the listening process; the response occurs afterward, and it sets another communication process into action in which the listener becomes the message sender.

The second step of Wolvin and Coakley's listening-process model can be called the "paying attention" component. Teachers spend a great deal of instructional time reminding students to pay attention; unfortunately, however, children often do not understand the admonition. When asked to explain what "paying attention" means, some children equate it with physical behaviors such as not kicking feet or cleaning off desks. Learning to attend to the speaker's message is especially important because researchers have learned that students can listen to 250 words per minute—two to three times the normal rate of talking (Foulke, 1968). This differential allows listeners time to tune in and out as well as to become distracted during listening.

### How important is listening?

Listening is often called the most important language art because it is the one we use the most. Researchers report that people spend as much time listening as they do reading, writing, and talking combined (Pinnell & Jaggar, 2003). Both children and adults spend approximately half of their communication time listening. Language researcher Walter Loban described the importance of listening this way: "We listen a book a day, we speak a book a week, we read a book a month, and we write a book a year" (cited in Erickson, 1985, p. 13).

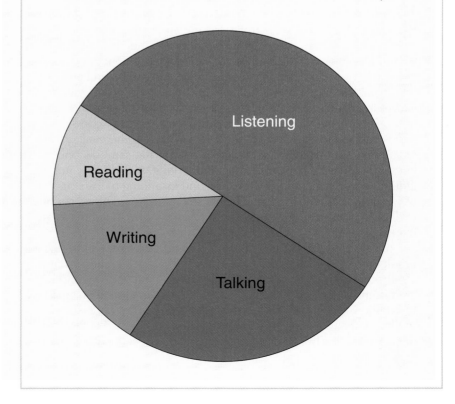

Furthermore, the intensity of students' need to attend to the speaker's message varies with their purpose for listening. Some types of listening require more attentiveness than others. Effective listeners, for example, listen differently to directions on how to reach a friend's home than they do to a poem or story being read aloud.

## ESSENTIAL #2: Purposes for Listening

Why do people listen? Children often answer that they listen to learn or to avoid punishment, but according to Wolvin and Coakley (1995), people actually use different types of listening for these four purposes:

- Discriminative listening to distinguish sounds
- Aesthetic listening for enjoyment
- Efferent listening to learn information
- Critical listening to evaluate information

**Discriminative Listening** People use discriminative listening to distinguish sounds and develop sensitivity to nonverbal communication. Teaching discriminative listening involves one sort of activity in the primary grades and a different activity for older students. Children use discriminative listening as they develop phonemic awareness, the ability to blend and segment the sounds in spoken words, identify rhyming words, and spell words.

Children also learn to "listen" to the nonverbal messages that people communicate. For example, young children quickly recognize the unspoken message when a parent's expression changes from a smile to a frown or when a teacher expresses puzzlement. Older students learn the meanings of more sophisticated forms of body language, such as people folding their arms over their chest to signify stubbornness or an invasion of their space. They also recognize how teachers emphasize that something they are teaching is important, such as by writing it on the chalkboard, speaking more loudly, or repeating information.

**Aesthetic Listening** People listen aesthetically when they're listening for enjoyment to stories being read aloud, as Mr. Hernandez's students did in the Classroom Close-Up. The focus of this type of listening is on the lived-through experience and the connections that listeners make to the literature.

As students listen to the teacher read aloud well-crafted stories such as *Charlotte's Web* (White, 1980) and *Thunder Cake* (Polacco, 1990), they engage with the text and step into the secondary world of the story. In *Charlotte's Web*, they feel the unlikely friendship between Charlotte and Wilbur, and in *Thunder Cake*, they understand the granddaughter's fear of thunderstorms and the urgency with which she and her grandmother collect the ingredients and prepare the thunder cake. The outcome of aesthetic listening is an emotional response. In addition to listening to teachers read stories aloud, children also listen aesthetically when they

- listen to storytellers tell stories
- listen to poets recite poems
- view puppet shows and plays
- listen to singers sing songs
- participate in choral reading and readers theatre
- view films and videotaped versions of stories

**Efferent Listening** People listen efferently to understand a message and remember important information. This type of listening is required in many instructional activities, particularly in thematic units. Students determine the speaker's purpose, identify the big ideas, and then organize the information in order to remember it.

Children often use efferent listening as they listen to teachers read books aloud or view videos as part of social studies and science thematic units. For instance, children learn how energy from the sun turns into energy for electricity as they listen to the teacher read *My Light* (Bang, 2004), learn about a historical mystery as they listen to the teacher read *The Lost Colony of Roanoke* (Fritz, 2004), and find out how dolphins communicate in *Dolphin Talk: Whistles, Clicks, and Clapping Jaws* (Pfeffer, 2003). Even though these books provide information, students may use a combination of aesthetic and efferent listening. Children often imagine that they're astronauts as they listen to the teacher read aloud *Exploring Our Solar System* (Ride & O'Shaughnessy, 2003), living in the secondary world of the book as they travel through space.

### What is phonemic awareness?

Phonemic awareness is the ability to hear and manipulate sounds in words. Children move through a continuum as they learn about the structure of language. First, they recognize that sentences are composed of words, and then that words rhyme and can be broken down into syllables and sounds. As their understanding grows, children learn to recognize words that begin or end with the same sound. Later, they learn to blend sounds into words and segment one-syllable words into sounds and longer words into syllables (Ehri et al., 2001).

Phonemic awareness is auditory; it's not the same as phonics because it doesn't involve reading and writing. It's critically important, however, that children link their understanding of the structure of words to their knowledge of letters so that they can blend sounds to decode words and segment sounds to spell words (National Reading Panel, 2000).

Researchers have found that phonemic awareness is the best predictor of whether children will learn to read successfully (Adams, 1990; Stanovich, 1993–1994). Children who learn to blend and segment sounds in kindergarten are likely to learn to read in first grade. In addition, reading instruction heightens children's understanding of phonemic awareness. Hallie Yopp (1992) concluded that phonemic awareness is both a prerequisite for and a consequence of learning to read.

**Critical Listening**

People listen critically to evaluate a message. Critical listening is an extension of efferent listening: As in efferent listening, listeners seek to understand a message, but they also filter the message to detect propaganda and emotional appeals. Students use critical listening to listen to debates, commercials, political speeches, and other arguments.

Teachers can help students think more critically as they read aloud and discuss books. When students listen to teachers read aloud stories such as *The True Story of the 3 Little Pigs!* (Scieszka, 1989) and *Witness* (Hesse, 2001), they critically analyze the characters' claims, and when they read informational books, such as *Antarctica* (Cowcher, 1990), and biographies, such as *My Hiroshima* (Morimoto, 1987), they can evaluate the authors' warnings about destroying the environment and about nuclear war. Students don't automatically think critically about these books, but teachers can guide them to consider the effects of viewpoint, persuasion, and emotional appeal.

**When Do Students Use Each Purpose?**

Students rarely use these purposes separately. For instance, as eighth graders listen to *Catherine, Called Birdy* (Cushman, 1994), the story of a strong-willed young noblewoman set in the Middle Ages, they use several purposes simultaneously. As they listen aesthetically, they step back into history and imagine they are Birdy and feel what she is feeling. At the same time, they use efferent listening as they think about geographic locations, historical events, kings and other historical figures, and additional information the author has

## What's the difference between *aesthetic* and *efferent*?

Louise Rosenblatt (1978, 2005) coined the term *aesthetic reading* to describe the stance readers take when they are reading for pleasure—involved in the lived-through experience and making connections to the literature they are reading. The focus is on their experience during reading. In contrast, Rosenblatt's term *efferent* means "to carry away." Efferent reading is practical: Students use it to identify and remember big ideas. Aesthetic and efferent reading, according to Rosenblatt, represent two ends of a continuum. Students rarely use one type of reading exclusively; instead, they use a combination of purposes. The terms *aesthetic* and *efferent* can also be used to describe two purposes of listening.

carefully included in the story. It's also possible that they use discriminative listening and notice rhyme, alliteration, and other types of wordplay. Critical listening plays a role, too, as students consider the author's viewpoint, assess emotional appeals, and think about the theme.

Teachers need to teach students about these purposes and help them set purposes for listening. Students need to know what teachers expect them to listen for, or teachers need to help students set their own purposes. When reading *Catherine, Called Birdy,* for example, teachers usually explain that students should listen aesthetically and enjoy the story, but they also point out that students should notice the historical information as they're listening. Teachers often begin discussions after reading aloud by talking about the aesthetic interpretation, but then move on to talking about the historical information children learned as they listened.

## The Four Purposes of Listening

| Type | Discriminative | Aesthetic | Efferent | Critical |
|---|---|---|---|---|
| **Purpose** | Distinguish among sounds | Listen for pleasure or enjoyment | Understand a message | Evaluate a message |
| **Examples** | • Participate in phonemic awareness activities<br>• Notice rhyming words in poems and songs<br>• Recognize alliteration and onomatopoeia<br>• Experiment with tongue twisters | • Listen to stories and poems read aloud<br>• View video versions of stories<br>• Watch students perform a play or a readers theatre reading | • Listen to informational books read aloud<br>• Listen to directions<br>• Listen to the teacher present information<br>• Use graphic organizers<br>• Listen to oral reports<br>• View informational videos<br>• Listen during mini-lessons | • Listen to debates and political speeches<br>• View commercials and advertisements<br>• Evaluate themes and arguments in books read aloud |

# Strategies

## Listening Strategies

Listening happens every day in every classroom. Students listen as the teacher reads stories aloud, and they listen to the teacher give directions and present information. Even though listening has been called the neglected language art, there's no doubt that it plays a significant role in classroom activities. However, what has been neglected is teaching students how to be more effective listeners. Most of what has traditionally been called listening instruction is merely practice: When students listen to the teacher present information during a science unit and then complete a worksheet, for example, teachers assume that students know how to listen and that they will be able to complete the assignment. Through activities like these, students only practice whatever listening strategies they already possess.

The best way to improve children's listening is by teaching listening strategies (Brent & Anderson, 1993; Opitz & Zbaracki, 2004). Teachers use Dorn and Soffos's (2001) four teacher behaviors—modeling, coaching, scaffolding, and fading—as they teach minilessons about listening strategies and guide students to become more effective listeners.

Students use some strategies, such as activating background knowledge and monitoring their understanding, for most types of listening, but others are particularly effective for certain listening purposes. Many of these strategies are the same ones that students use for reading and viewing, the other receptive language arts.

**Strategies for Discriminative Listening** As young children develop phonemic awareness, they learn to blend and segment sounds. These two strategies are especially useful when children are learning to read and spell: As they sound out words, students pronounce individual sounds and then blend them to decode the words, and when they are spelling an unfamiliar word, they pronounce the word slowly, segmenting individual sounds. Two other strategies that students acquire are savoring word play and noticing verbal and nonverbal cues. Children enjoy telling jokes and riddles and repeating tongue twisters. They apply what they've learned about wordplay when they appreciate poems they're reading and write their own wordplay and poetry.

Children also learn to notice verbal and nonverbal cues when they're listening to parents, teachers, and classmates. They learn that careful listening is enhanced by observation. Speakers direct their listeners' attention with a combination of visual and verbal cues. Visual cues include gesturing, writing

or underlining important information on the chalkboard, and changing facial expressions. Verbal cues include pausing, raising or lowering the voice, slowing down speech to stress key points, and repeating important information. Surprisingly, many students are not aware of these attention-directing behaviors, so teachers must point them out. Once students are aware of these cues, they can use them to increase their understanding of a message.

**Strategies for Aesthetic Listening** Children learn to use predicting, visualizing, connecting, and summarizing strategies through minilessons, and they apply what they're learning as they listen to the teacher read stories aloud. These are the same comprehension strategies that students use when they read, but learning them through listening is often more effective.

The second graders in the Classroom Close-Up, for instance, used aesthetic listening strategies as they listened to Mr. Hernandez read aloud *Cook-a-Doodle-Doo!* (Stevens & Crummel, 1999). Mikey offered predictions spontaneously, and at key points in the story, Mr. Hernandez asked the students to make additional predictions. They revised their understanding of the story as they made predictions and listened to see if they were correct. Students refined their understanding of the story as they offered comments and listened to the comments their classmates made, such as when students reflected on the pig's role in the story. The students made personal connections to their families' cooking experiences and literary connections to the "Little Red Hen" stories they had read. The title of the book provided an opportunity for language play when

### Strategies Students Use as They Listen

| Discriminative Listening | Efferent Listening |
|---|---|
| • blending<br>• segmenting<br>• savoring word play<br>• noticing verbal and nonverbal cues | • organizing<br>• recognizing big ideas<br>• questioning<br>• summarizing |
| **Aesthetic Listening** | **Critical Listening** |
| • predicting<br>• visualizing<br>• connecting<br>• summarizing | • determining the author's viewpoint<br>• identifying persuasive techniques<br>• evaluating<br>• drawing conclusions |

Mr. Hernandez and his students compared "cock-a-doodle-doo" to "cook-a-doodle-doo." Students also noticed the similarity between the names *Big Brown Rooster* and *Little Red Hen* and the "not I" refrain from "The Little Red Hen" story. The students used the visualizing and summarizing strategies when they made character charts after listening to Mr. Hernandez read the story.

Students do not always use every strategy as they listen to a story, but *Cook-a-Doodle-Doo!* provided opportunities for the students to use all of them, and Mr. Hernandez knew how to take advantage of teachable moments.

<table><tr><td>**Strategies for Efferent Listening**</td><td>When students listen efferently, they focus on the big ideas and use strategies that help them recognize these ideas and organize them so they are easier to remember. For</td></tr></table>

example, they use the questioning strategy to help them pick out what's important and understand the relationships among the big ideas. Summarizing is another strategy students use to help them remember the big ideas.

Teachers often have students complete graphic organizers to highlight the big ideas and the relationships among them (Yopp & Yopp, 2001). When sixth graders listened to a presentation comparing amphibians and reptiles, for example, they made a T-chart to organize the information; they chose this graphic organizer because it emphasizes the comparison structure. They labeled one column "Amphibians" and the other "Reptiles" and wrote notes in each column while they listened to the presentation.

<table><tr><td>**Strategies for Critical Listening**</td><td>Listening critically means listening to evaluate or judge the message, and the most impor-</td></tr></table>

tant strategy for critical listening is evaluating (Lundsteen, 1979). Students use the evaluating strategy to think about these questions:

- ◆ What is the speaker's or author's purpose?
- ◆ Is there an intellectual or emotional appeal?
- ◆ Are illustrations persuasive?
- ◆ Are propaganda devices being used?
- ◆ Are deceptive words or inflated language used?

As students listen to books read aloud, view commercials and advertisements, and listen to speakers, they need to ask themselves these questions in order to evaluate the message. Students also use efferent listening strategies during critical listening because critical listening is an extension of efferent listening: They organize ideas, ask questions, recog-

nize the big ideas, and summarize the presentation so that they can evaluate the message.

<table><tr><td>**The Listening-Reading-Viewing Connection**</td><td>Not only is it important that students learn strategies to improve their ability to listen, but students also use many of the same strategies for listening that they use for</td></tr></table>

reading and viewing. Listening serves as a bridge to reading: Once students learn to use a listening strategy, they can apply what they have learned to reading and viewing. These strategies affect comprehension, no matter whether students are comprehending what they are listening to or what they are reading or viewing. Students need to learn to vary how they listen to fit their purpose for listening and develop specific strategies to use for different types of listening (Brent & Anderson, 1993; Jalongo, 1991). Capable listeners often use predicting and visualizing when listening aesthetically to stories, but many less capable listeners have only one approach to listening, no matter what the purpose: They listen as hard as they can and try to remember everything. This strategy is destined to fail for at least two reasons. First, trying to remember everything places an impossible demand on short-term memory; and second, many items in a message are not important enough to remember. Often students equate listening with intelligence, and less capable listeners assume that they are poor listeners because they "just aren't smart enough."

**Sixth Graders' T-Chart**

| Amphibians | Reptiles |
|---|---|
| Metamorphosis $H_2O \downarrow$ land | Only one form |
| Skin is moist | Dry skin |
| Smooth or warty skin | Have scales |
| Lay eggs in water in jelly | Lay eggs on land in shells |
| Gills then lungs | Just lungs |
| Only males ♂ have voices! | Only the Gecko has a voice! |

# MINILESSON *Visualizing*

## Mrs. Armstrong Teaches Visualizing to Her Fourth Graders

1. **Introduce the topic**   Mrs. Armstrong introduces visualizing to her fourth-grade class. She explains that when she listens to a story read aloud, she makes pictures in her mind that go along with the story. She asks if they, too, make pictures in their minds, and many children agree that they do.

2. **Share examples**   Mrs. Armstrong begins reading Judy Blume's *Tales of a Fourth Grade Nothing* (1972) and demonstrates how to create mind pictures of the characters and story events while reading aloud the first two chapters.

3. **Provide information**   Mrs. Armstrong explains the steps she uses in creating mind pictures:

   1. Close your eyes.
   2. Draw a picture of a scene or character in your mind.
   3. Listen for details and add them to your picture.
   4. Add colors to your mind picture.

   She creates a chart about visualizing, draws a person's head with a picture in it, and writes these four steps on the chart.

4. **Supervise practice**   As Mrs. Armstrong continues reading the book aloud, students practice making mind pictures. She stops reading periodically to ask students to describe how they are using the strategy. The fourth graders especially enjoy creating mind pictures near the end of the book when Peter finds out that his little brother Fudge ate his turtle.

5. **Assess learning**   After finishing the book, Mrs. Armstrong asks students to reflect on how they used the visualization strategy. One fourth grader explains:

   *I made a picture in my mind of how upset Peter was that Fudge ate his turtle. He was crazy for wanting to find his turtle and mad at his brother and because no one cared about his turtle, only about his brother. His face was red because he was crazy mad and he was yelling at Fudge and at his mom. He was crying and wiping at his eyes because his turtle's been eaten. Then I had a new picture in my mind when Peter got the big box with a puppy in it at the end. He was calm but not really happy. He was still sad about his turtle being dead. He had a smart look on his face because he knew it had to be a puppy and he thought to name him Turtle so he wouldn't forget. I see him holding the black and white dog and that dog is licking him all over his face.*

Kucer (1991) urges teachers to talk with students about their understanding of strategies because he found that students' interpretations often don't match those of the teacher.

Because reading and listening involve many of the same strategies, teachers can teach strategies through listening and then have students apply them during reading (Pearson & Fielding, 1982; Sticht & James, 1984). As they read aloud, teachers model how to use these strategies, and after listening, students can reflect on how well they used them. It is easier for students to focus on strategy use during listening than during reading because they don't have to decode written words when listening.

# MINILESSON *Getting Clues*

## Mrs. Rodriquez's Students Watch for Clues

1. **Introduce the topic**   Mrs. Rodriquez explains to her second graders that she often does some special things to get their attention and to tell them what information is most important when she teaches a lesson.

2. **Share examples**   Mrs. Rodriquez asks her students to watch her carefully as she begins a lesson about the body of an insect as part of a thematic unit on insects. Mrs. Rodriquez begins to speak, and she holds up three fingers as she explains that insects have three body parts. Next, she points to the three body parts on a nearby chart and names them, tapping each part with a pointer. Then she writes the names of the body parts on the chalkboard. Afterward, Mrs. Rodriquez asks students to recall what she did during the presentation, and the students correctly point out the three clues she used.

3. **Provide information**   Mrs. Rodriquez explains to students that teachers or other presenters often use clues to help listeners understand what is most important in a lesson. She explains that teachers use a variety of clues and asks her students to look for more clues as she continues the lesson. She demonstrates several more clues, including repeating an important fact and raising her voice for emphasis. Afterward, Mrs. Rodriquez asks students to identify the clues.

4. **Supervise practice**   The next day, Mrs. Rodriquez presents a lesson comparing insects and spiders, and she asks students to watch for her clues and to raise their hands to indicate that they noticed them. Afterward, she reviews the clues she used. She repeats this step for several additional lessons about insects.

5. **Assess learning**   To check their understanding about clues, Mrs. Rodriquez has her second graders make a list of the clues she used during a lesson, and they draw pictures to illustrate each clue they add to the list.

# Classroom Practice

## INTERACTIVE READ-ALOUDS: Getting Students Engaged in Listening

Reading aloud to students is a cherished classroom routine. In a recent study of sixth graders' reading preferences, an overwhelming 62% of students reported that they enjoy listening to the teacher read aloud (Ivey & Broaddus, 2001). Children's author Mem Fox (2001) and reading-aloud guru Jim Trelease (2001) both urge teachers to make time to read aloud to students every day because as they listen, students gain valuable experiences with books, enrich their background knowledge and vocabulary, and develop a love of reading. Reading aloud is art; effective readers are familiar with the book they're reading, and they read fluently and with expression, changing the tone of their voices and using pauses to enhance students' listening experience.

Reading aloud has been an informal activity in most classrooms: Teachers pick up a book, read the title aloud, and begin reading while students listen quietly. Often young children sit in a group on the floor around the teacher, and older students sit attentively at their desks. The students are passive as they listen, but afterward, they become more engaged as they talk briefly about the story and perhaps participate in a follow-up activity. The focus is on the sharing of literature with little or no student involvement until after the reading is over. Researchers who have studied reading aloud, however, have concluded that students are better listeners when they are involved while the teacher is reading, not afterward (Dickinson & Tabors, 2001). This conclusion has led to the development of the interactive read-aloud procedure (Barrentine, 1996).

In an interactive read-aloud, teachers introduce the book and activate children's background knowledge before they begin to read. They model listening strategies and fluent oral reading as they read aloud, and they engage students while they read. Then after reading, they provide opportunities for students to respond to the book. The most important component, however, is how teachers involve students while they are reading aloud (Fisher, Flood, Lapp, & Frey, 2004).

One way that teachers engage students is to stop reading periodically to discuss what has just been read. What matters is when teachers stop reading: When they're reading stories aloud, it's more effective to stop at points where students can make predictions and suggest connections, after reading episodes that students might find confusing, and just before it becomes clear how the story will end. When they're reading informational books aloud, teachers stop to talk about big ideas as they are presented, briefly explain technical terms, and emphasize connections among the big ideas. When they reading poems, teachers often read the entire poem once, and then stop as they read the poem a second time for students to play with words, notice poetic devices, and repeat favorite words and lines. Deciding how often to stop for discussion and knowing when to end the discussion and continue reading develop through practice and vary from one group of students to another. In the Classroom Close-Up, Mr. Hernandez actively involved his second graders in listening by encouraging them to talk about the story as he read it aloud.

## INTERACTIVE READ-ALOUDS

**1 Pick a book**
Teachers choose award-winning and other high-quality books that are appropriate for students and fit into their instructional programs.

**2 Preview the book**
Teachers practice reading the book to ensure that they can read it fluently and to decide where to pause and engage children with the text; they write prompts on self-stick notes to mark these pages. Teachers also think about how they will introduce the book and select difficult vocabulary words to highlight.

**3 Introduce the book**
Teachers activate students' background knowledge, set a clear purpose for listening, and preview the text.

**4 Read the book interactively**
Teachers read the book aloud, modeling fluent and expressive reading. They stop periodically to ask questions to focus students on specific points in the text and involve them in other activities.

**5 Involve students in after-reading activities**
Students participate in discussions and other types of response activities.

In addition to discussion, teachers use these activities to involve children as they read stories aloud:

- ◆ Make and revise predictions at pivotal points in the story
- ◆ Share personal, world, and literary connections
- ◆ Talk about what they're visualizing or how they're using other strategies
- ◆ Draw a picture of a character or an event
- ◆ Assume the persona of a character and share what the character might be thinking
- ◆ Reenact a scene from the story

In addition, young children who are reading patterned stories often recite repetitive refrains while the teacher is reading.

While teachers read aloud informational books or chapters in content-area textbooks, children participate in these ways:

- ◆ Ask questions or share information
- ◆ Raise their hands when they hear specific information
- ◆ Restate headings as questions
- ◆ Take notes
- ◆ Complete graphic organizers

Teachers often read a poem aloud several times. During the first reading, children often listen without participating, and then teachers invite them to participate in these ways as they listen a second time:

- ◆ Add sound effects
- ◆ Mumble read along with the teacher, if they can read the poem
- ◆ Repeat lines after the teacher
- ◆ Clap when they hear rhyming words, alliterations, onomatopoeia, or other poetic devices

Teachers don't have children do all these things, of course, with any one interactive read-aloud, but they choose participatory activities based on their students' interests and the material they are reading.

Children—especially kindergartners and primary-grade students—often beg to have a familiar book reread. Although it's important to share a wide variety of books with children, researchers have found that children benefit in specific ways from repeated readings (Yaden, 1988). Through repetition, students gain control over the parts of a story and are better able to synthesize those parts into a whole.

The quality of children's responses to a repeated story changes, too. Martinez and Roser (1985) examined young children's responses to stories and found that as stories became increasingly familiar, children's responses indicated a greater depth of understanding. They found that children

## Theory to Practice
### Using Interactive Read-Alouds in a Third-Grade Classroom

During a unit on the rain forest, Mrs. Cooper uses the interactive read-aloud procedure to share stories, informational books, and poems with her third graders. She varies the engagement techniques she uses according to the book's genre and her purposes.

**Book 1: *One Day in the Tropical Rain Forest***

Mrs. Cooper reads Jean Craighead George's chapter-book story *One Day in the Tropical Rain Forest* (1990). As she begins, Mrs. Cooper asks the students to listen aesthetically and to imagine that they are Tepui, an Indian boy living in the Venezuelan rain forest, who helps scientists find a new species of butterfly. The next day, she asks them to listen critically—to determine the author's message about preserving the rain forest. After she finishes reading, Mrs. Cooper invites students to draw pictures of Tepui that emphasize the author's message.

**Book 2: *Nature's Green Umbrella***

Next, Mrs. Cooper reads *Nature's Green Umbrella: Tropical Rain Forests* (Gibbons, 1994), an informational book. The students divide into small groups, and each group takes responsibility for locating the answer to one of the questions about the rain forest that the class brainstormed in an earlier activity. As Mrs. Cooper reads aloud, students raise their hands when they hear the answer to their question, and she helps them write notes. Afterward, the students in each group summarize their notes and write a paragraph-length answer to their question, which they copy on chart paper, post in the classroom, and share with the class.

**Book 3: *The Tree***

Several days later, Mrs. Cooper reads aloud *The Tree* (Vyner, 1994), a cumulative story about a rain forest tree. Even though it's a story, *The Tree* reads like a poem following the cumulative pattern of "This is the house that Jack built." Mrs. Cooper invites students to play with the language by reading along with her once they figure out the author's pattern. The students enjoy the book so much that Mrs. Cooper rereads it several times, with the third graders chanting as she reads. Later, many of the third graders write new versions of *The Tree* as their end-of-unit project.

talked almost twice as much about familiar books that had been reread many times as they did about unfamiliar books that had been read only once or twice. The form and focus of children's talk changed, too: Children tended to ask questions about unfamiliar stories, but they made comments about familiar ones. Children's talk about unfamiliar stories focused on characters; the focus changed to details and word meanings when they talked about familiar stories.

The researchers also found that children's comments after repeated readings were more probing and more specific, suggesting that they had greater insight into the story. Researchers investigating the value of repeated readings have focused mainly on preschool and primary-grade students, but rereading favorite stories and other types of books many have similar benefits for older students as well.

**How to Choose the Best Books**

Choosing books to read aloud can be difficult because teachers have access to literally thousands of books today. The most important guideline for choosing books for interactive read-alouds is to choose books that you like. A second guideline is to choose books that children will like but cannot read independently. A number of guides are available to help teachers select books, including:

- *Adventuring With Books: A Booklist for Pre-K–Grade 6* (McClure & Kristo, 2002)
- *Kaleidoscope: A Multicultural Booklist for Grades K–8* (Hansen-Krening, Aoki, & Mizokawa, 2003)
- *The New York Times Parent's Guide to the Best Books for Children* (Lipson, 2000)
- *The Read-Aloud Handbook* (Trelease, 2001)
- *Your Reading: An Annotated Booklist for Middle School and Junior High School* (Brown & Stephens, 2003)

Teachers also can check journals, including *Language Arts, The Reading Teacher, The Horn Book,* and *Book Links,* for reviews of newly published trade books for children.

Books that have received awards or other acclaim from teachers, librarians, and children make good choices. The two most prestigious awards are the Caldecott Medal and the Newbery Medal, which are awarded annually by the American Library Association. Books receive special notice in other ways, too. In many states, for example, children vote for favorite books to receive recognition, such as the Buckeye Book Award in Ohio and the Sequoyah Book Award in Oklahoma. The International Reading Association also sponsors a Children's Choices competition, in which children select their favorite books, and a similar Teachers' Choices competition; lists of these books are published annually in *The Reading Teacher.*

**Benefits of Reading Aloud**

It's easy to take reading aloud for granted, assuming that it is something teachers do for fun in between instructional activities. However, reading aloud to students is an important instructional activity with numerous benefits:

- Children's interest in reading is stimulated
- Children's reading interests and their taste for quality literature are broadened
- Children are introduced to the sounds of written language
- Children's knowledge of vocabulary and sentence patterns is expanded
- Children are introduced to books that are "too good to miss"
- Children listen to books that might be too difficult for them to read on their own or that are "hard to get into"
- Children see their teachers model what capable readers do
- Children's background knowledge is expanded
- Children are introduced to genres and elements of text structure
- Children are more likely to become lifelong readers
- Children become a community of learners through a pleasurable, shared experience

---

### Can a book be too difficult to read aloud?

Teachers often read aloud grade-appropriate books that are too difficult for some students to read independently. The idea is that even if students can't read the words, they can understand the ideas presented in the book. This read-aloud strategy works for many students, but for others, it does not. For example, students may lack sufficient background knowledge on the topic or may be overwhelmed by unfamiliar vocabulary in the book. They may not listen strategically, or they may not be interested in the book.

You can solve these problems. You can build background knowledge before reading by showing a video, reading a picture book, or sharing a story box of objects. At the same time you're building background knowledge, introduce key vocabulary words, and while reading, briefly explain unfamiliar words; sometimes providing a synonym is enough. In addition, struggling students may not know how to listen. It's important to teach the listening process and ask students to use strategies, such as visualizing, while they listen.

Finally, struggling students often complain that a book is "boring," but what they generally mean is that they don't understand it. Making sure that students understand often takes care of their seeming lack of interest; however, if the book really doesn't interest students, you can create interest by making connections with their lives, showing the video version of the story, or asking students to assume a role as a character and dramatize events from the story. If none of these strategies work, then choose a different book to read.

Reading stories aloud to children has always been an important component in most kindergarten and first-grade classrooms. Sometimes teachers think they should read to children only until they learn to read for themselves, but reading aloud to share the excitement of books should remain an important part of the language arts program at all grade levels. Upper-grade students report that when they listen to the teacher read aloud, they get more interested in the book and understand it better, and the experience often makes them want to read the book themselves (Ivey, 2003). In addition, Albright (2002) examined her seventh graders' responses during interactive read-alouds of picture books, and she found that through this activity, her students were more engaged in learning, they exhibited higher-level thinking, and they enriched their content-area knowledge.

## LEARNING TO "DO" SCHOOL: Ways to Improve Students' Efferent Listening

Efferent listening is the most common type of listening that students use in school: They listen efferently when teachers present information and give directions. Students may be learning about homonyms during language arts, for example, the water cycle during a science unit, or the Bill of Rights during a social studies unit. No matter the topic, teachers want students to remember the big ideas and understand the relationships among them. They can use five techniques to improve students' listening by piquing their curiosity and encouraging them to be more actively involved in listening. By incorporating these techniques into their presentations, teachers make their oral presentation more like interactive read-alouds.

**Activate Background Knowledge** Teachers encourage students to activate background knowledge and build on that knowledge by having them explore the topic. They can brainstorm ideas while the teacher takes notes on chart paper, in list or cluster format. As students share ideas, the teacher asks them to elaborate, and the teacher clarifies any misconceptions. Or, students can quickwrite on the topic and then share their writing with the class. Teachers also use anticipation guides to stimulate students' interest in a topic and activate their background knowledge. They present a set of statements related to the topic, some of which are true and will be confirmed by the presentation, and others that are false and will be corrected by the presentation. Before the presentation, students read and disuss each statement and mark whether they think it is true or false. Then they listen to the presentation and mark each statement again after listening (Readence, Bean, & Baldwin, 2004).

**Set a Clear Purpose** Teachers explain the purpose for listening and tell students to listen efferently, to remember information. For example, their purpose

might be to learn how to identify prefixes or to identify four reasons why pioneers traveled west in covered wagons.

**Use Manipulatives** Teachers choose objects, pictures and photos, or word cards for students to examine or use in activities during the presentation. Using manipulatives increases students' interest and makes abstract ideas more concrete.

**Create Graphic Organizers** Teachers create diagrams using circles, boxes, lines, and arrows to show the relationships among the big ideas, and students complete the graphic organizer by adding words during the presentation.

**Have Students Take Notes** Students take notes to help them remember the big ideas as they listen to oral presentations.

Upper-grade students often use a special kind of note taking in which they divide their papers into two columns, labeling the left column *Take Notes* and the right column *Make Notes*. They take notes in the left column, but, more important, they think about the notes, make connections, and personalize the notes in the right column (Berthoff, 1981). The right column should be more extensive than the left one because this column shows students' thinking.

### Teaching Students to Take Notes

Students are more active listeners when they take notes. Their interest in note taking begins when they realize that they can't store unlimited amounts of information in their minds: They need some kind of external storage system.

Teachers introduce note taking by demonstrating the procedure. They set a clear purpose, and during the oral presentation, they stop periodically, ask students to identify the big idea that was presented, and list their responses on the chalkboard. Teachers often begin by writing notes in a list format, but the notes can also be written in an outline or diagram. After an introduction to various note-taking approaches, students develop personal note-taking systems in which they write notes in their own words and use a consistent format.

Children's awareness that note taking is a strategy "to help you remember what you are listening to" starts in the primary grades. Teachers begin demonstrating the usefulness of note taking on charts with kindergartners and first graders, and second and third graders begin taking notes in their learning logs as a part of thematic units.

Teachers often teach students to take notes from informational books and reference materials. However, taking notes from a speaker is equally important, and it presents special challenges. When they are taking notes from a speaker, students cannot control the speed at which information is presented. They usually cannot listen more than once to a speaker to complete their notes, and the structure of oral presentations is often less formal than that of printed materials. Students need to become aware of these differences so that they can adapt their note-taking system to the mode of presentation.

## Scaffolding English Learners

### Why is listening so important for English learners?

Listening is a key to language development because children learn English as they listen to the teacher and classmates talk and read aloud.

**Reason 1: Language Models**

When teachers read aloud, the books provide language models. English learners acquire new vocabulary and more sophisticated language patterns and sentence structures through listening. Gibbons (2002) warns, however, that classrooms are noisy places, and the background buzz may make it harder for English learners to hear, under-stand, and learn. Teachers can alleviate this problem by sitting English learners close to where they often talk and read to the whole class and by insisting that classmates be courteous listeners.

**Reason 2: Expanding Knowledge**

Students also develop background knowledge through listening. They learn new information and the vocabulary to express the ideas, and they also make new connections between the ideas and past experiences. This contri-bution is especially important for children of poverty, including English learners, who have limited background knowledge.

**Reason 3: Transfer to Reading**

Listening is an important instruc-tional tool because it is a receptive process, like reading. Students can transfer the listening strategies they learn to reading, and both listening and reading involve the active construction of meaning.

Effective listening depends on expectations and predictions about the content, language, and genre that the listener brings to the text. In addition, whether students are successful listeners depends on their background knowledge and familiarity with the topic teachers are talking or reading about.

---

Minilessons are a good example of an interactive presenta-tion of information. In a minilesson, teachers:

- Set a purpose for the lesson and connect it to ongoing activities in the classroom
- Interest students in the lesson by using student examples or examples from literature
- Involve students in activities, including brainstorming ideas, locating examples, manipulating words and sen-tences, discussing the topic, and making charts and posters
- Put students in small groups to experiment with the new information
- Have students make personal connections to the new in-formation by applying it in language arts activities

Teachers improve students' efferent listening by enhancing their interest in the topic and by increasing their active in-volvement during listening.

### Developing a Critical Ear

Students—even those in the primary grades—need to become critical listeners because they are exposed to persuasion and propaganda all around them; the biggest culprit is probably tel-evision commercials. It's essential that they listen critically in order to judge the advertising claims. For instance, do the jog-ging shoes actually help you run faster? Will the breakfast ce-real make you a better football player? Will owning a particular pair of shoes or video game make you more popular? At school, students use critical listening to understand many stories that teachers read aloud, and social studies and science lessons on topics such as pollution, political candidates, and drugs de-mand that students listen and think critically.

**Persuasion and Propaganda**

There are three ways to persuade people. The first is by reason. We seek logical con-clusions, whether from absolute facts or from strong possibilities; for example, we can be persuaded to practice more health-ful living as the result of medical research. It is necessary, of course, to distinguish between reasonable arguments and un-reasonable appeals. To suggest that diet pills will bring about extraordinary weight loss is an illogical appeal.

A second way is an appeal to character. We can be per-suaded by what another person recommends if we trust that person. Trust comes from personal knowledge or the reputa-tion of the person who is trying to persuade. We can believe what scientists say about the dangers of nuclear waste, but can we believe what a sports personality says about the taste of a particular brand of coffee?

The third way is by appealing to people's emotions. Emotional appeals can be as strong as intellectual appeals. We have strong feelings and concern for ourselves and other people and animals. Fear, a need for peer acceptance, and a desire for freedom of expression are all potent feelings that influence our opinions and beliefs.

Any of these types of appeals can be used to try to persuade someone. For example, when a child tries to convince her parents that her bedtime should be delayed by 30 minutes, she might argue that neighbors allow their children to stay up later—an appeal to character. It is an appeal to reason when the argument focuses on the amount of sleep a 10-year-old needs. And when the child announces that she has the earliest bedtime of anyone in her class and it makes her feel like a baby, the appeal is to emotion. The same three appeals apply to in-school persuasion. To persuade classmates to read a particular book in a book talk "commercial," a student might argue that classmates should read the book because it is short and interesting (reason); because it is hilarious and they'll laugh (emotion); or because it is the most popular book in the seventh grade and everyone else is reading it (character).

## Propaganda Devices

### Glittering Generality
Propagandists use generalities such as "environmentally safe" to enhance the quality of a product. Even though the generality is powerful, listeners think beyond the generality to assess the product.

### Testimonial
Advertisers associate a product with an athlete or movie star. Listeners consider whether the person offering the testimonial has the expertise to judge the quality of the product.

### Name Calling
Persuaders try to pin a bad label on someone or something they want listeners to dislike, such as calling a person "unpatriotic." Listeners then consider the effect of the label.

### Card Stacking
Propagandists often use only items that favor one side of an issue; unfavorable facts are ignored. To be objective, listeners seek information about other viewpoints.

### Bandwagon
Advertisers claim that everyone is using their product. For example, "four out of five physicians recommend this medicine." Listeners consider whether everyone really does use this product.

### Rewards
Propagandists offer rewards for buying their products. Children are lured by toys in fast-food meals, and adults by rebates from manufacturers. Listeners ask whether the reward makes the product worth buying.

## What is media literacy?

Today, our information and entertainment come more from the visual media—television, films and DVDs, CD-ROMs, and the Internet—than from print sources. For instance, children spend an average of 21 hours each week watching television, and they will have spent more time in front of the television than in the classroom by the time they graduate from high school (Lembo, 2000). Children's interest in the media is reflected in the books and magazines they choose to read and the topics they write about (Dyson, 2003). Because of the prevalence of media today, it's essential that children learn to both comprehend and evaluate a message rather than simply accept it at face value.

*Media literacy* is the ability to interpret media messages (Silverblatt, 2001). Children use critical listening, viewing, and thinking skills to analyze the media messages that inform, entertain, and sell to us every day. Children use media literacy strategies and skills, for example, when they question whether violence being depicted is normal and acceptable, examine digital photo manipulation in magazines and on the Internet, notice special effects and the placement of paid products in films, explore possible bias in news reports, and ponder the public relations "spin" on events.

Media literacy involves teaching children to ask the right questions. Teachers encourage children not to accept media presentations at face value. Instead, they should ask probing questions about the purposes, viewpoints, and motives of a message:

- What perspective is used?
- What values are conveyed?
- Which media techniques are used?
- Who is the intended audience?
- Who profits from this message? (Brunner & Tally, 1999)

Children can also ask themselves what has been omitted from the message. When children ask questions like these, they become more critical thinkers and understand that the developer's purposes, viewpoints, and motives influence the content of media productions. They also use these questions when they are listening critically to stories and informational books.

The media play an important role in children's lives (Alvermann, Moon, & Hagood, 1999; Dyson, 1997). In fact, they are some of the most powerful cultural forces today. Because of their importance, it's crucial that teachers make time in their language arts programs for media literacy lessons so that children become savvy media consumers.

It's essential that children become critical consumers of commercials and advertisements because they are bombarded with them (Lutz, 1997). Advertisers use appeals to reason, character, and emotion just as other persuaders do to promote products, ideas, and services; however, advertisers may also use propaganda to influence our beliefs and actions. Propaganda suggests something shady or underhanded. Like persuasion, propaganda is designed to influence people's beliefs and actions, but propagandists may use certain techniques to distort, conceal, and exaggerate.

People seeking to influence us often use words that evoke a variety of responses. They claim that something is "improved," "more natural," or "50% better"—loaded words and phrases that are deceptive because they are suggestive. When a product is advertised as 50% better, for example, consumers need to ask, "50% better than what?" Advertisements rarely answer that question.

Doublespeak is another type of deceptive language characterized as evasive, euphemistic, confusing, and self-contradictory. It is language that only pretends to communicate (Lutz, 1997). Two types of doublespeak that students can understand are euphemisms and inflated language. Euphemisms are words or phrases (e.g., "passed away") that are used to avoid harsh realities, often out of concern for someone's feelings rather than to mislead. Inflated language includes words intended to make the ordinary seem extraordinary. Thus, car mechanics become "automotive internists," and used cars become "pre-owned" or even "experienced" cars.

Children need to learn that people sometimes use words that only pretend to communicate; sometimes they use words to intentionally misrepresent, as when someone advertises a vinyl wallet as "genuine imitation leather" or a ring with a glass stone as a "faux diamond." When children can interpret deceptive language, they can avoid being deceived.

To sell products, advertisers use propaganda devices, such as testimonials, the bandwagon effect, and rewards. Students can listen to commercials to find examples of each propaganda device and discuss the effect the device has on them. They can also investigate to see how the same devices vary in commercials directed toward youngsters, teenagers, and adults. For instance, a commercial for a snack food with a sticker or toy in the package will appeal to a youngster, and an advertisement for a videotape recorder offering a factory rebate will appeal to an adult. The propaganda device for the ads is the same: a reward! Propaganda devices can be used to sell ideas as well as products. Public service announcements about smoking or wearing seat belts, as well as political advertisements, endorsements, and speeches, use these devices.

**Critical Thinking About Books** Many stories, informational books, and poems that teachers read aloud encourage critical thinking. When teachers read aloud stories such as *The Giver* (Lowry, 1993) and *The True Story of the 3 Little Pigs!* (Scieszka, 1989), students use a combination of aesthetic and critical listening: They use critical listening to evaluate the theme of *The Giver* and to determine whether the wolf's story is believable. When students listen to informational books such as *Antarctica* (Cowcher, 1990) and

---

## Books That Encourage Critical Listening

Avi. (1991). *Nothing but the truth.* New York: Orchard Books. (U)

Babbitt, N. (1975). *Tuck everlasting.* New York: Farrar, Straus & Giroux. (U)

Bunting, E. (1994). *Smoky night.* San Diego: Harcourt Brace. (P–M)

Cohen, B. (1983). *Molly's pilgrim.* New York: Lothrop, Lee & Shepard. (M)

Cowcher, H. (1990). *Antarctica.* New York: Farrar, Straus & Giroux. (P–M)

Creech, S. (2004). *Heartbeat.* New York: HarperCollins. (M–U)

Ellis, D. (2000). *The breadwinner.* Toronto: Groundwood. (M–U)

Gantos, J. (2000). *Joey Pigza loses control.* New York: Farrar, Straus & Giroux. (M)

Haddix, M. P. (1998). *Among the hidden.* New York: Aladdin Books. (U)

Hesse, K. (2001). *Witness.* New York: Scholastic. (U)

Lobel, A. (2004). *Potatoes, potatoes.* New York: Greenwillow. (P–M)

Lowry, L. (1993). *The giver.* Boston: Houghton Mifflin. (U)

Morimoto, J. (1987). *My Hiroshima.* New York: Puffin Books. (M)

Naylor, P. R. (1991). *Shiloh.* New York: Macmillan. (M–U)

Scieszka, J. (1989). *The true story of the 3 little pigs!* New York: Viking. (P–M)

Siebert, D. (1991). *Sierra.* New York: HarperCollins. (M–U)

Spinelli, J. (1997). *Wringer.* New York: HarperCollins. (M–U)

Turner, A. (1987). *Nettie's trip south.* New York: Macmillan. (M)

Van Allsburg, C. (1986). *The stranger.* Boston: Houghton Mifflin. (M)

Whelan, G. (2000). *Homeless bird.* New York: HarperCollins. (U)

Yolen, J. (1992). *Encounter.* Orlando: Harcourt Brace. (M)

---

P = primary grades (K–2); M = middle grades (3–5); U = upper grades (6–8)

---

*Encounter* (Yolen, 1992), they confront important ecological and social issues. The books provide information about the issues, and classmates share their ideas during discussions. Through these activities, students think more deeply about controversial issues and challenges and expand their own beliefs. Even some books of poetry stimulate critical listening. *Sierra* (Siebert, 1991), for example, a book-length poem about this western mountain range, ends with a warning about the threat people pose to the environment.

## A IS FOR AUTHENTIC ASSESSMENT: Does Anyone Assess Listening?

Even though teachers ask their students to listen for a variety of instructional activities each day, listening is almost never assessed. Because it's an invisible cognitive process, it's hard to judge how well children are listening. Usually teachers assume that children are listening if they can apply the content they listened to as they participate in a discussion, write a journal entry, or complete a graphic organizer. The problem is that even when students apply the content successfully, teachers don't know for sure that it was the result of how well they listened; it could be that they already knew the information or that they've learned to compensate for their weak listening skills by using classmates' comments to their advantage. Even more troubling is that when children can't apply the content they have heard presented, teachers don't know why. They may be ineffective listeners, but it's also possible that they didn't understand the purpose for listening, didn't activate background knowledge, or didn't have adequate knowledge about the topic. A classmate may have distracted them, or a personal problem may have occupied their thoughts. In addition, English learners might have been unfamiliar with key vocabulary words or been overwhelmed by the teacher's speed of presentation or sophisticated sentence structure.

With the current testing mandates, teachers might consider assessing listening a low priority, but because so much instruction is presented orally, that's a mistake. Assessment is an integral component of listening instruction (Opitz & Zbaracki, 2004). Teachers commonly assume that students can understand the books they read aloud—if the topic of the book is appropriate for the students' grade level but the text is too difficult to for them to read themselves, then students should be able to understand the book if they listen to it read aloud. Often that is the case, but not for everyone. For children who are not successful listeners, teachers may want to check their listening capacity level using an informal reading inventory.

Assessment and instruction are linked, so teachers need to do these things to be able to assess their students' listening:

- Teach listening; don't assume that students know how to listen. Teach students about the purposes for listening and how to use the listening strategies.
- Set expectations for listening. Tell students what to listen for, and hold them accountable for listening.
- Use interaction techniques for involving students. For both reading aloud and giving oral presentations, find ways to involve students more actively.
- Monitor students' listening so that you know when listening has broken down; then you can teach them how to get back on track.
- Expect students to assess their own listening. Have them reflect on their purpose, the strategies they use, how actively they were involved, and whether they understood what they listened to.

Once teachers become more involved in teaching listening, they'll begin to assess students' listening. The purpose of this assessment is rarely to assign a grade; instead, it is to determine whether students are listening effectively so teachers can take action when students aren't successful.

### Checking Children's Listening Capacity Level

Teachers can determine whether students are likely to understand grade-level books by checking their listening capacity level using an informal reading inventory (IRI), such as *The Critical Reading Inventory: Assessing Students' Reading and Thinking* (Applegate, Quinn, & Applegate, 2004). Teachers follow the instructions in the IRI manual, but instead of having students read the grade-level passage, they read it aloud to students and then ask the comprehension questions. If students answer the questions correctly, then they can usually listen to grade-level books and understand them. If students can't answer the questions, then teachers repeat the listening test using a passage for a lower grade level. Sometimes teachers find that students' listening capacity is one or more levels lower than their current grade level; for these students to listen to and understand the books that are read aloud, teachers must teach listening strategies and provide extra support while they are reading.

# Review

## The Big Ideas

Listening is the most basic and most used of the language processes. Despite its importance, listening instruction is neglected because teachers assume that children already know how to listen. Students need to learn how to vary the way they listen according to their purpose, and to consider their purpose as they choose which strategies to use.

These big ideas were presented in Part 2:

- Listening is a three-step process: receiving, attending, and assigning meaning.
- The four types of listening are discriminative, aesthetic, efferent, and critical.
- Teachers use interactive read-alouds to actively engage students in listening to stories, informational books, and poetry.
- Teachers also use techniques to actively involve students in listening to oral presentations.
- Teachers teach students to listen critically because they are exposed to many types of persuasion and propaganda.
- Teachers also teach students to use critical thinking in order to understand complex issues in books that teachers read aloud.

## Classroom Inquiry

Because listening is going on all around you, you're likely to be interested in learning how actively involved your students are in listening. You can examine what you and your students do in the classroom and interview students to learn what they know about listening. Consider investigating one of these topics.

**Purposes for Listening**

Children spend nearly half of the school day listening to you and their classmates for a variety of purposes. To examine how your students use listening and what they understand about listening, you might be interested in exploring these questions:

- What types of listening activities do my students engage in?
- What listening purposes do I set for my students?
- Can my students articulate their own purposes for listening?
- How do my students vary the way they listen according to their purpose?

**Listening Strategies**

Students learn strategies to listen more effectively and then apply many of these strategies to reading. To explore what strategies your students use when they listen, think about these questions:

- Which listening strategies have I taught and modeled?
- How do I teach a listening strategy?
- Which listening strategies do my students use?
- Can my students explain what they do when they listen?

**Interactive Read-Alouds**

It's essential that students are actively involved when teachers read aloud stories, informational books, and poetry. To examine how you read aloud, ask yourself these questions:

- What steps do I follow in doing interactive read-alouds?
- How do I engage my students during interactive read-alouds?
- Which engagement techniques do my students prefer?
- Are all of my students engaged during the read-alouds?

# 3

# Talking

## INTRODUCTION

When they come to school, most children are fluent oral language users, no matter what language they speak. They've had 4 or 5 years of extensive practice talking and listening in social settings. Because children have acquired basic oral language competencies, teachers often assume that they don't need to emphasize talk; however, children's talk is an essential part of language arts and is crucial for academic success in all content areas.

In addition to social or conversational language that children learn at home and use with friends, they learn more formal academic English, the language of instruction, at school. It's also the language used on standardized achievement tests. Teachers are responsible for teaching academic English—the complex concepts, technical vocabulary and jargon, and sophisticated sentence structures for expressing abstract ideas—through language arts and content-area study. One way teachers do this is through talk. They move beyond asking literal-level questions to structuring grand conversations to stimulate and support higher-level thinking about literature and instructional conversations to study and analyze content-area topics.

It's difficult for students to be successful if they don't understand and use academic language. Everyone needs to learn academic language to be successful in school, and it's especially challenging for many English learners. Decreasing the achievement gap among ethnic and social class groups has become a national priority, and talk is an important way to address the problem.

# Classroom Close-Up

## Third Graders Participate in Literature Circles

The students in Mrs. Zumwalt's third-grade class participate in literature circles because she knows that these students need lots of reading practice and opportunities to talk about books. For 30 minutes each day, they read or talk about the easy chapter books they are reading in small groups. Most of Mrs. Zumwalt's students are English learners who read a year below grade level, so she works hard to find easy-to-read chapter books that will interest them.

Students in one small group are reading *The Cat's Meow* (Soto, 1987), the story of a white cat named Pip who speaks Spanish to Graciela, the little girl who owns her. Spanish words are included in the text. All but one of the students in this group speak Spanish at home, so they feel very comfortable with the inclusion of the Spanish words.

Yesterday, the five students in the group read the first chapter, and now they're talking about the story; Mrs. Zumwalt joins the group for a few minutes. The discussion focuses on whether the cat can really speak Spanish or whether it is just Graciela's imagination at work.

| | |
|---|---|
| *Armando:* | That girl knows Spanish, so it could be that she is just pretending. She really could be just thinking those Spanish words. And it says that her mom and dad are weird. Maybe she comes from a weird family. That's what I think. |
| *Maricela:* | I think Pip can speak Spanish, but she will just speak to that girl and no one else. |
| *Marcos:* | Yeah, I think Pip can talk in Spanish. That would be cool. |
| *Rubin:* | No, Armando. It's for real, man. The cat—what's his name? |
| *Linda:* | Pip, and she's a girl, not a boy. |
| *Rubin:* | Yeah, Pip. I think he, I mean she, can talk. And Linda, how do you know it's a girl cat? |
| *Linda:* | Look, I'll show you. (She turns to the first page of the first chapter, scanning for a word.) Look, on page 1, here it is. It says "looked at her empty bowl." Her. That's how I know. |

Mrs. Zumwalt redirects the conversation and asks: "Do you think you'll find out for sure whether Pip can talk by the time you finish reading the book?" The students are sure they will find out. Then she asks them to consider possible story lines: "So, what do you think might happen in the story?"

| | |
|---|---|
| *Linda:* | I think the story might be like the one about Martha the talking dog that we read last year. Martha got in trouble for talking too much so she stopped talking but then at the end when some robbers came, she called the police and was a hero. |
| *Mrs. Zumwalt:* | I know that story! It's called *Martha Speaks* (Meddaugh, 1995), right? (The students agree.) |
| *Armando:* | I don't think Pip will talk in front of anyone except for Graciela. Not that Juanita. Pip doesn't want to be sent to be in a circus because she's a freak. She wants to be a normal white cat. I think maybe it will stay her secret. |
| *Rubin:* | I think people will find out about Pip and she will be famous. Then she'll win a million dollars on "Who Wants to Be a Millionaire." |

After everyone laughs at Rubin's comment, Mrs. Zumwalt asks about Juanita and the students respond.

| | |
|---|---|
| *Armando:* | Juanita is the girl that Graciela talks to and tells that Pip can talk Spanish. She doesn't believe her, but she could still gossip about it at school. |
| *Mrs. Zumwalt:* | Is Juanita a friend of Graciela's? |
| *Linda:* | I think so. |
| *Maricela:* | They play together. |
| *Armando:* | No, I don't think they are friends. They just know each other and maybe they play together, but they are not friends. They don't act like friends. |
| *Maricela:* | I think Graciela wants to be friends. That's what I think. |

---

### What can you learn by listening to students talk about a book?

Teachers know that they can learn a great deal through observing students as they work, listening to students participate in discussions, and talking with students during conferences. As you read this Classroom Close-Up about a small group of third graders discussing a book they are reading, notice Armando's role in the discussion and how the students use talk to clarify their understanding. In addition, think about how the students talk about their use of reading strategies and the connections they are making between the book and their lives, the world around them, and other literature.

Mrs. Zumwalt moves the conversation around to Juanita because the students seemed unaware of her when Armando mentioned her and because she will figure prominently in the book. As several of the students suggested, people will find out about Pip the talking cat, and a big problem develops.

The students continue reading and talking about the book as they learn that Graciela's neighbor, Sr. Medina, is the one who taught Pip to speak Spanish. In chapter 6, they read that Sr. Medina's nosy neighbor has called the television stations and told them about Pip and her special ability. During their discussion, the students talk about the television news crews coming to interview Sr. Medina and Pip. The students are angry that the neighbor called the television stations.

| | |
|---|---|
| *Linda:* | It's not fair that that lady across the street was so nosy and she ruined everything. It got so bad that Sr. Medina had to move away. |
| *Maricela:* | I like that Graciela sprayed that lady with the hose and she got all wet. And Graciela called her a "sour old snoop." That's funny. |
| *Mrs. Zumwalt:* | In the book, it says that Graciela hoped the lady would "shrink into a puddle of nothing like the evil witch in *The Wizard of Oz*." What does that mean? |
| *Armando:* | That's what happened in *The Wizard of Oz*. I saw the movie so I know. |
| *Rubin:* | This chapter reminds me of when my uncle got killed. His name was Manuel. He was 16, I think. He got killed by some gang bangers. They were in a car and they came by his house and they shot him. He was in the house and the bullet came in through the window. Then the ambulance came but he was dead. So the police came and they put up this yellow ribbon all around the house. My mom and dad made me stay in the house but I wanted to go outside and watch. Then the television reporters came and it was crowded with people. Just like in this chapter. |
| *Marcos:* | Sr. Medina had to move away and he took Pip with him. |
| *Linda:* | No, he didn't take Pip. She's Graciela's cat. |
| *Marcos:* | Look on page 69. It says, "He moved out last night and took his cat with him." |
| *Linda:* | Well, it's not his cat. |

Mrs. Zumwalt asks the students to predict whether Graciela will get her cat back, and then they read the last chapter of the book and learn that Pip does come back, and now she's black, not white, and she speaks French, not Spanish! They talk about the ending.

| | |
|---|---|
| *Linda:* | I'm happy. I knew Pip would come back. I would be so, so, so sad if anyone stole my cat. |
| *Marcos:* | I liked this book. It was funny. |
| *Rubin:* | I wish it would happen to me. |
| *Maricela:* | I would like to be Graciela. |

## Twenty Easy-to-Read Chapter Books

Bang-Campbell, M. (2002). *Little rat sets sail*. San Diego: Harcourt Brace.

Benchley, P. (1994). *Small wolf*. New York: HarperCollins.

Brenner, B. (1978). *Wagon wheels*. New York: HarperCollins.

Coerr, E. (1986). *The Josefina story quilt*. New York: HarperCollins.

Coerr, E. (1988). *Chang's paper pony*. New York: HarperCollins.

Coerr, E. (1999). *Buffalo Bill and the Pony Express*. New York: HarperCollins.

Cushman, D. (2000). *Inspector Hopper*. New York: HarperCollins.

Dahl, R. (1990). *Esio trot*. New York: Puffin Books.

Danziger, P. (1994). *Amber Brown is not a crayon*. New York: Putnam.

Haas, J. (2001). *Runaway radish*. New York: Greenwillow.

Horowitz, R. (2001). *Breakout at the bug lab*. New York: Dial Books.

Laurence, D. (2001). *Captain and Matey set sail*. New York: HarperCollins.

Lewis, T. P. (1983). *Hill of fire*. New York: HarperCollins.

Livingstone, S. (2001). *Harley*. New York: North-South Books.

Lottridge, C. B. (2003). *Berta: A remarkable dog*. Toronto: Groundwood.

Lowry, L. (2002). *Gooney bird Greene*. Boston: Houghton Mifflin.

McDonald, M. (2002). *Judy Moody*. Cambridge, MA: Candlewick Press.

Roop, P., & Roop, C. (1985). *Keep the lights burning, Abbie*. Minneapolis, MN: Carolrhoda.

Seuling, B. (2001). *Robert and the great pepperoni*. Chicago: Cricket Books.

Turner, A. (1995). *Dust for dinner*. New York: HarperCollins.

| | |
|---|---|
| *Mrs. Zumwalt:* | Why? |
| *Maricela:* | Well, her parents are weird; that's for sure. But, she does some interesting things. And I wish I had a cat who could talk to me in Spanish or in English. |
| *Armando:* | I liked the Spanish words. I'm going to write a story and put Spanish words in it. Those Spanish words made it fun to read this book. |

Mrs. Zumwalt moves from group to group as they discuss the books they are reading. Her focus in these conversations is helping students to use talk to deepen their comprehension. She watches to make sure that all students are participating and that the conversation explores important elements of plot, character, and theme. She asks questions to probe their thinking or redirect their attention. She also watches students' growing involvement with the story. Mrs. Zumwalt is pleased that Rubin became more involved with *The Cat's Meow:* After reading the first chapter, he didn't seem interested in the story, but by the end, he was hooked. Mrs. Zumwalt believes that it is the conversation that brings about the change.

As you continue reading Part 3, think about how Mrs. Zumwalt incorporates the topics being presented. Here are three questions to guide your reading:

- ◆ How did these third graders' conversations exemplify the characteristics of small-group conversations?
- ◆ How did Mrs. Zumwalt use questions to scaffold the students' discussions?
- ◆ Which talk strategies did Mrs. Zumwalt's students show evidence of using?

# Essentials

## ESSENTIAL #1: Small-Group Conversations

Conversations should be common occurrences in classrooms. As students converse with classmates, they use talk for different purposes: to control classmates' behavior, maintain social relationships, convey information, and share personal experiences and opinions (Wilkinson, 1984). Students meet in small groups to respond to literature they have read, respond to each other's writing, work on projects, and explore big ideas they are learning. The most important feature of small-group conversations is that they promote thinking. Teachers take students' ideas seriously, and students are validated as thinkers (Nystrand, Gamoran, & Heck, 1993).

Students learn and refine their strategies for conversing with classmates as they participate in small-group conversations (Cintorino, 1993; Kaufman, 2000). Students learn how to begin conversations, take turns, keep the conversation moving forward, support comments and questions that group members make, deal with conflicts, and bring the conversation to a close. And, they learn how powerful talk is in making meaning and creating knowledge.

To begin the conversation, students gather in groups at tables or in other areas in the classroom, bringing with them any necessary materials. One student in each group begins the conversation with a question or comment; students then take turns making comments and asking questions, and they support the other group members as they elaborate on and expand their comments. The tone is exploratory, and throughout the conversation, the group is progressing toward a common goal (Cintorino, 1993)—deepening students' understanding of a book they have read, responding to a question the teacher has asked, or creating a project. From time to time, the conversation slows down, and there may be a few minutes of silence (Sorenson, 1993); then a group member asks a question or makes a comment that sends the conversation in a new direction.

## Characteristics of Small-Group Conversations

### The Group
Effective groups have three to six members. The groups can be permanent or be established for specific activities. Students form a cohesive group and are courteous and supportive of each other.

### Purpose
The purpose of the small-group conversation or work session is to deepen understanding and create knowledge. Students talk to solve problems and discover answers to authentic questions—questions that require critical thinking.

### Strategy Use
Students learn to use strategies to begin the conversation, keep it moving forward and on task, and end it.

### Students' Roles
Group members may have assigned roles or jobs. Sometimes students keep the same roles for a period of time, or specific roles are assigned for a particular purpose.

### Ownership
Small-group conversations are student centered. Students feel ownership of and responsibility for the activities they are involved in and the projects they create.

### The Teacher's Role
Teachers establish groups and teach students to work collaboratively. They clearly define the purpose of the group work and outline the activities to be completed.

Students try to support one another in groups, and two of the most important ways they do this is by calling each other by name and maintaining eye contact. They also cultivate a climate of trust in the group by expressing agreement, sharing feelings, voicing approval, and referring to comments that group members made earlier. Conflict is inevitable, but students need to learn how to deal with it so that it doesn't get out of control. They learn to accept that there will be differing viewpoints and to make compromises. Cintorino (1993) reported that her eighth graders used humor to defuse disagreements in small-group conversations.

At the end of a conversation, students reach consensus and conclude that they have finished sharing ideas, explored all dimensions of a question, or completed a project. Sometimes students create a product during the conversation—it may be a brainstormed list, a chart, or something more elaborate, such as a set of puppets. Group members are responsible for collecting and storing materials they have used and for reporting on the group's work.

## ESSENTIAL #2: Levels of Questions

Asking and answering questions are common types of talk in classrooms. Researchers have found that teachers ask as many as 50,000 questions a year, whereas students ask as few as 10 (Watson & Young, 2003). The most common questions are literal questions, those that require simple recall, even though the most useful questions ask students to analyze, interpret, evaluate, and offer opinions.

Questions can be grouped into three levels: literal, inferential, and critical. Literal or "on the page" questions have a single factual answer and can usually be answered with a few words or "yes" or "no." When the questions refer to a book that students are reading, the answers are directly stated in the text.

The second level of questions is inferential or "between the lines." To answer these questions, students synthesize information and form interpretations with both their background knowledge and clues in the text. The answers are implicitly stated in the text.

The third, most complex level of questioning is critical or "beyond the page." These questions are open ended. They require students to go beyond the text and think creatively and abstractly about global ideas, issues, and concerns. At this level, students apply information, make connections, evaluate and value the text, and express opinions.

Teachers use these three levels of questions for different purposes. They use literal questions during a conversation to check that students have learned basic information and understand the meaning of words. Literal questions are easy to ask and answer, but because they are the most frequently asked questions, teachers need to be careful not to overuse them. To help students think more deeply and to challenge their thinking, teachers ask inferential and critical questions. When they are talking about literature, teachers ask inferential questions to probe students' understanding of a story and make interpretations, and when they are talking about big ideas during a thematic unit, they ask students to analyze the ideas, make comparisons, and summarize information. Teachers ask critical questions that challenge students' thinking to go beyond the story to make connections, evaluate the story, reflect on the overall theme, and delve into the author's craft. They ask critical questions during thematic units for similar purposes: to consider different viewpoints, examine issues, and draw conclusions.

**Questioning Patterns** — Teachers commonly use the IRF (Initiate-Response-Feedback) cycle when they ask questions:

- Initiate: The teacher asks a question.
- Response: A student answers the question.
- Feedback: The teacher responds to the student's answer.

This cycle is teacher centered because teachers do most of the talking and control the flow of the conversation. It's the primary way teachers involve students in discussions; in fact, researchers report that more than half the instructional talk in classrooms occurs in IRF cycles (Watson & Young, 2003). Teachers often use this cycle for assessment, to check on students' attention and understanding rather than to promote learnng.

## Levels of Questioning

| | |
|---|---|
| **Literal or "On the Page" Questions** | Literal questions are factual. The answers to these questions are stated explicitly in the text. Students answer these questions with "yes" or "no" or with a few words taken directly from the text. |
| **Inferential or "Between the Lines" Questions** | Inferential questions require analysis and interpretation. The answers are implicitly stated in the text. To answer these questions, students use a combination of background knowledge and clues in the text. |
| **Critical or "Beyond the Page" Questions** | Critical questions go beyond the text and focus on global issues, ideas, and problems. Often there are no correct answers. To answer these questions, students think creatively; make personal, world, and literary connections; evaluate the text; and express opinions. |

Even though the IRF cycle is common, it's less conducive to learning than other procedures that involve students in asking questions and doing more of the talk. Here are suggestions to make discussions more effective:

- Teach students how to participate in small-group conversations.
- Provide frequent opportunities for students to talk to explore ideas in small groups.
- Relax your control so that students can talk among themselves.
- Alternate small-group and teacher-led discussions.
- Have students talk about the answer with partners before responding in a teacher-led discussions.
- Examine the types of questions you ask and your purpose for asking them.
- Have students ask questions in a discussion.
- Teach students to ask higher-level questions.

When the classroom community changes and students become more actively involved in a discussion by asking questions or having opportunities to talk about the answers to questions that teachers ask, discussions become much more effective.

**Question-Answer Relationships** Questions at the end of reading assignments, including chapters in content-area textbooks, replicate the teacher question–student answer cycle commonly used in discussions. Students can apply their knowledge about the levels of questions in order to answer these questions. Teachers help students make connections between oral and written questions using the Question-Answer Relationships (Raphael, 1986) procedure. Questions are organized into four levels; the questions at the two highest levels both require critical thinking:

- **Right There Questions.** Readers find the answer to these literal questions "right there" in the text.
- **Think and Search Questions.** Readers search for the answer to these inferential questions in different parts of the text.
- **Author and Me Questions.** Readers use a combination of the author's ideas and their own ideas to answer these critical-level questions.
- **On My Own Questions.** Readers use their own ideas to answer these critical-level questions.

Understanding the type of thinking required to answer the question helps the students complete the assignment.

Students usually read the list of questions before beginning to read the text and predict how they will answer them by categorizing them according to level. For example, students might say, "That question sounds like a 'right there' question," or "That question begins 'why do you think,' so I'm guessing that's an 'on my own' question." Then they read the text, noticing information that's related to the questions. Afterward, they answer the questions and then share their answers with the class and explain how they answered them.

## Theory to Practice
### Third Graders Ask Higher-Level Questions About a Story

After reading *Amber Brown Is Not a Crayon* (Danziger, 1994), the story of two best friends and what happens to their friendship when one of them moves to another state, a group of Mrs. Zumwalt's third graders wrote questions to ask when the class got together to have a grand conversation. These students know the difference between "easy" questions and questions that "make you think." They also know that questions that can be answered with a single word or with "yes" or "no" aren't very effective.

### The Procedure

The third graders flipped through the pages of *Amber Brown Is Not a Crayon,* jotting possible questions on small self-stick notes that they attached to the pages. Then they shared their ideas, refining the questions through feedback from classmates. The students told each other when they thought the questions were too easy or were only tangentially related to the story.

### The Questions

Here is the list of questions the students developed:

- Why do you think Amber and Justin are best friends?
- Do you think Mr. Cohn is sort of like Ms. Frizzle [in the Magic School Bus series]?
- Why is Amber being mean to Justin?
- What do you think will happen to Amber and Justin after he moves away?
- Can they still be best friends after Justin moves away?

### Levels of Questions

Most of these questions delve into the "best friends" theme of the book and require students to use higher-level thinking skills. They go beyond the factual level and ask students to explore big ideas about friendship.

### The Grand Conversation

The students in the small group led the class discussion on *Amber Brown Is Not a Crayon.* They took turns asking questions and encouraging classmates to expand on their answers and make personal connections between the story and their own lives. Later, the students posted their list of questions in the classroom, and students each chose a question to respond to in their reading logs.

# Strategies

## Talk Strategies

Children participate in a variety of talk activities: They engage in conversations, ask questions, retell stories, and perform in dramatic activities. Even though students are familiar with many of these activities, teachers show them how to be more strategic and make their talk more purposeful. When students organize the ideas they want to share, for example, their talk is more worthwhile, or when students consider the level of question they've been asked, their answer is likely to be more effective.

**Strategies for Participating in Conversations**
Successful conversations don't just happen. Students need to know how to begin, sustain, and end conversations so that they can participate effectively in small-group and whole-class conversations. Teachers teach conversation routines—how to make a comment, take turns, encourage classmates to participate, and redirect the conversation—and students practice using these strategies in conversations. Students learn how to stick to the topic and how to be polite and supportive of their classmates. They also learn about the kinds of comments they can make—sharing ideas, presenting information, asking questions, offering opinions, and making suggestions—and how to build on classmates' comments.

In the Classroom Close-Up, Mrs. Zumwalt's students demonstrated many of these strategies. With their teacher's guidance, the third graders are learning to make comments, take turns, build on classmates' comments, and stick to the topic. Mrs. Zumwalt has taught minilessons on talk strategies, modeled their use in conversations, and insisted that students be respectful and supportive of their classmates. Mrs. Zumwalt's classroom is a community of learners where the children respect each other and assume responsibility for working and learning together.

**Strategies for Asking Questions**
Questioning is an important strategy that students use in different ways:

- Asking questions as part of conversations and other discussions
- Analyzing both the questions that teachers ask and the questions in content-area textbooks
- Asking self-questions to monitor understanding as they read and during oral presentations

Students use questioning for the first two purposes during talk activities. What's important is that students recognize the level of questions they're asking or that are being asked of them because questions are answered differently depending on their level.

Students learn how to ask questions that are clear and to the point and about the differences among literal, inferential, and critical questions. They learn to evaluate the level of a question and the type of thinking required to answer questions representing each level. Once students become more familiar with the levels of questions, they learn to value inferential and critical questions that emphasize high-level thinking because the answers are more stimulating.

**Strategies for Retelling Stories**
When children read stories and listen to stories read aloud, they use comprehension strategies, including organizing, visualizing, identifying big ideas, and summarizing. They use the same strategies for retelling stories because the focus in this activity is on comprehension—having children demonstrate their understanding.

When students retell stories, they organize the ideas into the beginning, middle, and end. They add description, dialogue, and word play to bring the setting and characters to life so listeners can easily visualize the story. They focus on the big ideas and summarize less important parts to create a coherent story that interests their listeners.

When teachers teach retelling strategies, they're teaching comprehension, and students can apply what they're learning to reading and listening. In fact, students also apply these comprehension strategies when they're writing stories.

## Strategies Students Use in Talk Activities

| Conversations | Retelling Stories |
|---|---|
| • taking turns | • organizing |
| • redirecting the talk | • visualizing |
| • sharing ideas | • identifying big ideas |
| • offering opinions and suggestions | • summarizing |

| Asking Questions | Dramatic Activities |
|---|---|
| • asking literal questions | • activating background knowledge |
| • asking inferential questions | • elaborating ideas |
| • asking critical questions | • responding to nonverbal cues |
| • evaluating | • monitoring |

Students use strategies as they perform in improvisations and puppet shows. To take on the role of a character, they activate their background knowledge and think about the person they're role-playing— his or her behavior, speech, and mannerisms. At the same time, they think about the scene or the events in the story they're dramatizing. They also monitor and respond to feedback, both verbal and nonverbal cues, from the other performers and the audience. They judge their effectiveness and modify their performance based on the feedback they receive.

As they learn about dramatization strategies, students become more effective at doing improvisations and puppetry. Teachers teach strategy minilessons, model how to use the strategies, provide feedback to students on how effectively they use the strategies, encourage students to reflect on their dramatic experiences, and then fade as students become more expert at using the strategies independently.

# MINILESSON
*Conversations*

## Ms. Shapiro Teaches Her Second Graders About Sustaining Conversations

1.  **Introduce the topic**   Ms. Shapiro explains to her second graders that she wants them to think about how they behave during grand conversations. She asks them to observe a grand conversation that she has planned with four students in the class. "We will be doing some good things to help the conversation and some bad things that hurt the conversation," she says. "Watch carefully so you will notice them."

2.  **Share examples**   Ms. Shapiro and four students have a grand conversation about a familiar story, *Hey, Al* (Yorinks, 1986). She chose a familiar story so that students could focus on the conversation itself and not get caught up in the story. The students participating in the conversation take turns making comments, but they don't expand on each other's comments nor do they call each other by name or look at classmates as they are talking. Also, some students are looking away from the group as though they are not listening.

3.  **Provide information**   Ms. Shapiro's students are eager to identify the strengths and weaknesses of the grand conversation they have observed. The "good things" were that "everyone talked about the story and

nothing else" and "everybody was nice." The "bad things" included that "some people didn't pay attention and look at the person talking," "some people didn't say other people's names," and "some people just said things but they didn't go next to what other people said." Ms. Shapiro agrees that the students have identified the problems, and she explains that she's seen some of these same problems in their conversations. Together they make a chart of "Good Things to Do in a Grand Conversation."

4.  **Supervise practice**   Ms. Shapiro's students participate in grand conversations as part of literature circles and after she reads a book aloud to the class. She explains that she will observe their grand conversations to make sure they are doing all the good things they listed on their chart. For the next 2 weeks, Ms. Shapiro briefly reviews the chart with them before each grand conversation and takes a few minutes afterward to talk about the changes in behavior she has observed.

5.  **Assess learning**   After 2 weeks of practice, Ms. Shapiro brings the students together to talk about their grand conversations, and she asks the second graders which of the good things from the chart they are doing better now. The students mention various points and conclude that their grand conversations have improved.

## ACADEMIC LANGUAGE: A Key to School Success

The type of English used for instruction is called *academic language*. It's different than the social or conversational language we speak at home and with friends in two ways. First, academic language is more cognitively demanding and decontextualized than social language in which speakers carry on face-to-face conversations about everyday topics (Wong-Fillmore & Snow, 2002). Teachers use academic language when they teach language arts, math, and other content areas and when they give directions for completing assignments. It's also the language used in content-area textbooks and standardized achievement tests.

Second, academic language has semantic, syntactic, and pragmatic features that distinguish it from social language. The ideas expressed are more complex; the meaning is less obvious and takes more effort to understand. The vocabulary is more technical and precise; many words are unfamiliar or used in new ways. The sentence structure is different: Academic language uses longer, complex sentences that may be difficult to understand. Academic language has a different style, too. Speakers and writers present detailed, well-organized information about complex and abstract topics, usually without becoming personally involved in the topic.

Even though children are proficient users of social language, they are likely to have difficulty understanding and using academic language in the classroom without instruction (Wong-Fillmore & Snow, 2002). Through instruction and frequent opportunities to use talk and the other language arts in meaningful ways, children learn the knowledge, vocabulary, and language patterns associated with academic English. Although learning academic English is essential for all children, the challenge is greater for English learners.

**BICS and CALP**
Jim Cummins (1996) theorized that English learners must develop two types of English proficiency. First, children learn

### Contrasts Between Social and Academic Language

| | Social Language | Academic Language |
|---|---|---|
| **Topics** | Topics are familiar, everyday, and concrete; they are often examined superficially, with few details being presented. | Topics are unfamiliar, complex, and abstract. More detail is provided, and they are examined in more depth. |
| **Vocabulary** | Everyday, familiar words are used. | Technical terms, jargon, and many multisyllabic words are used. |
| **Sentence Structure** | Sentences are shorter and dependent on the context. | Sentence structure is longer and more complicated. |
| **Viewpoints** | One opinion or viewpoint is shared, and it is often subjective or biased. | Multiple viewpoints are considered and analyzed, usually objectively. |

### Learn More About Academic Language

Adger, C. T., Snow, C. E., & Christian, D. (Eds.). (2002). *What teachers need to know about language.* Washington, DC: The Center for Applied Linguistics.

Boyd, F. B., & Brock, C. H. with M. S. Rozendal. (2004). *Multicultural and multilingual literacy and language.* New York: Guilford Press.

Burke, J. (2005). *School smarts: The four C's of academic success.* Portsmouth, NH: Heinemann.

Chamot, A. U., & O'Malley, J. M. (1994). *The CALLA handbook: Implementing the cognitive academic language learning approach.* Reading, MA: Addison-Wesley.

Diaz-Rico, L. T., & Weed, K. Z. (2001). *The cross cultural, language, and academic development handbook: A complete K–12 reference guide* (2nd ed.). Boston: Allyn & Bacon.

social or everyday language, which Cummins called *Basic Interpersonal Conversational Skills* (BICS). Social language is characterized as context embedded because contextual cues that make the language easier to understand are available to speakers and listeners. This type of language is easy to learn, according to Cummins, because it is cognitively undemanding and can usually be acquired in only 2 to 3 years.

Cummins's second type of language is called *Cognitive Academic Language Proficiency* (CALP). CALP is academic English, the type of language that children need to understand and use for academic success, and it's much harder for English learners to understand because it is context reduced and more cognitively demanding. *Context reduced* means that the language is more abstract and less familiar, and *cognitively demanding* means that technical terms, complex sentence structures, and less familiar topics are involved. English learners require 5 to 7 years or more to become proficient in this type of English, and too many English learners never reach proficiency.

How quickly English learners learn academic English depends on many factors, including their native language proficiency, school experiences, motivation, and personality. The family's literacy level, their socioeconomic status, and their cultural isolation are other considerations. In addition, when families flee from social unrest or war in their native countries, children often take longer to learn English because of the trauma they experienced.

**Instructional Recommendations**

So that children can grow in their knowledge of and use of academic language, Courtney Cazden (2001) challenges teachers to make changes in classroom language use to incorporate more academic language. Finding ways to help all students develop academic language has become more urgent because of the enactment of the No Child Left Behind Act of 2001.

It's essential that teachers set high standards for themselves and for their students. The activities they organize should challenge students to use higher-order thinking as they listen, talk, read, and write. Whether students use higher-order thinking is dependent on the level of questions teachers ask and on the types of activities in which students are involved. Teachers should incorporate academic language into their instruction, even with young children and English learners; too often, in an attempt to be kind, they simplify the words and sentence structures they use. What happens, however, is that students don't have the opportunity to learn the technical vocabulary and sophisticated sentence patterns that are part of academic English.

Students' school success is dependent on their proficiency with academic English. Learning academic English is a challenge for all students; however, it's especially difficult for English learners who are developing and refining their conversational English abilities at the same time they are learning academic English.

## *Scaffolding English Learners*

### Teach Academic English Through Thematic Units

The best way to teach academic English to English learners is through thematic units because language development is linked with content-area learning (Gibbons, 2002). In thematic units, students are involved in meaningful activities and broadening their knowledge of the world. Academic English is described as context reduced in comparison to context-embedded social language, but teachers can adapt their instruction to scaffold students' learning to make academic English more comprehensible. Teachers provide support in these ways:

- Involve students in hands-on, active learning opportunities
- Have students work with classmates in small groups
- Link lessons to students' prior experiences, or build needed background knowledge

- Clarify meaning with objects, photos, and demonstrations
- Teach technical vocabulary related to the topic
- Use graphic organizers
- Have students talk, read, create visuals, and write about the topic
- Teach students to recognize when they're confused and how to take action
- Demonstrate how to ask and answer higher-level questions
- Teach students how to listen to and read informational books and content-area textbooks
- Involve students in making projects to demonstrate their learning

With these instructional supports in place, students are better able to learn age-appropriate content knowledge along with their classmates.

Anna Chamot and Michael O'Malley's Cognitive Academic Language Learning Approach (CALLA) (1994) is a good way to promote English learners' academic English in connection with content-area learning. CALLA integrates content-area instruction with language development and incorporates these instructional supports.

It's not possible to postpone instruction for up to 10 years as English learners develop CALP proficiency and catch up with their monolingual classmates. Teaching academic English through meaningful content-area activities is effective because students grow in their English language proficiency and knowledge of content-area topics, and they become more interested in learning as they experience success.

To deepen their comprehension, students talk about stories they are reading in literature focus units and literature circles in discussions that are often called *grand conversations* (Peterson & Eeds, 1990). They are different than traditional discussions because they are child centered. Students take responsibility for their own learning and do most of the talking as they voice their opinions and support their views with examples from the story: They talk about what puzzles them, what they find interesting, their personal connections to the story, connections to the world, and connections they see between this story and others they have read. Students usually don't raise their hands and wait to be called on by the teacher; instead, they take turns and speak when no one else is speaking, much as adults do when they talk with friends. Students also encourage their classmates to contribute to the conversation. Even though teachers often sit in on conversations, the talk is primarily among the students.

Grand conversations can be held with the whole class or in small groups. When students meet as a class, there is a feeling of community. Young children usually meet as a class, and older students get together when they're learning literature conversation procedures, participating in a literature focus unit, or listening to the teacher read a book aloud to the class. But during literature circles, small groups meet because they are reading different books and students want to have more opportunities to talk. When the entire class meets, students have only a few opportunities to talk, but when they meet in small groups, they have many, many more opportunities to share their responses.

Grand conversations have two parts. The first part is open ended: Students talk about their reactions to the book, and their comments determine the direction of the conversation. Teachers do participate; they share their responses, ask questions, and provide information. Later in the grand conversation, teachers focus students' attention on one or two aspects of the book that they did not talk about in the first part of the conversation.

After the grand conversation, students often write in their reading logs, or write again if they wrote before the grand

## GRAND CONVERSATIONS

**1 Read the book** Students read a picture book or a chapter in a novel or listen to the teacher read a story aloud.

**2 Prepare for the grand conversation** Students think about the story by drawing pictures or writing in reading logs. This step is especially important when students don't talk much because with this preparation, they are more likely to have ideas to share with classmates.

**3 Have small-group conversations** Students form small groups to talk about the story before getting together as a class. This step is optional and is generally used when students don't talk much.

**4 Begin the grand conversation** Students form a circle for the class conversation so that everyone can see each other. Teachers begin by asking, "Who would like to begin?" or "What are you thinking about?" One student makes a comment, and classmates take turns talking about the idea the first student introduced.

**5 Continue the conversation** A student introduces a new idea, and classmates talk about it, sharing ideas, asking for clarifications, and reading excerpts from the story to make a point. Students limit their comments to the idea being discussed, and after students finish discussing this idea, a new one is introduced. To ensure that everyone participates, teachers often ask students to make no more than three comments until everyone has spoken at least once.

**6 Ask questions** Teachers ask questions to direct students to an aspect of the story that has been missed; for example, they might focus on an element of story structure or the author's craft. Or, they may ask students to compare the book to the film version of the story, or to other books by the same author.

**7 Conclude the conversation** After all of the big ideas have been explored, teachers end the conversation by summarizing and drawing conclusions about the story or the chapter of the novel.

**8 Reflect on the conversation** Students often write in reading logs to reflect on the ideas discussed in the grand conversation.

conversation. Then they continue reading the book if they have read only part of it. Both participating in grand conversations and writing entries in reading logs help students think about and respond to what they have read.

From their observational study of fifth and sixth graders conducting conversations about stories, Eeds and Wells (1989) found that students extend their individual interpretations of books through talk, and even create a better understanding of of them. Students talk about their understanding of the story and can change their opinions after listening to classmates' alternative views. They share personal stories related to their reading in poignant ways that trigger other students to identify with them. Students also gain insights about how authors use the elements of story structure to develop their message.

Martinez and Roser (1995) researched the content of students' grand conversations, and they found that students often talk about story events and characters or explore the themes of the story but delve less often into the author's craft to explore the way he or she structured the book, the arrangement of text and illustrations on the page, or the author's use of figurative or repetitive language. The researchers called these three directions conversation can take *experience, message,* and *object.*

Drawing students' attention to the "object" is important because they apply what they've learned about the author's craft when they write their own stories. Students who know more about leads, pacing, figurative language, point of view, imagery, surprise endings, voice, and flashbacks write better stories than those who don't. One way teachers help students examine the author's craft is through the questions they ask during grand conversations. For example, teachers ask students to think about why Kate DiCamillo directs comments to the readers in *The Tale of Despereaux* (2003) and the way Paul Fleischman features a different character's viewpoint in each chapter of *Seedfolks* (1997).

The stories you choose to share with students matter, too. Martinez and Roser (1995) noticed that some books lend themselves to talk about message and others to talk about experience or object. Stories with dramatic plots or stories that present a problem to which students can relate, such as *Chrysanthemum* (Henkes, 1991) and *Jeremy Thatcher, Dragon Hatcher* (Coville, 1991), focus the conversation on the book as experience. Multilayered stories or books in which main characters deal with dilemmas, such as *Smoky Night* (Bunting, 1994) and *The Giver* (Lowry, 1993), focus the conversation on the message. Books with distinctive structures or language features, such as *Black and White* (Macaulay, 1990) and *Maniac Magee* (Spinelli, 1990), focus the conversation on the object.

An additional benefit of grand conversations is that when students talk in depth about stories, their writing shows the same level of inferential comprehension (Sorenson, 1993). Students seem to be more successful in grand conversations if they have written in reading logs first, and they are more successful in writing entries if they have talked about the story first.

## INSTRUCTIONAL CONVERSATIONS: Using Talk to Learn

Instructional conversations provide opportunities for students to talk about the big ideas they are learning in thematic units;

## INSTRUCTIONAL CONVERSATIONS

**1 Choose a focus**
Teachers choose a focus for the instructional conversation that's related to the goals of a thematic unit.

**2 Present information**
Teachers present information or read an informational book or an excerpt from a content-area textbook in preparation for the discussion.

**3 Prepare for the instructional conversation**
Sometimes teachers have students complete a graphic organizer together as a class or in small groups before beginning the conversation.

**4 Have small-group conversations**
Sometimes students respond to a question in small groups before beginning the whole-class instructional conversation.

**5 Begin the instructional conversation**
Teachers begin by asking a question related to the focus they have identified. Students take turns sharing information, asking questions, and making connections. Teachers often write students' comments on chart paper in a list or create a graphic organizer.

**6 Continue the conversation**
Teachers continue the conversation by asking additional questions, and students take turns responding to the questions and exploring the big ideas.

**7 Conclude the conversation**
Teachers bring the conversation to an end by reviewing the big ideas that were discussed, using the charts they have developed.

**8 Reflect on the conversation**
Students record big ideas discussed during the instructional conversation by writing and drawing in learning logs.

through these conversations, students enhance their academic language proficiency (Goldenberg, 1992/1993). As in grand conversations, students are active participants, sharing ideas and building on classmates' ideas with their own comments. Teachers are participants, too, making comments much as the students do, but they also clarify misconceptions, ask questions, and provide instruction.

Instructional conversations deepen students' content-area knowledge and develop their academic language proficiency in these ways:

- Students deepen their knowledge about the topic during the instructional conversation.
- Students use technical and precise vocabulary and more complex sentence structures to express the ideas being discussed.
- Students learn to provide support of the ideas they present with information found in informational books, content-area textbooks, and other resources in the classroom.
- Students ask inference and critical-level questions, those with more than one answer, during instructional conversations.
- Students participate actively in the instructional conversation and make comments that build on and expand classmates' comments.

Students use efferent talk in instructional conversations to accomplish goals, learn information, and work out problems in thematic units. As they talk, students pose hypotheses; ask questions; provide information and clarify ideas; recall ideas presented earlier; make personal, world, and literary connections; make inferences; and evaluate the text and the information presented in it (Roser & Keehn, 2002). In contrast to grand conversations about stories, in which students use primarily aesthetic talk to create and deepen their interpretations, here students use primarily efferent talk to create knowledge and understand relationships among the big ideas they are learning.

Researchers have compared the effectiveness of small-group conversations with other instructional approaches and have found that students' learning is enhanced when they relate what they are learning to their own experiences—especially when they do so in their own words (Wittrock & Alesandrini, 1990). Similarly, Roser and Keehn (2002) reported a fourfold increase in students' learning when they had opportunities to clarify and elaborate ideas through talk.

After the discussion ends, students often write and draw in learning logs to record the important ideas discussed during the instructional conversation. Students may refer to the brainstormed list or graphic organizer the teacher made earlier.

Instructional conversations are useful for helping students grapple with big ideas they are learning in social studies, science, and other content areas. When students are discussing literature, they generally use grand conversations, which facilitate response to literature. An exception is when students focus on analyzing plot, characters, theme, and other elements of story structure; technically speaking, because they are thinking efferently, they are participating in an instructional conversation, not a grand conversation.

## K-W-L CHARTS: Building Knowledge Through Talk

Teachers use K-W-L charts (Ogle, 1986) to activate and build students' background knowledge during thematic units. In K-W-L, the letter *K* stands for *know*, *W* for *wonder*, and *L* for *learned*. Students share what they know and ask questions about a topic, and teachers write students' comments and questions on a chart. Through this activity, students become curious and more engaged in the learning process, and teachers have opportunities to introduce complex ideas and technical vocabulary in a nonthreatening way.

**The Procedure** Teachers divide a large chart into three columns and label them "K—What We Know," "W—What We Wonder," and "L—What We Learned." At the beginning of a unit, teachers introduce the chart and complete the first two columns as students think about the topic, share information, and ask questions. Then at the end of the unit, teachers complete the third column of the chart to summarize and review students' learning.

## K-W-L CHARTS

**1 Post a K-W-L chart**
Teachers post a large chart on the classroom wall, divide it into three columns, and label the columns "K—What We Know," "W—What We Wonder," and "L—What We Learned."

**2 Complete the K column**
At the beginning of the thematic unit, teachers have students brainstorm what they know about the topic and then record their responses in this column. If students suggest any incorrect information, teachers help them reword the information as a question and add it to the W column.

**3 Complete the W column**
Teachers write students' questions about the topic in this column.

**4 Complete the L column**
At the end of the unit, students reflect on what they have learned, and teachers record this information in the L column.

## Kindergartners' K-W-L Chart About Fish

| What We Know About Fish | What We Wonder About Fish | What We Learned About Fish | |
|---|---|---|---|
| Fish live in water. | Are sharks fish? | Sharks are fish. | Fish will die if they are not in the water because they cannot breathe. |
| Fish can swim. | How does a fish breathe underwater? | Fish have backbones. | |
| Tuna is a fish. | How long does a fish live? | Fish breathe through gills. | Fish hatch from eggs in the water. |
| My Grandpa likes to fish. | Why don't fish have arms and legs? | Fish live any place there is water. | |
| There are different kinds of fish. | Are whales fish? | Some fish like salt water. | Fish have all the colors of the rainbow. |
| Fish are slippery if you hold them. | Where do fish live? | Some fish like fresh water with no salt. | Fishes' skin is covered with scales. |
| You can eat fish. | Do fish sleep? | Fish eyes don't have eyelids. | Some fish live for 50 years or more. |
| Fish are pretty. | What do they eat? | Fish swim by moving their tails. | Yes, fish can hear. |
| | Can fish hear me talk? | | |

Teachers direct, scribe, and monitor the development of the K-W-L chart, but it is the students' talk that makes this such a powerful activity. Students use talk to explore and question ideas as they complete the K and W columns and to share new knowledge as they complete the L column.

**Ways to Use K-W-L Charts**
K-W-L charts are very adaptable. Even though each of the three columns on a K-W-L chart plays an important role in learning, sometimes teachers adapt the K-W-L format and use only two columns, either the K and L columns or the W and L columns, depending on available time and curricular needs. When teachers use only the W and L columns, for example, they have students brainstorm questions after previewing a chapter in a social studies textbook and then add what they learn in the L column to complete the chart after reading the chapter.

Sometimes teachers add a fourth column to the K-W-L chart, inserting an H—How do we find information?—between the W and the L columns. After they brainstorm a list of questions, students list the appropriate resources—an informational book, a dictionary, a community member, an atlas, the Internet, an encyclopedia, for example—for answering the questions in this column. The K-W-H-L chart is especially useful when students use K-W-L charts as a research tool.

Teachers also can organize the information on the K-W-L chart into categories to highlight the big ideas and to help students remember more of what they're learning; this procedure is called *K-W-L Plus* (Carr & Ogle, 1987). Teachers either provide three to six big-idea categories when they introduce the chart, or they ask students to determine the categories after they brainstorm information about the topic in the K column. Students then focus on these categories as they complete the L column, classifying each piece of information according to one of the categories. For example, if students are studying fish, the information might be organized into these big-idea categories: what fish look like, where fish live, how they breathe, how they move, and how they reproduce. Afterward, students often create a graphic organizer using the categories and the information in the L column. When categories are used, it's easier to make sure that students learn about each of the big ideas.

**Individual K-W-L Charts**
Students also make individual K-W-L charts as part of thematic units. As with class K-W-L charts, students brainstorm what they know about a topic, identify questions, and list what they've learned. They can make their charts on a page in their learning logs, or they can construct posters or flip books with K, W, and L columns. Sometimes teachers have students make their own charts after creating a class chart, or they have the students work together in small groups or individually. Checking how students complete their L columns is a good way to monitor their learning, too.

Students at all grade levels can create K-W-L charts as part of thematic units; young children learn about topics such as fish and the four seasons, and upper-grade students study the Constitution and the cell. No matter the grade level or whether they work individually or together as a class, students have knowledge to share and questions to ask about the topic.

## The Power of Drama

Drama provides a medium for students to use language in a meaningful context. Not only is drama a powerful form of communication, it also is a valuable way of learning. When children participate in dramatic activities, they interact with classmates, share experiences, and explore their own understanding. According to Dorothy Heathcote, a highly acclaimed British drama teacher, drama "cracks the code" so that the message can be understood (Wagner, 1999). Drama has this power for three reasons: It involves a combination of logical and creative thinking, it requires active experience, and it integrates the language arts. Research confirms that drama has a positive effect on both students' oral language development and their literacy learning (Wagner, 2003). Too often, however, teachers ignore drama because it seems unimportant compared to reading and writing.

Drama activities range from quick improvisations that are child centered to polished theatrical performances that are audience centered. Instead of encouraging children to be spontaneous and use drama to explore ideas, theatrical performances require that students memorize lines and rehearse their presentations. Our focus here is on child-centered dramatizations that are used to enhance learning.

## HOT SEAT

**1 Learn about the character**
Students prepare for the hot seat activity by reading a story or a biography to learn about the character they will impersonate.

**2 Create a costume**
Students design a costume appropriate for the character. In addition, students often collect objects or create artifacts to use in their presentation.

**3 Prepare opening remarks**
Students think about the most important things they'd like to share about the character and plan what they will say at the beginning of the activity.

**4 Introduce the character**
The student sits in front of classmates in a chair designated as the "hot seat," tells a little about the character he or she is role-playing using a first-person viewpoint (e.g., "I was the first person to step onto the moon's surface"), and shares artifacts.

**5 Ask questions**
Classmates ask thoughtful questions to learn more about the character, and the student remains in the role to answer them.

**6 Summarize the ideas**
The student doing the role play selects a classmate to summarize the important ideas that were presented about the character. The student in the hot seat clarifies any misunderstandings and adds any big ideas that classmates didn't mention.

**Improvisation** Students step into someone else's shoes and view the world from that perspective as they reenact stories. These activities are usually quick and informal because the emphasis is on learning, not performance. Students assume the role of a character and then role-play as the teacher narrates or guides the dramatization. Students usually don't wear costumes, and there's little or no rehearsal; it's the spontaneity that makes improvisation so effective.

Students often reenact stories during literature focus units. Sometimes they dramatize episodes while they are reading to examine a character, understand the sequence of events, or clarify a misunderstanding. As students dramatize an episode, teachers often direct the class's attention by asking questions, such as "What's (*character's name*) thinking?" and "Why is (*character's name*) making him do this?" For example, while seventh graders read *Holes* (Sachar, 1998), the story of a boy named Stanley Yelnats who is sent to a juvenile detention center for a crime he didn't commit, they often reenact Stanley digging a hole on his first day at Camp Green Lake to analyze the effect the experience had on him. Later, as they continue reading, they focus on pivotal points in the story: when Stanley finds the small gold lipstick tube while he's digging a hole, when he claims he stole a bag of sun-

flower seeds and is taken to the Warden's office, when he escapes from the camp and meets up with another escaped boy nicknamed "Zero," and finally, when the two boys return to camp and find the "treasure" suitcase. Through these improvisations, students understand individual episodes better as well as the overall structure of the story.

At other times, students, especially young children, dramatize an entire story after they finish reading it or listening to the teacher read it aloud. Teachers often break stories into three parts—beginning, middle, and end—to organize the dramatization and provide more opportunities for students to participate in the activity. Through improvisation, children review and sequence the events in the story and develop their concept of story. Folktales, such as *One Grain of Rice: A Mathematical Folktale* (Demi, 1997) and *Two of Everything: A Chinese Folktale* (Hong, 1993), are easy for younger children to dramatize.

**Sitting in the Hot Seat** Students assume the persona of a character from a story or biography they're reading and sit in the "hot seat" to be interviewed by classmates. It's called the

# PROCESS DRAMA

**1** **Set the purpose**
Teachers identify the purpose for the dramatic activity.

**2** **Create the dramatic context**
Teachers explain the dramatic context for the activity, and everyone assumes a role. Sometimes teachers share artifacts they have collected that relate to the characters and the event.

**3** **Dramatize the event**
Students partici-pate in the dramatization, staying in the role of the character they have chosen and building on the experience. Teachers create tension or present a challenge during the dramatization.

**4** **Ask questions**
Teachers ask questions or they invite students to ask questions about the dramatic context, and then students respond to them, usually from the viewpoint of their characters.

**5** **Prompt reflection**
Students write simulated journal entries or letters in the persona of their characters. They include details and insights they've gained through the dramatization.

**6** **Discuss the activity**
Teachers and students talk about the dramatization, reflecting on the experience and sharing their writing in order to gain new insights about the event.

hot seat because students are expected to respond to their classmates' questions. Students aren't intimidated by the activity; in fact, in most classrooms, it's very popular. Students are usually eager for their turn to sit in the hot seat. They answer the questions they're asked from the viewpoint of the character; through this activity, they deepen their comprehension as well as their classmates'. Students often wear a costume they've created when they assume the character's persona and share information about the character with classmates. They also collect objects and make artifacts to share.

**Process Drama**  British educator Dorothy Heathcote has developed an imaginative and spontaneous dramatic activity called *process drama* to help students explore stories they're reading, social studies topics, and current events (Tierney & Readence, 2005; Wagner, 1999). Teachers create an unscripted dramatic context about a story episode or a historical event, and the students in the class assume roles to experience and reflect on the episode or event (Schneider & Jackson, 2000).

For example, if the class is studying the Underground Railroad, the teacher might create a dramatic context on the moment when the escaped slaves reach the Ohio River. They'll be safe once they cross the river, but they're not safe yet. It's important that the teacher focus on a particular critical moment—one that is tension filled or that creates challenges. Most of the students would play the role of escaped slaves, but others would be conductors guiding the slaves to safety or the Quakers who risked their lives to hide the slaves. Either the teacher or other students would be bounty hunters or plantation owners trying to capture the escaped slaves.

With everyone participating in a role, the class dramatizes the event, examining the critical moment from their viewpoint. The teacher moves the action forward by recounting the event and asking questions. After reliving the experience, students reflect on it by writing a simulated journal entry or a simulated letter. They write in the persona of their character, sharing information about the experience and reflecting on it. Afterward, students step out of their roles to discuss the experience and share what they have learned.

Process drama goes beyond improvisation: Not only do the students reenact the episode or event, but they explore the topic from the viewpoint of their character as they respond to the teacher's questions and when they write simulated journal entries or letters. The discussion that follows the reenactment also deepens students' understanding. Heathcote believes that process drama is a valuable activity because it stimulates children's curiosity and makes them want to read books and learn more about historical or current events.

**Playing With Puppets**  Children become characters from favorite stories when they put puppets on their hands. A second grader pulls a green sock on one hand and a brown sock on the other hand, and with these simple puppets that have buttons sewn on for eyes, the characters of Frog and Toad from Arnold Lobel's award-winning books *Frog and Toad Are Friends* (1979a) and *Frog and Toad Together* (1979b) come to life. The second grader talks in the voices of the two characters and uses the puppets to retell events from the stories. Even though many adults often feel self-conscious playing with puppets, children do not.

Children can create puppet shows with commercially manufactured puppets, or they can make their own hand and finger puppets. When children create their own puppets, they are limited only by their imaginations, their ability to construct things, and the materials at hand. Simple puppets provide children with the opportunity to develop both creative and dramatic ability. The simpler the puppet, the more is left to the imagination of the audience and the puppeteer.

After students have made their puppets, they can create and perform puppet shows almost anywhere; they don't even need a script or a stage. Several children can sit together on

# Theory to Practice
## Fifth Graders Become Pilgrims on the *Mayflower*

Ms. Edge's fifth graders are studying the Pilgrims, and her purpose in this activity is to examine the difficulties the Pilgrims faced on their voyage. The activity is set on the night of November 10, 1620, 11 weeks after the Pilgrims set sail from England on the *Mayflower* and the night before the ship reached the New World.

The students assume roles as Pilgrims and sailors. They want Ms. Edge to become William Bradford, but she chooses to become a sailor named Jake. The classroom becomes the *Mayflower*. To simulate a cold November night, Ms. Edge turns off the lights, and the students huddle together on the floor, Pilgrims in one area and sailors in another, trying to sleep on the rocking ship. The tension mounts as students consider the hardships they're facing.

### Questions

Next, Ms. Edge asks questions to probe the fifth graders' understanding. Her questions for Pilgrims include:

- What has has been hard for you on this voyage?
- Will you reach the New World safely?
- What kind of life do you dream of in the new land?

Her questions for sailors include:

- What have you learned from the Pilgrims?
- What do you think will happen to them in the New World?

### Reflections

After the students dramatize life on the *Mayflower*, Ms. Edge asks them to write an entry in their simulated journals for November 10, 1620. Here is one child's "Pilgrim" entry:

*Dear Diary,*

*Today it is Nov. 10, 1620. My father signed the Mayflower Compact. One boy tried to explode the ship by lighting up a powder barrel. Two of my fiends died of Scurvy. Other than that, we had a good day.*

The dramatization ends when Ms. Edge announces that it is morning and turns on the lights.

### Discussion

As students share their reflections about the Pilgrims' suffering, they gain new understanding of the Pilgrims' determination to find a new home so that they could worship God in their own way.

the floor holding their puppets and invent a story that they tell to other classmates who sit nearby, listening intently. Or, students can make a stage from an empty appliance packing crate and climb inside to present their puppet show. What matters is that students can use their puppets to share a story with an appreciative audience.

## A IS FOR AUTHENTIC ASSESSMENT: Retelling Stories to Check Comprehension

Children often retell and dramatize familiar stories they've read or watched on television, and they invent new stories using familiar characters and episodes. When they retell a story, children organize the information they remember to provide a personalized summary (Hoyt, 1999). Their stories usually have a beginning, middle, and end: In the beginning, they describe the characters, identify the setting, and explain the problem; in the middle, they describe how the problem gets worse and how the characters attempt to solve the problem; finally, at the end of the story, they explain how the characters succeed at solving the problem. These retelling activities have three benefits: Children expand their oral language abilities, enhance their use of comprehension strategies, and deepen their knowledge of story structure. In addition, they prepare students to write retellings and new stories.

Teachers can capitalize on children's interest in retelling stories and use it to assess their comprehension. Retelling is an authentic assessment tool because it's similar to the language arts activities that take place in classrooms every day (McKenna & Stahl, 2003). As they listen to children retell a story, teachers use a scoring sheet or rating scale to evaluate the cohesiveness and completeness of the retellings. This activity is especially valuable for English learners because teachers can assess both the students' comprehension and their oral language fluency (O'Malley & Pierce, 1996).

Once you begin listening to children retell stories, you'll notice that children who understand a story retell it differently than those who don't. Good comprehenders' retellings make sense: They reflect the organization of the story, and they mention all of the important story events. In contrast, weak com-

> "When they retell a story, children organize the information they remember to provide a personalized summary.

## Types of Puppets

**Stick Puppets**
Attach pictures students have drawn or pictures cut from magazines to sticks, tongue depressors, or popsicle sticks to make these simple puppets.

**Paper Bag Puppets**
Place the puppet's mouth at the fold of the paper bag and draw or paint on faces, add clothes and yarn for hair, and attach arms and legs.

**Cylinder Puppets**
Paint faces on cardboard tubes, add yarn for hair, and decorate with clothing. Insert fingers in the bottom of the tube to manipulate the puppet.

**Cup Puppets**
Glue facial features, hair, wings, and other decorations on a styrofoam cup. Then attach a stick or heavy-duty straw to the inside of the cup as the handle.

**Paper Plate Puppets**
Use crayons or paint to make a face on the paper plate and add junk materials for decorations. Tape a stick or ruler to the back of the plate as the handle.

**Finger Puppets**
Draw, color, and cut out small figures, add tabs to either side of the figure and tape the tabs together to fit around a finger. Or, cut the finger section from a glove and add decorations.

prehenders often recall events haphazardly or omit important events, often those in the middle of the story.

**Three Children's Retellings**

A first-grade teacher reads aloud *Hey, Al* (Yorinks, 1986), the award-winning picture-book story about Al, a hardworking janitor, and his loyal dog, Eddie, who yearn for a better life. At the beginning of the story, Al is discouraged because he has to work so hard, and

then a bird offers him an easy life. Al accepts the bird's offer, and in the middle of the story, the bird flies Al and Eddie to an island paradise where they have a wonderful time—until they start turning into birds. They escape and fly toward their home in the city. Al reaches home safely, but Eddie almost drowns. At last Al and Eddie are reunited, and they realize that it's up to them to make their own happiness. After the teacher finishes reading the story, the children draw pictures of their favorite parts and talk about the story in a grand conversation. Afterward, the first graders individually retell the story to her, but they aren't prompted to add more information.

Here are three children's retellings:

*Retelling #1:* The story is about Al and Eddie. A bird took them to Hawaii and they had a lot of fun there. They were swimming and playing a lot. Then they came back home because they didn't like being birds.

*Retelling #2:* Al and Eddie are at the island. They like it and they are changing into birds. They have wings and feathers and stuff that made them look funny. That makes them scared so they fly back to their old home. I think Eddie crashed into the ocean and drowned. So Al buys a new dog and they have lots of fun together.

*Retelling #3:* This man named Al and his puppy named Eddie wanted more excitement so they went to an island. It was wonderful at first, but then they started changing into birds and they hated that. They wanted to go back home. They started flying home, and they were flying and they were changing back into their real selves. Al made it home, but Eddie almost drowned because he was smaller. All in all, they did learn an important lesson: You should be happy with yourself just the way you are.

These three retellings show children's differing levels of comprehension. The first child's brief retelling is literal: It includes events from the beginning, middle, and end of the story, but it lacks an interpretation. Many details are missing; in fact, this child doesn't mention that Al's a man (or a janitor) or that Eddie's a dog.

Even though the second retelling is longer than the first one, it shows only partial comprehension. It's incomplete because it lacks a beginning: This child focuses most of the retelling on the middle and misunderstands the end of the story because Eddie doesn't drown. With some prompting from the teacher, this child might have added more information about the beginning of the story or corrected the ending.

The third child's retelling, in contrast, is quite complete. This child retells the beginning, middle, and end of the story and explains the characters' motivation for going to the island. Most important, this child establishes a purpose for the story by explaining its theme-making your own happiness.

After examining the strengths and weaknesses of each retelling, teachers can use what they learn to plan instruction. For example, the first student might benefit from learning to add more details in a retelling, and the second student needs to learn more about organizing the retelling into beginning, middle, and end parts. They both need to learn more about how to recognize the theme of a story. Because the third child's retelling was so complete, this child might be interested in reading more challenging stories where the theme is less obvious.

# RETELLING STORIES

**1 Introduce the story**
The teacher introduces the story by reading the title, examining the cover of the book, or talking about a topic related to the story. The teacher also explains that students will be asked to retell the story afterward.

**2 Read the story**
Students read the story or listen to the teacher read it aloud. When students are reading the story themselves, it is essential that the story be at their reading level.

**3 Discuss the story**
Students and the teacher talk about the story, sharing ideas and clarifying confusions. (This step is optional, but discussing the story usually improves the students' retelling.)

**4 Create a graphic organizer**
Students can create a graphic organizer or a series of drawings to guide their retelling. (This step is optional too, but it's especially helpful for students who have difficulty retelling stories.)

**5 Have a student retell the story**
The teacher asks students to individ-ually retell the story in their own words, and asks prompting questions to elicit more information:

- What happened next?
- Where did the story take place?
- What did the character do next?
- How did the story end?
- What was the author's message?

**6 Mark the scoring guide**
The teacher scores the retelling using a scoring guide as the student retells the story.

**Guidelines for Retelling**

Teachers sit one-on-one with individual children in a quiet area of the classroom and ask them to retell the story. While the child is retelling, teachers use a scoring sheet to mark the components that the child includes in the retelling. If the child hesitates or doesn't finish retelling the story, teachers ask questions, such as "What happened next?"

Teachers can't assume that children already know how to retell stories, even though many children do. Through a series of minilessons on retelling strategies and demonstrations of the retelling procedure, children will understand what's expected of them. Children also need to practice retelling stories before they'll be good at it. They can retell stories with a classmate and to their parents at home.

Children who continue to have difficulty retelling stories may need to learn more about story structure, especially beginning, middle, and end. It may also be helpful to have them make graphic organizers and draw pictures to scaffold their retellings. As their comprehension improves, so will their retelling abilities.

<table>
<tr><td>**Can Children Retell Informational Books, Too?**</td><td>Children also can retell informational books they've read or listened to the teacher read aloud; in these retellings, they focus on summarizing the big ideas and the relationships among them rather than on characters and story events (Flynt & Cooter, 2005).</td></tr>
</table>

Their retellings should address these questions:

What are the big ideas?
How are the big ideas structured?
What is the author's purpose?
What connections do students make?
What did students learn that they didn't already know?

As children recall the big ideas, it's important that they recognize the structural pattern the author used (e.g., sequence, cause and effect, or comparison) and organize their retelling the same way. Recognizing the author's structural pattern usually provides a clue to the author's purpose, another component that good comprehenders include in their retellings.

For children to remember the big ideas they're learning, it's essential that they make personal, world, or textual connections to them. They need some background knowledge about a topic in order to make connections—and if they can't make any connections, it's unlikely they'll understand and remember the big ideas.

<table>
<tr><td>**Judging Children's Retellings**</td><td>Most children enjoy retelling stories, and their rubric scores provide a useful measure of their comprehension. Some children, however, are shy or uncomfortable talking with teachers, so their scores may underesti-</td></tr>
</table>

## Ten Ways to Help Children Who Have Difficulty Retelling Stories

- Demonstrate how to retell a story effectively.
- Have children dramatize the story as they retell it.
- Have children make puppets and other props to use in retelling the story.
- Teach children about story structure, especially the beginning, middle, and end.
- Divide the story into the beginning, middle, and end, and then have children retell each part.
- Have children draw a series of pictures to use in retelling the story.
- Create graphic organizers to use in retelling the story.
- Have children look at the illustrations when retelling a picture-book story.
- Practice retelling stories with a partner or in a small group.
- Write the retelling as a book.

### Scoring Guide: Retelling Stories

Name _Cassie_     Date _Mar. 10_
Book _Ruby Lu, Brave and True_

| 4 | ___ Names and describes all characters. |
|---|---|
| | ___ Includes specific details about the setting. |
| | ___ Explains the problem. |
| | ___ Describes attempts to solve the problem. |
| | ___ Explains the solution. |
| | ___ Identifies the theme. |
| **(3)** | ✓ Names all characters and <u>describes</u> some of them.   *P* |
| | ___ Identifies more than one detail about the setting (location, weather, time). |
| | ✓ Recalls events in order. |
| | ✓ Identifies the problem. |
| | ✓ Includes the beginning, <u>middle</u>, and end.   *P* |
| 2 | ___ Names all characters. |
| | ✓ Mentions the setting. |
| | ___ Recalls most events in order. |
| | ___ Includes the beginning and end. |
| 1 | ___ Names some characters. |
| | ___ Recalls events haphazardly. |
| | ___ Includes only beginning or end. |

P = prompted

mate how well they comprehend (McKenna & Stahl, 2003). The same is true for English learners.

As teachers listen to children retell stories, they can think more deeply about the children's comprehension ability as they ask themselves questions like these:

Does the child make personal connections to the story?
Does the child make inferences?
Does the child make evaluative statements? (Hoyt, 1999)

These questions go beyond the literal comprehension typically measured on rubrics and checklists.

Teachers also can assess the effectiveness of children's retelling by asking these questions:

Does the child speak with expression?
Is the retelling coherent?
Does the child need prompting?
Does the child incorporate vocabulary and sentence structure from the story?

They also can examine children's use of visualizing, summarizing, and other retelling strategies as they listen to the retelling or ask children to reflect on their retelling.

Retelling is an instructional tool as well as a useful assessment tool. When students participate regularly in retelling activities, their comprehension improves as they focus on the big ideas in the story, and their oral language abilities are enhanced as they incorporate sentence patterns, vocabulary, and phrases from stories and informational books into their own talk (McKenna & Stahl, 2003).

# Review

## The Big Ideas

Too often, teachers assume that students already know how to talk, so they concentrate on reading and writing, but it's crucial that teachers develop students' ability to understand and use academic English, the language of schooling.

The key points in Part 3 include:

- Talk is a necessary ingredient for learning.
- Students learn to talk in small-group conversations.
- Students learn to understand and use academic language.

- In grand conversations, students use aesthetic talk to deepen their understanding of stories.
- Students use efferent talk as they participate in instructional conversations about content-area topics.
- Students retell stories to demonstrate their comprehension.
- Students activate and build background knowledge as they make K-W-L charts during thematic units.
- Students use improvisation and process drama as tools for learning in literature focus units and thematic units.

## Classroom Inquiry

No matter whether you're a practicing teacher or a preservice teacher observing in kindergarten through eighth-grade classrooms, you're likely to be interested in learning more about the talk that goes on in the classroom. Consider creating a classroom inquiry to investigate one of these topics.

**Types of Talk**  Providing opportunities for students to talk is important for social, linguistic, and academic purposes. To delve into this concept, ask yourself these questions:

- How much time do students spend talking?
- Do boys and girls get equal opportunities to talk?
- Do I exclude any students?
- In what types of talk activities are students involved?

**Levels of Questions**  Higher-level questions help students to think more deeply about stories they are reading and topics they are learning. To explore this topic, consider these questions:

- What types of questions do I ask?
- What types of questions do students ask?
- Is my questioning style teacher centered or child centered?

**Grand and Instructional Conversations**  Students use talk as they respond to books they are reading and what they are learning in thematic units. To examine how students use talk in these two instructional procedures, think about these questions:

- Do students follow the procedures for grand conversations?
- Do students follow the procedures for instructional conversations?
- How do students elaborate their knowledge through these conversations?

Once you identify an inquiry question, make plans for your classroom inquiry, collect and analyze data, and draw conclusions to improve your classroom practice.

# 4

# Reading

## INTRODUCTION

Reading is a meaning-making process. Readers use their life and literature experiences and knowledge of written language as they interact with the text they're reading. It is quite common for two people to read the same story and come away with different interpretations. Louise Rosenblatt (2005) explains that meaning does not exist on the pages of the book that a reader is reading; instead, meaning is created through the transaction between readers and what they are reading.

This text is based on a balanced view of reading instruction: Children learn to read through a combination of direct instruction about reading strategies and skills and opportunities to read and respond to authentic literature (Baumann, Hoffman, Moon, & Duffy-Hester, 1998; Pressley, 1998). It's the combination of instruction and opportunities to read authentic texts that creates the balance.

Literature should be at the heart of reading instruction. Sometimes basal readers are thought of as the most appropriate material for reading instruction, but it's not a good idea to limit children's reading materials to basals because many selections lack authenticity or are excerpted from longer texts. For children to become lifelong readers, they need to read a variety of stories, informational books, and poems.

Reading should be integrated with the other language arts: Children *listen* to books read aloud, *talk* about books they're reading, use books as models for *writing, view* film versions of books, and make posters to *visually represent* books. Reading and responding to literature don't occur in a vacuum.

## Fifth Graders Read *Number the Stars*

Mrs. Ochs teaches a literature focus unit on *Number the Stars* (Lowry, 1989), a Newbery award–winning story of two girls, one Christian and one Jewish, set in Denmark during World War II. In this unit, she wants to help her fifth-grade students use their knowledge of genre and story structure to deepen their comprehension of the story. She rereads the story, analyzes the elements of story structure in the book, and considers how she wants to teach the unit.

To begin the unit, Mrs. Ochs asks students about friendship: "Would you help your friend if he or she needed help?" The students talk about friendship and what it means to them. They agree that they would help their friends in any way they could—helping friends get medical treatment if they were ill, and sharing their lunch if they were hungry, for example. One child volunteers that he is sure that his mom would let his friend's family stay at his house if the friend's house burned down. Then Mrs. Ochs asks, "What if your friend asked you to hold something for him or her, something so dangerous that 60 years ago you could be imprisoned or killed for having it?" Many say they would, but doubt they would ever be called on to do that. Then she shows them a broken Star of David necklace, similar to the one on the cover of *Number the Stars,* and one student says, "You're talking about the Nazis and the Jews in World War II." The prereading stage continues for 2 more days as students share what they know about the war, and Mrs. Ochs presents information, reads several picture-book stories about the war, and shows a video.

Mrs. Ochs reads the first chapter of *Number the Stars* aloud as students follow along in individual copies of the book; she almost always introduces a book this way because she wants to get all students off to a good start and because so many concepts and key vocabulary words are introduced in the beginning of a book. After the first chapter, students continue reading the second chapter. Most of the students read independently, but some read with buddies, and Mrs. Ochs continues reading with a group of the six lowest readers.

Then Mrs. Ochs brings all the students together for a grand conversation. The students make connections between the information they have learned about World War II and the story events. Mrs. Ochs reads aloud *The Yellow Star: The Legend of King Christian X of Denmark* (Deedy, 2000), a picture-book story about the Danish king who defies the Nazis, be-

cause the king is the focus of the second chapter. The students predict that the Nazis will take Ellen and her family to a concentration camp even though Annemarie and her family try to hide them. After the grand conversation, the students write in reading logs. For this entry, Mrs. Ochs asks them to write predictions about what will happen in the story based on what they know about World War II and what they read in the first two chapters.

Mrs. Ochs continues having the students read and respond to the chapters. Some students continue to read independently, but many of the students form reading groups so that they can read and talk about the story as they are reading. Mrs. Ochs continues reading with the lowest readers. The whole class comes together after reading each day to talk about the story in a grand conversation. Afterward, they write in reading logs.

During the grand conversations, Mrs. Ochs probes students' understanding of the story and asks them to think about how the author used plot, characters, setting, and other elements of story structure. Mrs. Ochs has taught the students about these elements, so they are able to apply their knowledge to the story they are reading. One day, she asks students about the conflict situation in the story. At first, the students say that the conflict is between people—Nazis and Danes—but as they continue talking, they realize that the conflict is not between individual people, but within society.

Another day, Mrs. Ochs talks about the setting. She asks if this story could have happened in the United States. At first, the students say no, because the Nazis never invaded the United States, and they use maps to make their point. But as they continue to talk, students broaden their discussion to the persecution of minorities and conclude that persecution can happen anywhere. They cite two examples—the mistreatment of Native Americans and the internment of Japanese Americans during World War II.

During the grand conversation after students finish reading *Number the Stars,* Mrs. Ochs asks about the theme. "Did Lois Lowry have a message in her book? What do you think

### How can teachers facilitate students' comprehension of stories?

As teachers teach literature focus units, they include activities at each stage of the reading process to ensure that all students in their classrooms comprehend what they are reading. This attention to comprehension is essential because when students don't understand what they are reading and can't relate the literature to their own lives and the world around them, the experience has been wasted. As you read this Classroom Close-Up, notice how Mrs. Ochs involves her fifth graders in a variety of language arts activities to deepen their understanding of World War II and to facilitate their comprehension of the story, *Number the Stars.*

## Analysis of the Structural Elements in *Number the Stars*

| Element | Story Analysis | Teaching Ideas |
|---|---|---|
| Plot | The beginning is before Ellen goes into hiding; the middle is while Ellen is in hiding; and the end is after Ellen and her family leave for the safety of Sweden. The problem is saving Ellen's life. The overarching conflict in the story is conflict with the Nazis, who represent society. | Before reading, students need background knowledge about World War II, the Nazis, Jews and the Holocaust, and Resistance fighters. There is so much interesting information in the story that can distract students, so it is important to focus on the problem and how it will be solved. |
| Characters | Annemarie and Ellen are the main characters in this story, and through their actions and beliefs, readers learn that these two girls are much more alike than they are different. The two girls are both courageous, one because she has to be, the other because she chooses to be. | Even though one girl is Christian and one is Jewish, the girls are more alike than they are different. A Venn diagram will emphasize this point. Students might make open-mind portraits from one girl's viewpoint. |
| Setting | The story is set in Denmark during World War II. The setting is integral to the plot and based on actual events, including fishermen ferrying Jews to safety in Sweden. | Use maps of Europe to locate the setting of the story. Students can draw maps and mark story locations, and they also can mark the spread of the German (and Japanese) forces during the war on a world map. |
| Point of View | The story is limited omniscient. It is told from the third-person viewpoint, and readers know only what Annemarie is thinking. | Students can retell important events from one of the girls' perspectives or from the parents' or the Nazis' viewpoints. |
| Theme | This story deals with the courage and bravery of: the Jews, the fishermen, the Resistance fighters, King Christian X and Danes who wore six-pointed yellow stars on their clothes, and Annemarie's family. One theme is that people choose to be courageous when they see others mistreated. | Students focus on the theme as they talk in grand conversations and collect favorite quotes from the story. Students might also read about other people who have been courageous to examine the universal qualities of courage. |

about the theme?" Several students comment that the theme was that the Nazis were bad people; others said "innocent people get killed in wars" and "peace is better than war." To move the students forward in their thinking, Mrs. Ochs suggests that one theme is about courage or being brave. She reads two sentences from the book: "That's all that brave means—not thinking about the dangers. Just thinking about what you must do" (p. 123). The students agree that both girls and their families were brave. Mrs. Ochs asks students to think back through the story and help her brainstorm a list of all the times they were brave. They brainstormed more than 30 instances of bravery!

Mrs. Ochs and her students continue their discussion about the theme for several more days. Finally, she asks them, "Do you think you're brave? Would you be brave if you were Annemarie or

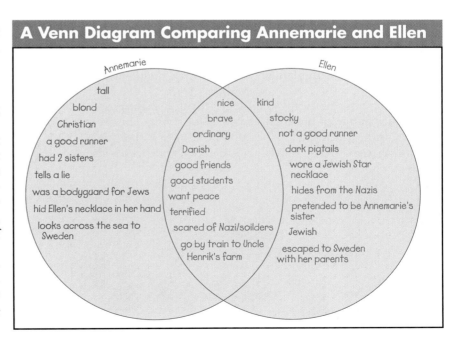

**A Venn Diagram Comparing Annemarie and Ellen**

Annemarie / Ellen

- tall
- blond
- Christian
- a good runner
- had 2 sisters
- tells a lie
- was a bodyguard for Jews
- hid Ellen's necklace in her hand
- looks across the sea to Sweden

- nice
- brave
- ordinary
- Danish
- good friends
- good students
- want peace
- terrified
- scared of Nazi/soilders
- go by train to Uncle Henrik's farm

- kind
- stocky
- not a good runner
- dark pigtails
- wore a Jewish Star necklace
- hides from the Nazis
- pretended to be Annemarie's sister
- Jewish
- escaped to Sweden with her parents

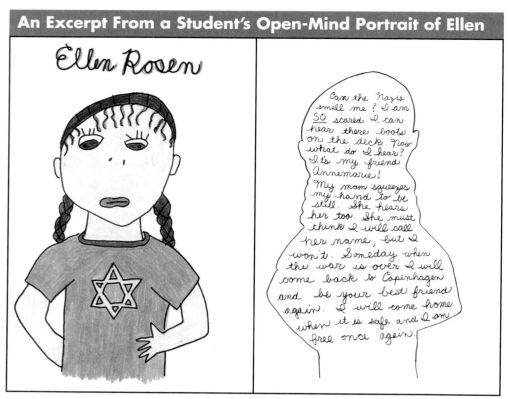

Ellen Rosen

Can the Nazis smell me? I am SO scared I can hear there boots on the deck. Now what do I hear? It's my friend Annemarie! My mom squeezes my hand to be still. She hears her too. She must think I will call her name, but I won't. Someday when the war is over I will come back to Copenhagen and be your best friend again. I will come home when it is safe and I am free once again.

Ellen?" They talk about war and having to be brave. "What about Ellen?" Mrs. Ochs asks. "Did she have to be brave?" The students agree that she did. "But what about Annemarie? Couldn't she and her family have stayed safely in Copenhagen?" The students are surprised at first by the question, but through their talk, they realize that Annemarie, her family, and the other Resistance fighters had chosen to be brave.

As the students read *Number the Stars*, Mrs. Ochs also involves them in several exploring-stage activities focusing on the story structure. They mark areas of Nazi and Japanese occupation on world maps and draw maps of Denmark. To compare Annemarie and Ellen, they make Venn diagrams and conclude that the girls are more alike than they are different. They also make open-mind portraits of one of the girls, showing what she is thinking at several pivotal points in the story.

The students plan an applying-stage activity after the great-grandfather of one of the children comes for a visit. This student brings his great-grandfather to school to talk about his remembrances of World War II, and then the students decide to each interview a grandparent, a great-grandparent, or an elderly neighbor who was alive during the war. The students develop this set of interview questions:

◆ What did you do during the war?
◆ How old were you?
◆ Were you on the home front or the war front?
◆ Did you know about the Holocaust then?
◆ What do you remember most from World War II?

Each student conducts an interview and then uses the writing process to write an essay about the person's wartime experiences. They word process their essays so that they have a professional look. Here is one student's essay:

My grandfather Arnold Ott was in college at the time the war started. All of a sudden after Pearl Harbor was attacked, all his classmates started to join the army. He did also and became an engineer that worked on B-24 and B-25 bombers. The military kept sending him to different schools so he would be able to fix all the bombers. He never had to fight because of that. He earned some medals, but he said the real ones were only given to those who fought. He said that he was glad that he did not fight because he had friends that never came back.

Mrs. Ochs duplicates the essays and binds them into books. She also makes extra copies for the interviewees. The students are so excited about the people they interviewed and the essays they wrote that they decide to have a party. They invite the interviewees and introduce them to their classmates, and they ask the interviewees to autograph the essays they have written about them.

As you continue reading Part 4, think about how Mrs. Ochs incorporates the topics being presented. Here are three questions to guide your reading:

◆ How does Mrs. Ochs use each stage of the reading process?
◆ Which language arts do the fifth graders use as they respond to *Number the Stars*?
◆ How does Mrs. Ochs ensure that her less capable readers are successful?

# Essentials

## ESSENTIAL #1:
## What's Important in Reading?

Everyone—parents, teachers, and politicians—has an opinion on what's important in reading instruction. Often the debate centers on phonics: Some people believe that phonics is the most important factor because students need to be able to decode the words they're reading, but others consider phonics to be less important than comprehension because the purpose of reading is to make meaning from text. The view taken in this text is that there are five important factors in developing capable readers:

- Word identification
- Comprehension
- Fluency
- Motivation
- Vocabulary

Teachers address all five of these factors through direct instruction, by reading aloud to students every day, and by pro-viding daily opportunities for students to read books at their own reading level.

**Word Identification**

Capable readers have a large bank of words that they recognize instantly and automatically because they can't stop and analyze every word as they read (LaBerge & Samuels, 1976). Students learn to read phonetically regular words, such as *baking* and *first*, and high-frequency words, such as *there* and *would*. In addition, they learn word-identification strategies to figure out unfamiliar words they encounter while reading. They use phonic analysis to read *raid*, *strap*, and other phonetically regular words, syllabic analysis to read *jungle*, *election*, and other multisyllabic words, and morphemic analysis to read *omnivorous*, *millennium*, and other words with Latin and Greek word parts. Through a combination of instruction and reading practice, students' knowledge of words continues to grow.

## Instructional Recommendations

| | |
|---|---|
| **Word Identification** | • Teach phoneme-grapheme correspondences, phonics generalizations, and other phonics concepts<br>• Teach high-frequency words<br>• Teach word-identification strategies (phonic analysis, syllabic analysis, and morphemic analysis) |
| **Fluency** | • Have students practice reading familiar texts to develop fluency<br>• Have students independently read texts at their reading level<br>• Involve students in choral reading activities |
| **Vocabulary** | • Have students independently read books at their reading level<br>• Read aloud to students every day<br>• Teach vocabulary words during literature focus units and thematic units<br>• Post vocabulary words on word walls<br>• Involve students in vocabulary activities |
| **Comprehension** | • Have students activate background knowledge before reading<br>• Build students' background knowledge when necessary before reading<br>• Encourage students to set purposes for reading<br>• Teach students to use comprehension strategies<br>• Show students how to make inferences<br>• Teach students about genres<br>• Teach students about the structure of stories, informational books, and poems |
| **Motivation** | • Encourage students to express their own ideas and opinions<br>• Have students choose books for independent reading<br>• Have students talk about books they're reading<br>• Involve students in authentic reading activities<br>• Have students work collaboratively with classmates in literature circles |

Phonics, the set of phoneme-grapheme relationships, is an important part of word-identification instruction in the primary grades, but it's only one part of word identification because English is not an entirely phonetic language. During the primary grades, children also learn to recognize at least 300 high-frequency words, such as *what, said,* and *come,* that can't be sounded out. Older students learn more sophisticated word-identification strategies about dividing words into syllables and recognizing root words and affixes.

### Fluency

Capable readers have learned to read fluently—quickly and with expression. Three components of fluency are reading speed, word recognition, and prosody (Rasinski, 2004). Students need to read at least 100 words per minute to be considered fluent readers, and most children reach this speed by third grade. Speed is important because it's hard for students to remember what they're reading when they read slowly. Word recognition is related to speed because readers who automatically recognize most of the words they're reading read more quickly than those who don't. Prosody, the ability to read sentences with appropriate phrasing and intonation, is important because when readers read expressively, the text is easier to understand (Dowhower, 1991).

Developing fluency is important because readers don't have unlimited cognitive resources, and both word identification and comprehension require a great deal of mental energy. During the primary grades, the focus is on word identification, and students learn to recognize hundreds of words, but in fourth grade—after most students have become fluent readers—the focus changes to comprehension. Students who are fluent readers have the cognitive resources available for comprehension, but students who are still word-by-word readers are focusing on word identification.

### Vocabulary

Capable readers have larger vocabularies than less capable readers do (McKeown, 1985). They learn words at the amazing rate of 7 to 10 per day. Learning a word is developmental: Children move from recognizing that they've seen or heard the word before to learning one meaning, and then to knowing several ways to use the word (Allen, 1999). Vocabulary knowledge is important in reading because it's easier to decode words that you've heard before, and it's easier to comprehend what you're reading when you're already familiar with some words related to the topic.

Reading is the most effective way that students expand their vocabularies. Capable readers do more reading than less capable students, so they learn more words. Not only do they do more reading, but the books capable students read contain more age-appropriate vocabulary than the easier books that

### Learn More About Comprehension

Blachowicz, C., & Ogle, D. (2001). *Reading comprehension: Strategies for independent learners.* New York: Guilford Press.

Gallagher, K. (2004). *Deeper reading: Comprehending challenging texts, 4–12.* York, ME: Stenhouse.

Harvey, D., & Goudvis, A. (2000). *Strategies that work: Teaching comprehension to enhance understanding.* York, ME: Stenhouse.

Miller, D. (2002). *Reading with meaning: Teaching comprehension in the primary grades.* York, ME: Stenhouse.

Owocki, G. (2003). *Comprehension: Strategic instruction for K–3 students.* Portsmouth, NH: Heinemann.

Sweet, A. P., & Snow, C. E. (Eds.). (2003). *Rethinking reading comprehension.* New York: Guilford Press.

lower-performing students read (Stahl, 1999).

### Comprehension

Readers use their past experiences and the text to construct comprehension, a meaning that's useful for a specific purpose (Irwin, 1991). Comprehension is a complex process that involves both reader and text factors (Sweet & Snow, 2003). While they're reading, readers are actively involved in thinking about what they already know about a topic. They set a purpose for reading, read strategically, and make inferences using cues in the text. Readers also use their knowledge about texts: They think about the genre and the topic of the text, and they use their knowledge of text structure to guide their reading.

Capable readers are strategic: They use predicting, visualizing, connecting, questioning, summarizing, and other strategies to think about and understand what they're reading (Pressley, 2002). They also learn to monitor whether they're comprehending and learn how to take action to solve problems and clarify confusions when they occur. Teaching comprehension involves introducing strategies through minilessons, demonstrating how capable readers use the strategies, and involving students in supervised practice activities.

Through these activities, teachers scaffold students and then gradually release responsibility for comprehending to students (Pearson & Gallagher, 1983). Teachers withdraw support slowly once students show that they can use strategies independently while they're reading. Of course, even when students are using strategies independently, they may need increased scaffolding when they're reading more difficult texts, texts about unfamiliar topics, or different genres (Pardo, 2004).

### Motivation

Capable readers are motivated. They're engaged while they're reading and expect to be successful. Motivation is intrinsic; it involves feeling self-confident and viewing the activity as pleasurable (Cunningham & Cunningham, 2002). Students are more likely to be motivated when they're reading high-interest texts, when they work collaboratively with classmates, when they have opportunities to make choices, when not everything is graded, and when they feel ownership of their work (Gallagher, 2003). Motivation isn't something that teachers can force on students; instead, it's an innate desire that students must develop themselves.

Teaching reading isn't as easy as deciding whether to focus on phonics or comprehension. Teachers need to focus on all five factors so that students develop a bank of instantly recognizable words, become fluent readers, acquire an extensive vocabulary, learn to comprehend effectively, and stay motivated to become capable readers.

## ESSENTIAL #2: The Reading Process

Reading is a process in which readers negotiate meaning in order to comprehend, or create an interpretation. During reading, the meaning does not go from the page to the reader. Instead, reading involves a complex negotiation between the text and the reader that is shaped by many factors: the reader's knowledge about the topic, the reader's purpose for reading, the language community the reader belongs to and how closely that language matches the language used in the text, the reader's culturally based expectations about reading, and the reader's expectations about reading based on his or her previous experiences (Weaver, 1994).

**Stage 1: Prereading**
The reading process begins before readers open a book to read: They activate or build background knowledge, set a purpose for reading, and preview the selection before beginning to read. In the Classroom Close-Up, Mrs. Ochs involved her students in prereading activities. She expanded their background knowledge about World War II and the Holocaust as they prepared to read *Number the Stars*.

**Stage 2: Reading**
Students read the book or other selection in one of these ways:
- Independent reading
- Shared reading
- Guided reading
- Reading aloud to students

## Types of Reading

**Independent Reading**
Students read silently by themselves and at their own pace (Taylor, 1993). The selections must be at students' reading level in order for them to comprehend what they're reading.

**Reading Aloud to Students**
Teachers use the interactive read-aloud procedure to share selections that are appropriate for students' interest level but too difficult for them to read by themselves (Barrentine, 1996).

**Guided Reading**
Teachers scaffold students' reading to teach reading strategies (Fountas & Pinnell, 1996, 2001). Guided reading is conducted with small groups of students who read at the same level.

**Shared Reading**
Students follow along as the teacher reads a selection aloud (Fisher & Medvic, 2000). Primary-grade teachers often use big books—enlarged versions of the selection—for shared reading (Holdaway, 1979).

When students can read the book easily, they use independent reading, and when the book is beyond their reading level, teachers read it aloud. Teachers use either shared or guided reading when students can read the book with teacher support.

**Stage 3: Responding**
Students respond to what they have read by writing in reading logs and participating in grand conversations (Peterson & Eeds, 1990) (or instructional conversations after reading informational books). As students read the book, they develop initial impressions, and through these two activities, they clarify their thinking, make personal, world, and literary connections, and elaborate their understanding.

Students often direct the flow of the discussions and choose their own topics for writing, but teachers play an important role, too: They ask questions, introduce new topics, provide information, and explain confusions during grand conversations, and they provide prompts for reading log entries when there's an important topic they want students to think about. Mrs. Ochs's students responded to these prompts when they were reading *Number the Stars* (Lowry, 1989):

| After Chapter 3 | What does "all of Denmark must be bodyguard for the Jews" mean? |
| After Chapter 5 | Do you think Annemarie and Ellen are safe? |
| After Chapter 9 | Do you think it's all right for Uncle Henrik and Mama to lie to Annemarie? |
| After Chapter 15 | What is so special in the lunch Annemarie carried to her Uncle? |

Teachers often wonder which response activity should come first. The order isn't important, but

## The Reading Process in Action: Stories

| Prereading | Students prepare to read by activating background knowledge and setting purposes for reading. When teachers are scaffolding the reading experience, they often build students' background knowledge and introduce key vocabulary words. |
| Reading | Students read the story independently or listen to the teacher read it aloud. Teachers also use shared reading or guided reading when they read with students. |
| Responding | Students deepen their comprehension by participating in grand conversations and writing in reading logs. |
| Exploring | Teachers post vocabulary on word walls and involve students in word-study activities. They also teach mini-lessons about story structure and share information about authors and illustrators. |
| Applying | Students create individual, small-group, or class projects to extend the reading experience. |

# GUIDED READING

**1 Choose a book** Teachers choose a book children in the group can read with 90–94% accuracy and collect copies of the book for each child.

**2 Introduce the book** Teachers show the cover, reading the title and the author's name, and activate children's background knowledge on a related topic. They use key vocabulary words as they talk about the book but don't directly teach them. Children also "picture walk" through the book, examining the illustrations.

**3 Have children read** Teachers provide support as children read the book independently. They help individual children decode unfamiliar words, deal with unfamiliar sentence structures, and comprehend ideas whenever assistance is needed.

**4 Respond to the book** Children talk about the book and relate it to others they have read, as in a grand conversation.

**5 Teach concepts** Teachers teach a phonics skill or comprehension strategy, review vocabulary words, or examine an element of story structure.

**6 Provide opportunities for independent reading** Teachers have children reread the book several more times during reading workshop.

---

not surprisingly, students' responses are better developed in the activity that comes second. So, to encourage powerful discussions, it's better to begin with reading logs, and for more complete journal entries, the discussion should come first.

**Stage 4: Exploring** This is the "teaching" stage, where students go back into the text to explore it more analytically. Teachers teach minilessons on reading strategies using excerpts from the book and minilessons on skills, including phonics, using words from the book (Cunningham, 2000; Duffy, 2003). Teachers add "important" vocabulary to word walls posted in the classroom, and students use these words for vocabulary activities. They make posters to highlight particular words and sort words to analyze related words (Bear, Invernizzi, Templeton, & Johnston, 2004). Researchers emphasize the importance of immersing students in words, teaching strategies for learning words, and personalizing word learning (Blachowicz & Fisher, 2002).

Teachers focus students' attention on the structure of the text and the literary language that authors use (Eeds & Peterson, 1995). They also share information about the author of the featured selection and introduce other books by that author. Some-times teachers have students read and compare several books written by a particular author.

**Stage 5: Applying** Readers move beyond comprehension to apply what they've learned and value the reading experience as they create projects. These projects can involve reading, writing, talk and drama, viewing, visually representing, or research, and can take many forms, including murals, readers theatre scripts, oral presentations, and individual books and reports, as well as reading other books by the same author (Luongo-Orlando, 2001). The variety of project options offers choices to students and takes into account Howard Gardner's (2000) theory of multiple intelligences, that students have preferred ways of learning and showing knowledge. Usually students choose which project they will do rather than working in small groups or as a class on the same project. Sometimes, however, the class decides to work together on a project, as Mrs. Ochs's students did in the Classroom Close-Up.

## ESSENTIAL #3: Elements of Story Structure

Stories have unique structural elements that distinguish them from informational books and poems. When students understand the role that each element plays, they are better able to comprehend what they are reading.

**Plot** Plot is the sequence of events involving characters in conflict situations. The main characters want to achieve a goal, and other characters oppose the main characters or prevent them from being successful (Lukens, 2002). The main events of a story can be divided into three parts—beginning, middle, and end. In the beginning, the characters are introduced and a problem is presented. In the middle, conflict intensifies as the characters face roadblocks that keep them from solving their problems. In the end, all that has happened in the story is reconciled, and readers learn whether the characters' struggles are successful.

The plot is developed through conflict that is introduced in the beginning of a story, expanded in the middle, and finally resolved at the end. Conflict occurs between a character and nature, between a character and society, between characters, or within a character (Lukens, 2002).

**Characters** Characters are the people or personified animals who are involved in the story. Authors usually create one or two well-rounded characters and several supporting characters. Main characters have many personality traits, but supporting charac-

## How Students Analyze Stories

| | |
|---|---|
| **Plot** | Students divide stories into three parts—beginning, middle, and end—and identify the problem confronting the characters that's usually introduced in the beginning. They notice how the problem creates a conflict situation and drives the plot. |
| **Characters** | Students identify the main characters and the supporting characters. Then they examine how the author developed the main characters and decide which attributes are most important. Students often make open-mind portraits to focus on one of the main characters. |
| **Setting** | Students consider whether the setting is integral to the story, and if it is, how it contributes to the story's effectiveness. They often draw maps of the story's setting. Students often talk about how the story would be different if it were set in another location or time period. |
| **Point of View** | Students determine who is telling the story and consider how the story would be different if it were being told from another viewpoint. Students often retell stories or excerpts from novels from the viewpoints of different characters. |
| **Theme** | Students think about the problem identified at the beginning of the story, the events in the story, and the attributes of the main characters to infer the theme. Identifying the theme is a challenge for many students, so teachers help them focus on the theme through the questions they ask during grand conversations and the topics they choose for reading log entries. |

## Stories Exemplifying the Story Elements

### Plot

Bunting, E. (1994). *Smoky night.* San Diego: Harcourt Brace. (P–M)

Dahl, R. (2001). *Charlie and the chocolate factory.* New York: Knopf. (M)

Sachar, L. (1998). *Holes.* New York: Farrar, Straus & Giroux. (U)

Soto, G. (1993). *Too many tamales.* New York: Putnam. (P)

### Characters

Avi. (1995). *Poppy.* New York: Orchard Books. (M)

Cushman, K. (1994). *Catherine, called Birdy.* New York: HarperCollins. (U)

Henkes, K. (1991). *Chrysanthemum.* New York: Greenwillow. (P)

Spinelli, J. (1990). *Maniac Magee.* New York: Scholastic. (U)

### Setting

Curtis, C. P. 1995). *The Watsons go to Birmingham—1963.* New York: Delacorte. (M–U)

Lowry, L. (1993). *The giver.* Boston: Houghton Mifflin. (U)

Meunier, B. (2003). *Pipolo and the roof dogs.* New York: Dutton. (P)

Whelan, G. (2000). *Homeless bird.* New York: Scholastic. (U)

### Point of View

Babbitt, N. (1975). *Tuck everlasting.* New York: Farrar, Straus & Giroux. (M–U)

Creech, S. (2000). *The wanderer.* New York: Scholastic. (M–U)

Meddaugh, S. (1995). *Hog-eye.* Boston: Houghton Mifflin. (P)

Ryan, P. M. (2000). *Esperanza rising.* New York: Scholastic. (M)

### Theme

Avi. (1991). *Nothing but the truth: A documentary novel.* New York: Orchard Books. (U)

Hesse, K. (2001). *Witness.* New York: Scholastic. (U)

Pinkney, J. (1999). *The ugly duckling.* New York: Morrow. (P)

White, E. B. (1980). *Charlotte's web.* New York: HarperCollins. (M)

P = primary grades (K–2); M = middle grades (3–5); U = upper grades (6–8)

ters are portrayed much less vividly. The extent to which supporting characters are developed depends on the author's purpose and the needs of the story.

Authors develop characters in four ways: by describing their physical appearance, narrating their activities, reporting what they say, and revealing their thoughts through monologue. Although all four sources of information about a character are important, information about what characters think and do is the most reliable.

**Setting**

Setting is where and when the story takes place. When the setting is crucial to the story's effectiveness, it's an integral setting, but when the setting is barely sketched, it's a backdrop setting (Lukens, 2002). The setting in many folktales, for example, is relatively unimportant, and these tales simply use the convention "Once upon a time . . . " to set the stage.

There are four dimensions of setting. One dimension is location—where the story takes place. Some stories could take place anywhere, but in others, the setting is integral to the story's effectiveness. A second dimension is weather. Some stories take place on sunny days, but when it's severe—a hurricane, a tornado, or a blizzard—weather becomes important. Next is the historical period: When stories take place in the past or future, setting often is important. The fourth dimension is time. Most stories ignore time of day, except for scary stories that take place after dark because night makes things scarier. Many short stories span a brief period of time, often less than a day, and sometimes less than an hour, but other stories span a long enough period for the main character to grow to maturity.

**Point of View**

The four points of view are first person, omniscient, limited omniscient, and objective (Lukens, 2002). The first-person viewpoint is used to tell a story through the eyes of one character; readers experience the story as the narrator tells it. The author uses the first-person pronoun *I*, but in the other three viewpoints, the third-person pronouns—*he* and *she*—are used. The author is godlike in the omniscient viewpoint, seeing and knowing all; the author tells readers about the thought processes of each character without concern for how the information is obtained. The limited omniscient viewpoint focuses on the thoughts of one character. In the objective viewpoint, readers are eyewitnesses to the story and are confined to the immediate scene. They learn only what is visible and audible, without knowing what any character thinks.

**Theme**

The theme is the underlying meaning of a story, such as telling the truth, being a true friend, overcoming struggles, and thinking of others first (Lehr, 1991). It emerges through the thoughts, speech, and actions of the characters as they seek to resolve their conflicts. The theme can be stated either explicitly or implicitly: Explicit themes are stated clearly in the story, but implicit themes are suggested rather than explicitly stated. Many themes focus on equality and social responsibility, and examining these themes provides an opportunity for students to consider critical-literacy issues.

# Strategies

## Reading Strategies

Reading is a strategic process, and children use a variety of word-identification, vocabulary, and comprehension strategies as they read. One of the most important word-indentification strategies that beginning readers use is blending the sounds in an unfamiliar word in order to pronounce it.

Children activate background knowledge during the prereading stage; they use this strategy to think about what they know about a topic and the vocabulary related to it. Also during the prereading stage, children set purposes for reading, which direct their attention during reading.

Fluent readers focus on comprehension as they read; they use a number of strategies, one of the most important of which is inferencing. When children make inferences, they draw conclusions using clues in the text and their own background knowledge.

**Strategies for Reading Stories**

Students' focus is on comprehension when they are reading stories. They make predictions about what will happen next in the story, and they visualize the story, bringing it to life in their minds. They make three types of connections—personal connections to events in their own lives, world connections to current and historical events, and literary connections to other books they've read. It might seem surprising that revising is another strategy that students use as they read stories, but they often revise their thinking about what will happen in the story and whether the characters will be successful. Students learn more as they continue reading, which often causes them to revise their opinions.

### Strategies Students Use as They Read

| General | Nonfiction |
|---|---|
| • blending | • identifying big ideas |
| • activating background knowledge | • questioning |
| • setting purposes | • summarizing |
| • inferencing | • evaluating |

| Stories | Poetry |
|---|---|
| • predicting | • reading interpretively |
| • visualizing | • noticing wordplay |
| • connecting | • using the poem as a model |
| • revising | |

# Scaffolding English Learners

## How to Improve Students' Comprehension

Many English learners have difficulty comprehending what they're reading. Sometimes the problem is due to students' limited knowledge of English or their lack of background knowledge about the topic, or cultural differences or affective factors may be responsible (Garcia, 2003). Despite the variety of difficulties that English learners may have with comprehension, researchers recommend that one of the best ways to help English learners improve their comprehension is by explicitly teaching them to use comprehension strategies (Hammerberg, 2004). The strategies most often recommended are activating background knowledge, predicting, connecting, visualizing, questioning, and summarizing.

Alvermann and Eakle (2003) recommend that teachers incorporate these seven components into their minilessons on comprehension strategies:

- Activate prior knowledge
- Engage students in the lesson
- Clearly explain the strategy, including how and when to use it
- Break the procedure for using the strategy into small steps
- Model how to use the strategy
- Provide plenty of opportunities for supervised practice
- Offer feedback to students

Through instruction, modeling, and supervised practice, teachers provide scaffolding so students can become more strategic readers. Once students are using a strategy effectively and understand that they are expected to use it as they read, teachers gradually withdraw their scaffolding. This step is important because as the scaffolding fades, students need to assume responsibility for using the strategy independently. If students stop using the strategy, then teachers need to step in, resume using scaffolds, and again try to move students to using the strategy independently.

English learners who learned to read in their native language can use for English reading the comprehension strategies they learned previously (Garcia, 1998). It's important to explain to these students that they can transfer to their English reading the strategies they acquired while reading in their native language. Thinking of what you already know about a topic before reading, drawing pictures in your mind as you read, and making connections between what you've read and your own life, for example, are strategies you use no matter whether you're reading Arabic, Russian, Hmong, or English.

To examine whether students are becoming strategic readers, teachers have students think aloud while they're reading a short passage. Think-alouds (Baumann, Jones, & Seifert-Kessell, 1993) reveal how readers are processing the text and thinking about the ideas in it as they are reading. Students verbalize their thought processes before, during, and after reading. Before they begin reading, students explain what they're thinking about, often talking about their background knowledge and making predictions. Then they read a chunk of text—a paragraph or a page—and stop and think aloud. Again, they explain what they're thinking—identifying the big ideas, making connections, attempting to identify unfamiliar words, and solving other problems they encountered. After they finish the text, students reflect on their reading experience. They evaluate the experience, commenting on the strategies they used, the problems they encountered and how they solved them, and the big ideas in the text.

Teachers explain how to think aloud, and they model the procedure as they read aloud to students: They think about the topic and the genre and make predictions before beginning to read, describe their visual images, make personal, world, and text connections, verbalize confusions, and demonstrate how to solve problems. Students who understand the procedure often demonstrate it for classmates, too. Then students work with partners to practice thinking aloud as they read a short passage. Once students are familiar with the procedure, teachers meet with individual students and ask them to think aloud as they read to assess their strategy use.

Using the think-aloud procedure is important for two reasons: Teachers model what strategic readers do when they demonstrate thinking aloud, and students use think-alouds to provide a window into their comprehension processes.

Readers often assume an efferent stance when they read nonfiction, and their focus is on remembering information. They identify the big ideas as they're reading and summarize the information so that they can remember it. It's important that students focus on the big ideas rather than on distracting details. Students use questioning to guide their learning. They ask self-questions to activate their background knowledge and set purposes for reading:

What do I already know about this topic?
What do I want to learn?
Why am I reading this?
How can I find the information I want to learn?

They ask other self-questions to identify big ideas and evaluate their comprehension:

What's the big idea here?
How does this idea relate to what I already know about the topic?

Do I understand this idea?
How does this idea relate to the other big ideas?

Students also direct questions to the teacher and their classmates during discussions to probe ideas, clarify misconceptions, and make connections. They also evaluate the effectiveness of their reading experience, judging whether they have accomplished their purpose for reading and have comprehended the big ideas.

Readers read poetry differently than stories and nonfiction. The arrangement of words on a page, the rhythm of the lines, and the images and sounds that the words make dictate how poems should be read. Poems are usually read aloud, and children learn to read interpretively. They vary how loud and how fast they read and change their voices to highlight particular words. Their goal is to make their reading interesting. Students also examine the poet's craft. They notice how the poem is structured and think about how they can use the poem as a model for their own writing.

# MINILESSON

*Theme*

## Mrs. Levin's Second Graders Learn About Theme

1. **Introduce the topic**   Mrs. Levin's second-grade class has just read *Martha Speaks* (Meddaugh, 1992), the story of a talking dog. Mrs. Levin rereads the last paragraph of the story, which exemplifies the theme, and says, "I think this is what the author, Susan Meddaugh, is trying to tell us—that sometimes we should talk and sometimes we should be quiet. What do you think?" The students agree, and Mrs. Levin explains that the author's message or lesson about life is called the theme.

2. **Share examples**   Mrs. Levin shows the students *Little Red Riding Hood* (Galdone, 1974), a story they read earlier in the year, and after briefly reviewing the story, she asks students about the theme of this story. One child quickly responds, "I think the author means that you shouldn't talk to strangers." Another child explains, "Little Red Riding Hood's mom probably tried to teach her to not talk to strangers but Little Red Riding Hood must have forgotten because she talked to the wolf and he was like a stranger." It is a message every child has heard, but they agree that they, too, sometimes forget, just like Little Red Riding Hood.

3. **Provide information**   The next day, Mrs. Levin shares three other familiar books and asks students to identify the theme. The first book is *The Three Bears* (Galdone, 1972), and students easily identify the "don't intrude" theme. The second book is *Chrysanthemum* (Henkes, 1991), the story of a young mouse named Chrysanthemum who doesn't like herself after her classmates make fun of her name. The students identify two variations of the theme: "you should be nice to everyone and not hurt their feelings" and "kids who aren't nice get in trouble." The third book is *Miss Nelson Is Missing!* (Allard, 1977), the story of a sweet teacher who transforms herself into a mean teacher after her students refuse to behave. The students identify the theme as "teachers are nice when you behave but they are mean when you are bad."

4. **Supervise practice**   Mrs. Levin asks students to choose one of the five stories they have examined and to draw pictures showing the theme. For example, students could draw a picture of Martha using the telephone to report burglars in the house or a picture of themselves ringing the doorbell at a friend's house. Mrs. Levin walks around as students work, helping them add titles to their pictures that focus on the theme of the story.

5. **Assess learning**   Teachers listen to students as they share their pictures with the class and explain how they illustrated the theme of the various stories.

# MINILESSON

## Making Predictions

### Mr. Voss's Kindergartners Learn to Predict

1. **Introduce the topic**   Mr. Voss explains to his kindergarten class that before he begins to read a book, he thinks about it. He looks at the illustration on the book cover, reads the title, and makes a prediction or guess about the story.

2. **Share examples**   Mr. Voss shows the cover of *The Wolf's Chicken Stew* (Kasza, 1987) and thinks aloud about it. He says, "This book is about a wolf who is going to cook some delicious chicken stew. Yes, that makes sense because I know that wolves like to eat chickens. I think the wolf on the cover is looking for chickens to cook in the stew." Then Mr. Voss asks the kindergartners to agree or disagree. Most agree, but one child suggests that the wolf is looking for a supermarket to buy the chickens.

3. **Provide information**   Mr. Voss reads the book aloud, stopping several times to confirm or revise predictions.

Children confirm the prediction once the hen and her chicks are introduced, but by the end, no one is surprised when the wolf befriends the chickens. After reading, they talk about how their predictions changed as they read the story.

4. **Supervise practice**   During story time for 5 days, the kindergartners make predictions before Mr. Voss reads aloud. If the prediction seems farfetched, Mr. Voss asks the child to relate it to the book or make a new prediction. Children confirm or revise predictions as they listen and discuss their predictions after reading.

5. **Assess Learning**   Mr. Voss listens to students' comments as they make a chart about predicting. The kindergartners dictate these sentences for the chart:

*You have to turn on your brain to think before you read. You can make a prediction. Then you want to find out if you are right.*

# MINILESSON

## Sequence

### Mrs. Miller Introduces Sequencing to Her Second Graders

1. **Introduce the topic**   Mrs. Miller explains to her second-grade class that authors organize informational books in special ways. One way is sequence, in which the author puts information in a certain order. She explains that they know many sequences: numbers, days of the week, grades in school, and months of the year.

2. **Share examples**   Mrs. Miller explains that she wants her students to be detectives to try to figure out the sequence in *From Plant to Blue Jeans* (L'Hommedieu, 1997). She begins to read the book aloud, and soon the students recognize that it describes the process of making blue jeans.

3. **Provide information**   Mrs. Miller explains that authors give some word clues about the sequence: She points out that in *From Plant to Blue Jeans,* the author uses the words *begin, then, last,* and *finally* to structure the book. These special words are called *cue words,* she explains, and other cue words are *first, second, third,* and

*next.* One student also points out that the title gives you an idea about the sequence. Then Mrs. Miller and the second graders make a poster, listing the steps and adding pictures to illustrate each step of the jeans-making process.

4. **Supervise practice**   The next day, Mrs. Miller divides the students into five small groups and passes out one of these books to each group: *Chicken and Egg* (Back & Olesen, 1986), *From Wax to Crayon* (Forman, 1997), *Honeybee* (Watts, 1990), *Postcards From Pluto: A Tour of the Solar System* (Leedy, 1993), and *Let's Find Out About Ice Cream* (Reid, 1996). The students read the book to figure out what is sequenced. Then they make posters, listing the steps in the sequence and drawing pictures to illustrate each step. Afterward, students explain the sequence in their books and share their posters with the class.

5. **Assess learning**   The students locate other books with the sequence pattern and bring them to show Mrs. Miller. She asks them what they have learned, and they respond that they have learned that some books have a special organization—sequence—but others do not.

# MINILESSON

*Reading Poems*

## Mr. Johnston Teaches His Third Graders How to Read Poems Interpretively

1. **Introduce the topic**   Mr. Johnston places a transparency of "A Pizza the Size of the Sun," by Jack Prelutsky (1996), on the overhead projector and reads it aloud in a monotone voice. He asks his third graders if he did a good job reading the poem, and they tell him that his reading was boring.

2. **Share examples**   Mr. Johnston asks what he could do to make his reading better, and they suggest that he read with more expression. He asks the students to tell him which words he should read more expressively and marks their changes on the transparency. He reads the poem again, and students agree that it is better. Then students suggest he vary his reading speed, and he marks their changes on the transparency. He reads the poem a third time, incorporating more changes. They agree that his third reading is the best!

3. **Provide information**   Mr. Johnston praises his students for their suggestions; they did help him make

this reading better. Then he asks what he can do to make his reading more interesting, and they suggest:

- Read some parts loud and some parts soft
- Read some parts fast and some parts slow
- Change your voice for some words

4. **Supervise practice**   Mr. Johnston divides the students into small groups and passes out transparencies of other poems. Students in each group decide how to read the poem and mark parts they will read in special ways. Mr. Johnston circulates around the classroom as students work, providing assistance as needed. Then students display their poems on the overhead projector and read them aloud with expression.

5. **Assess learning**   Mr. Johnston has students write about what they have learned. One student writes:

*I learned two ways to read poems. One is boring and the other is fun.*

In their reflections, the students write that they have learned how to read the fun way so that they can share their enjoyment of poems with others.

# Classroom Practice

## LANGUAGE EXPERIENCE APPROACH: It's Almost Foolproof!

The idea behind the Language Experience Approach (LEA) is simple: Children dictate words and sentences about an experience that the teacher writes for them, and the resulting text is used for reading instruction (Allen, 1976). Because the ideas and language come from the children themselves, they are usually able to read the text even if they haven't been successful with other types of reading. LEA was designed for young children who are learning about the direction of print on a page, concepts of "word" and "letter," and how to use letters to represent sounds in words, but this approach is effective for all emergent readers—whether they be fourth-grade struggling readers or 13-year-old immigrant students who are dictating in their native language or in English (Crawford, 2003; Sutton, 1998).

"Foolproof" is a strong word, but that's how successful the Language Experience Approach is for emergent readers, and especially those children who haven't been successful in grasping basic beginning reading concepts through other instructional methods. LEA has been used successfully to introduce children to reading for more than 40 years (Ashton-Warner, 1965; Stauffer, 1980).

**Instructional Recommendations**   Teachers can use the Language Experience Approach with individual children, with small groups, or with entire classes. When teachers are working with struggling students or with older English learners, they usually work one-on-on with them, but when they're working with whole classes of emergent readers, they often do group activities.

**Working With Individual Children.**   Teachers meet individually with children to reread familiar texts and create new

94    Part 4

ones. Then children practice reading words and sentences both in and out of context and explore concepts of written language and phonics concepts using the texts.

Topics for these texts come from children's own lives and school activities. Sometimes children write about playing with friends after school, and at other times, they write about a story the teacher read aloud or something they're learning in a science unit. The texts that children dictate are often called "stories," but they can be descriptions, explanations, directions, or letters as well as stories.

It's tempting to change children's language to Standard English when taking their dictation, but editing should be minimal so that children don't get the impression that their language is inferior or inadequate. If a child dictates "Me and him be runnin' real fast," for instance, the teacher writes *Me and him be running real fast.* The child's sentence structure is preserved but the teacher spells words such as "runnin'" conventionally. Teachers usually add past tense and plural markers even though English learners might not pronounce them, so that "Yesterday two boy play ball" is written *Yesterday two boys played ball.* Preserving children's language is important for another reason, too: Children will reread the text the way they dictated it, so they will be confused if the words they're saying don't match the words in the text.

Children collect their LEA texts in a notebook or folder so that they can practice rereading them and use them for word-study activities. They reread the texts each day, pointing at each word as they read. Afterward, teachers often ask children to pick out particular words or phrases or to underline the words they recognize in the text.

Teachers prepare small sentence strips and word cards that are kept in an envelope attached to the back of the page with the text. After reading the text in context, children sequence the sentence strips and read them. Then they practice reading the word cards, sometimes arranging them to re-create the text.

Teachers focus children's attention on high-frequency words they use again and again or words exemplifying a phonics concept children are studying, such as short *a* (e.g., *man, sat*) or consonant digraphs (e.g., *the, chin, shop*). Then children go back into the LEA texts to search for other examples of the focus word or concept (Rasinski & Padak, 2000). Teachers also have children sort word cards according to a particular phonics concept.

Children also have small boxes called *word banks* that are personal files of "known" words. As children learn to read new words, teachers write them on small cards, and children add them to the word bank. Children practice reading the words and use them for writing activities.

Once children understand basic concepts about how written language works and learn to read 25 high-frequency words

## LANGUAGE EXPERIENCE APPROACH

**1 Provide an experience**
Teachers provide an experience, or remind children of an experience, to serve as the stimulus for the writing.

**2 Talk about the experience**
Children talk about the experience to clarify and organize ideas and generate words for their dictation.

**3 Record the dictation**
Teachers write the text that children dictate. They print neatly and spell words correctly,

but they preserve children's word choice and syntax. If a child hesitates, the teacher rereads what has been written and encourages the child to continue.

**4 Read the text**
Teachers read the text aloud to remind children of the content and to demonstrate how to read with expression. Next, children read with the teacher, and finally, they read on their own.

**5 Examine the text**
Children sequence sentence strips to re-create the text, read words from the text that have been written on word cards, sort the word cards according to phonics concepts, and participate in writing activities.

**6 Add to the word bank**
Children identify words that they've learned to read, and teachers write these words on small cards for children to add to their word banks.

out of context, they are likely to be successful reading books for beginning readers. When teachers continue to use LEA, they use it to supplement other reading approaches.

**Working With Groups.** Teachers often take children's dictation to create class charts, letters, and other texts. For example, after the teacher reads aloud a picture book such as *Mister Seahorse* (Carle, 2004), children write about what they've learned about this unique ocean animal. Here is a first-grade class's chart about seahorses:

> Seahorses are good fathers. They take care of the eggs before they hatch into babies. They keep them safe in a pouch on their bodies. We wonder why seahorse fathers have pouches like kangaroo moms do.

Or, they can write a class letter to pen pals, an invitation to the principal to visit their class, or a thank-you note to the firefighters who visited their class to talk about their job.

Teachers follow the same steps to create the LEA text, but children take turns suggesting sentences to write. Teachers record children's dictation, stopping to point out when they capitalize the first letter in a sentence or add punctuation marks. Children reread the chart together for several days, often highlighting high-frequency words they recognize or words exemplifying a particular phonics concept. Sometimes teachers also make individual copies of the text for children to read, but they don't usually make sentence strips or word cards for each child.

When children write chart-size letters, they are delivered, but otherwise the charts remain in the classroom for children to reread. As more charts are written, older charts are hung together on a chart rack in a corner of the classroom, but children often want to get the charts out and reread them.

**Benefits** The Language Experience Approach emphasizes the connections among talk, reading, and writing. Children watch as teachers record their dictation, learning concepts about how written language works and how to apply phonics skills to spell words. They acquire a repertoire of high-frequency words for both reading and writing. Even children who have not been successful with other types of reading instruction can read what they have dictated, and this success builds children's feelings of confidence and interest in learning to read and write.

Children learn to gather ideas and organize them for writing, and LEA provides a natural lead-in to interactive writing, as children begin to assume responsibility for writing some of the words themselves.

## Three Ways to Promote Reading

The volume of reading that children do at school and at home is related positively to their reading achievement. In fact, higher-achieving students read three times as much each week as their lower-achieving classmates (Allington, 2001). Students who spend more time reading and read more words develop the ability to read fluently and comprehend what they're reading better than students who do less reading. Richard Allington recommends that teachers dramatically increase the quantity of reading that children do at school to at least an hour and a half. He emphasizes, however, that he's talking about actual reading—guided reading, buddy reading, independent reading—not related activities such as talking about books they've read or completing workbook pages.

**Free Voluntary Reading** One way to provide daily opportunities for in-school recreational reading is what Stephen Krashen (1993) calls free voluntary reading (FVR). Researchers have confirmed again and again that children, including English learners, who do more reading become more capable readers, and that's the point behind FVR (Cohen, 1999; Krashen, 1993, 2001). Two ways to provide this independent reading at school are Sustained Silent Reading and reading workshop. No matter which program teachers use to provide students with independent reading, these guidelines are followed:

- Children choose the books they read.
- Children have access to a large collection of books from which to choose those they want to read and are able to read.

- Children have daily uninterrupted time to read.
- Children have a comfortable, quiet location in which to read.
- Children receive encouragement from their teachers.

**Sustained Silent Reading.** In Sustained Silent Reading (SSR), students read independently for 10 to 15 minutes in books they've chosen themselves that are at their reading level, and teachers model independent reading at the same time (Pilgreen, 2000). Children don't write book reports, and teachers don't keep records of which books children read; instead, the emphasis is on reading for pleasure. This popular reading activity goes by a variety of names, including "drop everything and read" (DEAR), "sustained quiet reading time" (SQUIRT), and "our time to enjoy reading" (OTTER).

Teachers often have concerns that students won't use the reading time productively or that they'll always choose books that are too easy for them, but that doesn't seem to be the case (Von Sprecken & Krashen, 1998). Most students do actually read during SSR, and students' reading tastes do mature gradually.

**Reading Workshop.** In reading workshop, children spend 30 minutes or more each day reading silently in books they have chosen themselves (Atwell, 1987). Unlike SSR, it is not a short block of time. The teacher's role is different, too: They conference with students, talking about the books they're reading to monitor their comprehension. They also teach minilessons on reading strategies. After the independent reading time, children get together to share books they've finished reading.

**Cross-Age Reading Buddies** A class of upper-grade students is paired with a class of beginning readers, and the children become reading buddies. Older students use shared reading to read books with younger children. The younger children gradually do more and more of the reading as they become familiar with the book. Research supports the effectiveness of cross-age buddies, and teachers report that children's reading fluency increases and their attitudes toward school become more positive (Caserta-Henry, 1996; Labbo & Teale, 1990; Morrice & Simmons, 1991).

Teachers arranging a buddy reading program decide when the students will get together, how long each session will last, and what the reading schedule will be. Primary-grade teachers explain the program to their students and talk about activities the buddies will be doing together. Upper-grade teachers teach a series of minilessons about how to work with young children, how to read aloud and encourage children to make predictions, how to use shared reading, how to select books to appeal to younger children, and how to help them respond to books. Then older students choose books to read aloud and practice reading them until they can read the books fluently.

At the first meeting, the students pair off, get acquainted, and read together. They also talk about the books they have read and perhaps write in special reading logs. Buddies also may want to go to the library and choose the books they will read at the next session.

There are significant social benefits to cross-age tutoring programs. Children get acquainted with other children that they might otherwise not meet, and they learn how to work with older or younger children. As they talk about books they have read, they share personal experiences. They also talk about reading strategies, how to choose books, and their favorite authors or illustration styles. Sometimes reading buddies write notes back and forth, or the two classrooms plan holiday celebrations together, and these activities strengthen the social connections between the children.

**Traveling Bags of Books** Children can take traveling bags of books home to read with their parents. Teachers collect text sets of three, four, or five books on various topics and put them into sturdy bags for children to take home and read (Reutzel & Fawson, 1990). For example, teachers might collect copies of *The Gingerbread Boy* (Galdone, 1975), *Flossie and the Fox* (McKissack, 1986), *Red Fox Running* (Bunting, 1993), and *Rosie's Walk* (Hutchins, 1968) for a traveling bag of fox stories. Then children and their parents read one or more of the books and draw or write a response to the books they have read in the reading log that accompanies the books in the traveling bag. One family's response after reading *The Gingerbread Boy* is shown on this page. In this entry, the kindergartner drew a picture of Gingerbread Boy, an older sibling wrote the sentence the kindergartner dictated to accompany the picture, and the children's mother also wrote a comment. Children keep the bag at home for several days and then return it to school so that another child can borrow it. Teachers can also add small toys, stuffed animals, audiotapes of one of the books, or other related objects to the bags.

Teachers often introduce traveling bags at a special parents' meeting or an open house get-together and explain how parents use shared reading to read with their children. It is important for parents to understand that their children may not be familiar with the books and that the children are not expected to be able to read them independently. Teachers also talk about the responses that children and parents write in the reading log and show sample entries from the previous year.

It's crucial that children do a lot of reading if they are to become good readers. Through free voluntary reading, cross-age reading buddies, and traveling bags of books, children have more opportunities to read at school and at home.

## READER RESPONSE: Dynamic Engagement With Literature

When you're reading a novel, do you imagine yourself as one of the characters? Do you laugh out loud or cry while you're reading? Do you wish the story wouldn't end because you're enjoying it so much? If you do, it's because you're having a dynamic engagement with literature. This powerful feeling of pleasure and desire to do more reading is reader response, and it's what we want our students to experience. Marjorie Hancock (2004) describes response to literature as "the unique interaction that occurs within the mind and heart of the individual reader through the literature event" (p. 9).

The three components of response are the reader, the text, and the context for response (Galda, 1988). Readers bring their background knowledge, past literary experiences, ability to use reading strategies and skills, and desire to read to the reading experience; these characteristics are part of the reason why students' responses are unique and personal. Text characteristics are topic, genre, structural patterns, and literary elements, and children's awareness of these characteristics affects their comprehension. The context is the setting for the response. Children's responses reflect their sociocultural background, their family's income level, their religious beliefs, and the classroom climate. When teachers involve students with literature through literature focus units, literature circles, and reading workshop, provide opportunities for response, and celebrate children's responses, children respond differently than when teachers don't highlight literature in their language arts programs.

**Rosenblatt's Theory of Reader Response** Louise Rosenblatt (2005) describes reading as a transaction between readers and the text. Readers and the text are viewed as equally important in this theory. This point is significant because traditionally, the text was considered to be more important. According to traditional theories, the readers' job was to read carefully to figure out the correct meaning of the text. Readers were viewed as passive, but in contrast, Rosenblatt describes readers as actively involved in the

## A Family's Reading Log Entry Written After Reading *The Gingerbread Boy*

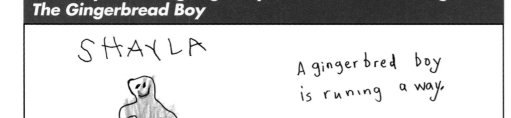

SHAYLA

A gingerbred boy is runing a way.

SHAYLA LOVES THIS BOOK! WE ALL DO! LAST NIGHT

WE MADE YUMMY GINGERBREAD COOKIES. THIS

WAS A FUN BOOK BAG. Alice Garcia

reading process, and they create responses as the result of the reading process. The responses represent readers' personal meaning.

According to Rosenblatt, readers vary how they read depending on their purpose. She identified two stances: aesthetic and efferent. Readers read aesthetically when they're reading for enjoyment, and at other times, they read efferently because they're reading to acquire information. Their stance is more private when they read aesthetically and more public when they read efferently.

When readers are reading aesthetically or for entertainment, they concentrate on the lived-through experience of reading. They focus on the thoughts, images, feelings, and associations evoked during reading rather than on remembering facts. As children read Kate DiCamillo's story *The Tale of Despereaux* (2003), for example, they suspend disbelief and root for Despereaux, a castle mouse who, armed with a needle and a spool of thread, makes a daring rescue; as they read *The Scrambled States of America* (Keller, 1998) or *Wait! No Paint!* (Whatley, 2001), they laugh at the improbable but hilarious text; or as they read Karen Cushman's *Rodzina* (2003), they imagine themselves traveling west on the orphan train with Rodzina Brodski.

When their purpose for reading is to acquire information, readers assume an efferent stance: They concentrate on the public, common referents of the words and symbols in the text. For example, as children read Doreen Rappaport's *Martin's Big Words: The Life of Dr. Martin Luther King, Jr.* (2001), with its breathtaking collage illustrations, their focus is on the events of Dr. King's life and his inspiring words, not on the experience of reading. This is also the stance students generally use when reading textbooks.

These two stances represent ends on a continuum—almost every reading experience calls for a balance between aesthetic and efferent reading (Rosenblatt, 2005). Readers do not simply read stories and poems aesthetically and informational books efferently; instead, as they read, they move back and forth between aesthetic and efferent stances, according to their purpose.

Rosenblatt's theory offers these recommendations for reading instruction:

- Teach children about the aesthetic and efferent stances and when to use them.
- Develop students' background knowledge about topic, genre, structural patterns, and literary devices so they can understand the texts they're reading.
- Teach students to be active, strategic readers.
- Ensure that students have daily opportunities for dynamic engagement with literature.
- Provide opportunities for students to respond to the text they're reading.
- Expect that students will comprehend texts differently because of their experiences, knowledge, and sociocultural backgrounds.

## Ways to Respond to Stories

### Listening
- Listen to the story on tape
- Listen to classmates talk in a grand conversation

### Talking
- Participate in a grand conversation
- Retell stories
- Perform a puppet show
- Reenact a story
- Sit on the hot seat and be interviewed as a character

### Reading
- Read sequels
- Read other books by the same author
- Read more about the topic
- Research the author

### Writing
- Write in reading logs
- Write a retelling
- Write a new version or a sequel
- Write a poem about the story or the character
- Write a letter to the author

### Viewing
- Watch film versions of stories
- Examine illustrations in picture books

### Visually Representing
- Create an open-mind portrait of a character
- Draw a diagram about the story
- Make puppets of characters

**Ways to Respond**

Many of the responses that students make are spontaneous, but others are planned by teachers. For example, kindergartners laugh (spontaneous response) while listening to their teacher read Thacher Hurd's hilarious picture book *Moo Cow Kaboom!* (2003). In the story, Moo Cow is cownapped by a space cowboy named Zork and taken to Planet 246 for the Inter-Galactic Rodeo. Afterward, children take turns dressing up as Farmer George (wearing a nightshirt), Moo Cow (wearing a cow mask), Zork (wearing a black cowboy hat) while classmates become a cast of supporting characters to reenact the beginning, middle, and end of the story (planned response). As eighth graders read *Crispin: The Cross of Lead* (Avi, 2002), the story of Crispin, a 13-year-old peasant boy who is falsely accused of being a thief and declared a "wolf's head" (which gives everyone in the country permission to kill him on sight), they compare Crispin's life to their own and comment on their compassion for him (spontaneous response). Students also make entries in their reading logs to explore the ideas in the story and make connections to what they're learning about the Middle Ages (planned response). And when the students reach the end of the story, where Crispin redeems himself, they cheer loudly (another spontaneous response).

**Spontaneous Responses.** Spontaneous responses are those that children make without prompting by the teacher. They make these responses because the text is so engaging. Young children, for example, clap their hands and tap their feet to the rhythm of Bill Martin and John Archambault's *Chicka Chicka Boom Boom* (1989) and chant along as the teacher reads and rereads the book. They spot the dangers facing two bugs named Frieda and Gloria in the illustrations in *Absolutely Not!*

(McElligott, 2004) and call out warnings to the bugs. Older students take action in their own neighborhoods after reading Paul Fleischman's *Seedfolks* (1997), a timeless story about a blighted community that's transformed after a girl plants some seeds and her neighbors are stirred to take action.

Janet Hickman (1980) examined young children's spontaneous responses and classified a variety of response behaviors, including:

- Children laugh, chant repetitive phrases, stretch to see illustrations, and clap with pleasure as they listen to the teacher read aloud.
- Children touch books as they browse in the classroom library, examine books in book baskets on their desks, and self-select books to read.
- Children eagerly talk about books, sharing discoveries and making connections.
- Children pretend to be characters and reenact stories.
- Children draw pictures of characters and events in the book.
- Children write their own books, often using the book as a model.

When children respond to books without being prompted by the teacher, their responses genuinely reflect their attention, understanding, and interest in the book.

**Planned Responses.** Teachers plan responses that are appropriate for the books that children are reading, and it's possible to design responses that address any of the language arts. Children often listen to a book on tape or view the film version of a story or examine the illustrations in a picture book. They talk about the story in a grand conversation, tell sequels, perform puppet shows, and dramatize the story while their classmates listen and watch. They read other books by the same author or on the same topic. They write in reading logs and write sequels, letters to the author, or books using the featured book as a model. They also make Venn diagrams, posters, open-mind portraits, and sketch-to-stretch drawings.

Teachers play a key role in encouraging students to respond to literature (Hancock, 2004). Successful teachers create a classroom climate where response is valued, and they infuse the curriculum with literature. Because they are knowledgeable about literature, they can select stimulating, high-quality books for instruction and stock the classroom library with additional books that will interest children and that are appropriate for their reading levels. They use effective techniques to share books with children and provide opportunities for children to interact with books. Oftentimes, teachers use literature focus units and literature circles to provide response opportunities.

When children participate in reader response activities, they grow as readers. Researchers report that students become more interested in books, and their reading abilities improve (Spiegel, 1998). In particular, they deepen their understanding of reading as a process, apply reading strategies that they're learning, grow in their appreciation of literary quality, and assume responsibility for learning. Another benefit is that children are more likely to become lifelong readers because of these successful reading experiences.

## Theory to Practice
### Seventh Graders Respond in Reading Logs

As Ms. Meinke's seventh graders participate in literature circles, they write in reading logs. One group is reading *The Great Gilly Hopkins* (Paterson, 1978), the story of an angry foster child who eventually finds acceptance. Ms. Meinke varies the types of entries her students write because she believes that the content of the chapter should determine the activity.

Timothy wrote this simulated-journal entry after reading Chapter 2:

> I can't live here, it's a dump. I have to live with Miss Trotter and that colored man Mr. Randolph. I will have to get out of this dump and fast. Today was the first day Mr. Randolph came and I can't escort him every day to dinner. I don't belong here, even Mrs. Nevin's house was better than here.

Johanna wrote about whether it is ever right to lie and steal after reading Chapter 7:

> I think she shouldn't be forgiven. I know she has had a horrible life, but it's never right. I kind of feel bad for her because of everything she's been through. She lies, cheats, and steals. I am not sure which side to take because in one way she should be forgiven but on another side she shouldn't be because she's done too many bad things.

After reading Chapter 13, Timothy wrote a found poem:

> He tore a piece of him and gave it to you.
> Don't make it harder for us baby.
> This was supposed to be a party, not a funeral.
> Sometimes it's best not to go visiting.
> You make me proud.
> Why would anybody leave peace for war?
> Stop hovering over me.
> Inside her head, she was screaming.

Steven reflects on the book in his last entry:

> I thought that at the end Gilly was going to go with her mom. I also thought Gilly's mom was going to be nice and sweet. I thought this was very good because it had an unexpected ending. I didn't think that Gilly's mom would be so rude and mean. Now I wish that Gilly would go back with Trotter because Courtney is mean.

Many students, like Steven, want Gilly to stay with Trotter, but others realize that Nonnie, who never knew of Gilly's existence, wants to provide a home for her granddaughter.

# NONFICTION BOOKS:
## More Than "Just the Facts"

Children are curious about the world—why the dinosaurs became extinct, Neil Armstrong's moon landing, differences between warm- and cold-blooded animals, how to decipher secret codes, threats to the rain forest, why snakes shed their skins, and how skyscrapers are built—and nonfiction books provide this information. Years ago, most nonfiction books were written for children in grades 4–8, but now they're available for everyone, including emergent and struggling readers (Palmer & Stewart, 2005). Because so many high-quality nonfiction books are available today, teachers are stocking their classroom libraries with them, and they're incorporating more nonfiction into their instruction.

Nonfiction books blend textual and visual information. They're visually appealing, and children often pick them up to look at the photos and graphic presentations of information. Children are excited about reading nonfiction books and are able to understand these texts as well as they do stories (Kristo & Bamford, 2004). They're more than just books of facts because once children start reading, they get interested in the topic and continue reading. They broaden their background knowledge through reading nonfiction books and become interested in learning more about content-area topics (Moss & Hendershot, 2002).

**Differences Between Stories and Nonfiction**

Stories and nonfiction books are different: They are written and read differently. It's important that children learn about these differences so that they can recognize whether a book is a story or nonfiction in order to read it effectively. To examine these differences, pick up a story and a nonfiction book on the same topic; Mary Pope Osborne's popular Magic Tree House series, for example, includes both stories and accompanying nonfiction research guides. The differences are easy to pick out when you read *The Knight at Dawn* (Osborne, 1993) and *Knights and Castles* (Osborne & Osborne, 2000). Here is a list of the differences that a class of third graders noticed after reading these Magic Tree House books:

- Nonfiction books are true, but stories are invented.
- You can start reading anywhere in a nonfiction book, but you read stories from beginning to end.
- Nonfiction books have photos and drawings, but stories have only drawings.
- Nonfiction books have a table of contents, but only some stories have it.
- Nonfiction books have indexes, but stories don't.

- Nonfiction books have extra things: notes in the margin, highlighted words, pronunciation guides, and diagrams with labels.
- At the end of nonfiction books, the author tells you how to learn more.

As they examine nonfiction books, children learn how to use the special features to enhance their comprehension. They learn to use an index to locate specific information, to use diagrams and margin notes to learn more about topics presented in the regular text, and to notice the vocabulary terms that are highlighted in the text.

There's another difference between nonfiction books and stories: They're structured differently. Stories are organized into three parts—the beginning, middle, and end—and solving the problem introduced in the beginning is the driving force. In contrast, nonfiction texts are organized to emphasize the relationships among the ideas being presented. There are five nonfiction organizational patterns, called *expository text structures*:

- Description
- Sequence
- Comparison
- Cause and effect
- Problem and solution

Some texts are organized around one of these patterns, such as a book about the life cycle of a frog that uses a sequence structure and one about the development of the polio vaccine that reflects a problem-and-solution structure, and children can often identify the pattern because it's signaled by the title or topic sentence. Other books, however, incorporate several patterns or don't appear to have any structure, and when there isn't a clear structure, children are more likely to have trouble comprehending and remembering the big ideas. To compensate for the lack of structure, teachers can help students set purposes for reading the text.

**Types of Nonfiction Books**

If you browse in a children's bookstore or school library, you'll notice how many different types of nonfiction books there are. The simplest way to classify them is that books about specific people are biographies and autobiographies: Biographies are stories of a person's life written by someone else, such as *Leonardo: Beautiful Dreamer* (Byrd, 2003), and autobiographies are written by the featured person. Many authors of children's books, including Stan and Jan Berenstain (2002), Tomie dePaola (2002), and Dick King-Smith (2002), have written autobiographies that appeal to children who have read their books. Other books about animals, places, and things are referred to simply as nonfiction.

## Learn More About Reading Nonfiction

Harvey, S. (1998). *Nonfiction matters: Reading, writing, and research in grades 3–8.* York, ME: Stenhouse.

Hoyt, L., Mooney, M., & Parkes, B. (2003). *Exploring informational texts: From theory to practice.* Portsmouth, NH: Heinemann.

Kristo, J. V., & Bamford, R. A. (2004). *Nonfiction in focus.* New York: Scholastic.

Moss, B. (2002). *Exploring the literature of fact: Children's nonfiction trade books in the elementary classroom.* New York: Guilford Press.

Zarnowski, M., Kerper, R. M., & Jensen, J. M. (2001). *The best in children's nonfiction: Reading, writing, and teaching Orbis Pictus Award books.* Urbana, IL: National Council of Teachers of English.

## Expository Text Structures

| Structure | Description | Examples |
|---|---|---|
| Description | A topic is delineated using attributes and examples. | Drez, R. J. (2004). *Remember D-Day: The plan, the invasion, survivor stories.* Washington, DC: National Geographic Association. (U)<br>Dowson, N. (2004). *Tigress.* Cambridge, MA: Candlewick Press. (P–M) |
| Sequence | Steps, events, or directions are presented in numerical or chronological order. | Hibbert, C. (2004). *The life of a grasshopper.* Chicago: Raintree. (P–M)<br>Zemlicka, S. (2004). *From fruit to jelly.* Minneapolis: Lerner. (P) |
| Comparison | Two or more things are compared or contrasted. | Ruth, M. M. (2004). *Hawks and falcons.* Carmel, IN: Benchmark Press. (M–U) |
| Cause and Effect | Causes and the resulting effects are described. | Pfeffer, W. (2004). *Wiggling worms at work.* New York: HarperCollins. (P–M) |
| Problem and Solution | A problem and one or more solutions are presented. Also includes question-and-answer format. | Allen, T. B. (2004). *George Washington, spymaster: How the Americans outspied the British and won the Revolutionary War.* Washington, DC: National Geographic Association. (M–U)<br>Skurzynski, G. (2004). *Are we alone? Scientists search for life in space.* Washington, DC: National Geographic Association. (M–U) |

Many nonfiction books are concept books—they explore a topic, such as *Spiders* (Simon, 2003) or *Mosque* (Macaulay, 2003). When the concept is explored mainly using photos, the book is called a photo essay. Others are arranged in special ways: For example, in alphabet books, such as *America: A Patriotic Primer* (Cheney, 2002), the information is organized around key words beginning with each letter of the alphabet. Information is organized in sequentially in how-to books, and the question-and-answer format is used in others, including . . . *If You Were There When They Signed the Constitution* (Levy, 1992) and other books in Scholastic's popular ". . . If You" series. Journals and collections of letters, such as *Searching for Anne Frank: Letters From Amsterdam to Iowa* (Rubin, 2003), are nonfiction books, too. The dividing line between stories and nonfiction isn't always clear; some nonfiction books are blended with story elements. *The Magic School Bus Explores the Senses* (Cole, 2001) and other books in the clever "Magic School Bus" series are good examples.

**How to Read Nonfiction Books**
To take full advantage of nonfiction books, students need to know how to read them: how to use the special features to locate information, how to read pages that combine textual and visual information, and how to use text structure to comprehend and remember what they've read. Kristo and Bamford (2004) call this "navigating" nonfiction books. Teachers teach students how to navigate nonfiction books through minilessons and demonstrations as they read books aloud.

Reading nonfiction begins in kindergarten; it shouldn't be postponed until students are older. Young children can distinguish fact from fiction and learn information from nonfiction books that teachers read aloud (Richgels, 2002). Primary-grade teachers often use nonfiction big books for read-alouds, and children are actively engaged in the reading experience. They listen intently, ask questions, share experiences, and notice nonfiction features in the text. In addition, the collections of leveled books that teachers use for guided reading in the primary grades include many nonfiction titles.

Teachers use the same reading process to read stories, nonfiction, and poems with students, but some of the activities vary because nonfiction books are different from other types of texts and place different demands on readers. When students read nonfiction, activating and building their background knowledge and introducing key vocabulary words become more important. Teachers often spend more time during the prereading stage to ensure that students are prepared to begin reading. Students also examine the special features of nonfiction texts so that they're prepared to use the features as comprehension aids while they're reading.

During reading, the focus is on helping students identify and remember the big ideas. Sometimes students read a nonfiction text one section at a time. They turn the heading of the section into a question to set a purpose for reading, and then read to find the answer. Students often stop to discuss each section of text after they've read it, rather than reading the entire book before talking about it. Their discussions are instructional conversations, not grand conversations.

## Types of Nonfiction

| Type | Description | Examples |
|------|-------------|----------|
| Concept books | A topic is delineated using a combination of text and illustrations. | Ballard, C. (2004). *How we use water.* Cambridge, MA: Candlewick Press. (P–M)<br>McWhorter, D. (2004). *A dream of freedom: The civil rights movement from 1954 to 1968.* New York: Scholastic. (U) |
| Photo essays | A photo display with minimal accompanying text. | Goodman, S. E. (2004). *Skyscraper: From the ground up.* New York: Knopf. (M)<br>Sobol, R. (2004). *An elephant in the backyard.* New York: Dutton. (P–M) |
| Alphabet books | Facts are presented in alphabetical order. | Grodin, E. (2004). *D is for democracy: A citizen's alphabet.* Chelsea, MI: Sleeping Bear Press. (M) |
| Directions | The steps in making or doing something are described. | LaFosse, M. G. (2004). *Origami activities: Asian arts and crafts for creative kids.* North Clarendon, VT: Tuttle. (M–U) |
| Question-and-answer books | A question-and-answer format to share information. | Crisp, M. (2004). *Everything dolphin: What kids really want to know about dolphins.* Minnetonka, MN: NorthWord. |
| Biographies | An account of a person's life, written by someone else. | Krull, K. (2004). *The boy on Fairfield Street: How Ted Geisel grew up to become Dr. Seuss.* New York: Random House. (M)<br>Robinson, S. (2004). *Promises to keep: How Jackie Robinson changed America.* New York: Scholastic. (M–U) |
| Autobiographies | An account of a person's life, written by that person. | Weber, E. N. R. (2004). *Rattlesnake mesa: Stories from a Native American childhood.* New York: Lee & Low. (U) |
| Journals, letters, and speeches | A collection of documents. | Al-Windawi, T. (2004). *Thura's diary: My life in wartime Iraq.* New York: Viking. (U) |
| Reference books | A comprehensive collection of articles on a topic. | Ransford, S. (2004). *The Kingfisher illustrated horse and pony encyclopedia.* Boston: Kingfisher. (M–U) |
| Blended story/ informational books | A book that combines narrative and expository elements. | Warren, A. (2004). *Escape from Saigon: How a Vietnam War orphan became an American boy.* New York: Farrar, Straus & Giroux. (U) |

After reading, the focus is on deepening their understanding of the big ideas. Students reread sentences with the big ideas, add vocabulary to the word wall, complete graphic organizers to emphasize the relationships among the big ideas, draw visual representations of the big ideas, and create projects to apply what they've learned.

There are many ways to incorporate nonfiction books into language arts. During literature focus units, teachers often pair nonfiction with fiction books to build students' background knowledge before they begin reading. In the Classroom Close-Up at the beginning of Part 4, Mrs. Ochs used a text set of books, including some nonfiction books, to build her students' knowledge about World War II. When stories are set in unfamiliar historical periods or geographic locations, when the characters are from little-known cultural groups, supplementing the story with real-life information becomes important.

Teachers can feature biographies or other nonfiction books, instead of stories, in literature circles (Stien & Beed, 2004). Students read these nonfiction books and then come together as a small group to talk about the book. Some of roles that students assume remain the same, such as discussion leader and word wizard, but students may choose different roles that are more appropriate for the genre they're reading. When students read a biography, for example, the roles might include creating a life line identifying important events in the person's life, drawing a series of portraits of the person, and identifying the personality traits, events, and opportunities that contributed to this person being remembered today.

Students also read nonfiction during reading workshop (Duthie, 1996). Sometimes teachers ask all students to read nonfiction so that they can study the genre. Teachers read aloud nonfiction and teach students about nonfiction fea-

## The Reading Process in Action: Nonfiction

**Prereading** — Students activate and build background knowledge before reading. They also preview the text and set purposes for reading.

**Reading** — Students read the book independently or participate in shared or guided reading. If the book's difficult, students listen to the teacher read it aloud.

**Responding** — Students participate in instructional conversations and write in learning logs.

**Exploring** — Students reread important parts of the text and identify important words and post them on the word wall. They analyze how the big ideas are organized, and they create a visual representations of the big ideas. Sometimes they form teams to research the topic.

**Applying** — Students create individual, small-group, or class projects

## WALKING IN ANOTHER'S FOOTSTEPS: Personalizing Reading and Learning

If you really enjoy reading, you probably imagine yourself as one of the characters in the novel you're reading. It's as though you were walking in that person's footsteps: You imagine that you're doing what the character is doing, and you feel the character's emotions. You're actively engaged in the reading experience and enjoying yourself. That's the experience you want your students to have when they read, and if they do, they're likely to become lifelong readers. Unfortunately, however, not all students become so engaged in their reading that they step into the story.

The same is true for reading biographies and learning history. When you're learning about the Lewis and Clark expedition to the northwestern wilderness, for example, do you imagine that you're one of the explorers or, perhaps, their Indian guide Sacagawea? Or are you an outsider, just memorizing the facts about the historic trip? You're likely to remember more when you're engaged in the experience because you are personalizing what you are learning. Perhaps even more important, you'll be curious, interested in learning more, when you're walking in the footsteps of a historical personality.

tures and expository text structures during minilessons. Or, those students who are interested in nonfiction can choose nonfiction books and magazines from the classroom library to read while their classmates read stories. Teachers conference with students and talk with them about the big ideas they're reading about and the nonfiction features they're finding useful.

Teachers also incorporate nonfiction into their thematic units. They create text sets with stories, nonfiction, and books of poetry. They read aloud some of these books, and students read other books themselves. When teachers read aloud, they have many opportunities to teach students about nonfiction books, special features in these books, and expository text structures. They also model how to use strategies to identify and remember the big ideas and how to notice relationships among the ideas. Even though teachers are teaching social studies or science, they're still teaching reading because students need to know how to read different types of texts.

**How to Personalize Reading and Learning** — Students can become more actively engaged in reading and learning by walking in the footsteps of a book character or a historical figure. During a literature focus unit, teachers invite students to assume the persona of one of the characters in the story, and when students are reading a biography, they can pretend to be the featured person. During a thematic unit, teachers ask students to become someone from that period, either an ordinary person or a famous person: Students can travel to China with Marco Polo, apprentice with the Renaissance ge-

**Why Use Nonfiction Books?** — According to Kristo and Bamford (2004), the most compelling reason for using nonfiction is the impact that it has on children. As they read and listen to the teacher read nonfiction books, children expand their background knowledge and enrich their vocabulary. Many of the words they're learning are academic English. The children often become more interested in reading and learning through reading nonfiction. Teachers notice that children participate more actively in class projects and show initiative in researching topics. More than just learning facts, children are often more motivated and better prepared for school success when they read nonfiction books.

## Ten Ways to Use Nonfiction

- Stock the classroom library with nonfiction books and magazines
- Read aloud nonfiction books
- Use nonfiction big books to teach about the genre
- Read companion fiction and nonfiction books
- Use nonfiction books in guided reading lessons
- Feature nonfiction books for literature circles
- Encourage students to read nonfiction during reading workshop
- Pair nonfiction with content-area textbooks
- Teach genre units on nonfiction and biography genres
- Study a nonfiction author

nius Leonardo da Vinci, become Harriet Tubman and conduct escaped slaves on the Underground Railroad, pretend to be an immigrant arriving at Ellis Island, campaign for the women's vote with Susan B. Anthony, or learn nonviolent resistance methods from Mohandas Gandhi.

When students assume the persona of a famous person, they check the information about that person in a biography, history book, or Internet resource, but if students are inventing the persona of an ordinary person, they begin by giving themselves an identity—a name, age, and occupation—and think about their role in history. If students are learning about Marco Polo's travels to China, for example, students might become the famous Italian trader himself, or they might become his brother Nicolo or Maffeo, a Venetian bodyguard, an Arab travel guide, a Persian camel driver, a Mongol cook, the Kublai Khan who befriended Marco Polo, or a Chinese sailor who traveled back to Venice with the Polos.

**Talk Activities.** Once students have assumed a persona, they're ready to participate in talk activities. During grand conversations, teachers ask students to talk about the events in the story from their character's viewpoint. They sometimes ask students what advice they'd give their character or that their character would give another character. Similarly, during a thematic unit, teachers ask students to assume the role of their historical figures to talk about a historical event.

Students also dress up as the characters or historical figures they're portraying and take a turn sitting on the hot seat. Students tell about their personality and answer classmates' questions as they think their character or historical figure would. For example, as part of a thematic unit on Ancient Egypt, a sixth grader named Matt who was pretending to be Mattus, Julius Caesar's servant, responded to these questions:

> What's your job?
> Are you scared of Julius Caesar?
> Is he a good general?
> Did he ever come to America?
> Do you think he wants to be king?
> Did you go to Egypt with him?
> Did you ever meet Cleopatra?
> What's the most famous thing he ever did?
> Were you there when he was assassinated?
> Why will people remember him in 2,000 years?

As students participate in talk activities, they deepen their understanding because they are personalizing the events in a book they're reading or the big ideas in a thematic unit.

**Writing Activities.** Students' talk activities serve as prewriting for their writing activities, and they can write simulated journal entries and simulated letters as they walk in the character's or historical figure's footsteps. A look at a series of diary entries written by a fifth grader who has assumed the role of Betsy Ross shows how she carefully chose the dates for each entry and wove in factual information:

May 15, 1773
Dear Diary,
This morning at 5:00 I had to wake up my husband John to get up for work but he wouldn't wake up. I immediately called the doc. He came over as fast as he could. He asked me to leave the room so I did. An hour later he came out and told me he had passed away. I am so sad. I don't know what to do.

June 16, 1776
Dear Diary,
Today General Washington visited me about making a flag. I was so surprised. Me making a flag! I have made flags for the navy, but this is too much. But I said yes. He showed me a pattern of the flag he wanted. He also wanted six-pointed stars but I talked him into having five-pointed stars.

July 8, 1776
Dear Diary,
Today in front of Carpenter Hall the Declaration of Independence was read by Tom Jefferson. Well, I will tell you the whole story. I heard some yelling and shouting about liberty and everyone was gathering around Carpenter Hall. So I went to my next door neighbors to ask what was happening but Mistress Peters didn't know either so we both went down to Carpenter Hall. We saw firecrackers and heard a bell and the Declaration of Independence was being read aloud. When I heard this I knew a new country was born.

June 14, 1777
Dear Diary,
Today was a happy but scary day. Today the flag I made was adopted by Congress. I thought for sure that if England found out that a new flag was taking the old one's place something bad would happen. But I'm happy because I am the maker of the first American flag and I'm only 25 years old!

Students can use simulated journals in two ways: as a tool for learning or as a project. When students use simulated journals as a tool for learning, they write the entries as they are reading a book in order to get to know the character better or during the thematic unit as they are learning about the historical period. In these entries, students are exploring concepts and making connections between what they are learning and what they already know. These journal entries are less polished than when students write a simulated journal as a project. Students might choose to write a simulated journal as a culminating project for a unit. As a project, students plan out their journals carefully, choose important dates, and use the writing process to draft, revise, edit, and publish their journals.

Students also write simulated letters from the character they're portraying to another character in the story or to another historical figure. They use the friendly letter format and try to use their character's voice in the letter. After reading *Sarah, Plain and Tall* (MacLachlan, 1985), a class of third graders assumed the persona of Sarah or of her brother William. Here is one third grader's letter written from Sarah's perspective:

Dear William,
I'm having fun here. There was a very big storm here. It was so big it looked like the sea. Sometimes I am very lonesome for home but sometimes it is very fun here in Ohio. We swam

in the cow pond and I taught Caleb how to swim. They were afraid I would leave. Maggie and Matthew brought some chickens.

Love,
Sarah

Then a classmate wrote back from William's perspective:

Dear Sarah,
You sound happy. That's good. I might come for a visit and bring my wife. I have never seen the prairie so I think I should come.

Your brother,
William

The letters show clearly how well these two students comprehend the story, and teachers can use them to monitor student's understanding.

**Using Books as Models** An amazing number of children's books have been written as journals and epistolary novels (collections of letters); in these books, the author assumes the role of a character and writes a series of journal entries or letters from that character's point of view. In *Catherine, Called Birdy* (1994), for example, author Karen Cushman took on the role of a disenchanted English noble woman of the 13th century and wrote a very convincing journal, chock full of details about life in the Middle Ages, and in *Regarding the Fountain: A Tale, in Letters, of Liars and Leaks* (1998), author Kate Klise crafted an epistolary novel about a fifth-grade class's efforts to replace the school's old water fountain using a collection of letters, postcards, memos, and newspaper articles. A story about replacing a water fountain might seem tame, but this book is laughing-out-loud funny and filled with intrigue as a school board member is implicated in a scheme to redirect the town's water supply.

Scholastic Books publishes four popular series of historical journals appropriate for fourth- through eighth-grade students. The "Dear America" series, including *The Winter of Red Snow: The Revolutionary Diary of Abigail Jane Stewart, Valley Forge, 1777* (Gregory, 1996), features courageous girls from the colonial period to the 20th century. The "My Name Is America" series, including *The Journal of Wong Ming-Ching, a Chinese Miner, California, 1852* (Yep, 2000), features the heroism of boys and young men. The "My America" series features more adventure-filled diaries of young pioneers, including *Our Strange New Land: Elizabeth's Diary, Jamestown, 1609* (Hermes, 2000). "The Royal Diaries," including *Kaiulani: The People's Princess, Hawaii, 1889* (White, 2001), describe the struggles and responsibilities of girls in royal families. These handsomely bound books look like journals, and they provide rich, detailed views into history that students can relate to because they're written from a girl's or a boy's perspective.

## Poems Are Like Onions

How is poetry like an onion? In *Peeling the Onion* (1993), Ruth Gordon explains that poems, like onions, have many layers that

### Journals

Altman, S. (1995). *My worst days diary.* New York: Bantam. (P).

Bowen, G. (1994). *Stranded at Plimoth plantation, 1626.* New York: HarperCollins. (M–U)

Cruise, R. (1998). *The top-secret journal of Fiona Claire Jardin.* San Diego: Harcourt Brace. (M)

Cushman, K. (1994). *Catherine, called Birdy.* New York: Clarion Books. (U)

Garland, S. (1998). *A line in the sand: The Alamo diary of Lucinda Lawrence.* New York: Scholastic. (M–U)

Gregory, K. (1999). *The great railroad race: The diary of Libby West.* New York: Scholastic. (M–U)

Hesse, K. (2000) *Stowaway.* New York: McElderry. (M–U)

Lasky, K. (1998). *Dreams in the golden country: The diary of Zipporah Feldman, a Jewish immigrant girl.* New York: Scholastic. (M–U)

Lewis, C. C. (1998). *Dilly's big sister diary.* New York: Millbrook Press. (P).

McKissack, P. C. (2000). *Nzingha: Warrior queen of Matamba.* New York: Scholastic. (M–U)

Moss, M. (1995). *Amelia's notebook.* New York: Tricycle Press. (P–M)

Moss, M. (2000). *Galen: My life in imperial Rome.* San Diego: Harcourt Brace. (M–U)

Murphy, J. (1998). *The journal of James Edmond Pease: A Civil War Union soldier.* New York: Scholastic. (M–U)

Myers, W. D. (1999). *The journal of Scott Pendleton Collins: A World War II soldier.* New York: Scholastic. (M–U)

Perez, A. I. (2002). *My diary from here to there/Mi diario de aquí hasta allá.* San Francisco: Childrens Book Press. (P)

Philbrick, R. (2001). *The journal of Douglas Allen Deeds: The Donner party expedition.* New York: Scholastic. (M–U)

Platt, R. (1999). *Castle diary: The journal of Tobias Burgess, page.* Cambridge, MA: Candlewick Press. (U)

Veciana-Suarez, A. (2002). *Flight to freedom.* New York: Scholastic. (U)

White, E. E. (1998). *Voyage on the great Titanic: The diary of Margaret Ann Brady.* New York: Scholastic. (M–U)

Yep, L. (2001). *Lady of Ch'iao Kuo: Warrior of the south.* New York: Scholastic. (U)

we uncover, one by one. Through repeated readings of a poem, we appreciate its layers of sound and meaning. There are other similarities, too. Both poems and onions can make us cry, but poems have a greater emotional impact: Some make us cry, some make us laugh, and others are simply unforgettable. A third way that poems are like onions is that they multiply: When we plant one onion, it will grow into a field of onions, and when we share poems with children, their appreciation of poetry will flourish.

## Epistolary Books

Ada, A. F. (1997). *Dear Peter Rabbit.* New York: Atheneum. (P)

Ada, A. F. (1998). *Yours truly, Goldilocks.* New York: Atheneum. (P)

Ada, A. F. (2001). *With love, Little Red Hen.* New York: Atheneum. (P)

Ahlberg, J., & Ahlberg, A. (1986). *The jolly postman, or other people's letters.* Boston: Little, Brown. (P)

Avi. (1991). *Nothing but the truth.* New York: Delacorte. (U)

Danziger, P., & Martin, A. M. (1998). *P.S. Longer letter later.* New York: Scholastic. (M)

Danziger, P., & Martin, A. M. (2000). *Snail mail no more.* New York: Scholastic. (M)

Klise, K. (1998). *Regarding the foundation: A tale, in letters, of liars and leaks.* New York: Avon. (U)

Klise, K. (2004). *Regarding the sink: Where, oh where, did Waters go?* San Diego: Harcourt Brace. (M–U)

Lyons, M. E. (1992). *Letters from a slave girl: The story of Harriet Jacobs.* New York: Scribner. (U)

Nagda, A. W. (2000). *Dear Whiskers.* New York: Holiday House. (M)

Nichol, B. (1994). *Beethoven lives upstairs.* New York: Orchard Books. (M–U)

Olson, M. W. (2000). *Nice try, tooth fairy.* New York: Simon & Schuster. (P)

Orlogg, K. K. (2004). *I wanna iguana.* New York: Putnam. (P–M)

Pinkney, A. D. (1994). *Dear Benjamin Banneker.* San Diego: Harcourt Brace. (M)

Teague, M. (2002). *Dear Mrs. LaRue: Letters from obedience school.* New York: Scholastic. (P–M)

Teague, M. (2002). *Detective LaRue: Letters from the investigation.* New York: Scholastic. (P–M)

Turner, A. (1987). *Nettie's trip south.* New York: Macmillan. (M–U)

Wheeler, S. (1999). *Greetings from Antarctica.* Chicago: Peter Bedrick Books. (M–U)

Woodruff, E. (1994). *Dear Levi: Letters from the Overland Trail.* New York: Knopf. (M–U)

**Take a Look at Poetry Books**

When you open a book of poetry, no matter whether it's Jack Prelutsky's classic *The Random House Book of Poetry for Children* (2000), Betsy Franco's clever *Mathematickles!* (2003), or *Popcorn* (1998), the first in James Stevenson's remarkable collection of "corn" books, you're likely to be amazed by the quality and variety of poetry available for children today. Books of poetry have been published on every topic imaginable, from baseball to American tap-dancer Bill Robinson to Halloween.

Poems can be classified in several ways. One way is by whether they rhyme. Poems that rhyme are called *rhymed verse,* and those that don't are called *free verse.* There are a variety of rhyme schemes, of course, but what matters is that children notice the rhyming words and their effect on the poem, not whether they can classify the rhyme scheme. Traditionally, poems rhymed, but many contemporary poems don't. In free verse, imagery, figurative language, and other poetic elements are used instead of rhyme.

A second way to classify poems is by poetic formula. Haiku and limericks are two types of poems that follow specific forms.

Arrangement is a third way to classify poems. Concrete poems and acrostics are two types of poems where the arrangement of the poem matters. In concrete poems, the words and lines are arranged on the page to create a design that reinforces the topic of the poem, and in acrostics, the lines are arranged so that the first letter of each line spells a word when read vertically. For example, in a poem about snowflakes, the first letter of the first word on each line might combine to spell the word *snowflakes* or a related word.

As you read poems, you'll realize their power. Some make you laugh, such as Kalli Dakos's *Put Your Eyes Up Here: And Other School Poems* (2003) and *Because I Could Not Stop My Bike: And Other Poems* (Shapiro, 2003), a collection of clever parodies of classic poems. Some make you think, such as the short poems about fanciful creatures from myths in *Creature Carnival* (Singer, 2004). Some are imaginative, such as *In the Spin of Things: Poetry in Motion* (Dotlich, 2003). Some tell a story, such as *Pumpkin Shivaree* (Agran, 2003), in which a pumpkin tells the story of its own life from seed to jack-o-lantern. Others play with words, such as *Bow Wow Meow Meow: It's Rhyming Cats and Dogs* (Florian, 2003), or create a strong rhythmic beat, such as the poems in *Hoop Queens* (Smith, 2003) that capture the energy of professional women's basketball players.

English learners who speak Spanish enjoy reading poems that incorporate some Spanish words, such as Gary Soto's *Neighborhood Odes* (1992) and *Canto Familiar* (1995) and Juan Felipe Herrera's *Laughing Out Loud, I Fly* (1998). The Spanish words are translated in a glossary, so non-Spanish speakers also can understand the poems. Other books of poetry are bilingual; the poems are printed side-by-side in Spanish and English, such as *Sol a Sol: Bilingual Poems* (Carson, 1998), *From the Bellybutton of the Moon and Other Summer Poems/Del Ombligo de la Luna y Otros Poemas de Verano* (Alarcón, 1998), and *The Tree Is Older Than You Are* (Nye, 1995). Students can read these poems in either language, or alternate reading one line in English and the next in Spanish.

Three types of poetry books are published for children. A number of picture-book versions of single poems (in which a line or stanza is illustrated on a page) are available, such as *Sailor Moo: Cow at Sea* (Wheeler, 2002) and *The Midnight Ride of Paul Revere* (Longfellow, 2001). Other books are specialized collections of poems, either written by a single poet, such as *Moon, Have You Met My Mother? The Collected Poems of Karla Kuskin* (Kuskin, 2003), or related to a single theme, such as *Poem Stew* (Cole, 1983), a popular collection of poems about food. Comprehensive anthologies are the third type, and they feature 50 to 500 or more poems arranged by category. Two of the best anthologies are *The Random House Book of Poetry for Children* (Prelutsky, 2000) and *The 20th Century Children's Poetry Treasury* (Prelutsky, 1999).

## Types of Poetry

| Type | Description | Examples |
|---|---|---|
| Rhymed verse | Poems with a rhyme scheme so that some lines end with the same sound. | Kirk, D. (2003). *Dogs rule!* New York: Hyperion Books.<br>Shields, C. D. (2003). *Almost late to school: And more school poems.* New York: Dutton. |
| Free verse | Poems that don't rhyme; images take on greater importance. | Medina, J. (2004). *The dream on Blanca's wall: Poems in English and Spanish.* Honesdale, PA: Boyds Mills Press.<br>Wong, J. S. (2002). *You have to write.* New York: McElderry. |
| Haiku | Japanese three-line nature poems containing 17 syllables. | Mannis, C. D. (2002). *One leaf rides the wind: Counting in a Japanese garden.* New York: Viking.<br>Prelutsky, J. (2004). *If not for the cat.* New York: Greenwillow. |
| Limerick | A five-line, rhymed verse form popularized by Edward Lear. | Ciardi, J. (1992). *The hopeful trout and other limericks.* Boston: Houghton Mifflin.<br>Livingston, M. C. (1991). *Lots of limericks.* New York: McElderry. |
| Concrete | Poems arranged on the page to create a picture or image. | Janeczko, P. B. (2001). *A poke in the I: A collection of concrete poems.* Cambridge, MA: Candlewick Press.<br>Roemer, H. B. (2004). *Come to my party and other shape poems.* New York: Holt. |
| Acrostic | Lines in a poem arranged so the first letter of each line spells a word when read vertically. | Powell, C. (2003). *Amazing apples.* New York: Whitman.<br>Schnur, S. (2001). *Summer: An alphabet acrostic.* New York: Clarion Books. |

Children also can access some classic poetry written for adults, including poems by Robert Frost, Langston Hughes, Edgar Allan Poe, and William Shakespeare. For instance, children enjoy reading Poe's "The Raven" and reciting Shakespeare's "The Witches' Song" from *Macbeth*. They enjoy the word play and appreciate the more sophisticated language and use of poetic elements in these poems; and this early introduction to classic poems builds children's background knowledge and prepares them for high school and college, where they undoubtedly study these poems.

Contemporary poets also are writing parodies of poems written by Edgar Allan Poe, Robert Frost, and others. Two collections of parodies to share with children are *Science Verse* (Scieszka, 2004) and *Because I Could Not Stop My Bike: And Other Poems* (Shapiro, 2003). These parodies provide the perfect opportunity to introduce children to the classic poems, discuss parody, and invite children to write their own humorous imitations.

**What Kinds of Poems Do Children Like?** Children have definite preferences about the poems they like best, just as adults do. Researchers have surveyed children's poetry preferences and found that the most popular forms of poetry are limericks and narrative poems (Fisher & Natarella, 1982; Kutiper, 1985; Terry, 1974). The least popular are haiku and free verse. In addition, children preferred funny poems, poems about animals, and poems about familiar experiences; they disliked poems with visual imagery and figurative language. The most important elements were rhyme, rhythm, and sound. Primary-grade students preferred traditional poetry, middle graders preferred modern poetry, and upper-grade students preferred rhyming verse. The researchers found that children really do like poetry, enjoy listening to poetry read aloud, and can explain why they like or dislike particular poems.

Researchers have also used school library circulation figures to examine children's poetry preferences. Kutiper and Wilson (1993) found that the humorous poetry of Shel Silverstein and Jack Prelutsky was the most popular. The three most widely circulated books were *The New Kid on the Block* (Prelutsky, 1984), *Where the Sidewalk Ends* (Silverstein, 1974), and *A Light in the Attic* (Silverstein, 1981); in fact, 14 of the 30 most popular books used in the study were written by these two poets. Both Silverstein and Prelutsky have used rhyme and rhythm effectively in their humorous narrative poems about familiar, everyday occurrences; these are the same qualities that children liked in the earlier poetry preference studies.

## Classic Poetry Accessible to Children

**Emily Dickinson**

Ackerman, K. (1990). *A brighter garden: Poetry by Emily Dickinson.* New York: Philomel.

Bolin, F. S. (1994). *Poetry for young people: Emily Dickinson.* Pittsburgh: Sterling House.

**Robert Frost**

Frost, R. (2001). *Stopping by woods on a snowy evening* (S. Jeffers, Illus.). New York: Dutton.

Frost, R. (2002). *Birches* (E. Young, Illus.). New York: Holt.

Schmidt, G. D. (Ed.). (1994). *Poetry for young people: Robert Frost.* Pittsburgh: Sterling House.

**Langston Hughes**

Burleigh, R. (2004). *Langston's train ride.* New York: Orchard Books.

Cooper, F. (1998). *Coming home: From the life of Langston Hughes.* New York: Putnam.

Hughes, L. (1996). *The dream keeper and other poems.* New York: Knopf.

Medina, T. (2002). *Love to Langston.* New York: Lee & Low.

**Henry Wadsworth Longfellow**

Longfellow, H. W. (2003). *Paul Revere's ride: The landlord's tale.* New York: HarperCollins.

Longfellow, H. W. (2003). *The song of Hiawatha.* Brooklyn, NY: Handprint Books.

**Edgar Allan Poe**

Bagert, B. (Ed.). (1995). *Poetry for young people: Edgar Allan Poe.* Pittsburgh: Sterling House.

Poe, E. A. (2002). *The raven and other poems.* New York: Scholastic.

**Carl Sandburg**

Bolin, F. S. (Ed.). (1995). *Poetry for young people: Carl Sandburg.* Pittsburgh: Sterling House.

Sandburg, C., & Niven, P. (2003). *Adventures of a poet.* Orlando: Harcourt Brace.

**Walt Whitman**

Kerley, B. (2004). *Walt Whitman: Words for America.* New York: Scholastic.

Reef, C. (2002). *Walt Whitman.* New York: Clarion Books.

Whitman, W. (1991). *I hear America singing.* (R. Sabuda, Illus.). New York: Philomel.

Whitman, W. (2003). *Nothing but miracles.* Washington, DC: National Geographic Society.

---

**Reading and Responding to Poems**

Children read poems aloud and often read them many times as they appreciate the word play and uncover the meaning. They also respond to poems by talking about them, picking out favorite words, phrases, and lines, and using the poem as a model for writing.

**How to Read a Poem.** Poetry is meant to be shared orally because the words and phrases lose much of their music when they are read with the eyes and not with the voice. As teachers and students read poems aloud, they read expressively, stressing and elongating words, adjusting reading speeds, and using musical instruments or props to accompany the reading (Elster & Hanauer, 2002). They consider these four aspects of expressive reading:

◆ Tempo: How fast or slowly to read the lines
◆ Rhythm: Which words to stress or say loudest
◆ Pitch: When to raise or lower the voice
◆ Juncture: When and how long to pause

Students experiment with tempo, rhythm, pitch, and juncture as they read poems in different ways; they learn that in some poems, reading speed may be more important and that in others, pausing is more important.

**Making Sense of Poems.** Some poems are very approachable, and students grasp the meaning during the first reading. For example, Jack Prelutsky's *The New Kid on the Block* (1984) is about a bully, but in the last line of the poem, students learn that the bully is a girl. What a kicker! Students laugh as they realize that they'd assumed the bully was a boy. They reread the poem to figure out how the poet set them up, and they pick out the words in the poem that created the image of a boy bully in their minds. As they talk about the poem, students discuss their assumptions about bullies and point out words in the text that led them to assume the bully was a boy. Some students also insist that the poet used the words *and boy* as an interjection early in the poem to mislead them.

Other poems are more difficult to understand. It might be helpful to think back to the "poems are like onions" comparison because understanding a poem often requires multiple readings. It really is like peeling an onion. From the first reading, students come away with an initial impression. Words and images stick in their minds: They giggle over silly rhymes, repeat alliterations and refrains, and ask questions about things that puzzle them. Sometimes they wonder about the title of the poem and why the poet chose it.

Students' comprehension grows as they explore the poem. In the primary grades, students often explore poems together as a class, but Dias (1996) recommends that older students work in small groups to reread and talk about the poem. At this point, it's important that students remain flexible and recognize that a fuller meaning is possible. They reread the poem, drawing on their personal experiences and their knowledge of poetry to look for clues to meaning. Then they share their ideas, and as they listen to classmates' comments and interpretations, their understanding grows. Teachers support students as they delve into a poem; they don't simply tell students what it means. They do provide information and ask questions to nudge students toward becoming independent, responsible readers.

The goal of comprehension is for students to answer the question, "What does this poem mean to you?" Poems often mean different things to different students because readers approach the poem with individual background knowledge and past experiences. Even so, a poem can't mean just anything; students' interpretations must be supported by the words in the text.

**Performing Poems.** Students share their understanding as they perform poems for classmates. One way for students to perform poems is using choral reading. Students arrange the poem for choral reading so that individual students, pairs of students, and small groups read particular lines or stanzas. Here are four possible arrangements:

- ◆ **Echo Reading.** The leader reads each line, and then the group repeats it.
- ◆ **Leader and Chorus Reading.** The leader reads the main part of the poem, and the group reads the refrain or chorus in unison.
- ◆ **Small-Group Reading.** The class divides into two or more groups, and each group reads one part of the poem.
- ◆ **Cumulative Reading.** One student or one group reads the first line or stanza, and another student or group joins in as each line or stanza is read so that a cumulative effect is created.

Then students rehearse their parts and, finally, they read the poem as an oral presentation. Students also can add props or play music in the background to enhance their presentation.

Performing poems is an important response activity because students become active participants in the poetry experience. As they prepare for their performance, they appreciate the sounds, feelings, and magic of poetry and deepen their comprehension of the poem they're rehearsing.

**Response Activities.** As children read poems or listen to them read aloud, they participate spontaneously in response actions: They move their bodies, tap their feet, or clap to the poem's rhythm, and they often repeat words, rhymes, and refrains, savoring the word choice and rhyme. Teachers also plan response activities that involve drawing, reading, talk, and writing to enhance students' appreciation of the poems they're reading.

One way students explore familiar poems is to sequence the lines of a poem. Teachers can copy the lines of the poem on sentence strips (long strips of chart paper), and then students sequence the lines in a pocket chart or by lining up around the classroom. Or, teachers can enlarge the text of the poem on a copy machine and then cut the lines apart. Then children arrange the lines in order on a tray or cookie sheet and read the familiar poem. As children sequence the poem, they check a copy of the poem posted in the classroom, if necessary. For a more challenging activity, teachers can cut apart the words on each line so that children build the poem word by word. Through these sequencing activities, children experiment with the syntactic structure of poems.

## The Reading Process in Action: Poems

|  |  |
| --- | --- |
| **Prereading** | Teachers activate children's background knowledge and introduce the poem by reading the title and the poet's name. |
| **Reading** | Poetry should be read aloud; children can read the poem aloud or listen to others read it. Children also use choral reading to read a poem together. Poems are usually read more than once. |
| **Responding** | Children talk about poems in grand conversations. They discuss what they like about a poem, including their favorite lines, and what confuses them. They also draw pictures and write journal entries about the poems they read. |
| **Exploring** | Children examine the poem more closely in this stage. They often reread the poem to notice the poetic devices the poet used. They also resequence lines of the poem, either to match the original version or in an order they prefer. |
| **Applying** | Children choose projects to develop, including delivering a choral reading presentation, creating a poster about the poem, learning about the poet, or writing a poem on the same topic or using the same structure. They also create a class collaboration book of the poem. |

A second way children respond to poems is by singing them. They pick a tune that fits the rhythm of the poem and sing it instead of reading it. Many teachers report that children quickly memorize poems when they sing them again and again. Alan Katz's hilarious book *Take Me Out of the Bathtub and Other Silly Dilly Songs* (2001) shows children how to fit new words to familiar tunes.

Children can celebrate a favorite poem by creating a class collaboration book of the poem. Students each prepare one page with a line or stanza of the poem written on it and add an illustration to complement the text. One student also makes a cover for the book with the title of the poem and the poet's name. The teacher compiles the pages and binds the book, and then the book is placed in the classroom library. Children enjoy rereading their illustrated version of the poem.

Writing is a fourth way that children respond to poems. They can write new poems following the format of the poem they've read. In this poem, a second grader uses "My Teacher" (Dakos, 1995) as a model:

My Mom
She loves to exercise at the gym
And watch romantic movies
And eat Mexican food
And get flowers painted on her nails
And sing in the choir at church
And most of all
ME!

# CHORAL READING

**1 Select a poem** Teachers choose a poem and copy it onto a chart or make multiple copies for students to read.

**2 Create the arrangement** Teachers work with students to decide how they will read the poem. They divide the poem into parts and identify who will read each part. Then the teacher adds marks to the chart, or students mark their copies so that they can follow the arrangement.

**3 Rehearse the poem** Teachers read the poem with students several times at a natural speed, pronouncing words carefully. Individual students and small groups are careful to read only their own parts.

**4 Perform the poem** Teachers empha-size that students pronounce words clearly and read with expression. Teachers can tape-record students' reading so that they can hear themselves.

**5 Revise the arrangement** Teachers work with students to fine-tune the arrangement to make it more effective, or they create another arrangement and read it again.

Children also can choose a favorite line from a poem and incorporate it in a poem they write.

| What About Memorizing Poems? |
|---|

Memorization is a useful mental exercise, but it's probably not a good idea to assign a particular poem for students to learn. Children vary in their poetry preferences, and requiring them to memorize a poem that they don't like risks killing their interest in poetry. A better approach is to encourage students who are interested in memorizing a favorite poem to do so and then recite it for the class; soon memorizing poems will become a popular response activity. In addition, as children rehearse for choral reading presentations, they often memorize the poem without even trying.

## A IS FOR AUTHENTIC ASSESSMENT: Making Comprehension Visible

Assessing how well students understand what they're reading is difficult because comprehension is an invisible process: As students read, there's little visible evidence of what strategies they're using—for example, whether they're activating background knowledge or letting the text structure guide their reading, or what inferences they're making. Teachers often give tests to assess students' comprehension, but a score of 90% or 65% correct doesn't tell you much except that one student knew more of the answers than the other one did. There are other ways to make comprehension visible that are effective instructional tools as well as useful assessment procedures.

As you continue reading, you'll learn about five procedures to teach and assess comprehension; some are used during reading to monitor students' strategy use, and others are used after reading as students deepen their understanding of the text. These procedures can be used with most types of texts and with students of all ages.

| Procedure 1: Coding the Text |
|---|

One way that students can show their thinking is by coding the text they're reading to record their strategy use (Harvey, 1998; Owocki, 2003; Tovani, 2000): They write letters or other symbols on small self-stick notes and place them beside the text while they're reading. This procedure can be used when students read stories, nonfiction, and poems. Although students use certain strategies, such as activating background knowledge, connecting, and questioning, for any type of reading, they also use other strategies for different types of texts.

Students use these codes when they read stories:

P = predict
C = connect
V = visualize
I = inference
T = theme
? = question

## An Excerpt From a Third-Grade Class Book Illustrating Shel Silverstein's Poem "Hug O' War"

Instead of tugs,

Or they can focus on the types of connections they're making and use these codes:

T-S = text to self
T-W = text to world
T-T = text to text

When students are reading nonfiction books, they often use these codes:

BK = background knowledge
BI = big idea
? = question
C = confused
R = reread
* = interesting

When students are reading poems, they use many of the same codes they used for stories, but they also use codes to mark where they notice the poet's use of specific poetic devices:

A = alliteration
I = image
M = metaphor
R = rhyme
RRR = repetition

Teachers introduce the coding procedure after they teach the strategies, and they post the codes on a chart in the classroom for students to refer to while they're reading. Teachers begin by modeling how to write the codes on self-stick notes and attach them to pages as they read. Then students try out the procedure with partners, and with practice, they learn to do the coding independently.

**Procedure 2: Charting the Text**

Students chart a text they're read by creating graphic organizers and other visual representations of the big ideas in the text (Hoyt, 1999). These maps make comprehension visible because the big ideas are highlighted, and even more important, the interrelationships are shown. Researchers have reported again and again that students' comprehension is increased when they create graphic organizers after reading (National Reading Panel, 2000).

Students create a graphic organizer or other visual representation by drawing a diagram that represents the structure of the text and then adding pictures and words to represent the big ideas. They add lines to point out the relationships among the ideas. Students divide charts for stories into three parts—beginning, middle, and end—and then they add pictures and words about the characters, events, and theme. For nonfiction, students identify the text structure, draw an appropriate diagram, and then add pictures and words to represent the big ideas. On poetry charts, students draw a picture to represent the poem, add a quote or key vocabulary from the poem, list the most important poetic devices used in the poem, and comment on the theme using a combination of words and symbols.

**Procedure 3: Double-Entry Journals**

Students often write in reading logs after they read a story, nonfiction text, or poem to deepen their understanding, and in these journal entries, they summarize the text, make connections, and evaluate their

## Excerpts From a Sixth Grader's Double-Entry Journal About *Seedfolks* (Fleischman, 1997)

| Quote | My Thinking |
|---|---|
| "I would show him that I was his daughter." P. 4 | I think this girl's wasting her time. I don't think those seeds will grow because it's a vacant lot full of trash and stuff. We have some vacant lots near our house and nothing grows there but weeds. |
| "There's plenty about *my* life that I can't change." P. 15 | I picked this sentence because it's really about how people feel. Wendell has lots of sadness in his life. I feel sorry for him. I'm wondering if this garden will take some of his sadness away. Can it help Kim and Ana, too? I don't see how a garden can help people, but maybe it will. |
| "Feel very glad inside." P. 50 | Poor lady! So many bad things have happened to her. She's so scared of everyone but the garden is helping her. I think the book should be called "The Miracle Garden". That's what it is. The lady bought these funnels and everybody is using them and I don't know why but that makes her feel good or maybe she feels useful. She says that the people in the garden are like a family and she likes being in a family. |
| "My father called them our seedfolks, because they were the first of our family there." P. 83 | So that's what seedfolks means. I was wondering so I just guessed seedfolks are people who plant seeds because I know "folks" is another name for "people". I'm really surprised this garden worked. I didn't think it would be good. I mean the whole neighborhood has changed and the people are different. Like Maricela who wanted her baby to die but now she has hope and Amir who didn't know his neighbors but now he does. |

reading experience. One type of journal that is especially effective in making comprehension visible is the double-entry journal (Barone, 1990): Students divide each journal page into two columns, and they write information from the text in the left column and their thoughts in the right column. They copy a sentence from the text in the left column that they think is important, interesting, or confusing, and in the right column write about why they chose this sentence, how they visualized it, what they predict will happen next, the connections they make to it, or why it confused them and how they clarified the confusion.

Teachers use double-entry journals to help students structure their thinking about a text (Tovani, 2000). When students are reading novels or nonfiction, they typically make one entry after reading each chapter or two, and when they're reading poems, they make one entry about each poem.

**Procedure 4: Sketch-to-Stretch**

Sketch-to-stretch is a small-group drawing activity that moves students beyond literal comprehension to think more deeply about a story, informational book, or poem (Short, Harste, & Burke, 1996). Students draw a picture to represent the theme or central message of the text, using shapes, colors, symbols, and words in their drawings to express the central meaning. Then students get into small groups to share their pictures and talk about them. As they share ideas with each other, students extend their comprehension and generate new ideas (Whitin, 1996).

Teachers can use a book with a clearly stated theme to introduce sketch-to-stretch. For example, in *Good Dog, Paw!* (Lee, 2004), the story of a veterinarian and her dog, Paw, the theme is that love is the secret to good health. After reading the book, talking about it, and identifying the theme, students can talk about different ways they can draw a picture of the theme. Many students draw hearts to represent love and add pictures of them taking good care their pets, but others focus on the love between parents and children.

Some students have difficulty representing an abstract theme in a drawing; instead, they draw a picture of a character or a big idea. Teachers can help students deepen their comprehen-

## SKETCH-TO-STRETCH

**1 Read a text**
Students read a story, nonfiction book, or poem.

**2 Discuss the text**
Students and the teacher discuss the text in a grand conversation or an instructional conversation, and they talk about ways to symbolize the theme using lines, colors, shapes, and words.

**3 Draw sketches**
Students draw sketches of the text they've read and discussed. Rather than drawing a picture of their favorite part, they focus on using symbols to represent what the text means to them.

**4 Share the sketches**
Students meet in small groups to share their sketches and talk about the symbols they used. Teachers encourage classmates to study each student's sketch and tell what they think the student is trying to convey.

**5 Share some sketches with the class**
Each group chooses one sketch from their group to share with the class.

sion by asking them to talk about how that character or big idea is important. Then students use more drawings and words to extend their comprehension. With scaffolding and lots of practice, students learn to move beyond the literal level when they read.

**Procedure 5: Projects**

Students extend their learning when they make projects. They can draw posters, give oral presentations, write reports, and create displays to make their comprehension visible. Not only do they show their comprehension, but they also demonstrate their ability to apply what they've learned in new ways (Luongo-Orlando, 2001). In the Classroom Close-Up, for example, Mrs. Ochs's students interviewed grandparents and community members about life during World War II. In this project, the questions students asked and the essays they wrote demonstrated their knowledge.

Teachers can use these activities instead of tests to examine how well their students understand what they're reading. They're more effective than tests because they serve instructional purposes in addition to being assessment tools.

# Review

## The Big Ideas

Teachers understand that reading is a meaning-making process and organize reading instruction to emphasize students' comprehension. They provide a variety of opportunities for students to read and respond to stories, informational books, and poems and integrate reading with the other five language arts.

The key points in Part 4 include:

- Five factors in developing capable readers are word identification, fluency, vocabulary, comprehension, and motivation.
- Reading is a five-stage process involving prereading, reading, responding, exploring, and applying.

- The Language Experience Approach is an effective way to introduce young children and other emergent readers to reading.
- Teachers promote reading through free voluntary reading, cross-age reading buddies, and traveling bags of books.
- When students respond to literature in both spontaneous and planned ways, their comprehension and interest in reading are enhanced.
- Students read aesthetically when they read for pleasure and efferently when they read to acquire information.
- Students use their knowledge of text features and expository text structures when they read nonfiction.
- Students follow the reading process as they read and respond to poems.

## Classroom Inquiry

Teachers put literature at the heart of language arts programs. After reading Part 4, you're probably interested in examining how students read stories, nonfiction, and poems, and how their reading experiences are integrated with the other language arts. Consider creating a classroom inquiry to investigate one of these topics.

### Stories

Teachers read stories aloud and provide opportunities for children to read stories themselves and with classmates. To examine how children read and respond to stories, ask yourself these questions:

- What do my students know about the elements of story structure?
- How much time do my students spend reading stories?
- How do my students respond to stories?

### Nonfiction

Children are interested in learning about the world and often choose to read nonfiction books. To examine the role of nonfiction in your classroom, choose one of these questions to explore:

- What types of nonfiction books do my students choose to read?
- What do my students know about text features or expository text structures?
- How do I incorporate nonfiction books in my instructional program?

### Poetry

Children like poetry, but too often, teachers don't make time to share poetry with their students. To reflect on your students' experiences with poetry, think about these questions:

- What types of poems do I share with students?
- What do my students know about how to read poems?
- Which poems do my students like best?

# 5 Writing

## INTRODUCTION

Are you a writer? If you are, you probably understand its power. Writing is more than the transcription of spoken words onto paper: It's a tool for discovery, self-expression, and communication. It's also a process. Bereiter and Scardamalia (1987) described writing as a knowledge-transforming process. Writers begin with tentative ideas; as they refine and rephrase the ideas, the text is transformed so that the finished composition hardly resembles those preliminary ideas. And in the process, the writer's knowledge has been transformed as well.

What happens in the classroom makes all the difference in developing students who like to write. The word *real* probably best describes effective writing instruction (Fox, 1988). Teachers create a "real"—nurturing—community of student-writers. The students write every day for "real"—authentic—purposes: to entertain, to present information, to share experiences, and to persuade. They write "real"—genuine—compositions instead of doing workbook exercises. They learn to use the genres or forms of writing: journal entries, stories, letters, reports, and poems. In addition, students share their writing with "real"—interested—audiences of their classmates (Graves, 1994). Teachers should never be the primary audience for students' writing because they typically read with red pens in hand, rather than as interested readers.

Teachers provide instruction, of course, but they connect what they're teaching with the writing students are doing. They teach strategy lessons, model what capable writers do, scaffold struggling writers, and provide feedback during revising and editing conferences. Through instruction and daily writing experiences, students learn the power of writing and become writers.

# Classroom Close-Up

## A Sixth-Grade Poetry Workshop

Mrs. Harris conducts a weeklong a poetry workshop in her sixth-grade classroom several times each year. The poetry workshop is a 2-hour block each day. The first hour, the reading workshop component, is devoted to reading and responding to poetry, and the second hour, the writing workshop component, to writing poetry. Students have folders for the poetry unit in which they collect papers to document the week's work.

During class meetings this week, Mrs. Harris draws students' attention to poetic devices. On Monday, she asks students to think about their favorite poems. What makes a poem a good poem? She reads aloud some favorite poems, and the students talk about why they like these poems. They also point out comparisons, onomatopoeia, which they call "sound effects," rhyme, and other poetic devices that the poets used.

On Tuesday, Mrs. Harris focuses on metaphors and similes. She reads aloud these poems from *The Random House Book of Poetry for Children* (Prelutsky, 2000): "The Toaster," "Steam Shovel," "The Dandelion," and "The Eagle." As she reads each poem, students notice these comparisons: The toaster is compared to a dragon, the steam shovel to a dinosaur, the dandelion to a soldier, and the eagle's dive to a bolt of lightning.

The next day, students come to the class meeting to share poems they have found that have comparisons; their classmates identify the comparisons. After they discuss the poems, Mrs. Harris explains the terms *metaphor* and *simile* and asks students to classify the comparisons in the poems they have shared.

On Thursday, Mrs. Harris reads aloud "The Night Is a Big Black Cat" (Prelutsky, 2000), a brief, four-line poem comparing night to a black cat, the moon to the cat's eye, and the stars to mice she is hunting in the sky. The students draw pictures illustrating the poem and add the lines or paraphrases of the lines to their pictures. On Friday, students finish their pictures and share them with the class.

Mrs. Harris points out the poetry section of the classroom library that has been infused with 75 more books of poetry. Students select books of poetry from the library to read during the independent reading time. Next, she introduces seven recently published books about poetry. *Love That Dog* (Creech, 2001), *Locomotion* (Woodson, 2003), and *A Bird About to Sing* (Montenegro, 2003) are stories written in poetic form about how children use poetry to write about their feelings. She also shares Janet Wong's book of poetry with advice about writing poems, *You Have to Write* (2002), and two informational books, *Poetry*

*Matters: Writing a Poem From the Inside Out* (Fletcher, 2002) and *Troy Thompson's Excellent Peotry* [sic] *Book* (Crew, 1998), books for middle school students about how to write poetry. She has several copies of each book, and she asks students to choose one to read during the week and to be prepared to participate in a grand conversation about the books on Friday.

During independent reading time, students also read poems and pick their favorites to share with classmates. Students make a list in their poetry notebooks of books they read. Students also choose their three favorite poems, and Mrs. Harris will make copies of these poems for them to paste into their notebooks. For each of their three favorite poems, students write a brief reflection on why they like the poem; whenever possible, they describe poetic devices in their explanations.

After reading, students get into small groups to share their favorite poems with classmates, and through this sharing they rehearse the poem they will read to the whole class; five or six students read one of their favorite poems aloud each day. During a previous poetry workshop, Mrs. Harris taught the students how to read poetry interpretively, or, as she says, "like a poet." They know how to vary the speed and loudness of their voices, how to emphasize the rhyme or other important words, and how to pause within lines or at the ends of lines. Mrs. Harris expects students to apply what they have learned when they read poetry aloud.

During the writing workshop minilessons this week, Mrs. Harris focuses on "unwriting," a strategy students can use to revise their poems. On Monday, she shares the rough draft of a color poem she has written: She has copied the poem onto a transparency that she displays on an overhead projector. She explains that she thinks she has too many unnecessary words in the poem, and she asks the students to help her unwrite it. The students make suggestions, and she crosses out words and substitutes stronger words for long phrases. Together they revise the poem and make it tighter. Mrs. Harris explains that poems are powerful because they say so much using only a few words. She encourages students to use unwriting as they revise their poems.

### How does poetry fit into the four instructional approaches?

Teachers incorporate poetry into all four instructional approaches. They share poems with students on topics related to literature focus units and thematic units, and in literature circles and reading workshop, students read books of poetry as well as stories and informational books. Students write poems in all four approaches, too. They write poems as projects during literature focus units, literature circles, and thematic units, and once students learn how to write poetry, they often choose to do so during writing workshop. As you read this Classroom Close-Up, notice how Mrs. Harris adapts reading and writing workshop for her weeklong poetry workshop.

## Poetry Workshop Schedule

| | |
|---|---|
| **Class Meeting** | Mrs. Harris leads a whole-class meeting to give a book talk on a new poetry book, talk about a poet, read several favorite poems using choral reading, or talk about a difficult or confusing poem. (15 minutes) |
| **Independent Reading** | Students choose books of poetry from the classroom library and read poems independently. As they read, students choose favorite poems and mark them with small self-stick notes. (30 minutes) |
| **Sharing** | Students form small groups and share favorite poems with classmates. Then several students read their favorite poems aloud to the whole class. They rehearse before reading to the class and try to "read like a poet" with good expression. (15 minutes) |
| **Minilesson** | Mrs. Harris teaches minilessons on poetry-writing strategies, such as how to use poetic devices, how to arrange the lines of a poem on a page, and how to use "unwriting" to revise poems. She also introduces and reviews poetry formulas during minilessons. (15 minutes) |
| **Writing** | Students write lots of rough-draft poems and choose the ones they like best to take through the writing process and publish. Students meet in revising groups and editing conferences with Mrs. Harris and classmates as they polish their poems. On Friday, the students have a poetry reading in which they read aloud one of the poems they have written. (45 minutes) |

On Tuesday and Wednesday, Mrs. Harris shares students' rough-draft poems, which she has copied onto transparencies. Then students suggest ways to unwrite their classmates' poems using the same procedure they practiced on Monday.

## A Sixth Grader's Visual Representation of a Poem

Several students ask to learn more about limericks, so on Thursday, Mrs. Harris reviews the limerick form and shares limericks from a book in the classroom library and other limericks that her students wrote in previous years. Then on Friday, students divide into small groups to try their hand at writing limericks. Mrs. Harris moves from group to group, providing assistance as needed. Afterward, they share their limericks with classmates.

Mrs. Harris's students record collections of words, quotes from poems they read, interesting phrases and images, lists of writing topics, and rough drafts of poems and other writings in their poetry notebooks. They also have a page describing the different types of poems that Mrs. Harris has taught them. During the indepen-dent writing time, they often use ideas, words and phrases, or even rough-draft poems from their writing note-books. Students write lots of rough drafts and then choose the most promising ones to take through the writing process and publish. During the week, they meet in revising groups and editing confer-ences with Mrs. Harris and a small group of class-mates. During the first half of the writing time, Mrs. Harris holds a revising group, and during the sec-ond half, she holds an editing group. Students sign up for the groups in advance. Students keep all their drafts of the poems they publish to document their use of the writing process and to trace the develop-ment of their poems.

On the last day of the poetry workshop, stu-dents type final copies of their poems, which they

## Poetry Workshop Grading Sheet

| Student's Check | | Teacher's Grade |
|---|---|---|
| _____ | 1. Read lots of poems. Keep a list of poetry books that you read. (15) | _____ |
| _____ | 2. Make copies of three favorite poems and write why you like the poems. (15) | _____ |
| _____ | 3. Read one poem aloud to the class. Be sure to read like a poet. (10) | _____ |
| _____ | 4. Write rough drafts of at least five poems. (25) | _____ |
| _____ | 5. Take one poem through the writing process to publication. (15) | _____ |
| _____ | 6. Read one of your poems during the poetry reading on Friday. (10) | _____ |
| _____ | 7. Other (10) | _____ |
| | Total | _____ |

contribute to the class book of poetry that Mrs. Harris compiles. The students move their desks into a circle and have a poetry reading. They read around, each taking a turn to read aloud one of the poems he or she has written.

Mrs. Harris posts the schedule for poetry workshop in the classroom so that students know what they are to be doing during the 2-hour time block. She also sets out her expectations for students at the beginning of the poetry workshop: They are to read and write lots of poems. She wants them to choose at least three favorite poems from the ones they read and to take at least one poem that they write through the writing process. She passes out copies of the grading sheet they will use that week, and students place them in their writing folders. This way, they know from the first day of the workshop what they are expected to accomplish.

As students complete the assignments, they add checkmarks in the left-hand column. After they finish the unit, they turn in their writing folders with the grading sheet and the papers they completed during the workshop. Mrs. Harris reviews their assignments and awards points to determine their grades using a 100-point grading scale.

As you continue reading Part 5, think about how Mrs. Harris incorporates the topics being presented. Here are three questions to guide your reading:

- How did Mrs. Harris's students use the writing process during writing workshop?
- Which writing strategies did Mrs. Harris's students use at they wrote poems?
- How could Mrs. Harris adapt writing workshop for her students to create multigenre projects (or another writing genre)?

# Essentials

## ESSENTIAL #1: Types of Journals

Students often write in journals, small booklets made from paper stapled together, to develop writing fluency or to deepen their comprehension as they read books or participate in thematic units. Their writing is usually spontaneous and loosely organized, and it often contains mechanical errors because students focus on thinking, not on spelling, capitalization, and punctuation. James Britton and his colleagues (1975) compare this type of writing to a written conversation, either with oneself or with trusted readers who are interested in the writer.

**Personal Journals** Students write in personal journals about events in their own lives and about other topics of special interest. They also collect ideas that can be used for longer writing projects. These journals are especially valuable for children who are novice writers still developing writing fluency, the ability to craft sentences, draft quickly, spell words automatically, and use capitalization and punctuation appropriately.

**Dialogue Journals** Dialogue journals are similar to personal journals except that they are written to be shared with the teacher or a classmate (Bode, 1989). Whoever receives the journal reads the entry and responds to it.

Dialogue journals are especially effective in promoting English learners' writing development. Researchers have found that these students are more successful writers when their teachers contribute to the dialogue with statements, requests for a reply, and other comments (Reyes, 1991). Not surprisingly, researchers found that students wrote more when teachers requested a reply than when they made comments that did not require a response. Also, when a student was particularly interested in a topic, it was less important what the teacher did, and when the teacher and the student were both interested in a topic, the topic seemed to take over as they shared and built on each other's writing. Reyes also found that bilingual students were much more successful in writing dialogue journal entries than other types of entries.

## The Purposes of Each Type of Journal

|  |  |
|------|----------|
| **Personal Journals** | • Record experiences<br>• Develop writing fluency<br>• Choose and develop a topic |
| **Dialogue Journals** | • Write for a specific audience<br>• Ask and respond to questions |
| **Reading Logs** | • Monitor comprehension<br>• Ask and respond to questions<br>• Make connections<br>• Summarize<br>• Analyze the structure of the text<br>• Evaluate a text |
| **Double-Entry Journals** | • Make connections<br>• Reflect on the reading or learning |
| **Language Arts Notebooks** | • Take notes about strategies and skills<br>• Develop a resource guide |
| **Learning Logs** | • Collect vocabulary words<br>• Use graphic organizers<br>• Take notes about the big ideas |
| **Simulated Journals** | • Write from another person's viewpoint<br>• Incorporate significant details |

**Language Arts Notebooks** In these notebooks, students take notes, write rules and examples, draw diagrams, and write lists of other useful information about language arts during minilessons. Later, they use the notebooks as resource guides and refer to the information when necessary.

**Learning Logs** Students write in learning logs as part of social studies and science thematic units and math units. They write quickwrites to activate background knowledge, and they draw diagrams, complete graphic organizers, and take notes to explore the big ideas.

**Simulated Journals** Students assume the role of a book character or a historical personality and write journal entries from that person's viewpoint. Students include details from the story or historical period in their entries. By assuming the role of a character, students deepen their comprehension.

Teachers use different types of journals for various classroom activities, and it isn't unusual for students to have several journals going at the same time. Second graders, for example, might write in a reading log as part of a literature focus unit, keep a math learning log to document their learning, and write in a learning log during a thematic unit. In contrast, sixth graders might make entries in a simulated journal while they read a novel in a literature circle, keep a language arts notebook, and write in a learning log during a thematic unit.

**Reading Logs** Students respond in reading logs to stories, poems, and informational books. They write and draw entries after reading, sometimes in response to the teacher's prompts and sometimes on a self-selected topic. They also make predictions, write lists of vocabulary words, summarize what they have read, and make charts and other diagrams to analyze the structure of the text or to examine the big ideas.

**Double-Entry Journals** Students divide each page of their journals into two columns and write different types of information in each column (Barone, 1990; Berthoff, 1981). Sometimes they write quotes from a story in one column and add reactions to the quotes in the other, or they write predictions in one column and what actually happened in the story in the other. The value of this format is that students make connections between the entries in the two columns.

### Learn More About the Writing Process

Atwell, N. (1998). *In the middle: New understandings about writing, reading, and learning.* Portsmouth, NH: Boynton/Cook.

Calkins, L. (1994). *The art of teaching writing.* Portsmouth, NH: Heinemann.

Graves, D. H. (1994). *A fresh look at writing.* Portsmouth, NH: Heinemann.

Johnson, B. (1999). *Never too early to write: Adventures in the K–1 writing workshop.* Gainesville, FL: Maupin House.

Ray, K. W., & Laminack, L. L. (2001). *The writing workshop: Working through the hard parts (and they're all hard parts).* Urbana, IL: NCTE.

## ESSENTIAL #2: The Writing Process

The writing process is a convenient way to describe what writers do as they compose. It's divided into five stages: prewriting, drafting, revising, editing, and publishing (Gillet & Beverly, 2001). This division can be misleading because the writing process isn't a linear series of neatly packaged activities. It actually involves recursive cycles; the stages merge and repeat as experienced writers draft and refine their writing (Barnes, Morgan, & Weinhold, 1997; Graves, 1994; Perl, 1994). The stages are useful, however, for introducing the writing process to children and for teaching specific writing activities.

**Stage 1: Prewriting** Children engage in activities to gather and organize ideas for writing during the prewriting stage. They brainstorm lists of words and ideas, read books, and conduct research. Young children often use drawing to gather their ideas; in fact, many young children can't write until they have drawn a picture because they don't know what they want to write about until they see what they draw (Dyson, 1986). Graves (1994) calls what writers do to prepare for writing "rehearsal" activities.

After gathering some ideas, children need to organize them. Sometimes they can simply sequence a list of ideas or make an outline and begin writing, but when children are writing about more complex topics, they make weblike diagrams called *clusters* to organize their ideas. They write the topic in a center circle and draw out rays for each main idea. Then they add details and other information on rays drawn out from each main idea. Clustering is more effective than outlining because it is nonlinear.

It's impossible to overestimate the importance of this stage. During prewriting, children activate and develop background knowledge in preparation for writing; it's as crucial to writers as a warm-up is to athletes. Donald Murray (1992) believes that at least 70% of writing time should be spent in prewriting, but too often, children begin writing without any planning.

### Stage 2: Drafting

Children get their ideas down on paper during the drafting stage. They begin with tentative ideas, developing them as they write a rough draft. Wide spacing is crucial on rough drafts, so children write on every other line to leave space for the revisions they'll make during the revising stage (Lane, 1993). Children stop periodically to reread what they've written to be sure it's making sense, but they shouldn't stop to check the spelling of a word or to worry about whether a sentence is grammatical; later, during the editing stage, they'll correct spelling, grammar, and other mechanical errors. When children stop to make corrections during drafting, they often lose their train of thought, and drafting becomes much more difficult. Sometimes teachers are tempted to point out mechanical errors during the drafting stage, but that sends the false message that mechanical correctness is more important than meaning (Sommers, 1994).

### Stage 3: Revising

During revising, children return to their rough drafts to refine the ideas and clarify meaning. They share their drafts with classmates and the teacher to get feedback that they use as they revise. Revision is a challenge because it's hard to be objective and to recognize the shortcomings in your own writing; however, as children gain experience with writing and sharing their writing with real audiences, they recognize the importance of "reader-friendly" text.

The first thing children do is to reread their rough drafts. They make some changes immediately—adding a sentence to finish a thought, substituting a more precise word, deleting extraneous text, and moving a sentence that seems out of place. They place question marks beside sections that need work.

Next, children share their drafts with small groups of classmates and ask for assistance with trouble spots (Calkins, 1994). They take turns reading their rough drafts aloud, and classmates in the group listen and respond, offering compliments, asking questions, and making suggestions for revision (Gere & Abbott, 1985). Sometimes the teacher joins the

writing group, but if the teacher is involved in something else, children work independently. Because writing must meet the needs of readers, feedback is crucial.

Then children make revisions. At first, children may make only several revisions, but as they gain more expertise, they may make 10 revisions or more. Children often use a blue pen for revisions so that they will show clearly on their rough drafts. They cross out, draw arrows, and write words, phrases, and sentences in the extra space left between the lines of their rough drafts.

Teachers often meet with children during the revising stage. Some teachers join small revising groups and offer their suggestions there, but others hold individual conferences with children either before or after they have made their revisions. When teachers meet with children before they revise, their purpose is to provide guidance and suggestions. When they meet after children have revised, their purpose is to monitor the children's revisions.

### Stage 4: Editing

The focus changes from meaning to mechanics in this stage. Children proofread their rough drafts, checking for misspelled words, misplaced punctuation marks, incorrectly capitalized words, run-on sentences and fragments, and grammar errors. Children reread their rough drafts several times, each time checking for a different type of error. To proofread, children read slowly, pointing to each word and looking for possible errors. They mark the errors they catch and their corrections with a red pen so that they stand out on the rough draft. Younger children typically circle errors, whereas older students use proofreaders' marks.

After proofreading their own papers, children trade papers with an editing partner and proofread each other's drafts. It's helpful to have a classmate proofread because the errors one child might miss, another would likely notice. By working together, children can identify and correct more of their mechanical errors.

Teachers often develop checklists to direct children's attention to particular types of errors. Children check off each category on the checklist after they search for that type of error, and then their editing partners also complete the checklist. Once the errors have been identified, children correct as many as they can individually or with their editing partner's assistance. Some errors are easy to correct, some require use of a dictionary, and others require assistance from another classmate or the teacher.

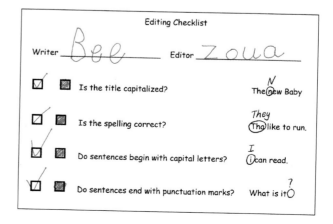

# Scaffolding English Learners
## Using the Writing Process Successfully

Learning to use the writing process is a challenge for all students, but it's greater for English learners because of cultural differences and linguistic demands. Writing doesn't involve simply thinking of an idea, choosing words to express it, and writing the words down; instead, students juggle myriad cognitive and linguistic components as they develop and refine their ideas.

As you continue reading, you'll learn about four problems many English learners face and three ways to solve them.

### Problem: Minimal Use of Strategies

Many English learners don't know how to use writing strategies, either because they haven't been taught or because they didn't understand the instruction (Chamot & O'Malley, 1994). Without strategy knowledge, students don't know how to make plans before beginning to write, pour out their ideas in rough drafts without censoring them, question the effectiveness of their rough drafts, elaborate and refine their ideas using feedback from classmates, or proofread to identify mechanical errors. In addition, they may not know how to work effectively with classmates to revise and edit their writing.

### Problem: Unfamiliar Organizational Patterns

Writing is organized in culturally specific ways, and even though people from different cultures use many of the same genres, they often organize them in different ways (Gibbons, 2002). That means that even though English learners are all familiar with story or report genres, they may organize them differently or use different linguistic features because they don't organize their thoughts in the same way. One of the most common organizational differences is that some English learners use a circular structure rather than a linear or hierarchical structure.

### Problem: Limited Vocabulary

English learners' limited vocabulary makes it much harder for them to express their ideas in writing (Chamot & O'Malley, 1994). Sometimes they can express an idea using conversational language, but they don't know the more sophisticated, academic language they need for writing. Even though teachers introduce technical vocabulary and write the words on word walls, English learners often don't practice the words enough to be able to use them in the sentences they're writing, or they may not know the related word forms that they need for the sentences they're writing.

### Problem: Excessive Concern With Mechanics

Even though English learners' writing contains many mechanical errors that reflect their developing knowledge of English, many English learners are overconcerned with correcting mechanical errors in their writing. These students equate good writing with spelling words correctly, capitalizing words and punctuating sentences appropriately, and using standard English grammar. Although it's important that students learn the mechanics of writing, the mechanics are not more important than the ideas students are expressing.

### Three Solutions

Three ways to scaffold English learners' development as writers are direct, planned instruction, class collaborations, and "real" writing experiences. Minilessons about writing strategies and genres are important for all students, but English learners often need additional scaffolding when they use writing strategies, examine genres, and participate successfully in writing process activities. The second suggestion is to write class collaborations with English learners before asking them to write independently. As they write a composition together, students review the genre, practice using the writing process, learn to use academic language, and balance their attention between developing ideas and correcting mechanical errors. And, finally, "real" writing experiences are essential so that students can apply what they're learning about writing in authentic compositions that they share with genuine audiences. An added benefit is that students build self-confidence and interest in writing as they become more successful writers.

Finally, children and their editing partners meet with the teacher to identify and correct any remaining errors in their drafts. Sometimes teachers quickly make the remaining corrections with the children, or teachers can make checkmarks in the margin to indicate errors for children to locate and correct on their own.

| **Stage 5: Publishing** | Children prepare the final copies of their compositions in this stage and share them with classmates or another appropriate audience. |

They often recopy their rough drafts using their best handwriting, or they can word process and print them. Often children compile their writing in booklets made by stapling sheets of paper together and adding construction paper covers. Sheets of wallpaper cut from old sample books also make sturdy covers.

Then children take turns sitting in the author's chair and reading their compositions aloud to classmates. Sharing writing this way is a valuable social activity that helps children develop sensitivity to audiences and confidence in themselves as authors. More than just providing opportunities for children to share writing, teachers need to teach children how to respond to their classmates. Teachers themselves serve as a model for responding positively to children's writing without dominating the sharing session.

Students also can share their writing with wide audiences at the Kids Online Magazine (www.kidsonlinemagazine.com), Frodo's Notebook (www.frodosnotebook.com), White Barn Press (www.whitebarnpress.com), and other Internet sites. Online 'zines vary in their submission requirements, so be sure to read the guidelines listed at each web site.

Children learn to use the writing process as they write compositions during literature focus units, writing workshop, and thematic units. Learning to use the process itself is more important than the success or failure of any particular writing project children might be involved in, because the writing process is a tool that they'll use and adapt all their lives.

## What is an author's chair?

Teachers designate a special chair in their classroom as "the author's chair" (Graves & Hansen, 1983). This chair might be a rocking chair, a lawn chair, a wooden stool, or a director's chair. Teachers often paint their author's chair bright colors, add comfortable cushions, and label it the "Author's Chair." Students sit in the chair to read aloud compositions they have written, and this is the only time anyone sits there.

When students share their writing, one student sits in the author's chair and classmates sit on the floor or in chairs in front of the author's chair (Karelitz, 1993). The student sitting in the author's chair reads his or her composition aloud and shows any accompanying illustrations. After the reading, classmates who want to comment raise their hands, and the author calls on several classmates to ask questions, give compliments, and make other comments. Then the author chooses another classmate to share and takes a seat in the audience.

Most students really enjoy sitting in the author's chair to read their writing aloud to classmates, and in the process, they learn about the importance of audience as they watch for their classmates' reactions. Classmates benefit from the experience as well: They get ideas for their own writing as they listen to how other students use sentence patterns and vocabulary that they might not be familiar with. The process of sharing their writing brings closure to the writing process and energizes students for their next writing project.

# Strategies

## Writing Strategies

Writing is a strategic process. Children use a variety of strategies as they write in journals and as they use the writing process. Five general strategies—those that children use for almost any type of writing activity—are activating background knowledge, organizing, drafting, revising, and proofreading. A few of these strategies are unique to writing, but others are the same ones that children use to listen, talk, and read.

As children prepare to write, no matter whether they're doing informal writing in journals or working on a writing project that they will take through the writing process, they ac-tivate their background knowledge to generate ideas for writing and then they organize their ideas. Sometimes they simply list and number the ideas, but at other times, they make clusters, outlines, or other graphic organizers to organize their ideas. Children use drafting as they begin writing. They let their ideas flow without censoring them. The ability to suspend judgment is critical in drafting; otherwise children will never write anything.

Children use the revising strategy to refine their writing. They have to distance themselves and become more objective in order to consider how effectively they are communicating and what they can do to make their writing more complete.

## Strategies Students Use as They Write

**General**
- Activating background knowledge
- Organizing
- Drafting
- Revising
- Proofreading

**Journals and Letters**
- Brainstorming
- Quickwriting
- Assuming a persona

**Reports**
- Identifying big ideas
- Asking questions
- Summarizing

**Poetry**
- Playing with language
- Unwriting
- Arranging words and lines

Revising is hard work because sometimes children have to scrap words, sentences, and paragraphs that they've already written and figure out better ways to develop their ideas.

Proofreading is an essential strategy for the editing stage. Children use proofreading to identify spelling, capitalization, punctuation, and grammar errors. This strategy is important because if children can't locate their errors, they can't correct them.

**Strategies for Writing Journals and Letters**

When children write journal entries and letters, they're writing to share ideas. Often the writing is informal. Children often brainstorm ideas as they prepare to write, sometimes making a mental list and sometimes making a list on paper.

Children often quickwrite when they write in journals: They write about a topic for 5 or 10 minutes, letting their thoughts flow without stopping to make revisions or correct misspelled words. This strategy, originally called *freewriting* and popularized by Peter Elbow (1973), helps children focus on generating ideas and developing writing fluency.

When children are making simulated journal entries or writing simulated letters, one of the most important strategies they use is assuming a persona. In order to write from another's viewpoint, children must step into the role of a character, and the information they share as well as their voice reflects the character.

**Strategies for Writing Reports**

Children use many of the same strategies for report writing that they use to read nonfiction. Two of the most important strategies are identifying big ideas and summarizing. As children prepare to write, they think about the big ideas they'll focus on in their composition, and

then they think about distilling the details they know about the topic. They ask themselves, "What's important?" and use the same kind of thinking that they use for summarizing. Students use these report-writing strategies along with other writing-process strategies as they develop and refine their reports.

**Strategies for Writing Poetry**

In addition to the other writing strategies, children use three "poetry" strategies: playing with language, unwriting, and arranging words and lines. Children use these three strategies for revision—to emphasize the meaning and improve the read-aloud quality of the poem. When they play with language, children experiment with word choice, substitute alliterative words, add rhymes, and rearrange lines of poetry to improve the rhythm.

Unwriting is one of the revision strategies that Mrs. Harris's sixth graders used in the Classroom Close-Up at the beginning of Part 5. In this strategy, children reduce wordiness in their poems and tighten lines of poetry by deleting unnecessary words and substituting more effective words or phrases. Sometimes words, such as *also, and, the,* and *very,* can be deleted, and the poem sounds better as a result. As children reread their poems, they look for one or more words they can "unwrite."

The third poetry strategy is arranging words and lines of poems. In contrast to stories and reports, poems are arranged

## QUICKWRITING

**1 Choose a topic** Students choose a topic (or the teacher assigns a topic) for the quickwrite, and they write it at the top of their papers.

**2 Write about the topic** Students write sentences or paragraphs to explore the topic. They focus on interesting ideas, make connections between the topic and their own lives, and reflect on their reading or learning. They rarely, if ever, stop writing to reread or correct errors in what they've written.

**3 Read the quickwrite** Students read their quickwrites in preparation for sharing them with classmates. They add any missing words and complete any unfinished thoughts.

**4 Share the quickwrite** Students share their quickwrites by reading them aloud to a partner or in a small group.

**5 Write a second time** Sometime students write a second time on the same topic or on a new topic that emerged through writing and sharing.

in special ways, and the arrangement helps to clarify the meaning. Children decide how many words to put on each line, where to place the lines on a page, and what capitalization and punctuation to use. Using a computer simplifies experimenting with a variety of arrangements, but children also can cut out the lines they've written and then tape them into place on another page once they're satisfied with the arrangement.

# MINILESSON
*Revising*

## Ms. Yarborough Introduces Revising to Third Graders

1. **Introduce the topic**   Ms. Yarborough names the five stages of the writing process as she points to the writing process charts hanging in the classroom. She explains that the focus today is on revising and points to that chart. She reminds students that the purpose of revising is to make their writing better and explains that writers add, delete, substitute, and move words and sentences as they revise.

2. **Share examples**   Ms. Yarborough shares this paragraph on the chalkboard and explains that she wrote it because they are studying about amphibians:

   *Amphibians live in water and on land. They live in water when they are babies. They live on land when they grow up. Frogs are some amphibians.*

   She reads the paragraph aloud and asks students to help her make it better by adding, deleting, substituting, and moving words and sentences.

3. **Provide information**   Students work with Ms. Yarborough to revise the paragraph. They add words and sentences and reorder sentences in the paragraph.

As students make suggestions, Ms. Yarborough writes the changes on the chalkboard. Here is the revised paragraph:

*Amphibians live part of their lives in water and part on land. Frogs, toads and salamanders are amphibians. They hatch from eggs in water, grow up, and live on land when they are adults. This process of changing is called metamorphosis.*

4. **Supervise practice**   Ms. Yarborough divides students into small groups and gives each group another paragraph about amphibians to revise. Students work together to make revisions, using blue pens and making marks as Ms. Yarborough demonstrated. Ms. Yarborough circulates as students work, and then students share their rough drafts and revised paragraphs with the class.

5. **Assess learning**   Ms. Yarborough asks students to compare the rough drafts and revised paragraphs and decide which are better. Then students brainstorm a list of reasons why revision is important. Their list includes: "The writing is more interesting," "It's more fun to read," and "The words are more scientific."

# MINILESSON *Quickwrite*

## Mrs. Ohashi Introduces Quickwriting to Her Fourth Graders

1. **Introduce the topic** Mrs. Ohashi tells her fourth graders that they are going to learn about a new kind of writing called quickwriting. She explains that it is the kind of writing you do after reading a book or learning something. In quickwriting, she says, you think and write fast.

2. **Share examples** Mrs. Ohashi demonstrates how to do a quickwrite. She holds up a book the students are very familiar with–*The True Story of the 3 Little Pigs!* (Scieszka, 1989), an outlandish version of "The Three Little Pigs," told from the wolf's viewpoint—and she says, "I don't believe that wolf! He's making up excuses for his horrible behavior." Then she begins to write the same words on the chalkboard. She pauses to think about the book. Then she rereads what she has written and continues writing. Here is her completed quickwrite:

   *I don't believe that wolf! He's not telling the truth. He's making up excuses for his horrible behavior. He knows that it is wrong to huff and puff and blow down other people's houses. I think he deserved what happened to him, but I like this story because it is so funny.*

   She reads her completed quickwrite aloud to the fourth graders.

3. **Provide information** Mrs. Ohashi explains that a quickwrite is a short piece of writing that is written quickly. You think and write, think and write, and then think and write some more. She explains that she begins by thinking about the topic and writing down the words she would say. She asks students to think about what they saw her do as she wrote the quickwrite, and they remember that she did a lot of thinking and writing.

4. **Supervise practice** Mrs. Ohashi asks the students what they would say if they were writing a quickwrite about the book. Students take turns offering suggestions. Then she asks them to write their own quickwrites about the familiar story. Mrs. Ohashi circulates, inviting students to think aloud when they have trouble thinking of something to say. The students write for 10 minutes, and then they share their writing with a partner.

5. **Assess learning** Mrs. Ohashi asks her fourth graders to reflect on what they have learned about writing a quickwrite. They talk about the cycle of thinking and writing.

# MINILESSON *Data Charts*

## Mr. Uchida Teaches His Fifth Graders How to Use Data Charts

1. **Introduce the topic** Mr. Uchida's fifth graders are preparing to write state reports. They have each chosen a state to research, and the class has developed a list of research questions such as, "What places should you visit in the state?" Mr. Uchida explains that students need to collect information to answer each question, and he has a neat tool to use to gather and organize the data: It's called a data chart.

2. **Share examples** Mr. Uchida shares three sample data charts that his students made last year to collect information for their state reports. He unfolds the large sheets of white construction paper that have been folded into many cells or sections; each cell is filled with information. The students examine the data charts and read the information in each cell.

3. **Provide information** Mr. Uchida folds a clean sheet of construction paper into four rows and five columns to create 20 cells. Then he unfolds the paper, shows it to the students, and counts the 20 cells. He explains how he folded the paper and traces over the folded lines so that students can see the cells. Then he writes the five research question in the top row of cells. He explains that students will write the information they locate to answer each question in the cells under the question. He demonstrates how to paraphrase information and take notes in the cell.

4. **Supervise practice** Mr. Uchida passes out large sheets of white construction paper and assists students as they divide the sheet into 20 cells and write the research questions in the top row. Then the fifth graders begin to take notes using resources they have collected. Mr. Uchida circulates in the classroom, helping students to locate information and take notes.

5. **Assess learning** After several days, Mr. Uchida brings the class together to check on the progress students are making with their data charts. Students show their partially completed charts and talk about their data collection. They ask what to do when they can't find information or when the information won't all fit into one box. Several students comment that they know how they will use their data charts when they begin writing their reports: They will use all the information in one column for one chapter of the report. They are amazed to have made this discovery!

## Mr. Rinaldi's Eighth Graders Write Simulated Letters

1. **Introduce the topic**   Mr. Rinaldi's eighth graders are studying the American Civil War, and each student has assumed the persona of someone who lived in that period. Many students have become Union or Confederate soldiers and given themselves names and identities. Today, Mr. Rinaldi asks his students to think about the war as their persona would. He explains that they will write simulated letters to Abraham Lincoln or Jefferson Davis, arguing an issue as their persona might. He explains that a simulated letter is a letter that is written as if the writer were someone else.

2. **Share examples**   Mr. Rinaldi assumed the persona of a Confederate bugle boy when his students assumed personas, and he reads a letter he has written to Abraham Lincoln as that bugle boy, begging Lincoln to end the war. He gives three reasons why the war should end: the South has the right to choose its own destiny; the South is being destroyed by the war; and too many boys are dying. He ends his emotional letter this way:

    *I 'spect I'm gonna die, too, Mr. President. What ya' gonna do when there be no more of us to shoot? No more Johnny Rebs to die. When the South has all died away, will you be a-smilin' then?*

The students are stunned by the power of their teacher's simulated letter.

3. **Provide information**   Mr. Rinaldi explains that he did three things in his simulated letter to make it powerful: He wrote in persona—the way a scared, uneducated boy might write—he included vocabulary words about the war, and he argued his point of view persuasively. Together they brainstorm a list of arguments or persuasive appeals—for better food and clothing for soldiers and to end the war or to continue the war. He passes out a prewriting form that students use to plan their simulated letters.

4. **Supervise practice**   The students write their letters using the writing process. The planning sheet serves as prewriting, and students draft, revise, and edit their letters as Mr. Rinaldi conferences with them, encouraging them to develop the voice of their personas. Afterward, students share their letters with the class.

5. **Assess learning**   After the lesson, Mr. Rinaldi talks with his students about their simulated letters. He asks them to reflect on what they have learned, and the students emphasize that what they learned was about the inhumanity of war, even though they thought they were learning about letters.

# Classroom Practice

## Young Children Can Write!

Many young children become writers before entering kindergarten, and others pick it up during their first year of school (Harste, Woodward, & Burke, 1984). Children move through a series of three stages during the primary grades. At first, children scribble randomly on a page and call it "writing." With more experience, they begin to intersperse letters in their scribbles, and line them up from left to right and from top to bottom. Children also begin to "read" or tell what their writing says. This first stage is emergent writing.

Next, in the beginning stage, children write strings of familiar letters, and their use of letters signals their new awareness of the alphabetic principle. Children use invented spelling to represent words, and as they learn more about phoneme-grapheme correspondences, their writing approximates conventional spelling. They move from writing single words to writing sentences and experiment with capital letters and punctuation marks.

On the next page, you'll see a kindergartner's letter to the Great Pumpkin. This emergent-stage writer wrote using scribbles that look like cursive handwriting and followed the left-to-

To: The Great Pumpkin
From: Melissa

I ♥ U ALL

mainly correct spelling and other conventions of written language, including capital letters and punctuation marks.

**How to Introduce Writing**

Young children's writing grows out of talking and drawing. As they begin to write, their writing is literally their talk written down, and children can usually express in writing the ideas they talk about. At the same time, children's letterlike marks develop from their drawing. With experience, children learn to differentiate between their drawing and their writing. Kindergarten teachers often explain to children that they should use crayons when they draw and pencils when they write. Teachers also differentiate where on a page children will write and draw: The drawing might go at the top of the page and the writing at the bottom, or children can use paper with space allocated for drawing and lines for writing.

Teachers help children emerge into writing when they give them pencils on the first day of school and say, "Let's write!" You can call young children's writing "kid writing" and contrast it with adult writing. When young children understand that their writing is allowed to look different from adults' writing, they are more willing to experiment with writing. Teachers show children how to hold a pencil and do kid writing with scribbles; random, letterlike marks; or letters. During kindergarten and first grade, children's writing gradually comes to approximate adult writing because teachers are modeling adult writing for them, teaching minilessons about written language, and involving them in writing activities.

Kid writing takes many different forms. It may be scribbles or a collection of random marks on paper. Sometimes children imitate adults' cursive writing as they scribble. Children string together letters that have no phoneme-grapheme correspondences, or they use one or two letters to represent entire words. Children who know more about phonics invent spellings that represent more sound features of words and apply some spelling rules.

Kid writing is important for young children. Too often, children assume that they should write and spell like adults do, but they can't. Without this freedom, children don't want to write, or they insist that teachers spell every word for them. Or, worse yet, they copy text out of books or from charts. Kid writing gives them permission to invent spellings that reflect their knowledge of written language.

right, top-to-bottom orientation. The Great Pumpkin's comment, "I love you all," can be deciphered. In another box is a page from a first grader's dinosaur book. The text reads, "No one ever saw a real dinosaur," and this beginning-stage writer used a capital letter to begin the sentence and a period to mark the end.

No one evur sae a rel dinsur.

The third stage is fluent writing, when children write in paragraphs and vary their writing according to genre. They use

**Interactive Writing**

Teachers use interactive writing to model adult or conventional writing (Button, Johnson, & Furgerson, 1996; Tompkins & Collom, 2004). Children collaborate on constructing the text to be written, and teachers reinforce concepts about written language, provide opportunities to create texts, and focus children's attention on individual words and sounds within words. This teaching strategy grew out of the Language Experience Approach, and conventional writing is used so that everyone can read the completed text.

Topics for interactive writing can come from stories students have read, classroom news, and information learned during thematic units. Children take turns holding the marking pen and doing the writing themselves. They usually sit in a

# INTERACTIVE WRITING

**1 Set a purpose**
The teacher presents a stimulus activity or sets a purpose, such as writing the daily news.

**2 Pass out writing supplies**
The teacher distributes white boards and dry-erase pens and erasers so children can write the text individually as it is written on chart paper.

**3 Choose a sentence to write**
Children create a sentence to write and repeat it several times, segmenting it into words. They also count the number of words in the sentence.

**4 Write the first sentence**
Children write the sentence word by word with the teacher's support. They slowly pronounce each word, "stretching" it out. Children take turns writing the letters to spell the word on chart paper. They write the letters using one color of pen, and the teacher uses another color to write the parts that children can't spell. Children use white correction tape to cover spelling errors and poorly formed letters. After each word is written, one child serves as the "spacer" and uses his or her hand to mark the space between words. Children reread the sentence from the beginning each time a new word is completed; when appropriate, the teacher points out capital letters, punctuation marks, and other conventions of print.

**5 Repeat for additional sentences**
The teacher repeats this procedure to write additional sentences to complete the message.

**6 Display the message**
Teachers display the message in the classroom and have children reread it often.

several days after a visit to a dentist. The children wrote in red and the teacher wrote in black. Notice that the children knew most beginning and ending sounds and the sight words *you* and *the*. The boxes around some letters indicate the use of correction tape.

**Writing Centers** Young children often write independently at a writing center that the teacher has set up in a corner of the classroom and equipped with a table and chairs, writing tools, and booklets and a variety of writing papers (Vukelich & Christie, 2004). A word wall with high-frequency words is posted nearby, and alphabet strips are available on the tables so children can hunt for and copy letters they need. A message board hangs on the wall, or mailboxes are set up so children can exchange messages with classmates. In many classrooms, computers with writing software programs such as Claris for Kids and printers are also available in the writing center.

Small groups of children often use the writing center while classmates are involved in other language arts activities with the teacher or working at other centers. Writing centers operate much like writing workshops: Children choose their own topics for writing, write independently, and share their writing with classmates also working at the center.

## GOOD, BETTER, BEST!
## Ways to Improve Students' Writing

Read through a stack of student compositions, and you'll notice right away that some papers are clearly better than others. In some compositions, the original ideas hold your attention as you read, striking words and phrases linger in your mind, and the writing has an easy flow and musical cadence. Other papers are disappointing; effective writing is thwarted by a lack of direction, a lifeless voice, awkward sentences, and mechanical errors that distract you as you read.

Vicki Spandel (2005) and her colleagues at the Northwest Regional Educational Laboratory examined student writing to identify the traits or qualities of effective writing. Through their research, they identified these six traits:

- Ideas
- Organization
- Voice
- Word choice
- Sentence fluency
- Conventions

circle on the carpet and take turns writing the text they construct on chart paper that is displayed on an easel. While one child is writing at the easel, the others are writing on small white boards in their laps.

When children begin interactive writing in kindergarten, they write letters to represent the beginning sounds in words and write familiar words such as *the, a,* and *is*. The first letters that children write are often the letters in their own names. As children learn more about sound-symbol correspondences and spelling patterns, they do more of the writing. Once children are writing words fluently, they can continue to do interactive writing as they work in small groups. Each child in the group uses a particular color pen, and children take turns writing letters, letter clusters, and words. They also get used to using the white correction tape to correct poorly formed letters and misspelled words.

On the next page, you'll see an interactive writing chart about brushing teeth, which a kindergarten class wrote over

Brushing Teeth
Brush your teeth after
you eat food.
Brush your teeth in the morning
and at night.
If you don't you will get
cavities.

Students grow in their understanding of what effective writing looks like and develop a vocabulary to talk about writing when they learn about these traits. In a multiyear study, Culham (2003) found that teaching students about the six traits improves the quality of their writing, especially when the instruction is systematic across the district.

**Trait 1: Ideas** Ideas are the "heart of the message" (Culham, 2003, p. 11). When ideas are well developed, the writing is clear and focused. Effective details elaborate the big idea and create images in readers' minds. As students examine this trait, they learn to

- Choose original and interesting ideas
- Narrow and focus ideas
- Choose details to develop an idea
- Use the senses to add imagery

*Esperanza Rising* (Ryan, 2000), the story of a girl and her mother who flee from Mexico and find work in California as migrant workers, demonstrates how effective authors develop ideas. The book's title emphasizes the theme: The main character's name is *Esperanza*, the Spanish word for *hope*, and she rises above her difficult circumstances. At the beginning of the book, Pam Muñoz Ryan chooses details carefully to paint a vivid picture of Esperanza's comfortable life on her family's ranch in Mexico, and later in the story, she creates a powerful contrast as she describes Esperanza's harsh existence in a migrant labor camp. Events in the story reinforce the theme, too: Esperanza's mother recovers from her illness, and her grandmother finally joins the family at the camp. As the story ends, Esperanza remains hopeful, telling her good friend Isabel never to be afraid of starting over.

**Trait 2: Organization** Organization is the internal structure of a composition. Its function is to enhance the central idea. Spandel (2001) explains that organization is putting "information

## Theory to Practice
### Mrs. Kirkpatrick's Students Write About Cookies

In Mrs. Kirkpatrick's kindergarten–first-grade classroom, the students participate in a weeklong literature focus unit on *If You Give a Mouse a Cookie* (Numeroff, 1985), a circular story about a mouse who, after receiving a cookie, wants a glass of milk, a straw, a napkin, other items, and finally another cookie. As the students read and respond to the book and other books in the series (e.g., *If You Take a Mouse to School* [2002]), they participate in three types of writing activities.

**Interactive Writing**

Before Mrs. Kirkpatrick reads the story aloud, the children sample cookies and talk about their favorite kinds of cookies. Then they use interactive writing to create this text about cookies on chart paper:

> We like to eat chocolate chip cookies, sugar cookies, and oatmeal cookies. The Cookie Monster says, "Cookies are a sometimes treat."

The children take turns writing words on chart paper, and Mrs. Kirkpatrick reviews spelling concepts as needed. Leo, for example, questioned how *cookie* is spelled; he thought it should be spelled phonetically—*kuke*.

**A Class Collaboration Book**

Children write pages for a class book following Laura Numeroff's pattern and using their own names. For example: *If you give Graciela a bag of popcorn, she will want a glass of juice.* After each child has made a page, Mrs. Kirkpatrick compiles the pages to make a book for the class library that children can read at school or take home to share with their parents.

**The Writing Center**

Children write their own books, drawing on ideas from the unit, at the writing center. In his book, "The Cookie Monster," Noah writes about how much he loves cookies. Here is his first page:

> I'm a cookie monsture. I love muching cookies. I cud eat about 3 milyun ofum.

Noah sounded out the words he didn't know how to spell. His text says: I'm a cookie monster. I love munching cookies. I could eat about 3 million of them.

After students write a book, they sit in the author's chair and share it with classmates.

together in an order that informs, persuades, or entertains" (p. 39). The logical pattern of the ideas varies according to genre; stories are organized differently than nonfiction or poetry. As students learn about organization, they develop the ability to

- Use structural patterns in their writing
- Craft leads to grab the readers' attention
- Use transition words to link ideas together
- Write satisfying endings

Louis Sachar's award-winning novel *Holes* (1998) is a well-organized story about a hapless boy named Stanley Yelnats who is wrongly convicted of theft and sent to Camp Green Lake, a juvenile detention facility where the boys spend every day digging holes. The beginning, middle, and end of the story are easy to pick out: The beginning is before Stanley arrives at Camp Green Lake, the middle is while he's at the camp, and the end is when he escapes and redeems himself. What makes this book unique is the second plot about a curse that has followed the Yelnats family for generations that Sachar wove throughout the book. As the book ends, Stanley fulfills his destiny by digging up the truth and unraveling the family curse.

**Trait 3: Voice** Voice is the writer's style; it's what breathes life into writing. Ruth Culham (2003) calls it "the soul of the piece" (p. 12). The writer's voice can be humorous or compelling, reflective or persuasive. What matters most is that the author connects with readers. Students develop their own voices as they

- Retell familiar stories from the viewpoints of different characters
- Assume a persona and write from that person's viewpoint
- Use strong verbs
- Avoid redundancy and vague wording

*Catherine, Called Birdy* (Cushman, 1994), the fictional diary of a rebellious teenage girl in medieval England, has a compelling voice that keeps you reading from the first page to the last. In this witty first-person account of daily life, Birdy recounts how she avoids marrying any of the rich suitors that her father brings to meet her. Her journal entries have an authentic ring because they're infused with period details and sprinkled with exclamations, such as "corpus bones" and "God's thumbs," that sound plausible.

**Trait 4: Word Choice** Carefully chosen words have the power to clarify meaning or to create a mood. It's important for writers to choose words to fit both their purpose and the audience to whom their writing is directed. Students increase their word knowledge through literature focus units and lots of reading. Teachers also teach students to

- Use precise nouns, vivid verbs, and colorful modifiers
- Consult a thesaurus to consider options
- Avoid tired words and phrases
- Use word play

Readers appreciate the importance of careful word choice in Pamela Duncan Edwards's collection of alliterative stories, including *Clara Caterpillar* (2001), *Some Smug Slug* (1996), *The Worrywarts* (2003b), and *Rosie's Roses* (2003a). These tongue-twister books are fun to read aloud.

**Trait 5: Sentence Fluency** Sentence fluency is "the rhythm and flow of carefully structured language that makes it both easy and pleasurable to read aloud" (Spandel, 2001, p. 101). Effective sentences vary in structure and length, and students are now encouraged to include some sentence fragments to add rhythm and energy to their writing (Culham, 2003). Teachers teach students about sentence structure and involve them in activities to manipulate sentences so that when they're writing, they can

- Vary sentence structure and length
- Include some sentence fragments
- Begin sentences in different ways
- Combine or expand sentences

In *Old Black Fly* (Aylesworth, 1992), a pesky fly goes on an alphabetical rampage until he is finally stopped by a fly swatter. The rhythm and flow of the snappy couplets make this a popular read-aloud book, and after reading, students are eager to try their hand at creating an imitative poem featuring an old grinning grasshopper or an old slippery seal.

**Trait 6: Conventions** Conventions guide readers through the writing. Mechanics, paragraphing, and design elements are three types of conventions. Writers check that they've used standard English mechanics—spelling, punctuation, capitalization, and grammar—as a courtesy to readers. They check that their division of the text into paragraphs enhances the organization of the ideas. They also create a design for their compositions and arrange the text on the page to enhance readability. Students apply what they've learned about conventions during the editing and publishing stages of the writing process when they

- Proofread to identify mechanical errors
- Use a dictionary when correcting spelling errors
- Check paragraphing
- Add design elements to the final copy

The importance of punctuation is highlighted in *Punctuation Takes a Vacation* (Pulver, 2003). After reading the book, teachers can remove the punctuation in excerpts from familiar books so students can see what happens when "punctuation takes a vacation."

The page layout is important in many picture books. In Jan Brett's *The Umbrella* (2004), a story set in the rain forest, and in many of her other books, illustrations on the edge of left-hand pages show what happened on the previous page, and illustrations of the edge of the right-hand pages show what will happen next. In *The Runaway Tortilla* (Kimmel, 2000), a southwestern version of "The Gingerbread Man" story, the tortilla's refrain is printed in red ink across the bottom of the page. These special design features add interest to the books.

**Instructional Recommendations**

A good way to introduce the six traits is by having students examine what makes a favorite book effective. For example, in Janet Stevens and Susan Stevens Crummel's *Jackalope* (2003), the story of a jackrabbit who wishes to be feared so his fairy god-rabbit gives him horns, there's a lot to like. A class of fourth graders identified these qualities:

- The story is told by an armadillo. (Ideas, Organization)
- Armadillo sounds like he's a cowboy. (Voice)
- The story mentions fairy tales and nursery rhymes. (Ideas)
- The beginning, middle, and end are easy to pick out. (Organization)
- Some of the sentences rhyme. (Sentence fluency)
- What the armadillo says is typed in colored boxes. (Conventions)
- The funny vegetable word plays are italicized so you are sure to notice them. (Word choice, Conventions)
- Jack is a good character because he saved the fairy go-drabbit. (Ideas)
- The theme is clear: You should be happy being yourself. (Ideas)
- We didn't find any spelling or punctuation or capitalization mistakes. (Conventions)

After learning about the six traits, the students reread their comments and classified them according to the traits they illustrate, and like many of the best books available for children today, *Jackalope* exemplifies all six traits.

Teachers introduce the six traits one by one through a series of minilessons. They explain the characteristics of the trait using stories and other trade books as models. Once students have some knowledge of the trait, they examine how students applied the traits in sample compositions and revise other sample compositions to incorporate the trait. Next, they apply what they've learned about the trait as they draft and revise their own writing. Students can also use rubrics based on the six traits to assess their writing.

**Linking the Six Traits to the Writing Process**

The writing process is a cyclical series of activities that students use as they draft and refine their writing, but it doesn't specify how to make writing better. That's where the six traits come in. Students apply what they've learned about the traits to improve the quality of their writing, particularly during the revising and editing stages (Culham, 2003).

As students reread their rough drafts, they can check that their writing exemplifies each of the traits. Teachers can develop checklists or rubrics that focus on one or all six traits that students can use to self-assess their writing. Students can also ask classmates in a revising group for feedback about how they might improve their sentence fluency, organization, or another trait. The six traits provide another reason for students to carefully proofread their rough drafts during editing: They learn that they correct mechanical errors and check paragraphing to improve the readability of their compositions.

Students also think about the design for their published compositions. They decide how to arrange the text on the page

## Books to Use in Teaching the Six Traits of Writing

### Ideas

Avi. (2002). *Crispin: The cross of lead.* New York: Hyperion Books. (U)
Bryan, A. (2003). *Beautiful blackbird.* New York: Atheneum. (P)
Bunting, E. (1996). *Going home.* New York: HarperCollins. (P–M)

### Organization

Allen, J., & Humphries, T. (2000). *Are you a snail?* Boston: Kingfisher. (P)
Pattison, D. (2003). *The journey of Oliver K. Woodman.* San Diego: Harcourt Brace. (M)
Paulsen, G. (1998). *My life in dog years.* New York: Delacorte. (M–U)

### Voice

Cronin, D. (2003). *Diary of a worm.* New York: HarperCollins. (P–M)
Fleischman, P. (1997). *Seedfolks.* New York: HarperCollins. (U)
Teague, M. (2002). *Dear Mrs. LaRue: Letters from obedience school.* New York: Scholastic. (M)

### Word Choice

Fisher, V. (2003). *Ellsworth's extraordinary electric ears and other amazing alphabet anecdotes.* New York: Atheneum. (M)
Long M. (2003). *How I became a pirate.* San Diego: Harcourt Brace. (P–M)
Snicket, L. (1999). *A series of unfortunate events: The bad beginning* (Book 1). New York: HarperCollins. (U)

### Sentence Fluency

DiCamillo, K. (2000). *Because of Winn-Dixie.* Cambridge, MA: Candlewick Press. (U)
Rash, A. (2004). *Agent A to Agent Z.* New York: Scholastic. (M)
Taback, S. (1997). *There was an old lady who swallowed a fly.* New York: Viking. (P)

### Conventions

Brett J. (1997). *The hat.* New York: Putnam. (P)
Hess, K. (2001). *Witness.* New York: Scholastic. (U)
Pulver, R. (2003). *Punctuation takes a vacation.* New York: Holiday House. (P–M)

P = primary grades (K-2); M = middle grades (3-5); U = upper grades (6-8)

in order to make their writing more understandable, and with word processing, students are able to make their compositions look very professional.

When students know about the six traits and how to use them to revise and edit their rough drafts, they can improve the quality of their writing.

## RESEARCH WORKSHOP: Asking Questions and Writing Answers

Isn't researching too difficult for children? Not according to Paula Rogovin (2001), who points out that children are naturally inquisitive. They enthusiastically pursue special interests and show genuine engagement with learning as they participate in research workshop. Asking and answering questions seem to be as empowering for children as they are for adults, and they help children develop into more thoughtful adults.

As children explore topics they're passionate about and search for answers to questions that puzzle them, they learn the inquiry process. Their understanding of the world deepens as they find answers and share what they've learned with classmates (Harvey, 1998).

**What Is a Research Workshop?** Research workshop is a 60- to 90-minute period where students identify questions and conduct research to find answers to the questions they've posed. Sometimes students choose questions that interest them. At other times, research workshop is connected to thematic units; in this case, the teacher identifies an umbrella topic, and students choose subtopic-questions. In addition to providing a large chunk of time for students to read, research, and write, teachers teach minilessons on research procedures and model how to do research as the class works together on collaborative projects. At the end of the workshop, students come together as a class to share what they've been working on and what they've learned.

When Rogovin (2001) conducts research workshops, she chooses broad topics, such as people at work and immigration, for her students to study, and then they choose subtopics, ask questions, and do research in small groups. The students collect information and share what they've learned by writing reports and giving oral presentations. Christine Duthie (1996) also has her primary-grade students conduct research during their writing workshop periods.

**The Inquiry Process** Students use this inquiry process as they ask questions and collect information to answer their questions:

1. **Questioning.** Students identify a question that interests them to research.
2. **Planning.** Students think about how they will be able to find answers to their questions. They identify people to interview, plan surveys and observations, and locate books, magazine articles, and Internet resources to use.
3. **Collecting.** Students gather information from a variety of resources and organize the information using a graphic organizer or outline.
4. **Synthesizing.** Students combine the big ideas to create a coherent report or other project.
5. **Evaluating.** Students examine their reports to judge the accuracy of their information, the completeness of their answers, and the effectiveness of their writing.
6. **Reporting.** Students share their completed reports with classmates and other audiences.

This process, which is similar to the writing process, nurtures students' curiosity, promotes questioning, and develops students' ownership of their research projects.

**Instructional Recommendations** For students to become capable researchers, teachers need to establish a climate of inquiry in their classrooms and teach students how to conduct research and write reports. It's not enough for them to do one research project during the school year.

**Class Collaboration Reports.** Too often, teachers assign reports without teaching students how to write them. An effective way to introduce report writing is to write a class collaboration report. The teacher presents a broad, "umbrella" topic, and then students brainstorm subtopics and identify questions related to them. Students choose questions, and those who are interested in the same questions gather in small groups to work together. Before they begin working, however, the teacher chooses one of the questions that no one chose and the class researches that question and writes the answer collaboratively. Then the groups work together to research their questions and write their sections of the report. Afterward, the teacher collects the completed sections, compiles them, and makes copies for each student.

A class of second graders researched crabs as part of a thematic unit about the seashore. First, they wrote this chapter as a class collaboration:

How Are Crabs Like Us?

We don't look anything like crabs, but we are alike in some ways. The most important thing is that crabs and people are both alive. Crabs eat, but they eat different foods than we do. Crabs

**Learn More About Research Workshops**

Allen, C. A. (2001). *The multigenre research paper: Voice, passion, and discovery in grades 4–6.* Portsmouth, NH: Heinemann.

Harvey, S. (1998). *Nonfiction matters: Reading, writing, and research in grades 3–8.* Portland: ME: Stenhouse.

Kristo, J. V., & Bamford, R. A. (2004). *Nonfiction in focus.* New York: Scholastic.

Portalupi, J., & Fletcher, R. J. (2001). *Nonfiction craft lessons: Teaching informational writing K–8.* Portland, ME: Stenhouse.

Robb, L. (2004). *Nonfiction writing: From the inside out.* New York: Scholastic.

Rogovin, P. (2001). *The research workshop: Bringing the world into your classroom.* Portsmouth, NH: Heinemann.

have arms but they look different. They have pincers instead of fingers. They have legs, but they have 6 more legs than we do. We can walk, run, and swim, and that's what crabs can do.

Then the second graders divided into small groups and wrote answers to these questions:

### Where Do Crabs Live?

Crabs live in lots of different places. Some crabs live in shallow pools. They also like to live under the sand and in the ocean. Each place is just perfect for the crabs to live and grow.

### How Do Crabs Move?

Crabs have eight legs. There are four on each side. We think that so many legs probably makes it hard to move. Crabs don't walk or run like we do. They actually move sideways.

### Do You Know Why Crabs Have Pincers?

Crabs have two claws called pincers. They use their pincers to catch food, and they use their pincers to fight predators like seagulls. The pincers are powerful.

### How Do Crabs Grow?

Crabs have hard shells. They grow and grow inside their shells. When they outgrow their shells, crabs shed it and grow a new one.

### Can Crabs Grow New Legs?

Yes! Crabs really can grow new legs. They can get new claws and new antennas, too. So if an animal bites off their leg, crabs grow new ones. They are small at first but they keep growing until they are normal. It's just remarkable!

---

## WRITING COLLABORATIVE REPORTS

**1 Choose a research question**
Students identify a question related to the umbrella topic to research.

**2 Model how to write a section**
The teacher chooses a different question to research. Students gather information and draft the section on chart paper. They move through the writing process, revising and editing their section, so that it's ready for inclusion in the class report.

**3 Gather and organize information**
Students working in small groups research their questions using books, the Internet, and other resources. They take notes and organize the information in a graphic organizer that's appropriate for their question.

**4 Write the sections**
Students use the writing process to write their sections. They write rough drafts and revise their sections. Next, the class comes together and reads the entire report aloud, checking for inconsistencies or redundancies. Then students edit their sections and meet with the teacher for a final check. Students word process the final copies of their section.

**5 Compile the report**
Students compile their sections, and as a class, they design the cover and make the title page and table of contents.

**6 Publish the report**
Students word process the final copy, and the teacher duplicates and binds copies for each student.

---

Students benefit in two ways from writing a group report: They learn the steps in writing a report, and they share the laborious parts of researching and writing because they're working in groups.

There's a gradual release of responsibility from the teacher to students before they tackle writing individual reports, which Perry and Drummond (2002) describe as moving from teacher-regulated to student self-regulated report writing. They have identified these characteristics of classrooms that promote responsible, independent writers:

- Students collaborate with classmates.
- Students are involved in meaningful research activities that require them to think strategically.
- Students increasingly assume responsibility for their learning by making choices, dealing constructively with challenges, and evaluating their own work.
- Students are evaluated on their research processes, their use of the writing process to prepare their reports, and the quality of their finished products.
- The teacher scaffolds students' learning by providing direct instruction about how to do research, modeling the process, having students do research in groups, and gradually releasing responsibility to the students to work independently.

**Individual Reports.** After students learn to conduct research and share what they learn in a collaborative report, they're ready to write individual reports. They use the inquiry process to find answers to their questions and the writing process to develop and refine their reports. Writing an individual report is similar to writing a collaborative report, except that students assume the entire responsibility themselves.

To begin, students identify several different research questions or an umbrella question with several subtopics, and then they conduct research to find the answers. Each question and answer usually becomes a chapter in the report.

Students use a variety of techniques as they conduct research: They interview experts, collect data through surveys, conduct experiments, make observations, and consult Internet sources in addition to reading nonfiction books (Kristo & Bamford, 2004). They learn to choose the techniques that are most appropriate for their questions (Harvey, 1998).

As students consult the books and other resources they've gathered, they collect lots of information that they need to remember, and they take notes. There's no single best way to take notes, but students often use self-stick notes to mark important information in books as they're reading. Then they go back and write short phrases, often in their own words, on note cards, or they complete graphic organizers. They don't try to take notes about everything they read, only about the big ideas. In addition, they're careful not to get distracted by other interesting information in the resources they're reading.

Students collect a lot of information, and they need to create categories to organize it. Choosing an appropriate organizational structure is important because it is reflected in the students' writing. The structure also influences which information is most important. Sometimes students complete graphic organizers, design charts, or write informal outlines.

As students begin to draft, they write sentences and paragraphs to present the information they collected. They also think about which special features to include to aid readers, such as chapter titles and headings. As they write, they summarize and synthesize the big ideas, being careful to distinguish between fact and opinion. They write leads to engage readers and summarize the big ideas in the conclusion. Students also create visuals to display other information, and sometimes identify additional information to highlight in sidebars (Kristo & Bamford, 2004).

When students revise their rough drafts, their first concern is whether they've answered their questions. They share their rough drafts with classmates and get feedback on how well they're communicating. They also double-check their notes to ensure the accuracy of their information and statistics, add details, revise their leads, and check transitions. Next, students finish the writing process by editing their reports to correct misspelled words, capitalization and punctuation errors, and nonstandard English usage.

Students usually word process the final copies of their reports, and they carefully format them, taking advantage of what they know about nonfiction features. They include a title page, a table of contents, chapter titles, illustrations with captions, photos downloaded from the Internet, a bibliography, and an index. They compile the pages and bind them into a book or display them on a chart.

Plagiarism isn't a big problem when children use the inquiry process, but they still need to understand what plagiarism is and why it's wrong. Children are less likely to plagiarize because they've collected information to answer questions that they care about, and because they have developed their compositions step by step—from prewriting and drafting to revising and editing. The two best ways to avoid having students copy work from another source and pass it

## The Writing Process in Action: Reports

**Prewriting** — Students choose a question to research, make plans, read and take notes, and organize the information to answer their question.

**Drafting** — Students write a rough draft, coherently presenting the information to answer their question.

**Revising** — Students meet in revising groups to get feedback about how effectively they have answered their question. Classmates offer suggestions for revising, and students use this feedback as they revise their rough drafts.

**Editing** — Students proofread their rough drafts and correct misspelled words, capital letters, punctuation marks, and other mechanical errors. They also meet with the teacher for a final editing conference.

**Publishing** — Students word process their final copies. They add illustrations, a table of contents, and a bibliography, and they compile their reports into books.

off as their own are to teach the inquiry process and to have children participate in research workshop rather than assigning reports as homework.

**Multigenre Projects.** A new approach to report writing is the multigenre project (Romano, 1995, 2000), in which students explore a topic through several genres. Tom Romano (1995) explains, "Each genre offers me ways of seeing and understanding that others do not" (p. 109). Grierson, Anson, and Baird (2002) explain that "research comes alive when students explore a range of alternate genres instead of writing the traditional research report" (p. 51).

An increasing number of multigenre books are being published today. Probably the best-known multigenre books are Joanna Cole's innovative Magic School Bus books. Information is presented in the context of Ms. Frizzle's class taking a field trip on their magic school bus and flying into the eye of a hurricane, traveling through the human body, exploring a beehive, and cruising under the ocean, too. Reports and diagrams are presented in sidebars on each page. Other multigenre books are stories and poems. Kate Klise's *Regarding the Fountain: A Tale, in Letters, of Liars and Leaks* (1998) and *Regarding the Sink: Where, Oh Where, Did Waters Go?* (2004) are stories told with a collection of letters, memos, and reports. And in Longfellow's poem *The Midnight Ride of Paul Revere* (2001), Christopher Bing adds maps and photos of artifacts from the Revolutionary War period to his illustrations.

When they create multigenre projects, students collect a variety of resources, including books, textbooks, Internet articles, charts, diagrams, and photos and then study the materials. As they conduct their research, students identify a repetend, or theme, for their multigenre project. Finally, students write several pieces, including essays, letters, journal entries, stories, and poems, and they incorporate the repetend in their pieces. They also collect photos, charts, and other visual representations that emphasize the repetend and compile all the pieces in a book or display them on a poster.

In a multigenre project on the planet Mars that focuses on the question Is life possible on Mars?, a group of sixth graders included the following pieces:

◆ A descriptive essay explaining that it is possible that life exists or has existed on Mars
◆ A data chart comparing Mars to other planets taken from an informational book students have read
◆ A photograph of the planet downloaded from the NASA Web site showing the polar regions where there might be ice
◆ A found poem questioning whether conditions necessary for life exist on Mars
◆ A simulated journal written from the perspective of an astronaut who is exploring the red planet, looking for evidence of life

Through these five pieces, students explore the repetend and reveal different kinds of information about Mars. This project is much more complete than it would have been if it were just a report (Allen, 2001).

Research workshop works: Students are actively engaged in language arts activities, and they use nonfiction reading and writing strategies. They also have opportunities to pursue special interests and develop responsibility for their own work.

## LIFE STORIES: Up Close and Personal

Children often wonder what it would be like to be someone else—an Olympic athlete, a test pilot, a knight in shining armor, a dancer, or the president, for example. One of the best ways to learn about other people's lives is by reading biographies and autobiographies. There are so many life-story books available today that children can read about a wide range of contemporary and historical personalities, including Confucius, Anna Pavlova, George W. Bush, Annie Oakley, J. K. Rowling, Alexander Graham Bell, Mother Teresa, Elvis Presley, Sandra Day O'Connor, and Houdini. At the same time children are reading about these people's lives, they also are learning about personal qualities such as courage and determination that they can apply to their own lives to help them reach their dreams and deal with both success and failure.

As they read life stories and listen to them read aloud, children learn about this genre and examine its structure. These books also serve as models for children's own writing. Biographies and autobiographies are life stories, and they combine expository writing with some elements of narration.

**Reading Biographies and Autobiographies**
Authors use several approaches in writing biographies and autobiographies (Fleming & McGinnis, 1985). The most common approach is historical: The writer focuses on events and presents them chronologically. Many autobiographies and biographies that span the person's entire life follow this pattern,

## Multigenre Books

### Stories

Avi. (1991). *Nothing but the truth.* New York: Avon. (U)
Cofer, J. O. (2004). *Call me Maria.* New York: Scholastic. (U)
Draper, S. (1994). *Tears of a tiger.* New York: Atheneum. (U)
Klise, K. (1998). *Regarding the fountain: A tale, in letters, of liars and leaks.* New York: Avon. (M–U)
Klise, K. (2004). *Regarding the sink: Where, oh where, did Waters go?* San Diego: Harcourt Brace. (M–U)
Teague, M. (2004). *Detective LaRue: Letters from the investigation.* New York: Scholastic. (P–M)

### Informational Books

Cheripko, J. (2004). *Caesar Rodney's ride: The story of an American patriot.* Honesdale, PA: Boyds Mills Press. (M–U)
Cole, J. (1996). *The magic school bus inside a hurricane.* New York: Scholastic. (Also other books in the series.) (P–M)
Keenan, S. (2004). *O, say can you see? America's symbols, landmarks, and inspiring words.* New York: Scholastic. (P–M)
Keller, L. (2000). *Open wide: Tooth school inside.* New York: Henry Holt. (P–M)
Tanaka, S. (2004). *D–Day: They fought to free Europe from Hitler's tyranny.* New York: Hyperion Books. (M–U)

### Poems

Crew, G. (1998). *Troy Thompson's excellent peotry* [sic] *book.* Victoria, Australia: Lothian. (M–U)
Longfellow, H. W. (2001). *The midnight ride of Paul Revere* (C. Bing, Illus.). Brooklyn, NY: Handprint Books. (M–U)
Thayer, E. L. (2000). *Casey at the bat: A ballad of the republic sung in the year 1888.* Brooklyn, NY: Handprint Books. (M–U)

## Genres for Multigenre Projects

- Alphabet books
- Cartoons
- Charts
- Diagrams
- Essays
- Graphic organizers
- Internet articles
- Letters
- Maps
- Newspaper articles
- Open-mind portraits
- Photos
- Poems
- Postcards
- Questions and answers
- Quotes
- Reports
- Simulated journals
- Stories
- Time lines

## Biographies and Autobiographies

### Biographies

Brown, D. (2004). *Odd boy out: Young Albert Einstein.* Boston: Houghton Mifflin. (P–M)

Collins, M. (2003). *Airborne: A photobiography of Wilbur and Orville Wright.* Washington, DC: National Geographic Society. (M–U)

Fleming, C. (2003). *Ben Franklin's almanac: Being a true account of the good gentleman's life.* New York: Atheneum. (M–U)

Freeman, R. (2002). *Confucius: The golden rule.* New York: Scholastic. (M–U)

Pinkney, A. D. (2002). *Ella Fitzgerald: The tale of a vocal virtuosa.* New York: Hyperion Books. (P–M)

Rappaport, D. (2001). *Martin's big words: The life of Dr. Martin Luther King, Jr.* New York: Hyperion Books. (P)

Rappaport, D. (2004). *John's secret dreams: The life of John Lennon.* New York: Hyperion Books. (M–U)

Sís, P. (2003). *The tree of life: A book depicting the life of Charles Darwin, naturalist, geologist, and thinker.* New York: Farrar, Straus & Giroux. (M–U)

St. George, J. (2004). *You're on your way, Teddy Roosevelt.* New York: Philomel. (M)

### Autobiographies

dePaola, T. (2002). *What a year.* New York: Putnam. (P)

Gantos, J. (2002). *Hole in my life.* New York: Farrar, Straus & Giroux. (M–U)

Jiménez, F. (2001). *Breaking through.* Boston: Houghton Mifflin. (M–U)

Numeroff, L. (2003). *If you give an author a pencil.* Katonah, NY: Richard C. Owen. (P)

Steig, W. (2003). *When everybody wore a hat.* New York: HarperCollins. (P–M)

including *Theodore Roosevelt: Champion of the American Spirit* (Kraft, 2003) and *Martin's Big Words: The Life of Dr. Martin Luther King, Jr.* (Rappaport, 2001).

Next is the sociological approach, in which the writer describes life during a historical period, providing supporting information about family life, food, clothing, education, economics, transportation, and so on. For instance, in *Woody Guthrie: Poet of the People* (Christensen, 2001), readers learn about the hard life many Americans faced during the Depression as they learn about the folk legend.

A third approach is psychological: The writer focuses on conflicts the central figure faces. Conflicts may be with oneself, others, nature, or society. The psychological approach has many elements in common with stories and is most often used in shorter autobiographies and biographies that revolve around particular events or phases in the person's life. One example is *You Want Women to Vote, Lizzie Stanton?* (Fritz, 1995), which is about one of the leaders in the women's rights movement.

This book focuses on Lizzie Stanton's role in the suffrage movement; it doesn't recount her entire life.

Biographies are accounts of a person's life written by someone else. To make the accounts as accurate and authentic as possible, writers consult a variety of sources of information during their research. The best source, of course, is the biography's subject, and writers can learn many things about the person through an interview. Other primary sources include diaries and letters, photographs, mementos, historical records, and recollections of people who know the person. Examples of secondary sources are books and newspaper articles written by someone other than the biographical subject.

Biographies are categorized as historical or contemporary. Contemporary biographies are written about a living person, especially someone the writer can interview, whereas historical biographies are about people who are no longer alive.

**Instructional Recommendations** It's important to link reading and writing in the classroom (Salesi, 1992). Children can create a variety of projects to showcase what they've learned by reading biographies, and they can create autobiography projects to document the events in their own lives. Sometimes the projects take the form of a report or book, but there are other types of projects as well.

**"Me" Boxes.** One way for children to focus on their own lives is to make a "me" box. Children collect objects and pictures representing their families, their hobbies, events in their lives, and special accomplishments. Next, they write explanations or reflections to accompany each object. Then children put all the objects in a shoebox, coffee can, or other container and decorate the outside of the container.

**Biography Boxes.** Children make biography boxes that are similar to "me" boxes. They identify items that represent the person, collect them, and put them in a box they have decorated. They also write papers to put with each object, explaining its significance. A fifth grader created a biography box for Paul Revere and decorated the box with aluminum foil, explaining that it looked like silver and that Paul Revere was a silversmith. Inside the box, he placed the following items:

- a spoon (to represent Revere's career as a silversmith)
- a toy horse (to represent his famous midnight ride)
- a tea bag (to represent his involvement in the Boston Tea Party)
- a copy of Longfellow's poem "The Midnight Ride of Paul Revere"
- an advertisement for Revere pots and pans (along with an explanation that Paul Revere is credited with inventing the process of layering metals)
- a portrait of the patriot
- photos of Boston, Lexington, and Concord that were downloaded from the Internet
- a life line the child drew marking important events in Paul Revere's life

The student wrote cards describing the relationship of each object to Paul Revere and attached them to the items.

## An Eighth Grader's Biography Poster

## A Page From a First Grader's "All About Me" Book

**Life Line Clotheslines.** Children collect objects that symbolize events in their life and hang them in sequential order on a "life line" clothesline, and then they write brief explanations about each object, explaining what the object is and how it relates to their lives (Fleming, 1985). Then they attach their explanations to the objects on the clothesline. Later, children can present their life lines to the class, or they can use the activity as prewriting for a longer autobiography project.

Children also can create biography life lines, showing the featured person's life from birth to death with the milestones identified by date. Later, if children are writing biography reports, they can use the information on the life line to identify topics to write about.

**"All About Me" Books.** Children in the primary grades often compile "All About Me" books. These autobiographies usually present basic information, such as the child's birthday, family members, friends, and favorite activities, using a combination of drawings and writing. To write these books, children and the teacher decide on a topic for each page; then, after brainstorming possible ideas for the topic, children draw a picture and write about it. Children may also need to ask their parents for information about their birth and events during their preschool years.

**Biography Posters.** Children can share the information they've learned by creating a poster. Posters often include a portrait of the person and information about his or her life and accomplishments. Students in an eighth-grade class made a biography quilt with paper squares, and each square was modeled after the illustrations in *My Fellow Americans,* by Alice Provensen (1995). They drew portraits set on an important day in the person's life, and around the outside added well-known sayings and other phrases related to person.

**Multigenre Biography Projects.** Students write and collect a variety of pieces about a person, including simulated jounals, open-mind portraits, photographs, poems, and quotes, to create a multigenre biography, which is like a mutigenre project. Then they compile their biographies on posters or in notebooks.

Life stories are interesting books because they weave information into a fascinating story. Some children who haven't been interested in other types of books grab on to these books and become readers. Through reading and writing biographies and autobiographies, children learn about the world and about themselves.

## Becoming a Poet

Children can write poetry! They write funny verses, vivid word pictures, powerful comparisons, and expressions of deep sentiment. One way to ensure successful poetry writing experiences is to use poetic forms; these structures serve as scaffolds, or temporary writing frameworks, so that students can focus on ideas rather than on rhyme schemes (Cecil, 1997).

People often link rhyme with poetry, but poets use a variety of techniques called *poetic devices,* including alliteration, onomatopoeia, and repetition, in addition to rhyme. Children often are more effective poets when they incorporate these other devices.

**Formula Poems**

The poetic forms may seem like recipes, but they are not intended to be followed rigidly. Rather, they provide a structure for students' poems. Meaning is always the most important consideration, and form follows the search for meaning. Perhaps a better description is that children "dig for poems" (Valentine, 1986) through words, ideas, poetic forms, rhyme, rhythm, and conventions.

## Poetic Devices

| | |
|---|---|
| **Alliteration** | Repeating the initial sound in consecutive words or words in close proximity. Example: *A right-handed rhinoceros wrote rhymes about rickshaws and rhubarb.* |
| **Assonance** | Repeating the vowel sound in consecutive words or words in close proximity. Example: *Dad slammed the bat . . .* |
| **Comparison** | Using similes and metaphors to compare one thing to another. Example: *People are like platypuses— unexplainable!* |
| **Onomatopoeia** | Adding words that sound like their meaning. Example: *The cars raced—varoom . . .* |
| **Repetition** | Repeating words and phrases. Example: *I am a little man/Standing all alone/In the deep, dark wood./I am standing on one foot/In the deep, dark wood . . .* |
| **Rhyme** | Ending lines of poetry with words having the same final sound. Example: *My feet/And seat/Are beat.* |

Poet Kenneth Koch (2000) developed some simple formulas that call for children to begin each line or stanza the same way. The formulas use repetition, a stylistic device that is often more effective for children than rhyme. Some forms may seem more like sentences than poems, but the dividing line between poetry and prose is a blurry one, and these poetry experiences move children toward more sophisticated poetic expression.

**"I Wish . . ." Poems.** Children begin each stanza with the words "I wish" and complete the line with a wish (Koch, 2000). Then they add more lines to describe or explain their wish. Here is a fourth grader's poem:

> I wish I were a star
> fallen down from Mars.
> I'm bursting through the sky
> like a firework
> on the fourth of July.

**Color Poems.** Children begin each stanza with a color and then describe the color using an event or a feeling (Koch, 2000). A second grader composed this poem:

> Orange is a pumpkin
> Big and roly-poly round
> Growing in a garden patch.
> Now that October's here
> I can tell you this:
> Soon you'll be a jack-o-lantern
> Looking out the window and
> Scaring kids on Halloween.

**"If I Were . . ." Poems.** Children begin each poem with "If I were . . ." and tell what it would be like to be someone or something else (Koch, 2000). Fifth graders wrote this poem from Annemarie's viewpoint after reading *Number the Stars* (Lowry, 1989):

> If I were Annemarie,
> I'd be brave.
> I'd hide my friends,
> and trick those Nazi soldiers.
> I would lie if I had to.
> If I were Annemarie,
> I'd be brave.

**Comparison Poems.** Children compare something to something else, and then expand on the comparison in the rest of the poem (Koch, 2000). A third grader wrote this poem after brainstorming a list of possible explanations for thunder:

> Thunder is a brontosaurus sneezing,
> that's all it is.
> Nothing to frighten you—
> just a dinosaur with a cold.

This student's comparison is a metaphor. She could have written "Thunder is like a brontosaurus sneezing," a simile, but her metaphor is a much stronger comparison.

**"I Am . . ." Poems.** Children write "I Am . . ." poems from the viewpoint of a book character or historical figure. They use repetition by beginning and ending each stanza with "I am . . ." and beginning the lines in between with "I . . ." First graders wrote this class collaboration poem after reading *Where the Wild Things Are* (Sendak, 1988), the story of a boy who imagines that he travels to the land of the wild things after he is sent to his bedroom for misbehaving:

> I am Max,
> wearing my wolf suit
> and making mischief.
> I turned into a Wild Thing.
> I became the king of the Wild Things.
> But I got homesick
> so I sailed home.
> I am Max,
> a hungry little boy
> who wants his mommy.

**Acrostic Poems.** Children write acrostic poems using key words. They choose a key word and write it vertically and then create lines of poetry, each one beginning with a letter of the word they have written vertically. After reading *Officer Buckle and Gloria* (Rathmann, 1995), the story of a police officer and his dog who give safety speeches at schools, a small group of first graders wrote this acrostic using the dog's name, Gloria, as the key word:

> **G**loria
> **L**oves to do tricks.
> **O**fficer Buckle tells safety
> **R**ules at schools.
> **I** wish I had
> **A** dog like Gloria.

Another small group composed this acrostic using the same key word:

> **G**ood dog Gloria
> **L**ikes to help
> **O**fficer Buckle teach safety
> **R**ules to boys and girls.
> **I** promise to remember
> **A**ll the lessons.

**Model Poems** Children model their poems on poems composed by adult poets, as Kenneth Koch suggested in *Rose, Where Did You Get That Red?* (1990). With these forms, children read a poem and then write their own, incorporating some key words and the theme expressed in the model poem. For other examples of model poems, see Paul Janeczko's *Poetry From A to Z: A Guide for Young Writers* (1994) and Nancy Cecil's *For the Love of Poetry* (1997).

**Apologies.** Using William Carlos Williams's "This Is Just to Say" as the model, children write a poem in which they apologize for something they are secretly glad they did (Koch, 1990). A seventh grader wrote this apology poem, "The Truck," to his dad:

> Dad,
> I'm sorry
> that I took
> the truck
> out for
> a spin.
> I knew it
> was wrong.
> But . . .
> the exhilarating
> motion was
> AWESOME!

Apology poems don't have to be humorous; they can be sensitive, genuine apologies, as another seventh grader's poem, "Open Up," demonstrates:

> I didn't
> open my
> immature eyes
> to see
> the pain
> within you
> a death
> had caused.
> Forgive me,
> I misunderstood
> your anguished
> broken heart.

**Invitations.** Children write poems in which they invite someone to a magical, beautiful place full of sounds and colors and where all kinds of marvelous things happen; the model is Shakespeare's "Come Unto These Yellow Sands" (Koch, 1990). A seventh grader wrote this invitation poem, "The Golden Shore":

> Come unto the golden shore
> Where days are filled with laughter,
> And nights filled with whispering winds.
> Where sunflowers and sun
> Are filled with love.
> Come take my hand
> As we walk into the sun.

**"If I Were in Charge of the World."** Children write poems in which they describe what they would do if they were in charge of the world; Judith Viorst's poem "If I Were in Charge of the World" (1981) is the model. Children are eager to share ideas about how they would change the world, as this fourth-grade class's collaborative poem illustrates:

> If I were in charge of the world
> School would be for one month,
> Movies and videogames would be free, and
> Foods would be McCalorieless at McDonalds.
> Poor people would have a home,
> Bubble gum would cost a penny, and
> Kids would have cars to drive.
> Parents wouldn't argue,
> Christmas would be in July and December, and
> We would never have bedtimes.
> A kid would be president,
> I'd meet my long lost cousin, and
> Candybars would be vegetables.
> I would own the mall,
> People would have as much money as they wanted, and
> There would be no drugs.

**Other Arrangements** Children can arrange poems in other ways, too. Once they have explored a variety of forms and models, they are better prepared to craft less structured poems and use poetic structures effectively.

**Found Poems.** Children collect words and phrases from a book or other text they are reading and then arrange them into lines to make a free-form poem. A sixth grader wrote this poem after reading *Hatchet* (Paulsen, 1987), the story of a boy who survives for months in the wilderness after his plane crashes:

> He was 13.
> Always started with a single word:
> Divorce.
> An ugly word,
> A breaking word, an ugly breaking word.
> A tearing ugly word that meant fights and yelling.
> Secrets.
> Visitation rights.
> A hatchet on his belt.
> His plane.
> The pilot had been sighted.
> He rubbed his shoulder.
> Aches and pains.
> A heart attack.
> The engine droned.
> A survival pack which had emergency supplies.
> Brian Robeson
> Alone.
> Help, p-l-e-a-s-e.

All of these words came from *Hatchet,* but the sixth grader did not plagiarize: He collected the words and phrases and arranged them into lines to create an original poem.

**Poems for Two Voices.** Children write poems to share contrasting viewpoints (Wilson, 1994). They arrange the poem in two columns, side by side on the page, and then one reader (or group) reads the left column while the other reader (or group) reads the right column. Sometimes the poem has words in only one column, but at other times, there are words—either the same words or different words—on the same line in both columns that the readers say simultaneously so that the poem sounds like a musical duet. After reading *Officer Buckle and Gloria* (Rathmann, 1995), a second-grade class wrote this poem for two voices. The voice on the left is Officer Buckle's and the voice on the right is Gloria's:

| | |
|---|---|
| I am Officer Buckle. | I am Gloria, |
| | a police dog in the |
| | K–9. |
| I teach safety tips | I teach safety tips |
| to boys and girls. | to boys and girls. |
| I say, | |
| "Keep your shoelaces tied." | |
| | I do a trick. |
| I say, | |
| "Do not go swimming | |
| during electrical storms." | |
| | I do a trick. |
| I say, | |
| "Stay away from guns." | |
| | I do a trick. |
| Bravo! | Bravo! |
| Everyone claps. | Everyone claps. |
| Do the kids love me? | |
| | Yes, they do. |
| No, the kids love you more. | |
| | The kids love both of us. |
| We're buddies! | We're buddies! |
| Always stick with your buddy. | Always stick with your buddy. |

To read other poems for two voices, check Paul Fleischman's Newbery Medal–winning *Joyful Noise: Poems for Two Voices* (1988), which is a collection of insect poems. And if two voices aren't enough, see Fleischman's *Big Talk: Poems for Four Voices* (2000), written for upper-grade students.

**Instructional Recommendations**
Students often have misconceptions that interfere with their ability to write poems. Many students, for instance, think poems must rhyme, and in their search for rhymes, they create inane verse. It is important that teachers help students develop an understanding of poetry and how poems look on a page as they begin writing poems.

**Introducing Students to Writing Poetry.** One way to introduce students to writing poetry is to read excerpts from

---

**The Writing Process in Action: Poems**

**Prewriting**
Students choose the type of poem they will write and then collect words and images to use in the poem.

**Drafting**
Students write a rough draft of the poem using the words and images they've collected. They experiment with poetic devices to sharpen the effect of their poems.

**Revising**
Students share their poems with classmates and get feedback about how to revise them. In particular, classmates comment on their choice of words and use of poetic devices. Then students use this feedback and their own ideas to revise their drafts.

**Editing**
Students proofread their poems and correct misspelled words. They also decide how they want to arrange the poems and how they will use capital letters and punctuation marks.

**Publishing**
Students sit in the author's chair to read their poems aloud to classmates, or classmates participate in a gallery walk to read the poems themselves.

---

the first chapter of *Anastasia Krupnik* (Lowry, 1979), in which 10-year-old Anastasia, the main character, is excited when her teacher, Mrs. Westvessel, announces that the class will write poems. Anastasia works at home for 8 nights to write a poem. Lowry does an excellent job of describing how poets search long and hard for words to express meaning and the delight that comes when they realize their poems are finished. Then Anastasia and her classmates bring their poems to class to read aloud. One student reads his four-line rhymed verse:

I have a dog whose name is Spot.
He likes to eat and drink a lot.
When I put water in his dish,
He laps it up just like a fish. (p. 10)

Anastasia is not impressed. She knows the child who wrote the poem has a dog named Sputnik, not Spot! But Mrs. Westvessel gives it an A and hangs it on the bulletin board. Soon it is Anastasia's turn, and she is nervous because her poem is very different. She reads her poem about tiny creatures that move about in tidepools at night:

hush hush   the sea-soft night is aswim
with wrinklesquirm creatures
listen (!)
to them   move   smooth   in the moistly dark
here in the      whisperwarm    wet. (pp. 11–12)

In this free-form poem without rhyme or capital letters, Anastasia has created a marvelous word picture with invented words. Regrettably, Mrs. Westvessel has an antiquated view that poems should be about only serious subjects, be composed of rhyming lines, and use conventional capitalization and punc-

## A Comparison Chart Created After Reading *Anastasia Krupnik*

### Rules About Writing Poetry

| Mrs. Westvessel's Rules | Our Rules |
|---|---|
| 1. Poems must rhyme. | 1. Poems do not have to rhyme. |
| 2. The first letter in each line must be capitalized. | 2. The first letter in each line does not have to be capitalized. |
| 3. Each line must start at the left margin. | 3. Poems can take different shapes and be anywhere on a page. |
| 4. Poems must have a certain rhythm. | 4. You can hear the writer's voice in a poem—with or without rhythm. |
| 5. Poems should be written about serious things. | 5. Poems can be about anything—serious or silly things. |
| 6. Poems should be punctuated like other types of writing. | 6. Poems can be punctuated in different ways or not be punctuated at all. |
| 7. Poems are failures if they don't follow these rules. | 7. There are no real rules for poems, and no poem is a failure. |

tuation. She doesn't understand Anastasia's poem and gives her an F because she didn't follow directions.

Although this first chapter presents a depressing picture of teachers and their lack of knowledge about poetry, it is a dramatic introduction about what poetry is and what it is not. After reading excerpts from the chapter, develop a chart with your students comparing what poetry is in Mrs. Westvessel's class and what poetry is in your class.

**Teaching a Poetic Structure.** Teachers follow a three-step approach to teach a poetic structure: They introduce a poetic form, write a class collaboration poem for practice, and then invite students to write poems individually or with partners. The best way to begin is with a minilesson that explains the poetic structure and includes examples of poems incorporating the structure that other children have written.

Once students understand the form and how to use it, they create a class collaboration poem. Teachers follow the writing process as students brainstorm words and phrases, craft the poem and write it on the chalkboard or chart paper, revise and edit the poem, and finally prepare a final copy. This practice step is essential to ensure that students are prepared to write poems on their own.

**Using the Writing Process.** Students use the writing process to draft and refine their poems. The final stage of the writing process is publishing: It's an important step because it brings closure to the writing process, and students are motivated by sharing and by receiving their classmates' approval. In addition, students gather ideas they can use in their own writing as they listen to or read their classmates' poems. Students share their poetry in two ways—by reading it aloud to classmates and by providing written copies of their poems for classmates to read.

The most common way that students share their poems is by reading them aloud from the author's chair. Classmates listen to the poems read aloud and then offer compliments about what they liked—the student's choice of words, topic, use of poetic devices and poetry forms. Another way that students share their poems with classmates is through a read-around, as Mrs. Harris's students did in the Classroom Close-Up at the beginning of Part 5.

Teachers also display copies of students' poems, often accompanied by an illustration, on a wall of the classroom and then have a gallery walk for students to read and respond to the poems. If there isn't enough wall space in the classroom to display the students' work for the gallery walk, teachers can post poems in the hallway or place them on students' desks. Students move from poem to poem and read and respond to them using small self-stick notes that they attach to the edge of a student's paper or on the wall next to the paper. This activity can be completed much more quickly than if each student were to share his or her poem in front of the class. Because classmates will view their work, students are often more motivated than when the teacher will be the only audience.

## A IS FOR AUTHENTIC ASSESSMENT: Using Rubrics to Assess Writing

Rubrics are scoring guides that teachers use to assess students' achievement on writing assignments (Farr & Tone, 1994). These guides usually have 4, 5, or 6 levels, ranging from high to low, and assessment criteria are described at each level. Students receive a copy of the rubric as they begin writing so that they understand what is expected and how they will be assessed. Depending on the rubric's intricacy, teachers mark the assessment criteria either while they're reading students' writing or immediately afterward, and then they determine the overall score for the piece of writing.

The assessment criteria on some rubrics describe general qualities of effective writing, such as ideas, organization, word choice, and mechanics, but in others, they focus on genre components and characteristics. Teachers often use genre-specific rubrics to assess letters, autobiographies, reports, and multigenre projects.

No matter which assessment criteria are used, the same criteria are addressed at each level. If a criterion addresses sentence fluency, for example, descriptors about sentence fluency are included at each level; the statement "contains short, choppy sentences" might be used at the lowest level, and "uses sentences that vary in length and style" at the highest level. Each level represents a one-step improvement in students' application of that criterion.

Rubrics can be constructed with any number of levels, but it's easier to show growth in student writing when the rubric has more levels. Much more improvement is needed for students to move from one level to another if the rubric has 4 levels than if it has 6 levels. A rubric with 10 levels would be even more sensitive to student growth, but rubrics with more levels are harder to construct and more time-consuming to use. Researchers usually recommend that that teachers use rubrics with either 4 or 6 levels so that there is no middle score—each level is either above or below the middle—because teachers are inclined to score students at the middle level, when there is one.

Rubrics are often used for determining proficiency levels and assigning grades. The level that is above the midpoint is usually designated as proficient, competent, or passing—that's a 3 on a 4-point rubric and a 4 on a 5- or 6-point rubric. The levels on a 6-point rubric can be described this way:

1 = minimal level
2 = beginning or limited level
3 = developing level
4 = proficient level
5 = commendable level
6 = exceptional level

Teachers also equate levels to letter grades.

**How to Use Rubrics**

Assessment isn't something that happens after students have finished writing; it begins before students pick up their pencils to draft their compositions and continues through the writing process. As part of prewriting activities, teachers distribute copies of the rubric to students and explain the criteria by which their writing will be assessed. Teachers read the proficiency-level criteria and explain the descriptors. The rubric sets the standard for the writing assignment.

Next, during revising, students use the rubric to self-assess their writing. They examine the quality of their writing according to the descriptive criteria on the rubric and consider whether they have included the required components. Students judge whether their writing is likely to meet the teacher's expectations and how it will score on the rubric. They ask their classmates to offer sug-

## GALLERY WALKS

**1 Display the work**
Students post the work on classroom walls or place it on desks for the gallery walk.

**2 Give directions**
Teachers explain the purpose of the gallery walk, how to view and/or read the work, and what comments to make to classmates. Teachers also set time limits and direct students to visit three, five, eight, or more students' work, if there is not time to read everyone's work.

**3 Model the procedure**
Teachers model how to view, read, and respond during the gallery walk, using one or two students' work as examples.

**4 Provide comment sheets**
Teachers give students small self-stick notes on which to write comments about each student's work. Students attach notes with their comments to the edges of classmates' work.

**5 Direct the flow of traffic**
Teachers direct students as they move around the classroom, making sure that all students' work is viewed, read, and responded to and that comments are supportive and useful.

**6 Conclude the gallery walk**
Teachers ask students to move to their own work and review the responses they have received.

gestions about how to improve their organization, voice, or any criterion they think might be weak. It's also an opportunity for students to conference with their teacher and ask for more clarification about the assignment or the assessment criteria.

After students complete their final copies, teachers assess the compositions by marking the descriptive criteria on the rubric that best describe the composition as they read or immediately afterward. It's rare when descriptors are marked in only one level; they usually range over two or three levels. The overall score is the level where most of the markings are. Then teachers meet with students to talk about the assessment, identify strengths and weaknesses, and set goals for the next writing assignment.

**Commercial Versus Teacher-Made Rubrics**

Many commercially prepared rubrics are currently available for teachers. State departments of education post rubrics for mandated writing tests on their Web sites, and school districts hire teams of teachers or consultants to develop writing rubrics for each grade level. Spandel (2005) has rubrics that assess the six traits of writing. Other rubrics are provided with reading textbook programs, in professional books for teachers, and on the Internet.

Even though commercially prepared rubrics are convenient, they may not be appropriate for some groups of students or for specific writing assignments. They may have only 4 levels when 6 would be better, or they may have been written for a different grade level. They also may not address a specific genre, or they may have been written for teachers, not in kid-friendly language. Because of these limitations, teachers often decide to develop their own rubrics adapt commercial rubrics to meet their own needs.

**How to Develop Your Own Rubric**

Teachers can develop their own rubrics, but it's not as easy as it might seem. Teachers begin by thinking about the assignment and their expectations for students. They decide how many levels to use in the rubric, and then identify the assessment criteria. Next, they examine student samples as they think about the criteria and how to describe performance at each level.

Teachers draw a grid, with one section for each level. They use the information from the student papers and their expectations to write the criteria descriptors at each level. As teachers write and revise the descriptors, they think about whether the descriptors are worded clearly and concisely, whether one descriptor can be differentiated from another, and whether the descriptors represent equal steps from low to high.

Students should participate in making rubrics or in changing the criteria descriptors from teacher to kid-friendly language. As they work rubrics, students become more aware of the characteristics of effective writing and understand the assessment criteria better.

**Why Use Rubrics?**

There are many reasons to recommend rubrics. These scoring guides help students become better writers because they lay out the qualities that constitute excellence and clarify teachers' expectations so students understand how the assignment will be assessed. Students can use rubrics to improve their writing. They can examine their rough drafts and decide how to revise their writing to make it more effective based on the criteria on the rubric. They can also assess their completed compositions and use the results to set goals for their next writing assignment.

Rubrics make teachers' grading valid and reliable. Teachers rely on the criteria enumerated on the rubric, rather than on distractors, such as neatness, to make judgments about writing quality. Also, when teachers use rubrics, the assessments are more consistent from student to student and from one assignment to the next.

In addition, Vicki Spandel (2005) claims that rubrics are time savers. She says that using rubrics drastically reduces the time it takes to read and respond to students' writing because the criteria on the rubric guide the assessment and reduce the need to write lengthy comments back to students.

## RUBRICS

**1 Choose a rubric**
Teachers choose a rubric that is appropriate to the writing activity or create one that reflects the assignment.

**2 Introduce the rubric**
Teachers distribute copies to students and talk about the criteria used at each level, focusing on the requirements at the proficiency level.

**3 Have students self-assess their writing**
Students use the rubric to self-assess their writing as part of the revising stage. They highlight phrases in the rubric or check off items that best describe their writing. Then they determine which level has the most highlighted words or checkmarks; that level is the overall score, and students circle it.

**4 Assess students' writing**
Teachers assess students' writing by highlighting phrases in the rubric or checking off items that best describe the composition. Then they assign the overall score by determining which level has the most highlighted words or checkmarks and circle it.

**5 Conference with students**
Teachers talk with students about the assessment, identifying strengths and weaknesses. Then students set goals for the next writing assignment.

## Rubric for a Multigenre Project

| | |
|---|---|
| 6 | \_\_\_\_ includes five or more genres<br>\_\_\_\_ shows focused, impressive understanding of the topic<br>\_\_\_\_ elaborates the theme in each genre<br>\_\_\_\_ varies the writing style to reflect each genre<br>\_\_\_\_ has almost no mechanical errors<br>\_\_\_\_ uses an enticing design with four or more graphics that extend the text<br>\_\_\_\_ lists five or more references, including Internet resources, in a bibliography |
| 5 | \_\_\_\_ includes four genres<br>\_\_\_\_ shows in-depth understanding of the topic<br>\_\_\_\_ incorporates the theme in each genre<br>\_\_\_\_ consistently uses a distinctive, engaging writing style<br>\_\_\_\_ has a few mechanical errors<br>\_\_\_\_ uses an eye-catching design with four graphics that extend the text<br>\_\_\_\_ lists four references, including Internet resources, in a bibliography |
| 4 | \_\_\_\_ includes three genres<br>\_\_\_\_ shows clear understanding of the topic<br>\_\_\_\_ incorporates the theme in most genres<br>\_\_\_\_ uses an engaging writing style in some pieces<br>\_\_\_\_ has some mechanical errors that don't interfere with understanding<br>\_\_\_\_ uses an attractive design with three graphics that support the text<br>\_\_\_\_ lists three or four references, including Internet resources, in a bibliography |
| 3 | \_\_\_\_ includes two genres<br>\_\_\_\_ shows incomplete understanding of the topic<br>\_\_\_\_ identifies the theme<br>\_\_\_\_ has an inconsistent writing style<br>\_\_\_\_ has noticeable mechanical errors that may interfere with understanding<br>\_\_\_\_ uses an overall design with two graphics<br>\_\_\_\_ lists two references in a bibliography |
| 2 | \_\_\_\_ includes one genre<br>\_\_\_\_ shows little understanding of the topic<br>\_\_\_\_ doesn't identify the theme<br>\_\_\_\_ has an "encyclopedia-like" writing style<br>\_\_\_\_ overloaded with many mechanical errors that cause confusion<br>\_\_\_\_ includes a title and one graphic<br>\_\_\_\_ lists one reference in a bibliography |
| 1 | \_\_\_\_ includes a brief text<br>\_\_\_\_ shows very little understanding of the topic<br>\_\_\_\_ has no theme<br>\_\_\_\_ lacks awareness of audience<br>\_\_\_\_ difficult to read because of mechanical errors<br>\_\_\_\_ lacks a design but may include one graphic<br>\_\_\_\_ has no bibliography |

# Review

## The Big Ideas

Children discover the power of writing as they learn to use the writing process to craft stories, letters, reports, poems, and other compositions. Teachers teach minilessons on writing strategies, model what capable writers do, share examples of writing from trade books, and provide opportunities for children to write independently.

These big ideas were presented in Part 5:

- ◆ The writing process involves five recursive stages: prewriting, drafting, revising, editing, and publishing.
- ◆ Children use the writing process as they write during literature focus units, writing workshop, and thematic units.
- ◆ Children write in reading logs, learning logs, and other types of journals to develop writing fluency and enhance their comprehension.
- ◆ Young children write using kid writing while they are learning concepts about written language.
- ◆ Children prepare multigenre projects using a combination of reports, stories, poems, photographs and other illustrations, and other materials.
- ◆ Because rhyme is a sticking point for many children, they use poetic formulas and other structures to write poems.
- ◆ Teachers use rubrics to assess children's writing.

## Classroom Inquiry

Writing is an important part of the language arts program. You can examine your students' writing, what they know about writing, and your own instructional approaches. You might want to develop a classroom inquiry to investigate one of these topics.

**The Writing Process**
As students learn to use the writing process, they become more strategic writers, better able to plan, draft, and refine their writing. To examine what your students know about the writing process, think about these questions:

- ◆ How do my students use the writing process?
- ◆ Which writing strategies do I observe them using?
- ◆ How do my students describe the writing process?
- ◆ Do they think the writing process is valuable?

**Genres**
Students learn to write using a variety of genres, including poems, letters, reports, and stories, and they incorporate several genres in multigenre projects. To examine what your students know about genres, consider these questions:

- ◆ How do I teach a genre?
- ◆ Which genres do my students use?
- ◆ How do my students vary the writing process for particular genres?
- ◆ How do my students decide which genre to use?

**Assessing Writing**
Rubrics are effective because they make evaluation more objective. Rubrics also clearly specify the standards against which the writing will be assessed. To examine how you assess writing, ask yourself these questions:

- ◆ How do I assess my students' writing?
- ◆ What do my students know about rubrics?
- ◆ What do my students think about how their writing is assessed?
- ◆ How does my assessment compare with students' own assessment?

# 6 Language Tools

## INTRODUCTION

Words are the building blocks of meaningful language use. No matter whether we're listening, talking, reading, or writing, we're using words to understand and express ideas. Children learn three things about words: what they mean, how to use them in sentences, and how to spell them. This knowledge about vocabulary, grammar, and spelling is crucial for children's academic achievement.

There's a clear relationship between vocabulary knowledge and achievement (Beck, McKeown, & Kucan, 2002). Children who know the words used in academic English (e.g., *furiously, polygon, domesticate*) are more likely to comprehend stories they're reading, solve math story problems, and understand the big ideas in thematic units. Children also learn the grammatical features of words, including verb forms (e.g., *bring–brought*), comparatives and superlatives (e.g., *funny–funnier–funniest*), noun and verb forms (e.g., *apology–apologize*), noun and adjective forms (e.g., *curiosity–curious*) and affixed forms (e.g., *response–responsibility–irresponsible*) to be able to use them appropriately in sentences.

Children learn how words function in sentences as they learn about the parts of speech, and they learn how to combine words into sentences and use punctuation to emphasize their meaning. They also learn about the role of sound, pattern, and meaning in spelling: They learn to sound out words (e.g., *chat, birth*), they learn spelling patterns (e.g., *babies, getting, handle*), and they learn that related words have similar spellings even though they are pronounced differently (e.g., *nation–national*).

## Mr. Martinez Individualizes Spelling Instruction

The 28 students in Mr. Martinez's fourth-grade classroom participate in a 30-minute spelling lesson sandwiched between reading and writing workshop. During this time, the teacher assigns spelling words, and students practice them for the Friday test. Mr. Martinez uses the words from a commercial spelling program, and each week's words focus on a topic—r-controlled vowels or compound words, for example. Mr. Martinez introduces the topic through a series of lessons a week in advance so that his students will understand the topic and be familiar with the words before they study them for the spelling test.

During the first semester, students studied vowel patterns (e.g., *strike, each*), r-controlled vowels (e.g., *first*), diphthongs (e.g., *soil*), more sophisticated consonant spellings (e.g., *edge, catch*), words with silent letters (e.g., *climb*), and homophones (e.g., *one–won*). Now in the second semester, they are learning two-syllable words. They have studied compound words (e.g., *headache*) and words with inflectional suffixes (e.g., *get–getting*), and now the topic is irregular verbs. It's a difficult topic because students need to know the verb forms as well as how to spell the words, so Mr. Martinez is teaching grammar and spelling together.

Because the students' spelling levels range from second to sixth grade, Mr. Martinez has divided them into three groups. Each month, the groups choose new food-related names for themselves. This month, the names are types of pizza; earlier in the year, they chose fruit names, Mexican food names, vegetable names, cookie names, and snack names. Of course, at the end of the month, they sample the foods. Mr. Martinez calls these food names his "secret classroom management tool" because students behave and work hard in order to participate in the tasting.

Students in the Pepperoni Pizza group spell at the second-grade level, and they are studying r-controlled vowels. They have already studied two-letter spelling patterns, and now they are learning three-letter patterns. This week, the focus is on *ear* and *eer* patterns. Students in the Sausage Pizza group are at and almost at grade level; they are reviewing ways to spell /ou/. Students in the Hawaiian Pizza group are above-grade-level spellers; they are studying Latin root words and examining noun and verb forms of these words. This week's focus is /shən/. Mr. Martinez meets with each group twice a week, and each group has a folder of activities to work on between meetings. Some of these group meetings are held during the spelling period (usually on Thursdays), and others are squeezed into reading and writing workshop. The teacher also encourages students to look for words they are studying in the books they're reading and to use them in their writing. They bring their examples to share at these meetings.

Mr. Martinez has compiled a master list of 30 spelling words for this week. Everyone studies the same 12 words—irregular verbs—taken from the spelling textbook plus six additional words related to their small-group work. On the Friday test, they will be asked to spell 15 of the 18 words they've been studying.

The fourth graders are involved in three types of activities during the 30-minute spelling period: Mr. Martinez teaches minilessons on the weekly topic, students study words for the weekly spelling test, and students meet in small-groups to study other spelling topics.

| This Week's Spelling List | | | |
|---|---|---|---|
| All Pizzas | Pepperoni Pizzas | Sausage Pizzas | Hawaiian Pizzas |
| *forget | *year | *smooth | educate |
| *forgot | fear | *group | *education |
| *forgotten | deer | soup | observe |
| *know | beard | *moving | *observation |
| *knew | *cheer | wood | admit |
| *known | *hear | would | *admission |
| *throw | | | |
| *threw | | | |
| *thrown | | | |
| *break | | | |
| *broke | | | |
| *broken | | | |

\* = words on the spelling test

### How can teachers incorporate textbooks into their spelling programs?

Teaching spelling is more than having students memorize a list of words and take a test on Friday. Students need to learn spelling concepts—not just practice words—in order to develop into competent spellers. In addition, a single list of words is usually not appropriate for all students in a class because students' level of spelling development varies. As you read about Mr. Martinez's spelling program, notice how he teaches spelling concepts, incorporates the textbook's weekly lists of spelling words, and takes into account his students' levels of spelling development.

## Mr. Martinez's Schedule

|  |  |  |
|---|---|---|
| Monday | 15 min.<br>15 min. | Introduce the topic for the week<br>Have students take the pretest and self-check it |
| Tuesday | 20 min.<br>10 min. | Teach a lesson on the week's topic<br>Have students practice spelling words |
| Wednesday | 15 min.<br>15 min. | Teach a lesson on the week's topic<br>Have students take the practice test and self-check it |
| Thursday | 20 min.<br>10 min. | Work with small groups on other spelling topics<br>Have students practice spelling words |
| Friday | 10 min.<br>20 min. | Give spelling test<br>Review topic for the week and/or meet with small groups |

This is the fourth week that Mr. Martinez is teaching verbs. During the first week, students brainstormed verbs, and Mr. Martinez listed them on one of four charts: verbs that do not change form (e.g., *set, hurt*), regular verbs (e.g., *walk–walked*), irregular verbs with three forms (e.g., *do–did–done*), and irregular verbs with two forms (e.g., *sell–sold*). The students reviewed verbs that do not change form and regular verbs whose past and past-participle forms are created by adding *-ed*. That week, students were tested on words with inflectional suffixes, the topic taught the previous week. Regular verbs were tested the week after they were taught. For the next 2 weeks, students studied irregular verbs with three forms; because it was a difficult concept for many of the students, Mr. Martinez took 2 weeks to teach it. Students sorted the words into present, past, and past participle columns, practiced spelling the words on white boards, and created posters using the words in sentences. One student chose *eat–ate–eaten* and wrote this paragraph:

> I like to EAT m & ms. They are my favorite candy. I ATE a whole bag of m & ms yesterday. Now I have a stomachache because I have EATEN too much candy.

The students created their posters during writing workshop. They used the writing process to draft and refine their sentences, word processed them, enlarged them to fit their posters, and printed them out. After sharing them during a spelling minilesson, the students displayed them on a wall in the classroom.

This week, the focus changes to irregular verbs with two forms, such as *sleep–slept, leave–left,* and *buy–bought*. On Monday, they review the list of verbs they created several weeks ago. Mr. Martinez observes that students are already familiar with these irregular verbs; the only difficult one is *wind–wound*. The students are familiar with the nouns *wind* and *wound*, but they don't know the verbs *wind* and *wound*. Mr. Martinez explains each word:

> *Wind* (noun; pronounced with a short *i*): air in motion
> *Wind* (verb; pronounced with a long *i*): to coil or wrap something or to take a bending course
> *Wound* (verb—past tense of *wind*; the *ou* is pronounced as in *cow*): having coiled or wrapped something or to have taken a bending course
> *Wound* (noun; the *ou* is pronounced as in *moon*): an injury

He sets out these objects to clarify the words: a small alarm clock to wind, a map showing a road that winds around a mountain, wind chimes to show

## Word Sort of Irregular Verbs With Three Forms

| Present | Past | Past Participle |
|---|---|---|
| forget | forgot | forgotten |
| eat | ate | eaten |
| sing | sang | sung |
| write | wrote | written |
| break | broke | broken |
| throw | threw | thrown |
| forgive | forgave | forgiven |
| grow | grew | grown |

the wind's motion, a skein of yarn to wind, and an elastic bandage to wind around a wound. Students examine each item and talk about how it relates to one or more of the words. Clayton explains the bandage and manages to include all four words:

> OK. Let's say it is a windy day. The wind could blow you over and you could sprain your ankle. I know because it happened to me. A sprain is an injury like a wound but there's no blood. Well, then you get a bandage and you put it around your ankle like this [he demonstrates as he talks]: You wind it around and around to give your ankle some support. Now [he says triumphantly], I have wound the bandage over the wound.

| Irregular Verbs With Two Forms | | | |
|---|---|---|---|
| *sleep–slept | meet–met | *leave–left | *bring–brought |
| shine–shone | fight–fought | *wind–wound | *buy–bought |
| *catch–caught | pay–paid | mean–meant | hang–hung |
| bleed–bled | *teach–taught | creep–crept | *build–built |
| dig–dug | tell–told | *think–thought | sell–sold |
| make–made | keep–kept | *sweep–swept | say–said |

\* = word (past-tense form) on next week's spelling list

On Tuesday, the students play the "I'm thinking of . . . " game to practice the words on the Irregular Verbs With Two Forms chart. They are familiar with the game and eager to play it. Mr. Martinez begins, "I'm thinking of a word where you delete one vowel to change the spelling from present to past tense." The students identify *bleed–bled* and *meet–met*. Next, he says, "I'm thinking of a word where you add one letter to the present-tense verb to spell the past-tense form," and the students identify *mean–meant*.

Then the students take turns being the leader. Simone begins, "I'm thinking of a word where you change one vowel for the past tense." The students identify *dig–dug, hang–hung*, and *shine–shone*. Next, Erika says, "I'm thinking of a word where you change one consonant to make past tense," and the students answer *build–built* and *make–made*. Joey offers, "I'm thinking of a verb where you change the *i* to *ou* to get the past tense." The students identify four pairs: *wind–wound, think–thought, bring–brought*, and *fight–fought*. Then Camille says, "I'm thinking of a verb where you take away an *e* and add a *t* to make the past tense," and the students reply with *keep–kept, sweep–swept, sleep–slept*, and *creep–crept*. The students

continue the game until they have practiced all the verbs.

Today, Mr. Martinez distributes white boards to the class. He says the past-tense form of an irregular verb and students write both the present- and the past-tense forms, without looking at the chart unless they need help: *slept, taught, paid, bought, built,* and *left*. Many of the words he chooses are the ones that will be on next week's spelling list, but he also includes other words from the chart. After they write each pair of words, students hold up their white boards so that Mr. Martinez can check their work; when necessary, he reviews how to form a letter or points out an illegible letter.

After 15 minutes of practice, the students return to their desks to take the practice test on this week's words. Mr. Martinez reads the list aloud while the students write using blue pens, and then he places a transparency of the words on the overhead projector so students can check their own tests. The students put away their blue pens and get out red pens to check their papers, so cheating is rarely a problem. Mr. Martinez walks around the classroom to monitor students' progress.

As you continue reading Part 6, think about how Mr. Martinez incorporates the topics being presented. Here are three questions to guide your reading:

- Which grammar concepts did Mr. Martinez teach as part of spelling lessons?
- How could Mr. Martinez use the same activities to teach vocabulary?
- How well does the developmental stage represented by the words on the weekly spelling test match Mr. Martinez's students' levels of spelling development?

# Essentials

## ESSENTIAL #1: Grammar Concepts

Teachers teach these five types of information about grammar: parts of speech, parts of sentences, types of sentences, capitalization and punctuation, and usage.

**Parts of Speech**

Grammarians have sorted English words into eight groups called parts of speech: nouns, pronouns, verbs, adjectives, adverbs, prepositions, conjunctions, and interjections. Words in each group are used in essentially the same way in all sentences. Nouns and verbs are the basic building blocks of sentences. Nouns are words that name a person, a place, or a thing; concepts, such as love, also are nouns. Pronouns substitute for nouns. Verbs are words that show action or link a subject to

another word in the sentence. Adjectives, adverbs, and prepositions build on and modify the nouns and verbs. Adjectives are words that describe a noun or a pronoun, and adverbs describe a verb, an adjective, or another adverb. Prepositions are words that show position or direction, or how words are related to each other. They introduce prepositional phrases.

The last two parts of speech are conjunctions and interjections. Conjunctions connect individual words, groups of words, and sentences, and interjections express strong emotion or surprise. They are set off with exclamation points or commas.

**Parts of a Sentence**

A sentence is composed of one or more words to express a complete thought; to express the thought, it must have a subject and a predicate. The subject names who or

## The Eight Parts of Speech

| Part of Speech | Definition | Examples |
|---|---|---|
| Noun | A word used to name something—a person, a place, or a thing. A proper noun names a particular person, place, or thing and is capitalized; a common noun does not name a particular person, place, or thing and is not capitalized. | Abraham Lincoln<br>United States<br>Kleenex<br>city |
| Pronoun | A word used in place of a noun. | I<br>me<br>who |
| Adjective | A word used to describe a noun or a pronoun. Adjectives can be common or proper; proper adjectives are capitalized. Some words can be either adjectives or pronouns; they are adjectives if they come before a noun and modify it, and they are pronouns if they stand alone. | the<br>American<br>fastest<br>slippery-fingered<br>better |
| Verb | A word used to show action or state of being. A verb's form varies depending on its number (singular or plural) and tense (present, past, future). Some verbs are helping verbs; they help to form some tenses. | eat–ate–eaten<br>is, are, were<br>have, will, can |
| Adverb | A word used to modify a verb, an adjective, or another adverb. An adverb tells how, when, where, why, how often, and how much. | quickly<br>now<br>outside<br>well |
| Preposition | A word or group of words used to show position, direction, or how two words or ideas are related to each other. | at<br>with<br>to<br>between |
| Conjunction | A word used to connect words and groups of words. Three types: coordinating conjunctions, which connect equivalent words, phrases, or clauses; correlative conjunctions, which are used in pairs; and subordinating conjunctions, which connect two clauses that are not equally important. | and<br>but<br>or<br>either–or<br>because<br>when |
| Interjection | A word or phrase used to express strong emotion, set off by commas or an exclamation point. | Wow!<br>Cool, dude! |

what the sentence is about, and the predicate contains the verb and anything that completes or modifies it. In a simple sentence with one subject and one predicate, everything that is not part of the subject is part of the predicate.

**Types of Sentences** Sentences are classified in two ways. First, they are classified according to structure, or how they are put together. The structure of a sentence can be simple, compound, complex, or compound-complex, according to the number and type of clauses. A clause consists of a subject and a predicate, and there are two types of clauses. If the clause presents a complete thought and can stand alone as a sentence, it is an independent clause. If the clause is not a complete thought and cannot stand alone as a sentence, it is a dependent clause—it depends on the meaning expressed in the independent clause.

A simple sentence contains only one independent clause, and a compound sentence is made up of two or more independent clauses. A complex sentence contains one independent clause and one or more dependent clauses. A compound-complex sentence contains two or more independent clauses and one or more dependent clauses. For example:

Simple: We're having a barbecue.
Compound: We're having a barbecue, and my grandpa is coming.
Complex: We're having a barbecue because my dad bought a new grill.
Compound-Complex: We're having a barbecue because my dad bought a new grill, and my grandpa is coming.

Second, sentences are classified according to their purpose or the type of message they contain: Sentences that make statements are declarative, those that ask questions are interrogative, those that make commands are imperative, and those that communicate strong emotion or surprise are exclamatory. The purpose of a sentence is often signaled by the punctuation mark placed at the end of the sentence: Declarative sentences and some imperative sentences are marked with periods, interrogative sentences are marked with question marks, and exclamatory sentences and some imperative sentences are marked with exclamation points.

**Capitalization and Punctuation** Children learn that capital letters divide sentences and signal important words within sentences (Fearn & Farnan, 1998). Consider how the use of capital letters affects the meaning of these three sentences:

They were going to the white house for dinner.

They were going to the White house for dinner.

They were going to the White House for dinner. (Wilde, 1993, p. 18)

Capital letters also express loudness of speech or intensity of emotion because they stand out visually.

Children often begin writing during the preschool years using only capital letters; during kindergarten and first grade, they learn the lowercase forms of letters. They learn to capitalize *I*, the first word in a sentence, and names and other proper nouns and adjectives. The most common problem for older children is overcapitalization, or capitalizing too many words in a sentence. This problem tends to persist into adulthood because students have trouble differentiating between common and proper nouns (Shaughnessy, 1977). Too often, students assume that important words in the sentence should be capitalized.

It's a common assumption that punctuation marks signal pauses in speech, but punctuation plays a greater role than that, according to Sandra Wilde (1993). Punctuation marks both signal grammatical boundaries and express meaning. Some punctuation marks indicate sentence boundaries; periods, question marks, and exclamation points mark sentence boundaries and indicate whether a sentence makes a statement, asks a question, or expresses an exclamation. In contrast, commas, semicolons, and colons mark grammatical units within sentences.

Quotation marks and apostrophes express meaning within sentences. Quotation marks are used most often to indicate what someone is saying in dialogue, but a more sophisticated use is to express irony, as in *My son "loves" to wash the dishes.* Apostrophes are used in contractions to join two words and in

possessive nouns to show relationships. Consider the different meanings of these phrases:

The monkey's howling (and it's running around the cage).

The monkey's howling (annoyed us; we wanted to kill it).

The monkeys' howling (annoyed us; we wanted to kill them).

(We listened all night to) the monkeys howling. (Wilde, 1993, p. 18)

Researchers have documented that learning to use punctuation is a developmental process. Beginning in the preschool years, children notice punctuation marks and learn to distinguish them from letters (Clay, 1991). In kindergarten and first grade, children are formally introduced to the end-of-sentence punctuation marks, which they learn to use conventionally about half the time (Cordeiro, Giacobbe, & Cazden, 1983). Many beginning writers use punctuation marks in more idiosyncratic ways, such as between words and at the end of each line of writing, but over time, children's usage becomes more conventional. Edelsky (1983) looked at first- through third-grade bilingual writers and found similar developmental patterns for English learners.

Students do learn to use punctuation marks correctly, and an important component is helping them discover how punctuation helps to clarify meaning. Angelillo (2002) suggests that to learn punctuation, students need to read and write every day and receive direct instruction.

## ESSENTIAL #2: Stages of Spelling Development

Based on Charles Read's (1975) seminal work, researchers began to systematically study how children learn to spell. After examining students' spelling errors and determining that their errors reflected their knowledge of English orthography, Bear, Invernizzi, Templeton, and Johnston (2004) identified five stages of spelling development that students move through as they learn to read and write. As they continued to study students' spelling development, Bear and his colleagues also noticed three principles of English orthography that children master as they move through the five stages of spelling development:

- **The Alphabetic Principle:** Letters represent sounds.
- **The Pattern Principle:** Letters are combined in predictable ways to spell sounds.
- **The Meaning Principle:** Related words have similar spellings even when they are pronounced differently.

Young children focus on the alphabetic principle as they learn to represent sounds with letters. They pronounce words and record letters to represent the sounds they hear, spelling *are* as *r* and *bed* as *bad,* for example.

Children learn the pattern principle next, as they study phonics. They learn to spell consonant and vowel patterns. They learn to spell the /k/ at the end of short-vowel words with *ck* so that they spell *luck* correctly, not as *luk*, and they learn the CVCe pattern, as in *shine*. They also learn the pattern for adding inflectional suffixes, so that they spell the plural of *baby* as *babies*, not *babys*.

## The Stages of Spelling Development

| Stage | Description | What Children Learn |
|---|---|---|
| Emergent Spelling | Children string letters and letterlike forms together without associating the marks they make with specific phonemes. Ages 3–5. | • the difference between writing and drawing<br>• the left-to-right progression of text<br>• some letter–sound matches<br>• to print letters |
| Letter-Name Spelling | Children apply the alphabetic principle as they use letters to represent phonemes in words. They learn consonant blends and digraphs and short vowels. Ages 5–7. | • the alphabetic principle<br>• short-vowel sounds<br>• consonant sounds<br>• consonant blends and digraphs |
| Within-Word Spelling | Students learn long-vowel patterns and *r*-controlled vowels but may confuse spelling patterns and reverse the order of letters in words. Ages 7–9. | • long-vowel spelling patterns<br>• complex consonant patterns<br>• *r*-controlled vowels<br>• diphthongs |
| Syllables and Affixes Spelling | Students continue to examine spelling patterns as they spell multisyllabic words. They also add inflectional endings and use apostrophes in contractions and possessives. Ages 9–11. | • inflectional endings<br>• syllabication<br>• possessives<br>• contractions |
| Derivational Relations Spelling | Students focus on the meaning principle and learn that words with related meanings are often related in spelling despite changes in sound. They also learn Latin and Greek root words and affixes. Ages 11–14. | • consonant and vowel alternations<br>• Greek affixes and root words<br>• Latin affixes and root words<br>• etymologies |

The third principle is meaning; students learn, for example, that the words *oppose* and *opposition* are related in both spelling and meaning. Once students understand this principle, they are less confused by irregular spellings (e.g., *sign*) because they don't expect words to be phonetically regular.

### Stage 1: Emergent Spelling

Emergent spelling represents children's natural, early expression of writing. They often scribble and make marks randomly across the page. Some emergent spellers have a large repertoire of letter forms to use in writing, but others repeat a small number of letters or letterlike forms over and over. Children typically use uppercase letters. Toward the end of this stage, children begin to notice that letters represent sounds in words and spell the beginning sound correctly. Example: M (*monkey*). This stage is typical of preschoolers, ages 3 to 5.

### Stage 2: Letter-Name Spelling

Children learn the alphabetic principle as they use letters to represent phonemes. At the beginning of this stage, their spellings are quite abbreviated and represent only the most prominent features in words. Then as they learn consonant sounds, including blends and digraphs and short-vowel sounds, their spellings become more conventional with beginning, middle, and ending sounds being represented in their spellings. Examples: DA (*day*), KLOZ (*closed*), BAD (*bed*), and CLEN (*clean*). These spellers slowly pronounce words they want to write, listening for familiar letter names and sounds, and they write letters to represent the sounds they hear without consideration of English spelling patterns. Letter-name spellers are 5- to 7-year-olds.

### Stage 3: Within-Word Spelling

Children focus on both letter-sound combinations and spelling patterns as they learn how to use long-vowel patterns, diphthongs and the less common vowel patterns, and *r*-controlled vowels. Examples: LIEV (*live*), SOPE (*soap*), HUOSE (*house*), and BERN (*burn*). Students experiment with long-vowel patterns and learn that words such as *come* and *bread* are exceptions that do not fit the vowel patterns. Children may confuse spelling patterns and spell *meet* as METE, and they reverse the order of letters, such as FORM for *from* and GRIL for *girl*. Students also learn about complex consonant sounds, including -*tch* (*match*) and -*dge* (*judge*), and they learn about diphthongs (*oi/oy*) and other less common vowel patterns, including *au* (*caught*), *aw* (*saw*), *ew* (*sew, few*), *ou* (*house*), and *ow* (*cow*). Students also notice homophones and compare long- and short-vowel combinations (e.g., *hop–hope*) as they experiment with vowel patterns. Spellers at this stage are typically 7- to 9-year-olds.

<table>
<tr><td>

**Stage 4: Syllables and Affixes Spelling**

</td><td>

Students apply what they have learned about one-syllable words to spell multisyllabic words, and they learn how to add inflectional endings (*-s, -es, -ed,* and *-ing*). The focus is on patterns as students learn to spell longer words. They also learn about

</td></tr>
</table>

compound words, possessives, and contractions. Examples: EAGUL (*eagle*), MONY (*money*), GETING (*getting*), BABYIES (*babies*), CA'NT (*can't*), and BE CAUSE (*because*). As these examples show, many of the errors that students make are at the point where two syllables come together. Spellers in this stage are generally 9- to 11-year-olds.

<table>
<tr><td>

**Stage 5: Derivational Relations Spelling**

</td><td>

Students' focus is on meaning as they learn that words with related meanings are often spelled in similar ways even though vowel and consonant sounds are pronounced differently (e.g., *wise–wisdom*). An example of

</td></tr>
</table>

a vowel alternation is *explain–explanation*, and a consonant alternation is *magic–magician*. Students' spelling errors often result from spelling words by how they sound rather than thinking about related words. Examples: CRITASIZE (*criticize*), APPEARENCE (*appearance*), and COMMITTE or COMMITEE (*committee*). Students also learn about Greek and Latin root words and affixes, and they begin to examine etymologies and the role of history in shaping how words are spelled. They learn about eponyms (words from people's names), such as *maverick* and *sandwich*. Spellers at this stage are 11- to 14-year-olds.

# Strategies

Children use many of the same strategies for vocabulary, grammar, and spelling that they use for listening, talking, reading, writing, viewing, and visually representing, but they use them to focus on words and sentences. Because words and sentences are the building blocks of language arts, it's critical that students become strategic in learning vocabulary words, using standard English grammar, and spelling words conventionally.

## Vocabulary Strategies

Vocabulary strategies, according to Baumann and Kame'enui (2004), promote independence when students are learning unfamiliar words. Students activate their background knowledge about the topic to unlock word meanings. They predict the meaning of words, based on context and what they know about root words and affixes.

Most words have more than one meaning, and students learn to choose among multiple meanings. They realize that when a word doesn't make sense in a sentence, it might be because the word has more than one meaning.

Students also use classroom resources—dictionaries, thesauruses, word walls, classmates, and the teacher—when they don't understand the meaning of a word. As they use these strategies, students develop word consciousness, a positive attitude about vocabulary that's necessary for independent word learning (Scott & Nagy, 2004).

## Grammar Strategies

Grammar is more than knowing the rules of Standard English; it's also knowing how to use Standard English to construct effective sentences. Two of the strategies that students use to craft more sophisticated sentences are combining and expanding sentences. As they use these strategies, they rearrange words in sentences and delete any unnecessary words. Punctuation also plays a role in constructing effective sentences: Students add commas to make their writing easier to read, and they use semicolons and colons to indicate relationships among ideas.

Students use proofreading to catch nonstandard forms and other grammatical errors in their writing. For example, when they're proofreading, students check for subject-verb agreement, verb tenses, objective-case pronouns in prepositional phrases, and double negatives. They also check for sentence fragments and run-on sentences. If they locate any errors, they correct them.

### Strategies Students Use in Language Activities

| Vocabulary | Grammar | Spelling |
|---|---|---|
| • activate background knowledge | • combine sentences | • "sound-it-out" |
| • predict | • expand sentences | • "think-it-out" |
| • choose among multiple meanings | • punctuate to clarify meaning | • proofread |
| • use resources | • proofread | • use resources |

## Spelling Strategies

Students use strategies to spell unfamiliar words (Laminack & Wood, 1996). Novice spellers often use a "sound-it-out" strategy for spelling, but because English isn't a completely phonetic language, this strategy is only somewhat effective. Students identify many of the sounds they hear in a word, but they can't spell unpronounced letters or spelling patterns (e.g., SIK–*sick*, BABES–*babies*). The "think-it-out" strategy is much more effective. Students who have more knowledge about spelling sound the word out and then think about what they know about English spelling patterns and meaning relationships among words to create a more conventional spelling. Specifically, they

- Break the word into syllables
- Sound out each syllable
- Add affixes to root words
- Look at the word to see if it looks correct
- Generate possible spellings based on spelling patterns and meaning relationships if the word doesn't look correct
- Choose the best alternative

Students also use other spelling strategies: They learn to proofread to identify and correct spelling errors in their writing. They also learn two ways to find the correct spelling of a word: First, they locate words they want to spell on word walls and other charts in the classroom; and second, they find the spelling of unfamiliar words in a dictionary.

> "Novice spellers often use a 'sound-it-out' strategy for spelling, but because English isn't a completely phonetic language, this strategy is only somewhat effective. . . . The 'think-it-out' strategy is much more effective."

# MINILESSON
## *Combining Sentences*

### Mrs. Reeves's Third Graders Learn to Combine Sentences

1. **Introduce the topic**   Mrs. Reeves makes a transparency of this paragraph and shares it with her third-grade class:

   *Recess is good. It is the best time of the day. I like to run. I like to kick the ball. It is fun. I like to play ball games like soccer. I like to play hard. I like to win. I dream of being on the winning team. I wish recess was longer. I wish it was two hours long.*

   She explains that this paragraph is like many of the paragraphs her students write. She asks them to tell her what is good about the paragraph and what they think should be changed. That the paragraph sticks to one topic is a plus, but the students agree that the "I like" sentences are repetitive and boring.

2. **Share examples**   Mrs. Reeves explains that they can revise the paragraph by putting some of the sentences together to make it more interesting. Here is their revision:

   *Recess is the best time of the day. I like to play ball games like soccer. Running and kicking are fun. I like to play hard and win. I dream of being on the winning team. I wish recess was two hours long.*

3. **Provide information**   Mrs. Reeves explains to students that what they did is called *sentence combining*. They can combine sentences to make them more interesting and reword them to vary the words they use.

4. **Supervise practice**   Mrs. Reeves divides the class into small groups and gives each group another paragraph to revise. She circulates as students work and provides assistance as needed. After they revise their sentences, students in each group share their revised paragraphs.

5. **Assess learning**   Mrs. Reeves asks the students to reread the paragraphs she gave them and their revised paragraphs. She asks, "Which ones are better?" The students conclude that their revised paragraphs are better because the sentences are not as repetitive and boring.

# MINILESSON

## Mrs. Hamilton Teaches the "Think It Out" Strategy to Her Second Graders

1. **Introduce the topic**  Mrs. Hamilton asks her second graders how to spell the word *because,* and they suggest these options: *beecuz, becauz, becuse,* and *becuzz.* She asks the students to explain their spellings. Aaron explains that he sounded the word out and heard *bee* and *cuz.* Molly explains that she knows there is no *z* in *because* so she spelled it *becuse.* Other students explain that they say the word slowly, listening for all the sounds, and then write the sounds they hear. Mrs. Hamilton explains that this is a good first-grade strategy, but now she is going to teach them an even more important second-grade strategy called "think it out."

2. **Share examples**  Mrs. Hamilton asks students to observe as she spells the word *make.* She says the word slowly and writes *mak* on the chalkboard. Then she explains, "I sounded the word out and wrote the sounds I heard, but I don't think the word is spelled right because it looks funny." The children agree and eagerly raise their hands to supply the right answer. "No," she says, "I want to 'think it out.' Let's see. Hmmm. Well, there are vowel rules. The *a* is long, so I could add an *e*

at the end of the word." The students clap, happy that she has figured out the spelling of the word. She models the process two more times, spelling *great* and *running.*

3. **Provide information**  Mrs. Hamilton shares a chart she has made with the steps in the "think it out" strategy:

   1. Sound the word out and spell it the best you can.
   2. Think about spelling rules to add.
   3. Look at the word to see if it looks right.
   4. If it doesn't look right, try changing some letters, asking for help, or checking the dictionary.

   The students talk about how Mrs. Hamilton used this strategy to spell *make, great,* and *running.*

4. **Supervise practice**  Mrs. Hamilton passes out white boards and dry-erase pens for the students to use as they practice the strategy. The students use the "think it out" strategy to write *time, what, walked, taking, bread,* and *people.* As they move through each step, they hold up their white boards to show Mrs. Hamilton their work.

5. **Assess learning**  Mrs. Hamilton ends the minilesson by asking students what they learned, and they explain that they learned the grown-up way to spell words. They explain the steps this way: First they sound it out, then they look it out, and then they think it out.

# Classroom Practice

## The Story of English

English is a historical language, which accounts for word meanings and some spelling inconsistencies (Tompkins & Yaden, 1986). English has a variety of words for a single concept, and the history of English in general and the etymology of the words in particular explain many apparent duplications. Consider these words related to water: *aquatic, hydrant, aquamarine, waterfall, hydroelectric, watercress, watery, aquarium, waterproof, hydraulic, aqualung,* and *hydrogen.* These words have one of three root words, each meaning "water": *water* is English, of course, *aqua* is Latin, and *hydro* is Greek. The root word used depends on the people who created the word, the purpose of the word, and when the word entered English.

The development of the English language is divided into three periods: Old English, Middle English, and Modern English. The beginning and end of each period are marked by a significant event—an invasion or an invention.

**The Old English Period**  The recorded history of the English language begins in A.D. 449, when Germanic tribes, including the Angles and the Saxons, invaded Britain. The invaders pushed the original inhabitants, the Celts, to the northern and western corners of the island; this annexation is romanticized in the King Arthur legends. Arthur is believed to have been a Celtic military leader who fought bravely against the Germanic invaders.

The English language began as an intermingling of the dialects spoken by the Angles, the Saxons, and other Germanic tribes who arrived in Britain. Many people assume that English is based on Latin, but it has Germanic roots and was brought to Britain by these invaders. Although 85% of Old English words are no longer used, many everyday words remain (e.g., *child, foot, hand, house, man, mother, old,* and *sun*). In contrast to Modern English, Old English had few loan words (words borrowed from other languages and incorporated into English) and had a highly developed inflectional system for indicating number, gender, and verb tense. The Anglo-Saxons added affixes to existing words, including *be-, for-, -ly, -dom,* and *-hood.* They also invented vividly descriptive compound words. The Old English word for "music," for example, was *ear-sport;* the word for "world" was *age of man;* and the word for "folly" was *wanwit.* The folk epic *Beowulf,* the great literary work of the period, illustrates the poetic use of words; for instance, the sea is described as a "whale-path" and a "swan's road."

Foreign words, from the Romans and the Vikings, made their way into the predominantly Germanic word stock. Contact between the Roman soldiers and traders and the Germanic tribes on the continent, before they invaded England, contributed some words, including *cheese, copper, mile, street,* and *wine.* The missionaries who reintroduced Christianity to Britain in 597 also brought many religious words (e.g., *angel, candle, hymn*).

In 787, the Vikings from Scandinavia began raiding English villages, and for the next 3 centuries, they attacked and occupied much of England. Their influence was so great that the Danish king Canute ruled England during the first part of the 11th century. The Vikings' contributions to the English language were significant: They provided the pronouns *they, their, them;* introduced the /g/ and /k/ sounds (e.g., *get, kid*); contributed most of our *sk-* words (e.g., *skin, sky*) and some of our *sc-* words (e.g., *scalp, score*); and enriched our vocabulary with more than 500 everyday words, including *husband* and *window.*

In Old English, some consonant combinations that are not heard today were pronounced, including the /k/ in words such as *knee.* The pronunciation of the vowel sounds was different, too; for example, during the Old English period, our word *stone* was spelled *stan,* and the vowel was pronounced like the *a* in *father.*

The structure, spelling, and pronunciation of Old English were significantly different from those of Modern English, so much so that we would not be able to read an Old English text or understand someone speaking Old English. The arrangement of words in sentences was different, too, with verbs often placed at the end of sentences. In many ways, Old English was more like Modern German than Modern English.

## What are homonyms?

Homonyms, words that have sound and spelling similarities, are divided into three categories: homophones, homographs, and homographic homophones. Homophones are words that sound alike but are spelled differently. Most homophones developed from different root words, and it is only by accident that they have come to sound alike. For example, the homophones *right* and *write* entered English before the year 900 and were pronounced differently. *Right* was spelled *riht* in Old English; during Middle English, the spelling was changed by French scribes to the current spelling. The verb *write* was spelled *writan* in Old English and *writen* in Middle English. *Write* is an irregular verb, suggesting its Old English heritage, and the *w* was pronounced hundreds of years ago. In contrast, a few words were derived from the same root words, such as *flea–flee, flower–flour,* and *stationary–stationery,* and the similar spellings were retained to demonstrate the semantic relationships.

Homographs are words that are spelled the same but pronounced differently; examples of homographs are *bow, close, lead, minute, record, read,* and *wind. Bow* is a homograph that has three unrelated meanings. The verb form, meaning "to bend in respect," was spelled *bugan* in Old English; the noun form, meaning "a gathering of ribbon" or "a weapon for propelling an arrow," is of Old English origin and was spelled *boga.* The other noun form of *bow,* meaning "forward end of a ship," is German and entered English in the 1600s.

Homographic homophones are words that are spelled and pronounced alike, such as *bark, bat, bill, box, fair, fly, hide, mine, pen, ring, row, spell, toast,* and *yard.* Some are related words; others are linguistic accidents. The meanings of *toast,* for example, came from the same Latin source word, *torrere,* meaning "to parch." The derivation of the noun *toast* as heated and browned slices of bread is obvious. However, the relationship between the source word and *toast* as a verb, "drinking to someone's honor or health," is not immediately apparent; the connection is that toasted bread was used to flavor the drinks used in toasts. In contrast, *bat* is a linguistic accident: *Bat* as a cudgel comes from the Old English word *batt;* the verb *bat* is derived from the Old French word *batre;* and the nocturnal *bat* derives its name from an unknown Viking word and was spelled *bakke* in Middle English. Not only do the three forms of *bat* have unrelated etymologies, but they were borrowed from three languages!

## The Middle English Period

An event occurred in 1066 that changed the course of the English language and ushered in the Middle English period: the Norman Conquest. In that year, William of Normandy crossed the English Channel and defeated the English king, Harold, at the Battle of Hastings. William claimed the English throne and established a French court in London. For nearly 300 years, French was the official language in England, spoken by the nobility and upper classes, although the lower classes continued to speak English. By 1300, the use of French had declined, and before the end of the 14th century, English was restored as the official language. Chaucer's *Canterbury Tales,* written in the late 1300s, provides evidence that English was also replacing French as the preferred written language. Political, social, and economic changes contributed to this reversal.

A large portion of the Old English vocabulary was lost as 10,000 French words were added to the

## Why do words have more than one meaning?

Many, many English words have more than one meaning. Sometimes the meanings are related and come from the same word, but at other times, the meanings come from different words and are unrelated. Consider these 10 uses of the word *break*:

- break a leg (V)
- break the law (V)
- break into a house (V)
- break a five-dollar bill (V)

- break a wild horse (V)
- break his fall (V)
- break for lunch (V)

- break the news (V)
- take a break (N)
- a lucky break (N)

Both the noun and verb forms are related in meaning, and they all come from the same Old English word, *brecan*. Other words use *break*, too, including *breakdown, breakfast, breakneck,* and *breakthrough.*

Now consider these meanings of *scale*:

- a machine for weighing (N)
- the small plates covering a fish's body (N)

- musical tones going up or down in pitch (N)
- to climb (V)

Only the last two seem related, so it shouldn't surprise you that these meanings came from three unrelated words that happen to have sound similarities. During the Old English period, the Vikings contributed the word *skal,* meaning "bowl," which evolved into our word for a weighing machine. The French word *escale,* meaning "shell," became our word for the plates covering a fish's body during the Middle English period. The last two meanings come from the Latin word *scalae,* meaning "ladder," which also entered our language during Middle English. That these three words with distinctly different meanings are pronounced and spelled the same way is a linguistic accident.

language, reflecting the Norman impact on English life and society (Baugh & Cable, 2002); they included military words (e.g., *soldier, victory*), political words (e.g., *government, princess*), medical words (e.g., *physician, surgeon*), and words related to the arts (e.g., *comedy, music, poet*). Many of the new French words duplicated Old English words. Typically, one word was eventually lost; often, it was the Old English word that disappeared. If both words remained in the language, they developed slightly different meanings, and we consider them synonyms today. Compare these pairs of synonyms: *end–finish, clothing–garments, forgive–pardon, buy–purchase,*

*deadly–mortal.* The first word in each pair comes from Old English; the second was borrowed from the Normans. The Old English words are more basic, and the French words are more sophisticated. Perhaps that is why both words in each pair have survived—they express slightly different ideas.

During this period, there was a significant reduction in the use of inflections, or word endings. Many irregular verbs were lost, and others developed regular past and past-participle forms (e.g., *climb, talk*), although Modern English still retains some irregular verbs (e.g., *sing, fly, be, have*) that contribute to usage problems. By 1000, *-s* had become the accepted plural marker, although the Old English plural form *-en* was used in some words. This artifact remains in a few plurals, such as *children.*

**The Modern English Period** William Caxton's introduction of the printing press in England marked the beginning of the Modern English period. The printing press was a powerful force in standardizing English spelling, as well as a practical means for providing people with books. Until the invention of the printing press, English spelling kept pace with pronunciation, but the printing press standardized spelling, and the lag between pronunciation and spelling began to widen.

The tremendous increase in travel to many parts of the world resulted in a wide borrowing of words from more than 50 languages (Tompkins & Yaden, 1986, p. 31):

## A Word With Multiple Meanings

scale

This is a scale.

A Fish has scales.

I can scale a Wall!

African (many languages): *banjo, cola, gumbo, safari, zombie*
Arabic: *alcohol, apricot, assassin, magazine*
Chinese: *chop suey, kowtow, tea, wok*
Dutch: *caboose, easel, pickle, waffle*
Eskimo: *igloo, parka*
French: *ballet, beige, chauffeur*
German: *kindergarten, poodle, pretzel, waltz*
Greek: *atom, cyclone, hydrogen*
Hawaiian: *aloha, hula, lei, luau*
Hebrew: *cherub, kosher, rabbi*
Hindi: *dungaree, juggernaut, jungle, shampoo*
Italian: *broccoli, carnival, macaroni, opera, pizza*
Japanese: *honcho, judo, kimono, origami*
Persian: *bazaar, divan, khaki, shawl*
Portuguese: *cobra, coconut, molasses*
Spanish: *alligator, guitar, mosquito, potato*
Turkish: *caviar, horde, khan, kiosk, yogurt*
Yiddish: *bagel, chutzpah, pastrami*

Many Latin and Greek words were added to English during the Renaissance to increase the language's prestige; for example, *congratulate, democracy,* and *education* came from Latin, and *catastrophe, encyclopedia,* and *thermometer* from Greek. Many modern Latin and Greek borrowings are scientific words (e.g., *aspirin, vaccinate*), and some of the very recently borrowed forms (e.g., *criterion, focus*) have retained their native plural forms, adding confusion about how to spell these forms in English. Also, some recent loan words from French have retained their native spellings and pronunciations, such as *hors d'oeuvre* and *cul-de-sac.*

Native Americans have also contributed a number of words to English. The early American colonists encountered many unfamiliar animals, plants, foods, and aspects of Native American life in North America; they borrowed the Native American terms for these things and tried to spell them phonetically. Native American loan words include *chipmunk, hickory, moccasin, moose, muskrat, opossum, raccoon, skunk, toboggan, tomahawk,* and *tepee.*

In addition to the considerable vocabulary expansion during the Modern English period, there was a striking change in the pronunciation of long vowels. This change, known as the Great Vowel Shift, has been characterized as "the most revolutionary and far-reaching sound change during the history of the language" (Alexander, 1962, p. 114). The change was gradual, occurring during the 1500s. Because spelling had become fixed before the shift, the vowel letter symbols no longer corresponded to the sounds. For example, the word *name* had two syllables and rhymed with *comma* during the Middle English period, but during the Great Vowel Shift, the pronunciation of *name* shifted to rhyme with *game* (Hook, 1975).

The Modern English period brought changes in syntax, particularly the disappearance of double negatives and double comparatives and superlatives. Eliminations came about slowly; for instance, Shakespeare still wrote, "the most unkindest cut of all." Also, the practice of using *-er* or *-est* to form comparatives and superlatives in shorter words and *more* or *most* with longer words was not standardized until after Shakespeare's time.

**How Do Words Enter English?**

Perhaps as many as 75% of our words have been borrowed from other languages and incorporated into English. Word borrowing has occurred during every period of language development, beginning when the Angles and Saxons borrowed over 400 words from the Romans. During the eighth and ninth centuries, the Vikings contributed approximately 900 words. The Norman conquerors introduced thousands of French words into English, reflecting every aspect of life; for example, *adventure, fork, juggler,* and *quilt.* Later, during the Renaissance, when scholars translated Greek and Latin classics into English, they borrowed many words from Latin and Greek to enrich the language, including *chaos, encyclopedia, pneumonia,* and *skeleton.*

New words continually appear in English, many of them created to describe new inventions, such as *e-mail* and *blog.* They are created in a variety of ways, including compounding, coining, and clipping. *E-mail,* for example, is clipped, or shortened, from *electronic mail.*

Compounding means combining two existing words to create a new word. *Friendship* and *childhood* are words that the Anglo-Saxons compounded more than a thousand years ago. Recent compoundings include *latchkey children* and *software.* Compound words usually progress through three stages: they begin as separate words (e.g., *ice cream*), then are hyphenated (e.g., *baby-sit*), and finally are written as one word (e.g., *splashdown*). There are many exceptions to this rule, such as the compound words *post office* and *high school,* which have remained separate words.

Creative people have always coined new words. Lewis Carroll, author of *Alice in Wonderland,* is perhaps the best-known inventor of words. He called his new words *portmanteau words* (borrowing from the British word for a suitcase that opens into two halves) because they were created by blending two words into one. His most famous example, *chortle,* a blend of *snort* and *chuckle,* is from the poem "Jabberwocky." Other examples of blended words include *brunch* (*breakfast* + *lunch*), *guesstimate* (*guess* + *estimate*), and *smog* (*smoke* + *fog*).

Clipping is a process of shortening existing words. For example, *bomb* is the shortened form of *bombard,* and *zoo* comes from *zoological park.* Most clipped words are only one syllable and are used in informal conversation.

Authors also create new words, so students should be alert to the possibility of finding a created word when they read stories. For example, the Howes (1979) created *Bunnicula* to name their spooky young rabbit (*bunny* + *Dracula*), and Chris Van Allsburg (1981) invented *Jumanji* to name his adventure game.

**Investigating Word Histories**

The best source of information about word histories is an unabridged dictionary, which provides basic etymological information about words: the language the word was borrowed from, the spelling of the word in that language or the transliteration of the word into the Latin alphabet, and the original meaning of the word. Etymologies are enclosed in brackets and appear at the beginning or the end of an entry. They are written in an abbreviated form to save space, using abbreviations for language names

## Books About Words

Agee, J. (2002). *Palindromania!* New York: Farrar, Straus & Giroux. (And many other books of palindromes.)

Amato, M. (2000). *The word eater.* New York: Scholastic.

Cleary, B. P. (2005). *How much can a bare bear bear: What are homonyms and homophones?* Brookfield, CT: Millbrook.

Clements, A. (1996). *Frindle.* New York: Simon & Schuster.

Fine, E. H. (2004). *Cryptomania! Teleporting into Greek and Latin with the cryptokids.* Berkeley, CA: Tricycle Press.

Frasier, D. (2000). *Miss Alaineus: A vocabulary disaster.* San Diego: Harcourt Brace.

Graham-Barber, L. (1995). *A chartreuse leotard in a magenta limousine: And other words named after people and places.* New York: Hyperion Books.

Gwynne, F. (1970). *The king who rained.* New York: Windmill Books.

Gwynne, F. (1976). *A chocolate moose for dinner.* New York: Windmill Books.

Gwynne, F. (1988). *A little pigeon toad.* New York: Simon & Schuster.

Leedy, L. (2003). *There's a frog in my throat: 440 animal sayings a little bird told me.* New York: Holiday House.

Pulver, R. (2003). *Punctuation takes a vacation.* New York: Holiday House.

*Scholastic dictionary of synonyms, antonyms, and homonyms.* (2001). New York: Scholastic.

Scieszka, J. (2001). *Baloney (Henry P.).* New York: Viking.

Terban, M. (1983). *In a pickle and other funny idioms.* New York: Clarion Books.

Terban, M. (1988). *Guppies in tuxedos: Funny eponyms.* New York: Clarion Books.

Terban, M. (1992). *The dove dove: Funny homograph riddles.* New York: Clarion Books.

Terban, M. (1993). *It figures! Fun figures of speech.* New York: Clarion Books.

Terban, M. (1996). *Scholastic dictionary of idioms.* New York: Scholastic.

such as *Ar* for Arabic and *L* for Latin. Let's look at etymologies for three words derived from very different sources: *king*, *kimono*, and *thermometer*. Each etymology is translated and elaborated, beginning with *king*:

king [bef. 900; ME, OE cyng]

The word *king* is an Old English word originally spelled *cyng*. It was used in English before the year 900. In the Middle English period, the spelling changed to its current form.

Next, let's consider *kimono*:

kimono [1885–1890; < Japn clothing, garb, equiv. to *ki* wear + *mono* thing]

Our word *kimono* comes from Japanese, and it entered English between 1885 and 1890. Kimono means "clothing" or "garb,"

and it is equivalent to the Japanese words *ki*, meaning "wear," and *mono*, meaning "thing."

Finally, we examine *thermometer*:

thermometer [1615–1625; thermo < Gr *thermos*, hot + meter < *metron*, measure]

The first recorded use of the word *thermometer* in English was between 1615 and 1625. Our word was created from two Greek words meaning "hot" and "measure."

Teachers can also research how idioms, such as "spill the beans," "an ace up your sleeve," "pay through the nose," "stick your neck out," and "rain cats and dogs," entered English. When you check Marvin Terban's *Scholastic Dictionary of Idioms: More Than 600 Phrases, Sayings, & Expressions* (1996), you'll find that some sayings are from ancient times, others come from medieval England, and still others are American. "Spill the beans," for instance, dates back to ancient Greece when many men belonged to secret clubs. If someone wanted to join the club, the members took a secret vote to decide whether to admit him. The men voted by placing a white bean (to vote *yes*) or a brown bean (to vote *no*) in a special jar. The club leader would then check the beans, and if all of them were white, the person was admitted to the club. Sometimes during the voting, one member would accidentally (or not so accidentally) knock the jar over, spilling the beans, and the vote would no longer be secret. The Greeks turned this event into a saying that we still use today. Another idiom with a different history but a similar meaning is "let the cat out of the bag."

English is a fascinating language when you look beyond sound-symbol correspondences. Teachers can locate information about words in dictionaries and other books about words and then share the stories with children so that they can appreciate the historical aspects of English.

## Word Smarts

Children's word knowledge plays a critical role in their academic success. Reading comprehension, for instance, depends on vocabulary knowledge: When many of the words are unfamiliar, children are unlikely to grasp the text's meaning. It's not surprising that high-achieving students know many more words than low-achieving students; in fact, researchers report that the vocabularies of high-achieving third graders are equal to the lowest-achieving high school seniors (Beck, McKeown, & Kucan, 2002).

Differences in children's word knowledge are apparent in kindergarten and first grade, and these differences appear to relate to the families' socioeconomic status (SES). Researchers have noticed that children from high SES homes know twice as many words as those from low SES homes (Beck, McKeown, & Kucan, 2002). How does a family's SES contribute to these differences? High SES children's vocabulary is enhanced in these ways:

- ◆ **Background Knowledge.** High SES children participate in a broader array of vocabulary-enriching experiences with their families.

- **Book Experiences.** High SES children are more likely to be read to every day, regularly visit the library and check out books, and have their own collection of books.
- **Parents' Vocabulary Level.** High SES parents use more sophisticated vocabulary when they talk with their children.

One way to demonstrate these differences is by comparing kindergartners' knowledge of color words: Some 5- and 6-year-olds know 25 color words or more, including *silver, magenta, turquoise, navy,* and *tan,* whereas others can't name the eight basic colors.

It's difficult for children with less vocabulary knowledge to catch up with their classmates because high achievers learn more words and they learn them more quickly than lower achievers. High SES children's vocabularies grow at an astonishing rate of 3,000 to 4,000 words a year, whereas low SES children learn words at a much slower rate. By the time children graduate from high school, high-achieving students' vocabularies range from 25,000 to 40,000 words or more.

> **What Does It Mean to "Know" a Word?**

Word knowledge isn't simple. It's not that you either know a word or you don't; instead, there's a continuum of word knowledge, moving from never having seen or heard the word before to knowing it well and being able to use it effectively in a variety of contexts (Allen, 1999). Isabel Beck and her colleagues (2002) suggest that there's a continuum of word knowledge that moves from not knowing a word to knowing it well:

- **No Knowledge.** Students are not familiar with the word.
- **Incidental Knowledge.** Students have seen or heard the word, but they don't know its meaning.
- **Partial Knowledge.** Students know one definition for the word or can use the word in one context.
- **Full Knowledge.** Students have a deep understanding of the word's multiple meanings and are able to use the word effectively in multiple contexts.

It takes time for students to move from having little or no knowledge of a word to full knowledge. During a week's study of a word, for example, students may move from the no knowledge or incidental knowledge level to partial knowledge, but it's unlikely they will reach the full knowledge level. In fact, it may take several years of using the word to develop a rich, decontextualized understanding of the word's meanings and related words.

To reach the full knowledge level, students have developed "ownership" of the word, meaning they know or can do these things:

- Pronounce the word correctly
- Understand the word's multiple meanings
- Use the word appropriately in sentences
- Apply the grammatical features of the word correctly
- Recognize related words (words that come from the same root word)
- Identify synonyms and antonyms

## The Grammatical Features of Words

There's more to learn about a word than its meaning. Many words have related noun, verb, and adjective forms, for example, and others have related forms that incorporate prefixes and suffixes. Here are seven common grammatical features of words:

- Plurals (*match–matches, bacterium–bacteria*)
- Verb tenses (*weep–wept, shrink–shrank–shrunk*)
- Comparative and superlative forms (*brief–briefer–briefest, careless–more careless–most careless*)
- Noun and verb forms (*breath–breathe, organization–organize*)
- Noun and adjective forms (*activity–active*)
- Verb and adjective forms (*regret–regrettable*)
- Affixes (*unexpected, reconsider, dishonest, conductor*)

Not all features pertain to all words, of course, but one or more of the features figure in almost every word students are learning. Consider the grammatical features of *vandalism,* taken from *Hoot,* by Carl Hiaasen (2002):

- Noun: *vandalism, vandals*
- Verb forms: *vandalize, vandalizing, vandalized*
- Adjective: *vandalized*

Or consider *lucky,* from *Kitten's First Full Moon* (Henkes, 2004):

- Noun: *luck*
- Adjective: *lucky*
- Adverb: *luckily*
- Affix: *unlucky*

When teachers introduce these related words, they help students move more quickly toward full word knowledge.

With this knowledge, students will be able to understand the word when they are listening and reading and use it to express ideas in talk and writing.

> **Choosing Words to Teach**

Teachers often feel overwhelmed when they think about all of the unfamiliar words in a book students are reading or in a thematic unit they are teaching. Of course, it's not possible to teach every unfamiliar word. Teachers need to choose the words that are most useful—those that are most important to understand the book or the big ideas in the unit. In addition, the words chosen for instruction should be common enough that students can use them in other contexts.

Words have different levels of usefulness. Some words, such as *comfortable* and *lonely,* are words that we use frequently, whereas words such as *brawny, frolic,* and *tolerate* are less common but still useful. Other words, such as *albumin* and *nebula,* are specialized and used infrequently. Beck, McKeown, and Kucan (2002) classified words into three tiers:

- **Tier 1 Words:** Basic, everyday words that don't usually have to be taught in school.
- **Tier 2 Words:** Useful words that students need to learn in school.
- **Tier 3 Words:** Less common, specialized words that not all students need to learn before high school.

The Tier 2 words are those that teachers should post on word walls and use for instruction. They are part of academic language—the words that students need to learn to be successful in school.

Instead of teaching 35, 60, or more unfamiliar words from a book or a thematic unit, teachers identify the Tier 2 words to focus on. Here are some questions to consider when choosing words:

- Is the word important to understanding the book or the big idea?
- Do students already understand the concept?
- Can students explain the unfamiliar word using words they already know?
- Do students know the root or any related words?
- Can students use the word in other contexts?

After considering these questions, teachers can choose 5 to 10 or 12 words, depending on the grade level, for direct instruction.

**Instructional Recommendations** Reading aloud to children and encouraging them to read are probably the most important ways teachers promote vocabulary growth (Nagy, 1988). Repeated exposure to words is crucial because students need to see and use a new word many times before they know it well. Even though students learn hundreds of words incidentally through reading and thematic units each year, teaching vocabulary directly is an essential part of language arts instruction for all students and especially for struggling students and English learners (Beck, McKeown, & Kucan, 2002).

Three characteristics of effective vocabulary instruction are repetition, integration, and meaningful use (Nagy, 1988). *Repetition* means that as students participate in language arts activities, they need to say, read, and write a word many times in order to learn it. *Integration* means that the words students are learning should be integral to what they are reading or studying; when teachers choose Tier 2 words from books or thematic units, they will be integral. *Meaningful use* means that students use the words in authentic language arts activities, not worksheets.

## WORD WALLS

**1 Prepare the word wall**
Teachers prepare a blank word wall in the classroom using sheets of construction paper or butcher paper, dividing it into 16 to 24 boxes and labeling the boxes with letters of the alphabet.

**2 Introduce the word wall**
Teachers introduce the word wall and write several key words on it during preparing activities before reading.

**3 Add words to the word wall**
Students suggest "important" words for the word wall as they are reading a book or participating in thematic-unit activities. The teacher or students write the words in the alphabetized blocks, making sure to write large enough so that most students can see the words. If a word is misspelled, it should be corrected. Sometimes teachers add a small picture or write a synonym for a difficult word, put a box around the root word, or write related words nearby.

**4 Refer to the word wall**
Students refer to the word wall when they are writing and use the words for a variety of vocabulary activities, including word posters and word sorts.

**Displaying Words on Word Walls.** Word walls are charts made from construction paper squares or sheets of butcher paper that are divided into alphabetized sections. Students and the teacher write on the word wall interesting, confusing, and other important Tier 2 words from books they are reading and about big ideas they are learning during thematic units. Usually students choose the words to write on the word wall during the exploring stage of the reading process, and they may even do the writing themselves. Teachers add any important words students have not chosen. Words are added to the word wall as they come up, not in advance.

**Defining Words on Word Posters.** Students choose a word from the word wall and write it on a small poster. Then they write the definition and draw a picture to illustrate the word. They may also want to use the word in a sentence.

**Categorizing Words in Word Sorts.** Students sort a collection of words taken from the word wall into two or more categories (Bear, Invernizzi, Templeton, & Johnston, 2004). For example, words from a story might be sorted by character, or words from a theme on machines might be sorted according to type of machine. Usually students choose which categories they will use for the sort, but sometimes the teacher chooses. The words can be written on cards, and then students sort a pack of word cards into piles. Or, students can cut apart a list

## A Fourth Grader's Word Poster

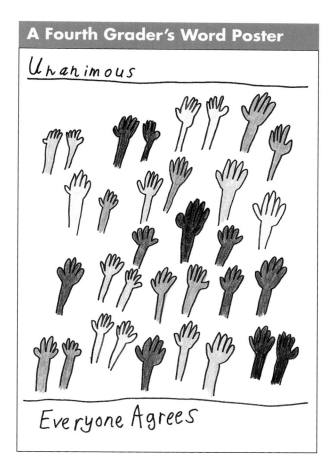

Unanimous

Everyone Agrees

of words, sort the words into categories, and then paste each group on a sheet of paper.

**Reading Words in a Tea Party.** Teachers prepare a set of cards with text (sentences or paragraphs) from a story or informational book students are reading; at least one Tier 2 word from the word wall is included in each excerpt, and that word is highlighted. Students have a "tea party" in which they read the cards to classmates: They walk around the classroom, reading the sentence or paragraph on their cards to a classmate, and then circulate to share with as many students as possible.

## Why Teach Grammar?

Grammar is probably the most controversial area of language arts. Teachers, parents, and the community disagree about the content of grammar instruction and how to teach it. Some people believe that formal instruction is unnecessary—if not harmful—for children; others believe that grammar instruction should be a key component of language arts instruction. Before getting into the controversy, let's clarify the terms *grammar* and *usage*. *Grammar* is the description of the syntax or structure of a language and prescriptions for its use (Weaver, 1996). It involves principles of word and sentence formation. In contrast, *usage* is correctness, or using the appropriate word or phrase in a sentence. It is the socially preferred way of using language within a dialect. *My friend, she; the man brung;* and *hisself* are

## *Theory to Practice*
### Ms. Vang Teaches Vocabulary Using *Smoky Night*

Ms. Vang reads Eve Bunting's *Smoky Night* (1994) aloud to her fourth and fifth graders early in the school year as she works to create an inclusive community in her multiethnic classroom. This Caldecott Medal book, set during the Los Angeles riots, is a touching story about getting along with others.

Ms. Vang teaches vocabulary during this literature focus unit. The words she chooses emphasize the concept of "riots" and are useful in helping students explore the meaning of the story.

### Tier 2 Words
*Smoky Night* includes many words that these fourth and fifth graders don't know, such as *gutter, cots,* and *squawking,* but Ms. Vang chooses to focus on these words about the riot: *rioting, destroy, angry, stealing, shelter,* and *hooligans.*

### Concept Cluster
Ms. Vang talks about "riots"—what they are, why they happen, and how people are affected—and shows some photos of a riot. Then she makes a cluster (a spider web–like diagram), writing *riots* in the center circle and drawing lines out from the circle. She writes a focus word at the end of each line and introduces it. The students talk about the words, their meanings and connections to the story.

### Word Posters
Students work with partners to create a poster about one of the focus words. They write the word at the top of the poster, define the word, and illustrate it. Then they share their posters and display them in the classroom.

### Synonym Study
Students examine synonyms for *angry.* They locate these synonyms in a thesaurus: *mad, furious, annoyed,* and *irate.* They talk about each one and the degree of anger it expresses. Then they sequence them from mild to extreme anger and make a chart to display what they have learned.

### Word Sort
Working in small groups, students sort a pack of word cards into "hooligans" and "neighborhood people" categories. These words are used in the sorting activity: *scared, escape, stealing, shelter, destroy, shouting, laughing, hopeful, strangers,* and *angry.* Because some words fit into both categories, this activity sparks discussion about the story and the words themselves.

examples of Standard English usage errors that children sometimes make. Fraser and Hodson explain the distinction between grammar and usage this way: "Grammar is the rationale of a language; usage is its etiquette" (1978, p. 52).

Children learn the structure of the English language—its grammar—intuitively as they learn to talk; the process is an unconscious one. They have almost completed it by the time they enter kindergarten. The purpose of grammar instruction, then, is to make this intuitive knowledge about the English language explicit and to provide labels for words within sentences, parts of sentences, and types of sentences. Children speak the dialect that their parents and community members speak. Dialect, whether Standard English or nonstandard English, is informal and differs to some degree from the written Standard English, or academic language, that students will read and write in school.

## *Scaffolding English Learners*

## How should I teach grammar to my English learners?

The goal of grammar instruction is to increase students' ability to structure and manipulate sentences and to expand their repertoire of sentence patterns. Teaching grammar is a controversial issue, and it is especially so for students whose native language is not English or for students who speak a nonstandard form of English, but learning academic English is crucial for these students' success in school.

### Correcting Students' Grammatical Errors

The best way to promote students' language development is to encourage all students to talk freely in the classroom. In the past, researchers have recommended that teachers not correct students' talk so as not to embarrass them; however, teachers are now finding that many English learners want to be corrected so that they can learn to speak Standard English correctly in order to do well in school (Scarcella, 2003).

The same is true with writing. During the editing stage of the writing process, teachers teach proofreading and help students identify and correct grammatical and usage errors. After teachers explain grammar concepts in minilessons, students should become responsible for identifying and correcting the errors themselves.

### Teaching Grammar Concepts

Teachers also provide direct instruction about grammar concepts through minilessons for English learners and other students who do not speak and write Standard English. The rationale for providing direct instruction is that many English learners have not been successful in acquiring Standard English through naturalistic approaches alone.

### Topics for Minilessons

The best way to choose topics for the minilessons is to identify the kinds of errors students are making and then teach lessons on those topics. In addition, teachers usually choose topics from state and district-level curriculum guides. Here are 10 of the most common topics:

| | |
|---|---|
| Plurals | Prepositions |
| Verb tenses | Possessives |
| Irregular verbs | Negatives |
| Contractions | Comparatives |
| Subject-verb agreement | Articles |

Teachers use the same approach for grammar minilessons that they use for other types of lessons. They introduce the topic using grammatical terms, provide examples from books students are reading and from students' own oral language and writing, explain the rules or provide guidelines for choosing the correct forms, involve students in practice exercises, and monitor students as they apply what they are learning in talk and writing activities.

Learning to speak, read, and write Standard English takes time, and it's unrealistic to assume that students will learn a grammar topic through a single minilesson. What's important is that teachers regularly teach Standard English to their English learners and expect them to assume responsibility for learning it.

Teachers, parents, and the community at large cite many reasons for teaching grammar. First, because using Standard English is the mark of an educated person, students should know how to use it. Many teachers feel that teaching grammar will help students understand sentence structure and form sentences to express their thoughts. Another reason is that parents expect that grammar will be taught, and teachers must meet these expectations. Other teachers explain that they teach grammar to prepare students for the next grade or for instruction in a foreign language. Others pragmatically rationalize grammar instruction because it is a part of norm-referenced achievement tests mandated by state departments of education.

Conventional wisdom is that grammar instruction will improve students' oral language and writing, but research since the early 20th century has not confirmed this assumption. Based on their review of research conducted before 1963, Braddock, Lloyd-Jones, and Schoer concluded that "the teaching of formal grammar has a negligible or, because it usually displaces some instruction and practice in actual composition, even a harmful effect on the improvement of writing" (1963, pp. 37–38). Since then, other studies have reached the same conclusion (Hillocks & Smith, 2003; Weaver, 1996).

Despite the controversy about teaching grammar and its value for children, grammar is a part of the curriculum and will undoubtedly remain so for some time. Given this fact, it's only reasonable that grammar should be taught in the most beneficial manner possible. Researchers suggest that integrating grammar study with reading and writing produces the best results (Beers, 2001; Weaver, McNally, & Moerman, 2001). They view grammar as a tool for writers and recommend integrating grammar instruction with the revising and editing stages of the writing process.

**Nonstandard Dialects** Students come to school speaking the dialects or varieties of English that their parents speak, and sometimes these dialects differ from Standard English; they are

## Ten Usage Errors That Students Can Correct

| | |
|---|---|
| **Irregular Verb Forms** | Students form the past tense of irregular verbs as they would a regular verb; for example, some students might use *catch + ed* to make *catched* instead of *caught*, or *swim + ed* to make *swimmed* instead of *swam*. |
| **Past-Tense Forms** | Students use present-tense or past-participle forms in place of past-tense forms, such as *I ask* for *I asked*, *she run* for *she ran*, or *he seen* for *he saw*. |
| **Nonstandard Verb Forms** | Students use *brung* for *brought* or *had went* for *had gone*. |
| **Double Subjects** | Students use both a noun and a pronoun in the subject, such as *My mom she*. |
| **Nonstandard Pronoun Forms** | Students use nonstandard pronoun forms, such as *hisself* for *himself*, *them books* for *those books*, and *hisn* for *his*. |
| **Objective Pronouns for the Subject** | Students use objective pronouns instead of subjective pronouns in the subject, such as *Me and my friend went to the store* or *Her and me want to play outside*. |
| **Lack of Subject-Verb Agreement** | Students use *we was* for *we were* and *he don't* for *he doesn't*. |
| **Double Negatives** | Students use two negatives when only one is needed; for example, *I don't got none* and *Joe don't have none*. |
| **Confusing Pairs of Words** | Some students confuse word pairs, such as *learn–teach*, *lay–lie*, and *leave–let*. They might say *I'll learn you to read* instead of *I'll teach you to read*, *go lay down* instead of *go lie down*, and *leave me do it* instead of *let me do it*. Other confusing pairs include *bring–take*, *among–between*, *fewer–less*, *good–well*, *passed–past*, *real–really*, *set–sit*, *than–then*, *who–which–that*, *who–whom*, *it's–its*, and *your–you're*. |
| **_I_ as an Objective Pronoun** | Students incorrectly use *I* instead of *me* as an objective pronoun—they say or write *It's for Bill and I* instead of *It's for Bill and me*. |

Adapted from Weaver, 1996.

nonstandard. For example, students may use double negatives rather than single negatives, so that they say "I ain't got no money" instead of "I don't have any money." Or they may use objective pronouns instead of subjective pronouns, so that they say "Me and him have dirt bikes" instead of "He and I have dirt bikes."

Students who speak nonstandard dialects learn Standard English forms as alternatives to the forms they already know. Rather than trying to substitute the standard forms for students' nonstandard forms, teachers explain that Standard English is the language of school. It is the language used in books, and students can easily locate Standard English examples in books they are reading. Calling Standard English "book language" also helps to explain the importance of proofreading to identify and correct usage errors in the books that students are writing. Moreover, many Standard English usage errors are status marking, and upper-grade students need to understand that Standard English is the language of privilege and prestige and that they can add it to their repertoire of language registers.

**Teaching Grammar Through Reading**

As they read, students learn about the structure of the English language: They learn more sophisticated academic language and ways of phrasing ideas and arranging words into sentences. In *Aunt Flossie's Hats (and Crab Cakes Later)* (Howard, 1991), for example, Susan tells about a visit to her great-aunt and how she and her sister play with her great-aunt's hats: "One Sunday afternoon, I picked out a wooly winter hat, sort of green, maybe" (p. 11). This sentence is particularly rich in modifiers: The hat is wooly, it is a winter hat, and it is green—sort of.

Students read sentences exemplifying all four sentence types in many books. One example is the Caldecott Medal–winning *Officer Buckle and Gloria* (Rathmann, 1995), the story of a police officer and his dog, Gloria. "Officer Buckle loved having a buddy" and "That night Officer Buckle watched himself on the 10 o'clock news" (n.p.) are statements, or declarative sentences. "How about Gloria?" and "Could she come?" (n.p.) are questions, or interrogative sentences. Officer Buckle's safety tips, such as "Keep your shoelaces tied" and "Do not go swimming during electrical storms!" (n.p.), are imperative sentences. The children loved Gloria and her tricks, and they cheered, "Bravo!" (n.p.)—an example of an exclamation, or exclamatory sentence.

Students read simple, compound, complex, and compound-complex sentences in books. William Steig includes all of these types of sentences in his Caldecott Medal book, *Sylvester and the Magic Pebble* (1988):

- ◆ **Simple Sentence:** "Suddenly Mr. Duncan saw the red pebble" (n.p.).
- ◆ **Compound Sentence:** "He felt he would be a rock forever and he tried to get used to it" (n.p.).
- ◆ **Complex Sentence:** "When he was awake, he was only hopeless and unhappy" (n.p.).
- ◆ **Compound-Complex Sentence:** "If he hadn't been so frightened, he could have made the lion disappear, or he

could have wished himself safe at home with his father and mother" (n.p.).

Students can pick out the subjects and predicates in sentences, too. The subject in "Officer Buckle loved having a buddy" (n.p.) is "Officer Buckle," and the remainder of the simple sentence is the predicate. In "He felt he would be a rock forever and he tried to get used to it" (n.p.), a compound sentence, there are two independent clauses, and "he" is the subject of each clause.

One way to help students focus on sentences in stories is sentence collecting (Speaker & Speaker, 1991): Students collect favorite sentences and share them with classmates. They copy their sentences on chart paper and post them in the classroom. Students and the teacher talk about the merits of each sentence, focus on word choice, and analyze the sentence types. Through this discussion, students gradually learn to comprehend more syntactically complex sentences. Students can cut the words in the sentences apart and rebuild them, either in the author's original order or in an order that appeals to them.

**Teaching Grammar Through Writing**

Students often apply in their own writing what they have noticed about sentences in books they're reading. Kathy Egawa (1990) reports that a first grader used the structure and rhythm of Jane Yolen's *Owl Moon* (1987) in writing "Salamander Sun." *Owl Moon* begins this way: "It was late one winter night, long past my bedtime when Pa and I went owling" (n.p.). The child's book, written in invented spelling, begins this way: "It was lat one spring afternoon a long time after lunch when ma tact me sawlumendering" (Egawa, 1990, p. 586). This first grader was not plagiarizing Yolen's book, but adapting and incorporating the structure and voice into his own writing.

Teachers use a problem-solving approach to deal with usage errors during the editing stage of the writing process. Students hunt for errors, trying to make their papers "reader-friendly." They recognize that it is a courtesy to readers to make their papers as correct as possible. During editing, classmates note errors and correct each other's papers, and teachers point out other errors. Sometimes teachers explain the correction (e.g., the past tense of *bring* is *brought*, not *brung*), and at other times, they simply mark the correction, saying, "We usually write it this way."

**Teaching the Parts of Speech**

Students learn about parts of speech through reading and writing activities. They can locate examples of the parts of speech in books they are reading so that they will understand that authors use parts of speech to express their ideas. They can read grammar concept books, including the popular books by Ruth Heller and Brian Cleary, and make their own books, too. Students can write sentences and experiment with words to see how parts of speech are combined to form sentences.

**Collecting Parts of Speech.** Students work in small groups to identify words representing one or all eight parts of speech from a book they are reading. For example, a group of fifth graders identified the following words representing each part of speech from Van Allsburg's *The Polar Express* (1985):

- ◆ **Nouns:** *train, children, Santa Claus, elves, pajamas, roller coaster, conductor, sleigh, hug, clock, Sarah*
- ◆ **Pronouns:** *we, they, he, it, us, you, his, I, me*
- ◆ **Verbs:** *filled, ate, flickered, raced, were, cheered, marched, asked, pranced, stood, shouted*
- ◆ **Adjectives:** *melted, white-tailed, quiet, no, first, magical, cold, dark, polar, Santa's*
- ◆ **Adverbs:** *soon, faster, wildly, apart, closer, alone*
- ◆ **Prepositions:** *in, through, over, with, of, in front of, behind, at, for, across, into*
- ◆ **Conjunctions:** *and, but*
- ◆ **Interjections:** *oh, well, now*

After identifying the parts of speech, teachers can make word cards that students can sort according to the part of speech. Because some words, such as *melted* and *hug*, can represent more than one part of speech depending on how the word is used in the sentence, words for this activity should be chosen carefully, or teachers can use the words in a sentence on the word card so that students can classify them correctly.

**Reading and Writing Grammar Concept Books.** Students examine concept books that focus on one part of speech or another grammar concept. For example, Brian Cleary describes adjectives and lists many examples in *Hairy, Scary, Ordinary: What Is an Adjective?* (2000). After students read the book and identify the adjectives, they can make posters or write their own books about parts of speech.

Students in an eighth-grade class divided into small groups to read Ruth Heller's books about parts of speech, including *Up, Up and Away: A Book About Adverbs* (1991) and *Mine, All Mine: A Book About Pronouns* (1997). After reading one of her books, students made a poster with information about a part of speech, which they presented to the class. Later, students divided into small groups to do a word sort. In this activity, students cut apart a list of words and sorted them into groups according to the part of speech. All the words had been taken from posters that students created, and students could refer to the posters if needed.

## Let's Play Sentence Games!

Experimenting with sentences helps students learn how the parts of speech work together. They experiment with sentences when they rearrange words and phrases in a sentence, combine several sentences to make a single, stronger sentence, or write sentences based on a particular sentence pattern. Through these activities, students learn about the structure of sentences and experiment with more sophisticated sentences than they might otherwise write.

## Grammar Concept Books

### Nouns

Cleary, B. P. (1999). *A mink, a fink, a skating rink: What is a noun?* Minneapolis: Carolrhoda.

Heller, R. (1990). *Merry-go-round: A book about nouns.* New York: Grosset & Dunlap.

Terban, M. (1986). *Your foot's on my feet! and other tricky nouns.* New York: Clarion Books.

### Verbs

Cleary, B. P. (2001). *To root, to toot, to parachute: What is a verb?* Minneapolis: Carolrhoda.

Heller, R. (1988). *Kites sail high: A book about verbs.* New York: Grosset & Dunlap.

Schneider, R. M. (1995). *Add it, dip it, fix it: A book of verbs.* Boston: Houghton Mifflin.

### Adjectives

Cleary, B. P. (2001). *Hairy, scary, ordinary: What is an adjective?* Minneapolis: Carolrhoda.

Heller, R. (1989). *Many luscious lollipops: A book about adjectives.* New York: Grosset & Dunlap.

### Conjunctions

Heller, R. (1998). *Fantastic! Wow! And unreal! A book about interjections and conjunctions.* New York: Penguin.

### Pronouns

Cleary, B. P. (2004). *I and you and don't forget who: What is a pronoun?* Minneapolis: Carolrhoda.

Heller, R. (1997). *Mine, all mine: A book about pronouns.* New York: Grosset & Dunlap.

### Prepositions

Cleary, B. P. (2002). *Under, over, by the clover: What is a preposition?* Minneapolis: Carolrhoda.

Heller, R. (1995). *Behind the mask: A book of prepositions.* New York: Grosset & Dunlap.

### Adverbs

Cleary, B. P. (2003). *Dearly, nearly, insincerely: What is an adverb?* Minneapolis: Carolrhoda.

Heller, R. (1991). *Up, up and away: A book about adverbs.* New York: Grosset & Dunlap.

### Interjections

Heller, R. (1998). *Fantastic! Wow! And unreal! A book about interjections and conjunctions.* New York: Penguin.

## An Eighth-Grade Poster on Adverbs

A third-grade class, for example, followed the rhyming pattern in Laura Numeroff's *Dogs Don't Wear Sneakers* (1993) and the sequel, *Chimps Don't Wear Glasses* (1995), to write verses. One group composed this verse, rhyming *TV* and *bumblebee*:

> Ducks don't have tea parties,
> Lions don't watch TV,
> And you won't see a salamander
> being friends with a bumblebee.

Another group wrote this verse, rhyming *cars* and *bars*:

> Sea otters don't go to church,
> Hummingbirds never drive cars,
> And you won't see a hermit crab
> munching on candy bars.

Don Killgallon (1997, 1998) recommends that teachers help students examine how authors write sentences through four types of activities: sentence unscrambling, sentence imitating, sentence combining, and sentence expanding. Sentence imitating is like the innovations and copy changes discussed earlier. Through sentence manipulation, students learn new syntactic structures and practice ways to vary the sentences they write.

**Sentence Unscrambling** Teachers choose a sentence from a book students are reading and divide it into phrases. Then they present the phrases in a random order, and students rearrange the phrases to re-create the author's original sentence. Although older students can do this activity with a list of phrases written on the chalkboard or on a sheet of paper, younger students need to have the phrases written on sentence strips so that they can actually arrange and rearrange them until they are satisfied with the order.

Here is a sentence from E. B. White's *Charlotte's Web* (1980), broken into phrases and scrambled:

> in the middle of the kitchen
> teaching it to suck from the bottle
> a minute later
> with an infant between her knees
> Fern was seated on the floor

Can you unscramble the sentence? This is E. B. White's original: "A minute later Fern was seated on the floor in the middle of the kitchen with an infant between her knees, teaching it to suck from the bottle" (pp. 6–7).

**Sentence Imitating** Students choose a sentence and then write their own sentence imitating the structure of the one they have chosen. Here is an original sentence from *Charlotte's Web:* "Avery noticed the spider web, and coming closer, he saw Charlotte" (p. 71). Can you create a sentence on a new topic that imitates E. B. White's sentence structure, especially the "and coming closer" part? A class of sixth graders created this imitation: "The fox smelled the poultry, and coming closer, he saw five juicy chickens scratching in the dirt."

Teachers begin sentence imitating by having students collect favorite sentences as they read, and then write them on sentence strips to post in the classroom and in their reading logs. After students gain experience collecting sentences, the teacher introduces sentence imitation as an oral activity. The teacher reads a sentence from those posted on the classroom wall, and then orally creates a new sentence using the same structure. The teacher says this new sentence aloud and points out that it follows the structure of the sentence posted on the wall. Then the teacher invites students to pick a sentence and create a new one using the same structure. Some students will quickly pick up on the idea and create sentences to share with the class, and with practice, more students will join in.

**Sentence Combining** Students combine and rearrange words in sentences to make the sentences longer and more conceptually dense (Strong, 1996). The goal of sentence combining is for students to experiment with different ways to join and embed words. Teachers choose a sentence from a book students are reading and break it apart into short, simple sentences. Then students combine the sentences, trying to recapture the author's original sentence. For example, try your hand at combining these short sentences that were taken from a more complex sentence written by E. B. White:

> No one ever had such a friend.
> The friend was so affectionate.
> The friend was so loyal.
> The friend was so skillful.

Here is the original sentence from *Charlotte's Web:* "No one ever had such a friend—so affectionate, so loyal, and so skillful"

(p. 173). You might wonder whether the *and* before "so skillful" is necessary: Students often discuss why the author may have added it.

Try this more complex sentence-combining activity, again using a sentence from *Charlotte's Web:*

They explored their home.
They crawled here and there.
They waved at Wilbur.
They crawled up and down.
They trailed tiny draglines behind them.
They crawled around and about.
They crawled for several days and several nights.

This is the original sentence: "For several days and several nights they crawled here and there, up and down, around and about, waving at Wilbur, trailing tiny draglines behind them, and exploring their home" (p. 178).

**Sentence Expanding** — Teachers choose a rich sentence from a book students are reading and present an abridged version to students. Then students expand the sentence so that the words and phrases they add blend in with the author's sentence. Here is an abridged sentence from *Charlotte's Web:* "There is no place like home. . . . " The original reads "There is no place like home, Wilbur thought, as he placed Charlotte's 514 unborn children carefully in a safe corner" (p. 172). A sixth grader wrote this expansion:

There is no place like home, like his home in the barn, cozy and warm straw to sleep on, the delicious smell of manure in the air, Charlotte's egg sac to guard, and his friends Templeton, the goose, and the sheep nearby.

Even though it is not the same as E. B. White's original sentence, the student's sentence retains the character of E. B. White's writing style.

These sentence-manipulation activities fit easily into exploring activities during the reading process. Whether students are involved in a literature focus unit, literature circles, or reading workshop, they often collect favorite sentences in their reading logs. Then students can use some of the sentences they have collected for these activities.

## Teaching Students to Spell Conventionally

The alphabetic principle suggests a one-to-one correspondence between phonemes and graphemes, but English spelling is phonetic only about half the time; other spellings reflect the language from which a word was borrowed. For example, *myth,* like most words with *y* where *i* would work, is a Greek word. Other words are spelled to reflect semantic relationships, not phonological ones. The spelling of *national* and *nation* and of *grade* and *gradual* indicates related meanings even though there are vowel or consonant changes in the pronunciations of the word pairs. If English were a purely phonetic language, it would be easier to spell, but at the same time, it would lose much of its sophistication.

**Invented Spelling— Good or Bad?** — Children's misspellings, called *invented spelling,* reflect their growing awareness of English orthography as they move through the stages of spelling development. Charles Read (1975, 1986), one of the first researchers to study preschoolers' efforts to spell words, discovered that they used their knowledge of phonology to invent spellings. These children used letter names to spell words, such as U (*you*), and they used consonant sounds rather consistently: GRL (*girl*), TIGR (*tiger*), and NIT (*night*). The preschoolers used several unusual but phonetically based spelling patterns to represent affricates: They spelled /tr/ with *chr* (e.g., CHRIBLES for *troubles*) and /dr/ with *jr* (e.g., JRAGIN for *dragon*), and they substituted *d* for /t/ (e.g., PREDE for *pretty*). Words with long vowels were spelled using letter names: MI (*my*), LADE (*lady*), and FEL (*feel*). The 3-, 4-, and 5-year-olds used several ingenious strategies to spell words with short vowels. For example, they rather consistently selected letters to represent short vowels on the basis of place of articulation in the mouth: Short *i* was represented with *e,* as in FES (*fish*); short *e* with *a,* as in LAFFT (*left*); and short *o* with *i,* as in CLIK (*clock*). These spellings may seem odd to adults, but they are based on phonetic relationships. The children often omitted nasals within words (e.g., ED for *end*) and substituted *-eg* or *-ig* for *-ing* (e.g., CUMIG for *coming* and GOWEG for *going*). Also, they often ignored the vowel in unaccented syllables, as in AFTR (*after*) and MUTHR (*mother*).

These children developed strategies for their spellings based on their knowledge of the phonological system and of letter names, their judgments of phonetic similarities and differences, and their ability to abstract phonetic information from letter names. These invented spellings are very useful— yes, they're a good thing—because they provide a glimpse into children's evolving understanding of English orthography.

Older children continue to create invented spellings for words they don't know how to spell conventionally. In fact, any word a child misspells is really an invented spelling, no matter whether they're spelling at the within-word stage or the derivational relations stage.

**Instructional Recommendations** — One goal of spelling instruction is for students to learn to spell words conventionally. A second, and equally important, goal is to help students develop a spelling conscience, a positive attitude toward spelling and a concern for using conventional spelling. Students learn to spell conventionally and develop a spelling conscience through a variety of language arts activities, in addition to minilessons on spelling strategies and skills and weekly spelling tests. Following are six of the most important ways to support children's spelling development.

**Provide Daily Writing Opportunities.** Children need daily opportunities to write informally in reading logs and other journals and use the writing process to draft, refine, and polish more formal compositions to become capable spellers.

As children write, they practice what they know about the English spelling system and experiment with sound-symbol correspondences, spelling patterns, and words with related meanings that they are learning.

**Encourage Daily Reading Opportunities.** Children learn the visual configurations of words as they read, and the ability to recall how words look helps them decide when a spelling they are writing is correct. Children learn about words as they read independently in reading workshop as well as in more teacher-led guided and shared reading.

**Post Words on Word Walls.** Teachers direct children's attention to words when they post lists of high-frequency words or important words from books they are reading or from social studies and science units on word walls, arranged alphabetically by first letter. Word walls are important reference tools because they are readily available in the classroom, and children can refer to them for language activities and when they are writing.

**Use Interactive Writing.** Teachers work with children to spell words conventionally when they "share the pen" and write the daily news, a story, or some other text interactively. Through the process of "stretching out" words and spelling them with the teacher's support, children learn how to go about spelling an unfamiliar word, and teachers provide useful information about high-frequency words and other words with unusual spellings. It's an important tool for teachers working with young writers who are learning the basics of writing and spelling.

**Do Making Words Activities.** Children arrange and rearrange a group of letter cards to spell words in a making words activity; while they are spelling words, they are practicing what they know about sound-symbol correspondences and spelling patterns (Cunningham & Cunningham, 1992). Primary-grade students used the letters *s, p, i, d, e, r* to spell *is, red, dip, rip, sip, side, ride,* and *ripe,* for example; with the letters *t, e, m, p, e, r, a, t, u, r, e,* fifth graders spelled these words:

2-letter words: *at, up*
3-letter words: *pet, are, rat, eat, ate, tap, pat*
4-letter words: *ramp, rate, pare, pear, meat, meet, team, tree*
5-letter words: *treat*
6-letter words: *temper, tamper, mature, repeat*
7-letter words: *trumpet*
8-letter words: *repeater*
9-letter words: *temperate, trumpeter*

Teachers often introduce making words as a whole-class lesson and then set the cards and the word list in a center for students to use again in small groups. Teachers can use almost any words for making words activities, but those related to lit-

---

**A Third Grader's Making Words Chart for *Friends***

## Making Words

| 2 | 3 | 4 | 5 | 6+ |
|---|---|---|---|---|
| in | fin | fine | rides | |
| if | red | find | dries | |
| | end | send | fried | |
| | sir | fire | | |
| | | ride | | |
| | | side | | |
| | | dine | | |

The word is: **friends**

---

erature focus units and thematic units work best; the words *spider* and *temperature* were selected from science units.

**Create Word Sorts.** In word sorts, children compare and contrast phoneme-grapheme correspondences, spelling patterns, and words related in meaning (Bear, Invernizzi, Templeton, & Johnston, 2004). Teachers make word cards for children to sort into two or more categories according to the spelling topic being studied. As children do the sorting, they read the words printed on the word cards, examine the sequence of letters in the word, and make judgments about how to classify the spelling based on how the word is pronounced, the letter patterns used, or the word's meaning, depending on their stage of spelling development. Sometimes teachers tell children which categories to use, making it a closed sort; at other times, children determine the categories themselves, making it an open sort. Children can sort word cards and then return them to an envelope for future use, or they can glue the cards onto a sheet of paper to make their sort permanent.

**What About Spelling Tests?** Spelling tests are controversial. Researchers report that spelling is best learned through meaningful reading and writing experiences (Gentry & Gillet, 1993; Wilde, 1993), and many teachers don't think these tests really teach students to spell. On the other hand, parents and administrators want students to take spelling tests because they see them as evidence that children are receiving spelling instruction.

Most teachers are expected to teach spelling using weekly tests today, but the tests should be only one part of the

## MAKING WORDS

**1 Make letter cards**
Teachers prepare a set of small letter cards with multiple copies of each letter, especially common letters such as *a, e, i, r, s,* and *t.* They print the lowercase letter form on one side of the cards and the uppercase form on the reverse.

**2 Choose a word**
Teachers choose a word to use in the activity, and without disclosing the chosen word, have a child distribute the needed letter cards to classmates.

**3 Name the letter cards**
Teachers ask children to name the letter cards and arrange them with consonants in one group and vowels in another.

**4 Make words**
Children use the letter cards to spell words containing two, three, four, or more letters and list the words they can spell on a chart. Teachers monitor children's work and encourage them to fix any misspelled words.

**5 Share words**
Teachers have children identify two-letter words they made with the letter cards and continue to report longer and longer words until they identify the chosen word made using every single letter card. After children share all of the words, teachers suggest any words they missed and point out recently taught spelling patterns and other concepts.

spelling program. In the Classroom Close-Up at the beginning of Part 6, you read about how Mr. Martinez teaches spelling using weekly spelling tests. He individualized his program so that his students receive instruction that better matches their instructional level while still addressing grade-level standards. The fourth graders did more than study a list of spelling words; they learned spelling patterns and rules through hands-on, small-group activities.

In an individualized approach, children study different lists of words; the lists are chosen according to their stage of spelling development. Often the words include some words that children are spelling incorrectly in their writing.

Children use this study strategy to practice their words efficiently:

1. Look at the word and say it to yourself.
2. Say each letter in the word to yourself.
3. Close your eyes and spell the word to yourself.
4. Write the word, and check that you spelled it correctly.
5. Write the word again, and check that you spelled it correctly.

Children take 10 minutes or less to practice their words each day, often writing them on white boards instead of on sheets of paper.

This brief practice is effective because students focus on the words themselves. In contrast, if children were using the words in sentences, they'd be spelling them only once, but this way they spell them four times—twice orally and twice in writing.

Even though students have been studying different words during the week, they take the final test on Friday together. Teachers read the common words first and then each group's words. Or, when students each have different words, teachers number the words on the master list. Students keep a list of their spelling words with the numbers, and before the test begins, they circle the numbers of their words on their spelling tests. Then they write only those words that correspond to the numbers they circled.

Spelling instruction would be much easier if all that teachers needed to do was to have students study spelling words and take a test on the words every Friday. Instead, teachers need to understand how children learn to spell, determine their students' stage of development, and match their instruction to their students' developmental level.

### A IS FOR AUTHENTIC ASSESSMENT: Analyzing Students' Spelling Development

When you think of spelling assessment, you probably think of weekly spelling tests, but the results of these tests tell you only how many of the assigned words students can spell. Students often memorize the words right before the test but forget how to spell some of them soon after. Many teachers notice that students misspell words in their writing that they spelled correctly on the spelling test several days earlier. In addition, knowing just that students spelled 45% or 90% of the words correctly doesn't provide a lot of information.

Examining the kinds of errors students make in their writing provides more useful information about what students already know about spelling, what they're using and confusing, and what they're ready to learn. For example, one student might spell *babies* as *babes,* and another might spell it as *babyes.* Although it's true that both students misspelled the word, the errors show that they differ in their level of spelling development and what they need to learn. The student who spells *babies* as *babes* is spelling phonetically—within-words spelling—and is ready to learn that *y* is used to spell the long *e* sound at the end of two-syllable words. On the other hand, the student who spells *babies* as *babyes* already knows about using *y* to spell the long *e* sound at the end of two-syllable words and is experimenting with ways to form plurals—syllables and affixes spelling. This student is ready to learn about changing the *y* to *i* and adding *es* to form plurals.

# INDIVIDUALIZED SPELLING TESTS

**1 Prepare a master list**
Teachers prepare a master list of 20–50 words, depending on students' grade level and the range of spelling levels in the classroom.

**2 Administer a pretest**
Teachers administer a pretest on Monday to all students in the class, using the words on the master list. Immediately afterward, students self-correct their pretests using red pens.

**3 Identify words to study**
Teachers have students choose 5 to 10 words to study from the words they misspelled on the pretest.

**4 Prepare study lists**
Teachers have students make two study lists, one to take home and one to use at school.

**5 Use the study strategy**
Teachers have students use the study strategy to practice spelling the words on their study lists each day during the week.

**6 Administer a practice test**
Teachers have students work with a partner to give each other practice tests on Wednesday or Thursday to check their progress in learning to spell the words.

**7 Administer the posttest**
Teachers administer a posttest on Friday, and students spell only the words they have practiced. Teachers collect and grade the tests.

**8 List misspelled words**
Teachers create a list of the words that students misspell to add to their master list for the following week.

**The Procedure**

Teachers examine the spelling errors in students' compositions and classify them according to the five stages of spelling development (Bear, Invernizzi, Templeton, & Johnston, 2004). This analysis provides information about students' current level of spelling development and the kinds of errors they're making. Knowing the stage of students' spelling development helps teachers provide appropriate instruction because students at different stages need to learn different things.

To analyze spelling errors, teachers read one or more compositions, depending on length, that a student has written and identify the errors in them. It's essential that the writings have some errors and that the student has proofread them to identify and correct as many spelling errors as possible. In compositions the student hasn't proofread, many of the errors may be due to carelessness or poor handwriting; the student may actually know how to spell the words, but if these known words are scored as errors, teachers will have a skewed understanding of the student's level of spelling development. Next, teachers classify the errors according to the five stages of spelling development; the stage with the most errors is the student's developmental level. Then teachers examine the spelling errors in each stage to identify patterns of error. Do some of the errors at one level reflect a common spelling concept—*r*-controlled vowels, past-tense markers, homophones, or Latin root words, for example? The patterns of error indicate instructional priorities for that student.

**Analysis of a Student's Spelling Errors**

Teachers choose a student's composition to analyze. Here is sixth-grade Ivan's story titled "Shadow," in which the spelling errors are highlighted:

You might think this story is about a big strong **musculer** guy. Well, **its** not, **its** about a small hedgehog named Shadow. His powers are amazing, some of them you won't **belive** are even powers. Let's start with his ability to run really, really, really fast. So fast that I **cant** even say really fast any more. His second power was to clone himself. This third power was to create a powerful shadow ball that would put his enemies in the shadow realm. His fourth power was to create an invisible shadow wave that would throw his **opponet** off balance so they would be easier to fight. Shadow had black hair with white tips. He was only about three feet tall.

OK now you know all about Shadow, but do you know about **Shadows villans**? Every **villan** Shadow ever fought was put in the shadow realm. All that was about to change because one of the villans Shadow fought he put in jail. That villan broke out of jail and freed all the villans Shadow put in the shadow realm. Your probobly thinking that they all went after Shadow to kill him. That's exactly what happen.

When all the **villans** went to kill Shadow, Shadow was ready for battle. They all socked Shadow but nothing happened because it was a clone. The next thing you know all the **villans** are on the floor. "I got **alot** stronger," Shadow said. **Your probobly** thinking this was going to be a long battle. I have to say it wasn't.

Shao Kahn the strongest **villan** held Shadow by the back. Shao Kahn let everyone do their strongest move on Shadow. When they got done Shadow fell to the ground like he was dead. All the **villans** left to go destroy the city. Nobody knew if Shadow was dead or alive. Then something came from the sky. It was the thunder god Raiden.

Raiden woke up Shadow and granted him the power of thunder and left. So Shadow ran to the spot where all the **villans** were at. They all tried to stop Shadow but they all died when they got shocked by him. Shadow put them all in the shadow realm where they belonged. Shadow had saved the city from destruction.

# ANALYZING SPELLING ERRORS

**1 Choose writing samples**
Teachers choose one long or several short writing samples by a single student to analyze.

**2 Identify misspelled words**
Teachers read the writing samples and identify the misspelled words, ignoring proper nouns, capitalization errors, and nonstandard grammatical constructions. When a word is hard to decipher, teachers check with the student to determine the intended word, and if it's not possible to figure it out, they skip it.

**3 Make an analysis chart**
Teachers draw a chart with five columns, one for each of the spelling stages, and label the columns with the names of the stages.

**4 Categorize the errors**
Teachers classify the spelling errors according to what they know about the stages of spelling development. They list each misspelling and its correct form in the appropriate column on the chart.

**5 Tally the errors**
Teachers count the number of errors in each column to determine the stage with the most errors: That stage is the student's current level of spelling development.

**6 Identify topics for instruction**
Teachers examine the student's misspelled words, looking at the kinds of errors (e.g., short *e*, homophones, schwa sound) to determine instructional priorities.

It's possible that he doesn't understand how to use apostrophes, even though he used them correctly in the contractions *let's* and *wasn't*. Third, he chose the wrong spelling for *your* in two sentences, so he may not understand that he's confusing the homophones *your* and *you're*. When he was asked whether any of the words in one of the sentences containing *your* was misspelled, he did not catch the error.

From this analysis, we can conclude that Ivan is making good progress in learning to spell, but he needs to learn to use more complex spelling strategies to move beyond sounding out words. He appears to need clarification about using apostrophes in contractions and possessives and choosing among homophones. Because some of his errors are in the derivational relations stage of spelling development, he might also benefit from learning more about root words and affixes. Ivan spelled seven three-syllable words correctly in his story, including *amazing, invisible,* and *destruction,* but after studying multisyllabic words, he might use more of them.

**What's an Acceptable Error Rate?** As students learn to read and write, they gradually reduce the number of misspelled words in their writing. The kinds of errors they make also change, reflecting the concepts they're learning.

Kindergartners spell a few high-frequency words correctly, such as *the, I, you,* and *is,* but they often use beginning letters or abbreviated spellings to represent entire words, so almost all of the words they write are misspelled by adult standards. Because kindergartners are learning important concepts about written language as they begin writing, it doesn't matter that most of their words are misspelled. In fact, if 5-year-olds were allowed to write only words that they knew how to spell, their spelling development would be hindered. Teachers nurture young children's spelling development when they encourage kindergartners to use their knowledge of phoneme-grapheme correspondences to invent spellings.

First graders grow quickly in their ability to spell words, learning to spell 50 to 100 high-frequency words (e.g., *said, want, who*) and growing in their knowledge of how to spell words with short- and long-vowel patterns. They usually reach the point where they spell correctly at least half of the words they write, and in second grade, students continue to spell more words correctly as their word knowledge increases. Through a combination of instruction and reading and writing experiences, children grow in their ability to spell words correctly. Their errors indicate what they don't understand about English spelling patterns, and teachers can use this information to provide appropriate instruction.

Ivan's spelling errors can be categorized according to the five stages of spelling development and then charted to gauge his spelling level and determine instructional priorities.

Ivan's story contains 377 words with 24 highlighted errors: That's an acceptable 6% error rate. Of his 24 errors, Ivan misspelled 12 different words. One misspelling was classified at the within-words stage, eight at the syllables and affixes stage, and three at the derivational relations stage. The word *villan* and its plural form were classified as one word because the error didn't involve the plural marker. More errors were classified at the syllables and affixes stage than at any other, so Ivan is a syllables and affixes–level speller.

Ivan's errors show three patterns. First, he misspelled these six words because he spelled them the way they sound to him: *musculer, exactily, alot, opponet, villan(s),* and *probobly;* he pronounces *exactly* as *exactily* and *opponent* as *opponet.* It's likely that he doesn't ask himself if words look right after spelling them. Second, he didn't use apostrophes in *its* and *cant,* both contractions, or in *Shadows,* a possessive.

## Classification of Spelling Errors in "Shadow"

| Emergent | Letter Name | Within-Words | Syllables and Affixes | Derivational Relations |
|----------|-------------|--------------|----------------------|------------------------|
|          |             | belive/believe | musculer/muscular<br>its/it's<br>cant/can't<br>Shadows/Shadow's<br>your/you're<br>exactily/exactly<br>happen/happened<br>alot/a lot | opponet/opponent<br>villan(s)/villain(s)<br>probobly/probably |

By third or fourth grade, most students reach the point where they misspell only about 10% of the words they write. The words they're misspelling are longer, and they often misspell them because they sound them out, rather than using more complex spelling strategies; for example, that's what the student who spells *because* as *becus* is doing. Teachers should focus their instruction on spelling multisyllabic words and other concepts such as homonyms that students continue to confuse.

Between fourth and eighth grades, students' error rates continue to decline to 2%, but almost all students continue to make a few errors. In fact, students who never misspell any words may be "safe spellers" who don't try to incorporate into their writing the more sophisticated academic language they're learning. They need to be encouraged to take risks even though it means they'll misspell some words. Students' error rates decline because they've learned to spell more words and use more complex spelling strategies. Another reason they reach this low error rate is that they've learned to proofread so that they can identify and correct most of their spelling errors during the editing stage of the writing process.

Not all students make satisfactory progress in learning to spell, and they don't reach the 50% error rate in first grade, the 10% error rate in third or fourth grade, or the 2% rate by eighth grade. Teachers can help these struggling spellers by analyzing their spelling errors to determine these students' level of spelling development and the kinds of errors they're making. With this knowledge, teachers can provide instruction to help struggling students grow in their spelling ability. Whole-class instruction isn't very useful when struggling students are more than one level behind their classmates. If a struggling sixth-grade speller is at the within-words stage, for example, grade-level instruction won't be very effective because it's likely to be aimed at students who are entering the derivational relations stage.

Analyzing students' spelling errors is a worthwhile authentic assessment tool that teachers can use to monitor students' growth through the school year and identify instructional priorities for students. Even though the analysis process is time-consuming and it can be difficult to determine the level of some spelling errors, this assessment tool helps teachers understand their students' instructional needs better than the results of weekly spelling tests do.

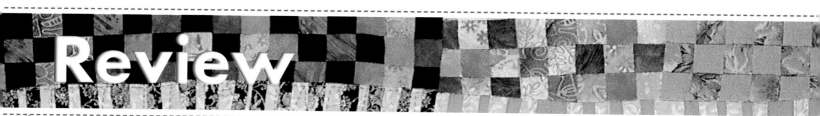

# Review

## The Big Ideas

Through a combination of authentic reading and writing experiences and instruction in vocabulary, grammar, and spelling, children learn about the meanings of words, how to arrange them in sentences, and how to spell them conventionally. The complex knowledge about words that children gain is academic language, and it's important to their school success.

These big ideas were presented in Part 6:

- ◆ Reading and writing are the most important ways students learn vocabulary, but direct instruction also is important.
- ◆ Teachers teach Tier 2 words and focus students' attention on the grammatical features of words.
- ◆ Vocabulary activities include word walls, word posters, and word sorts.
- ◆ Teachers teach grammar using sentences from books students are reading and from students' own writing.

- Students move through a series of five stages of spelling development as they learn the sound, pattern, and meaning principles.
- Teachers can analyze students' misspellings to determine their stage of spelling development and then plan appropriate instruction.
- Spelling instruction includes daily opportunities to read and write, posting words on word walls, and word-making and word-sorting activities.
- Teachers individualize weekly spelling tests so that students can be successful.

## Classroom Inquiry

Teachers develop their students' academic English through language-study activities. Because of the relationship between academic English and school success, it's important that teachers examine how they teach vocabulary, grammar, and spelling, and the effect of their instruction on students' learning. Consider developing a classroom inquiry to investigate one of these topics.

**Tier 2 Words** Researchers recommend that teachers teach Tier 2 words, the high-frequency words that are used in classroom instruction. To examine the words you're teaching and the effect of your instruction, you might be interested in exploring these questions:

- How do I choose words for vocabulary instruction?
- Which instructional approaches do my students prefer?
- Are my instructional approaches effective?
- Do my students remember the words a month or two after they've been taught?

**Standard English** Students come to school speaking the language of their homes, and at school they learn Standard English, if that isn't their home language. Teachers need to value children's home language while teaching them Standard English—the language of school. To examine your students' use of Standard English and the effect of your instruction, investigate these questions:

- Which non-Standard English errors do my students, English-only students as well as English learners, make in talking and writing?
- Are my instruction and my corrections effective?
- Is it my responsibility to teach Standard English?
- Do my students value learning Standard English?

**Stages of Spelling Development** Students move through the stages of spelling development as they learn about English orthography, and because students focus on different concepts at each stage, it's important to match instruction to students' developmental level. To examine your students' stage of spelling development, consider these questions:

- What do my students' writing samples show about their spelling development?
- How do I match my students' stage of development to their instructional activities?
- Which students have reached a plateau and are not progressing through the stages?

# References

## Professional References

Adams, M. J. (1990). *Beginning to read: Thinking and learning about print*. Cambridge, MA: MIT Press.

Albright, L. K. (2002). Bringing the Ice Maiden to life: Engaging adolescents in learning through picture book read-alouds in content areas. *Journal of Adolescent & Adult Literacy, 45,* 418–428.

Alexander, H. (1962). *The story of our language*. Garden City, NY: Doubleday.

Allen, C. A. (2001). *The multigenre research paper: Voice, passion, and discovery in grades 4–6*. Portsmouth, NH: Heinemann.

Allen, J. (1999). *Words, words, words*. Portsmouth, NH: Heinemann.

Allen, R. V. (1976). *Language experiences in communication*. Boston: Houghton Mifflin.

Allington, R. L. (2001). *What really matters for struggling readers: Designing research-based programs*. New York: Longman.

Alvermann, D. E., & Eakle, E. J. (2003). Comprehension instruction: Adolescents and their multiple literacies. In A. P. Sweet & C. E. Snow (Eds.), *Rethinking reading comprehension* (pp. 12–29). New York: Guilford Press.

Alvermann, D. E., Moon, J. S., & Hagood, M. C. (1999). *Popular culture in the classroom: Teaching and researching critical media literacy*. Mahwah, NJ: Erlbaum.

Angelillo, J. (2002). *A fresh approach to teaching punctuation*. New York: Scholastic.

Applegate, M., Quinn, K., & Applegate, A. (2004). *The critical reading inventory: Assessing students' reading and thinking*. Upper Saddle River, NJ: Merrill/Prentice Hall.

Ashton-Warner, S. (1965). *Teacher*. New York: Simon & Schuster.

Atwell, N. (1987). *In the middle: Writing, reading, and learning with adolescents*. Upper Montclair, NJ: Boynton/Cook.

Atwell, N. (1998). *In the middle: New understandings about writing, reading, and learning* (2nd ed.). Portsmouth, NH: Heinemann.

Banks, J. A. (1994). *Multiethnic education: Theory and practice* (3rd ed.). Boston: Allyn & Bacon.

Banks, J. A. (2001). *An introduction to multicultural education* (5th ed.). Boston: Allyn & Bacon.

Barnes, D., Morgan, K., & Weinhold, K. (Eds.). (1997). *Writing process revisited: Sharing our stories*. Urbana, IL: National Council of Teachers of English.

Barone, D. (1990). The written responses of young children: Beyond comprehension to story understanding. *The New Advocate, 3,* 49–56.

Barrentine, S. J. (1996). Engaging with reading through interactive read-alouds. *The Reading Teacher, 50,* 36–43.

Baugh, A. C., & Cable, T. (2002). *The history of the English language* (5th ed.). Upper Saddle River, NJ: Prentice Hall.

Baumann, J. F., Hoffman, J. V., Moon, J., & Duffy-Hester, A. M. (1998). Where are teachers' voices in the phonics/whole language debate? Results from a survey of US elementary teachers. *The Reading Teacher, 51,* 636–650.

Baumann, J. F., Jones, L. A., & Seifert-Kessell, N. (1993). Using think alouds to enhance children's comprehension monitoring abilities. *The Reading Teacher, 47,* 184–193.

Baumann, J. F., & Kame'enui, E. J. (Eds.). (2004). *Vocabulary instruction: Research to practice*. New York: Guilford Press.

Bear, D. R., Invernizzi, M., Templeton, S., & Johnston, F. (2004). *Words their way: Word study for phonics, vocabulary, and spelling instruction* (3rd ed.). Upper Saddle River, NJ: Merrill/Prentice Hall.

Beck, I. L., McKeown, M. G., & Kucan, L. (2002). *Bringing words to life: Robust vocabulary instruction*. New York: Guilford Press.

Beers, K. (2001). Contextualizing grammar. *Voices From the Middle, 8*(3), 4.

Bereiter, C., & Scardamalia, M. (1987). *The psychology of written composition*. Hillsdale, NJ: Erlbaum.

Berthoff, A. E. (1981). *The making of meaning*. Montclair, NJ: Boynton/Cook.

Blachowicz, C., & Fisher, P. (2002). *Teaching vocabulary in all classrooms* (2nd ed.). Upper Saddle River, NJ: Merrill/Prentice Hall.

Bode, B. A. (1989). Dialogue journal writing. *The Reading Teacher, 42,* 568–571.

Bowser, J. (1993). Structuring the middle-school classroom for spoken language. *English Journal, 82,* 38–41.

Braddock, R., Lloyd-Jones, R., & Schoer, L. (1963). *Research in written composition*. Champaign, IL: National Council of Teachers of English.

Brent, R., & Anderson, P. (1993). Developing children's classroom listening strategies. *The Reading Teacher, 47,* 122–126.

Britton, J., Burgess, T., Martin, N., McLeod, A., & Rosen, H. (1975). *The development of writing abilities, 11–18*. London: Schools Council Publications.

Brown, J. E., & Stephens, E. C. (Eds.). (2003). *Your reading: An annotated booklist for middle school and junior high school* (11th ed.). Urbana, IL: National Council of Teachers of English.

Bruner, J. (1986). *Actual minds, possible worlds*. Cambridge, MA: Harvard University Press.

Brunner, C., & Tally, W. (1999). *The new media literacy handbook*. New York: Anchor Books.

Button, K., Johnson, M. J., & Furgerson, P. (1996). Interactive writing in a primary classroom. *The Reading Teacher, 49,* 446–454.

Calkins, L. M. (1994). *The art of teaching writing* (2nd ed.). Portsmouth, NH: Heinemann.

Carr, E., & Ogle, D. (1987). K-W-L Plus: A strategy for comprehension and summarization. *Journal of Reading, 31,* 626–631.

Caserta-Henry, C. (1996). Reading buddies: A first-grade intervention program. *The Reading Teacher, 49,* 500–503.

Cazden, C. B. (2001). *Classroom discourse: The language of teaching and learning* (2nd ed.). Portsmouth, NH: Heinemann.

Cecil, N. L. (1997). *For the love of poetry: Literacy scaffolds, extension ideas, and more.* Winnipeg, MB: Portage and Main Press.

Chamot, A. U., & O'Malley, M. (1990). *Learning strategies in second language acquisition.* Cambridge, UK: Cambridge University Press.

Chamot, A. U., & O'Malley, J. M. (1994). *The CALLA handbook: Implementing the cognitive academic language learning approach.* New York: Addison-Wesley.

Ciardiello, A. V. (2004). Democracy's young heroes: An instructional model of critical literacy practices. *The Reading Teacher, 58,* 138–149.

Cintorino, M. A. (1993). Getting together, getting along, getting to the business of teaching and learning. *English Journal, 82,* 23–32.

Clay, M. M. (1991). *Becoming literate: The construction of inner control.* Portsmouth, NH: Heinemann.

Cleary, L. M. (1993). Hobbes: "I press rewind through the pictures in my head." In S. Hudson-Ross, L. M. Cleary, & M. Casey (Eds.), *Children's voices: Children talk about literacy* (pp. 136–143). Portsmouth, NH: Heinemann.

Cobb, C. (2003). Effective instruction begins with purposeful assessments. *The Reading Teacher, 57,* 386–388.

Cohen, K. (1999). Reluctant eighth grade readers enjoy Sustained Silent Reading. *California Reader, 33*(1), 22–25.

Cohle, D. M., & Towle, W. (2001). *Connecting reading and writing in the intermediate grades: A workshop approach.* Newark, DE: International Reading Association.

Cordeiro, P. , Giacobbe, M. E., & Cazden, C. (1983). Apostrophes, quotation marks, and periods: Learning punctuation in the first grade. *Language Arts, 60,* 323–332.

Crawford, A. (2003). Communicative approaches to second-language acquisition: The bridge to second-language literacy. In G. G. Garcia (Ed.), *English learners: Reaching the highest level of English literacy* (pp. 152–180). Newark, DE: International Reading Association.

Culham, R. (2003). *6 + 1 traits of writing: The complete guide, grades 3 and up.* New York: Scholastic.

Cummins, J. (1996). *Negotiating identities: Education for empowerment in a diverse society.* Ontario, CA: California Association for Bilingual Education.

Cunningham, P. M. (2000). *Phonics they use: Words for reading and writing* (3rd ed.). New York: Longman.

Cunningham, P. M., & Cunningham, J. W. (1992). Making words: Enhancing the invented spelling-decoding connection. *The Reading Teacher, 46,* 106–115.

Cunningham, P. M., & Cunningham, J. W. (2002). What we know about how to teach phonics. In A. E. Farstrup & S. J. Samuels (Eds.), *What research has to say about reading instruction* (3rd ed., pp. 87–109). Newark, DE: International Reading Association.

Daniels, H. (2002). *Literature circles: Voice and choice in book clubs and reading groups* (2nd ed.). Portland, ME: Stenhouse.

Day, J., Spiegel, D. L., McLellan, J., & Brown, V. (2002). *Moving forward with literature circles.* New York: Scholastic.

Dias, P. X. (1996). *Reading and responding to poetry: Patterns in the process.* Portsmouth, NH: Boynton/Cook.

Dickinson, D. K., & Tabors, P. O. (2001). *Beginning literacy with language.* Baltimore: Brookes.

Dixon-Krauss, L. (1996). *Vygotsky in the classroom: Mediated literacy instruction and assessment.* White Plains, NY: Longman.

Dorn, L. J., & Soffos, C. (2001). *Shaping literate minds: Developing self-regulated learners.* York, ME: Stenhouse.

Dowhower, S. L. (1991). Speaking of prosody: Fluency's unattended bedfellow. *Theory Into Practice, 30,* 165–173.

Duffy, G. G. (2003). *Explaining reading: A resource for teaching concepts, skills, and strategies.* New York: Guilford Press.

Duthie, C. (1996). *True stories: Nonfiction literacy in the primary classroom.* York, ME: Stenhouse.

Dyson, A. H. (1986). The imaginary worlds of childhood: A multimedia presentation. *Language Arts, 63,* 799–808.

Dyson, A. H. (1997). *Writing superheroes: Contemporary childhood, popular culture, and classroom literacy.* New York: Teachers College Press.

Dyson, A. H. (2001). Relational sense and textual sense in a US urban classroom: The contested case of Emily, girl friend of a ninja. In B. Comber & A. Simpson (Eds.), *Negotiating critical literacies in classrooms* (pp. 3–18). Mahwah, NJ: Erlbaum.

Dyson, A. H. (2003). *The brothers and sisters learn to write: Popular literacies in childhood and school cultures.* New York: Teachers College Press.

Edelsky, C. (1983). Segmentation and punctuation: Developmental data from young writers in a bilingual program. *Research in the Teaching of English, 17,* 135–136.

Eeds, M., & Peterson, R. L. (1995). What teachers need to know about the literary craft. In N. L. Roser & M. G. Martinez (Eds.), *Book talk and beyond: Children and teachers respond to literature* (pp. 10–23). Newark, DE: International Reading Association.

Eeds, M., & Wells, D. (1989). Grand conversations: An exploration of meaning construction in literature study groups. *Research in the Teaching of English, 23,* 4–29.

Egawa, K. (1990). Harnessing the power of language: First graders' literature engagement with *Owl Moon. Language Arts, 67,* 582–588.

Ehri, L. C., Nunes, S. R., Willows, D. M., Schuster, B. V., Yaghoub-Zadeh, Z., & Shanahan, T. (2001). Phonemic awareness instruction helps children learn to read: Evidence from the National Reading Panel's meta-analysis. *Reading Research Quarterly, 36,* 250–287.

Elbow, P. (1973). *Writing without teachers.* London: Oxford University Press.

Elster, C. A., & Hanauer, D. I. (2002). Voicing texts, voices around texts: Reading poems in elementary school classrooms. *Research in the Teaching of English, 37,* 89–134.

Erickson, A. (1985). Listening leads to reading. *Reading Today, 2,* 13.

Ernst, K. (1993). *Picturing learning.* Portsmouth, NH: Heinemann.

Farr, R., & Tone, B. (1994). *Portfolio and performance assessment: Helping students evaluate their progress as readers and writers.* Fort Worth, TX: Harcourt Brace.

Fearn, L., & Farnan, N. (1998). *Writing effectively: Helping children master the conventions of writing.* Boston: Allyn & Bacon.

Fisher, B., & Medvic, E. F. (2000). *Perspectives on shared reading: Planning and practice.* Portsmouth, NH: Heinemann.

Fisher, C. J., & Natarella, M. A. (1982). Young children's preferences in poetry: A national survey of first, second, and third graders. *Research in the Teaching of English, 16,* 339–354.

Fisher, D., Flood, J., Lapp, D., & Frey, N. (2004). Interactive read-alouds: Is there a common set of implementation practices? *The Reading Teacher, 58,* 8–17.

Flavell, J. H. (2001). *Cognitive development* (4th ed.). Upper Saddle River, NJ: Merrill/Prentice Hall.

Fleming, M. (1985). Writing assignments focusing on autobiographical and biographical topics. In M. Fleming & J. McGinnis (Eds.), *Portraits: Biography and autobiography in the secondary school* (pp. 95–97). Urbana, IL: National Council of Teachers of English.

Fleming, M., & McGinnis, J. (Eds.). (1985). *Portraits: Biography and autobiography in the secondary school.* Urbana, IL: National Council of Teachers of English.

Fletcher, R., & Portalupi, J. (1998). *Craft lessons: Teaching writing K–8.* Portland, ME: Stenhouse.

Fletcher, R., & Portalupi, J. (2001). *Writing workshop: The essential guide.* Portsmouth, NH: Heinemann.

Flynt, E. S., & Cooter, R. B., Jr. (2005). Improving middle-grades reading in urban schools: The Memphis Comprehension Framework. *The Reading Teacher, 58,* 774–780.

Foss, A. (2002). Peeling the onion: Teaching critical literacy with students of privilege. *Language Arts, 79,* 393–403.

Foulke, E. (1968). Listening comprehension as a function of word rate. *Journal of Communication, 18,* 198–206.

Fountas, I. C., & Pinnell, G. S. (1996). *Guided reading: Good first teaching for all children.* Portsmouth, NH: Heinemann.

Fountas, I. C., & Pinnell, G. S. (2001). *Guiding readers and writers, grades 3–6.* Portsmouth, NH: Heinemann.

Fox, M. (1988). Notes from the battlefield: Towards a theory of why people write. *Language Arts, 65,* 112–125.

Fox, M. (2001). *Reading magic: Why reading aloud to our children will change their lives forever.* San Diego: Harcourt Brace.

Frank, C. R., Dixon, C. N., & Brandts, L. R. (2001). Bears, trolls, and pagemasters: Learning about learners in book clubs. *The Reading Teacher, 54,* 448–462.

Fraser, I. S., & Hodson, L. M. (1978). Twenty-one kicks at the grammar horse. *English Journal, 67,* 49–53.

Freire, P., & Macedo, D. (1987). *Literacy: Reading the word and the world.* South Hadley, MA: Bergin & Garvey.

Galda, L. (1988). Readers, texts, and contexts: A response-based view of literature in the classroom. *The New Advocate, 1,* 92–102.

Gallagher, K. (2003). *Reading reasons: Motivational mini-lessons for middle and high school.* York, ME: Stenhouse.

Garan, E. (2004). *In defense of our children: When politics, profit, and education collide.* Portsmouth, NH: Heinemann.

Garcia, G. E. (1998). Mexican-American bilingual students' metacognitive reading strategies: What's transferred, unique, problematic? *National Reading Conference Yearbook, 47,* 253–263.

Garcia, G. E. (2003). Reading comprehension development and instruction of English-language learners. In A. P. Sweet & C. E. Snow (Eds.), *Rethinking reading comprehension* (pp. 30–50). New York: Guilford Press.

Gardner, H. (2000). *Intelligence reframed: Multiple intelligences for the 21st century.* New York: Basic Books.

Gentry, J. R., & Gillet, J. W. (1993). *Teaching kids to spell.* Portsmouth, NH: Heinemann.

Gere, A. R., & Abbott, R. D. (1985). Talking about writing: The language of writing groups. *Research in the Teaching of English, 19,* 362–381.

Gibbons, P. (2002). *Scaffolding language, scaffolding learning: Teaching second language learners in the mainstream classroom.* Portsmouth, NH: Heinemann.

Gillet, J. W., & Beverly, L. (2001). *Directing the writing workshop: An elementary teacher's handbook.* New York: Guilford Press.

Giroux, H. (1988). *Teachers as intellectuals: Toward a critical pedagogy of learning.* South Hadley, MA: Bergin & Garvey.

Goldenberg, C. (1992/1993). Instructional conversations: Promoting comprehension through discussion. *The Reading Teacher, 46,* 316–326.

Graves, D. H. (1983). *Writing: Teachers and children at work.* Portsmouth, NH: Heinemann.

Graves, D. H. (1994). *A fresh look at writing.* Portsmouth, NH: Heinemann.

Graves, D., & Hansen, H. (1983). The author's chair. *Language Arts, 60,* 176–183.

Grierson, S. T., Anson, A., & Baird, J. (2002). Exploring the past through multigenre writing. *Language Arts, 80,* 51–59.

Hammerberg, D. E. (2004). Comprehension instruction for socioculturally diverse classrooms: A review of what we know. *The Reading Teacher, 57,* 648–658.

Hancock, M. R. (2004). *A celebration of literature and response: Children, books, and teachers in K–8 classrooms* (2nd ed.). Upper Saddle River, NJ: Merrill/Prentice Hall.

Hansen-Krening, N., Aoki, E. M., & Mizokawa, D. T. (Eds.). (2003). *Kaleidoscope: A multicultural booklist for grades K–8* (4th ed.). Urbana, IL: National Council of Teachers of English.

Harste, J. (1993, April). Inquiry-based instruction. *Primary Voices K–6, 1*, 2–5.

Harste, J. C., Woodward, V. A., & Burke, C. L. (1984). *Language stories and literacy lessons.* Portsmouth, NH: Heinemann.

Harvey, S. (1998). *Nonfiction matters: Reading, writing, and research in grades 3–8.* Portland, ME: Stenhouse.

Heffernan, L. (2004). *Critical literacy and writer's workshop.* Newark, DE: International Reading Association.

Hickman, J. (1980). Children's responses to literature: What happens in the classroom. *Language Arts, 57*, 524–529.

Hillocks, G., Jr., & Smith, M. W. (2003). Grammars and literacy learning. In J. Flood, D. Lapp, J. R. Squire, & J. M. Jensen (Eds.), *Handbook of research on teaching the English language arts* (2nd ed., pp. 721–737). Mahwah, NJ: Erlbaum.

Holdaway, D. (1979). *The foundations of literacy.* Portsmouth, NH: Heinemann.

Hook, J. N. (1975). *History of the English language.* New York: Ronald Press.

Hoyt, L. (1999). *Revisit, reflect, retell: Strategies for improving reading comprehension.* Portsmouth, NH: Heinemann.

Hymes, D. (1972). On communicative competence. In J. B. Pride & J. Holmes (Eds.), *Sociolinguistics* (pp. 269–285). Harmondsworth, Middlesex, UK: Penguin.

Irwin, J. W. (1991). *Teaching reading comprehension processes* (2nd ed.). Boston: Allyn & Bacon.

Ivey, G. (2003). "The teacher makes it more explainable" and other reasons to read aloud in the intermediate grades. *The Reading Teacher, 56*, 812–814.

Ivey, G., & Broaddus, K. (2001). "Just plain reading": A survey of what makes students want to read in middle school classrooms. *Reading Research Quarterly, 36*, 350–377.

Jalongo, M. R. (1991). *Strategies for developing children's listening skills* (Phi Delta Kappan Fastback Series #314). Bloomington, IN: Phi Delta Kappa Educational Foundation.

Johnston, P. (2005). Literacy assessment and the future. *The Reading Teacher, 58*, 684–686.

Karelitz, E. B. (1993). *The author's chair and beyond: Language and literature in a primary classroom.* Portsmouth, NH: Heinemann.

Kaufman, D. (2000). *Conferences and conversations: Listening to the literate classroom.* Portsmouth, NH: Heinemann.

Killgallon, D. (1997). *Sentence composing for middle school.* Portsmouth, NH: Heinemann.

Killgallon, D. (1998). Sentence composing: Notes on a new rhetoric. In C. Weaver (Ed.), *Lessons to share: On teaching grammar in context* (pp. 169–183). Portsmouth, NH: Heinemann.

Koch, K. (1990). *Rose, where did you get that red?* New York: Vintage.

Koch, K. (2000). *Wishes, lies, and dreams.* New York: Harper Perennial.

Krashen, S. (1993). *The power of reading: Insights from the research.* Englewood, CO: Libraries Unlimited.

Krashen, S. (2001). More smoke and mirrors: A critique of the National Reading Panel report on fluency. *Phi Delta Kappan, 83*, 119–123.

Kristo, J. V., & Bamford, R. A. (2004). *Nonfiction in focus.* New York: Scholastic.

Kucer, S. B. (1991). Authenticity as the basis for instruction. *Language Arts, 68*, 532–540.

Kutiper, K. (1985). *A survey of the poetry preferences of seventh, eighth, and ninth graders.* Unpublished doctoral dissertation, University of Houston.

Kutiper, K., & Wilson, P. (1993). Updating poetry preferences: A look at the poetry children really like. *The Reading Teacher, 47*, 28–35.

Labbo, L. D., & Teale, W. H. (1990). Cross-age reading: A strategy for helping poor readers. *The Reading Teacher, 43*, 362–369.

Laberge, D., & Samuels, S. J. (1976). Toward a theory of automatic information processing in reading. In H. Singer & R. Ruddell (Eds.), *Theoretical models and processes of reading* (pp. 548–579). Newark, DE: International Reading Association.

Laminack, L. L., & Wood, K. (1996). *Spelling in use: Looking closely at spelling in whole language classrooms.* Urbana, IL: National Council of Teachers of English.

Landry, D. (1969). The neglect of listening. *Elementary English, 46*, 599–605.

Lane, B. (1993). *After the end: Teaching and learning creative revision.* Portsmouth, NH: Heinemann.

Lehr, S. S. (1991). *The child's developing sense of theme: Responses to literature.* New York: Teachers College Press.

Leland, C. H., Harste, J. C., & Huber, K. R. (2005). Out of the box: Critical literacy in a first-grade classroom. *Language Arts, 82*, 257–268.

Lembo, R. (2000). *Thinking through television.* Cambridge, UK: Cambridge University Press.

Lewin, L. (1992). Integrating reading and writing strategies using an alternating teacher-led/student-selected instructional pattern. *The Reading Teacher, 45*, 586–591.

Lewison, M., Flint, A. S., & Van Sluys, K. (2002). Taking on critical literacy: The journey of newcomers and novices. *Language Arts, 79*, 382–392.

Lipson, E. R. (2000). *The New York Times parent's guide to the best books for children.* New York: Crown/Three Rivers Press.

Loban, W. (1976). *Language development: Kindergarten through grade twelve* (Research Report No. 18). Urbana, IL: National Council of Teachers of English.

Lukens, R. J. (2002). *A critical handbook of children's literature* (7th ed.). Boston: Allyn & Bacon.

Luongo-Orlando, K. (2001). *A project approach to language learning: Linking literary genres and themes in elementary classrooms.* Markham, ON: Pembroke.

Lundsteen, S. W. (1979). *Listening: Its impact on reading and the other language arts* (Rev. ed.). Urbana, IL: National Council of Teachers of English.

Lutz, W. (1997). *The new doublespeak: Why no one knows what anyone's saying anymore.* New York: HarperCollins.

Lyon, G. R., & Chhabra, V. (2004). The science of reading research. *Educational Leadership, 61*(6), 12–17.

Martinez, M. G., & Roser, N. L. (1985). Read it again: The value of repeated readings during storytime. *The Reading Teacher, 38,* 782–786.

Martinez, M. G., & Roser, N. L. (1995). The books make a difference in story talk. In N. L. Roser and M. G. Martinez (Eds.), *Book talk and beyond: Children and teachers respond to literature* (pp. 32–41). Newark, DE: International Reading Association.

Martinez, M., & Teale, W. H. (1988). Reading in a kindergarten classroom library. *The Reading Teacher, 41,* 568–572.

Mazzoni, S. A., & Gambrell, L. B. (2003). Principles of best practice. In L. M. Morrow, L. B. Gambrell, & M. Pressley (Eds.), *Best practices in literacy instruction* (2nd ed., pp. 9–22). New York: Guilford Press.

McCabe, P. P. (2003). Enhancing self-efficacy for high-stakes reading tests. *The Reading Teacher, 57,* 12–20.

McClure, A. M., & Kristo, J. V. (Eds.). (2002). *Adventuring with books: A booklist for pre-K–grade 6* (13th ed.). Urbana, IL: National Council of Teachers of English.

McKenna, M. C., & Stahl, S. A. (2003). *Assessment for reading instruction.* New York: Guilford Press.

McKeown, M. G. (1985). The acquisition of word meaning from context by children of high and low ability. *Reading Research Quarterly, 20,* 482–496.

Morrice, C., & Simmons, M. (1991). Beyond reading buddies: A whole language cross-age program. *The Reading Teacher, 44,* 572–578.

Moss, B., & Hendershot, J. (2002). Exploring sixth graders' selection of nonfiction trade books. *The Reading Teacher, 56,* 6–17.

Muhammad, R. J. (1993). Mario: "It's mostly after I read a book that I write." In S. Hudson-Ross, L. M. Cleary, & M. Casey (Eds.), *Children's voices: Children talk about literacy* (pp. 92–99). Portsmouth, NH: Heinemann.

Murray, D. H. (1982). *Learning by teaching.* Montclair, NJ: Boynton/Cook.

Nagy, W. E. (1988). *Teaching vocabulary to improve reading comprehension.* Urbana, IL: ERIC Clearinghouse on Reading and Communication Skills and the National Council of Teachers of English and the International Reading Association.

National Council of Teachers of English. (1996). Exploring language arts standards within a cycle of learning. *Language Arts, 73,* 10–13.

National Reading Panel. (2000). *Teaching children to read: An evidence-based assessment of the scientific research literature on reading and its implications for reading instruction, reports of the subgroups.* Washington, DC: National Institute of Child Health and Human Development.

Novinger, S., & Compton-Lilly, C. (2005). Telling our stories: Speaking truth to power. *Language Arts, 82,* 195–203.

Nystrand, M., Gamoran, A., & Heck, M. J. (1993). Using small groups for response to and thinking about literature. *English Journal, 82,* 14–22.

Ogle, D. M. (1986). K-W-L: A teaching model that develops active reading of expository text. *The Reading Teacher, 39,* 564–570.

O'Malley, J. M., & Pierce, L. V. (1996). *Authentic assessment for English language learners: Practical approaches for teachers.* Boston: Addison-Wesley.

Opitz, M. F., & Zbaracki, M. D. (2004). *Listen hear! 25 effective comprehension strategies.* Portsmouth, NH: Heinemann.

Owocki, G. (2003). *Comprehension: Strategic instruction for K–3 students.* Portsmouth, NH: Heinemann.

Palmer, R. G., & Stewart, R. A. (2003). Nonfiction trade book use in primary grades. *The Reading Teacher, 57,* 38–48.

Palmer, R. G., & Stewart, R. A. (2005). Models for using nonfiction in the primary grades. *The Reading Teacher, 58,* 426–434.

Pardo, L. S. (2004). What every teacher needs to know about comprehension. *The Reading Teacher, 58,* 272–280.

Paris, S. G., & Jacobs, J. E. (1984). The benefits of informed instruction for children's reading awareness and comprehension skills. *Child Development, 55,* 2083–2093.

Paris, S. G., Wasik, B. A., & Turner, J. C. (1991). The development of strategic readers. In R. Barr, M. L. Kamil, P. B. Mosenthal, & P. D. Pearson (Eds.), *Handbook of reading research* (Vol. 2, pp. 609–640). New York: Longman.

Pearson, P. D., & Fielding, L. (1982). Research update: Listening comprehension. *Language Arts, 59,* 617–629.

Pearson, P. D., & Gallagher, M. (1983). The instruction of reading comprehension. *Contemporary Educational Psychology, 8,* 317–344.

Perl, S. (1994). Understanding composition. In S. Perl (Ed.), *Landmark essays on the writing process* (pp. 99–106). Davis, CA: Heragoras Press.

Perry, N., & Drummond, L. (2002). Helping young students become self-regulated researchers and writers. *The Reading Teacher, 56,* 298–310.

Peterson, R., & Eeds, M. (1990). *Grand conversations: Literature groups in action.* New York: Scholastic.

Pilgreen, J. (2000). *The SSR handbook: How to organize and maintain a Sustained Silent Reading program.* Portsmouth, NH: Heinemann.

Pinnell, G. S., & Jaggar, A. M. (2003). Oral language: Speaking and listening in the classroom. In. J. Flood, D. Lapp, J. R. Squire, & J. M. Jensen (Eds.), *Handbook of research on the teaching of the English language arts* (2nd ed., pp. 881–913). Mahwah, NJ: Erlbaum.

Pressley, M. (1998). *Reading instruction that works: The case for balanced teaching.* New York: Guilford Press.

Pressley, M. (2002). Comprehension strategies instruction: A turn-of-the-century status report. In C. C. Block & M. Pressley (Eds.), *Comprehension instruction: Research-based practices* (pp. 11–27). New York: Guilford Press.

Raphael, T. E. (1986). Teaching question answer relationships, revisited. *The Reading Teacher, 39,* 516–522.

Rasinski, T. V. (2004). Creating fluent readers. *Educational Leadership, 61*(6), 46–51.

Rasinski, T. V., & Padak, N. D. (1990). Multicultural learning through children's literature. *Language Arts, 67,* 576–580.

Rasinski, T., & Padak, N. (2000). *Effective reading strategies: Teaching children who find reading difficult* (2nd ed.). Upper Saddle River, NJ: Merrill/Prentice Hall.

Read, C. (1975). *Children's categorization of speech sounds in English* (NCTE Research Report No. 17). Urbana, IL: National Council of Teachers of English.

Read, C. (1986). *Children's creative spelling.* London: Routledge & Kegan Paul.

Readence, J. E., Bean, T. W., & Baldwin, R. S. (2004). *Content area reading: An integrated approach* (8th ed.). Dubuque, IA: Kendall/Hunt.

Reutzel, D. R., & Fawson, P. C. (1990). Traveling tales: Connecting parents and children in writing. *The Reading Teacher, 44,* 222–227.

Reyes, M. de la L. (1991). A process approach to literacy using dialogue journals and literature logs with second language learners. *Research in the Teaching of English, 25,* 291–313.

Richgels, D. J. (2002). Informational texts in kindergarten. *The Reading Teacher, 55,* 586–595.

Rief, L. (1999). *Vision and voice: Extending the literacy spectrum.* Portsmouth, NH: Heinemann.

Rogovin, P. (2001). *The research workshop: Bringing the world into your classroom.* Portsmouth, NH: Heinemann.

Romano, T. (1995). *Writing with passion: Life stories, multiple genres.* Portsmouth, NH: Boynton/Cook-Heinemann.

Romano, T. (2000). *Blending genre, altering style: Writing multigenre papers.* Portsmouth, NH: Boynton/Cook-Heinemann.

Rosenblatt, L. M. (1978). *The reader, the text, the poem: The transactional theory of the literary work.* Carbondale: Southern Illinois University Press.

Rosenblatt, L. (2005). *Making meaning with texts: Selected essays.* Portsmouth, NH: Heinemann.

Roser, N. L., & Keehn, S. (2002). Fostering thought, talk, and inquiry: Linking literature and social studies. *The Reading Teacher, 55,* 416–426.

Salesi, R. A. (1992). Reading and writing connection: Supporting content-area literacy through nonfiction trade books. In E. B. Freeman & D. G. Person (Eds.), *Using nonfiction trade books in the elementary classroom: From ants to zeppelins* (pp. 86–94). Urbana, IL: National Council of Teachers of English.

Samway, K. D., & McKeon, D. (1999). *Myths and realities: Best practices for language minority students.* Portsmouth, NH: Heinemann.

Scarcella, R. C. (2003). *Accelerating academic English: A focus on the English learner.* Oakland: Regents of the University of California.

Schmitt, M. C. (1990). A questionnaire to measure children's awareness of strategic reading processes. *The Reading Teacher, 43,* 454–461.

Schneider, J. J., & Jackson, S. A. W. (2000). Process drama: A special space and place for writing. *The Reading Teacher, 54,* 38–51.

Scott, J. A., & Nagy, W. E. (2004). Developing word consciousness. In J. F. Baumann & E. J. Kame'enui (Eds.), *Vocabulary instruction: Research to practice* (pp. 201–217). New York: Guilford Press.

Shanahan, T. (2003). Research-based reading instruction: Myths about the National Reading Panel report. *The Reading Teacher, 56,* 646–655.

Shaughnessy, M. P. (1977). *Errors and expectations: A guide for teachers of basic writing.* New York: Oxford University Press.

Short, K., Harste, J., & Burke, C. (1996). *Creating classrooms for authors and inquirers.* Portsmouth, NH: Heinemann.

Silverblatt, A. (2001). *Media literacy: Keys to interpreting media messages* (2nd ed.). Westport, CT: Praeger.

Sipe, L. R. (2002). Talking back and taking over: Young children's expressive engagement during storybook read-alouds. *The Reading Teacher, 55,* 476–483.

Sommers, N. (1994). Revision strategies of student writers and experienced adult writers. In S. Perl (Ed.), *Landmark essays on the writing process* (pp. 75–84). Davis, CA: Heragoras Press.

Sorenson, M. (1993). Teach each other: Connecting talking and writing. *English Journal, 82,* 42–47.

Spandel, V. (2001). *Books, lessons, ideas for teaching the six traits: Writing in the elementary and middle grades.* Wilmington, MA: Great Source Education Group.

Spandel, V. (2005). *Creating writers: Through 6-trait writing assessment and instruction* (4th ed.). Boston: Allyn & Bacon.

Speaker, R. B., Jr., & Speaker, P. R. (1991). Sentence collecting: Authentic literacy events in the classroom. *Journal of Reading, 35,* 92–95.

Spiegel, D. L. (1998). Reader response approaches and the growth of readers. *Language Arts, 76,* 41–48.

Squires, D., & Bliss, T. (2004). Teacher visions: Investigating beliefs about literacy learning. *The Reading Teacher, 57,* 756–763.

Stahl, S. A. (1999). *Vocabulary development.* Cambridge, MA: Brookline Books.

Stanovich, K. E. (1993–1994). Romance and reality. *The Reading Teacher, 47,* 280–291.

Stauffer, R. G. (1980). *The language-experience approach to the teaching of reading* (2nd ed.). New York: Harper & Row.

Steinbergh, J. W. (1993). Chandra: "To live a life of no secrecy." In S. Hudson-Ross, L. M. Cleary, & M. Casey (Eds.), *Children's voices: Children talk about literacy* (pp. 202–214). Portsmouth, NH: Heinemann.

Stewart, M. T. (2003). Building effective practice: Using small discoveries to enhance literacy learning. *The Reading Teacher, 56,* 540–547.

Sticht, T. G., & James, J. H. (1984). Listening and reading. In P. D. Pearson (Ed.), *Handbook of reading research* (pp. 293–318). New York: Longman.

Stien, D., & Beed, P. L. (2004). Bridging the gap between fiction and nonfiction in the literature circle setting. *The Reading Teacher, 57,* 510–518.

Strong, W. (1996). *Writer's toolbox: A sentence-combining workshop.* New York: McGraw-Hill.

Sutton, C. (1998). Helping the nonnative English speaker with reading. In M. F. Opitz (Ed.), *Literacy instruction for culturally and linguistically diverse students* (pp. 81–86). Newark, DE: International Reading Association.

Sweet, A. P. , & Snow, C. E. (2003). Reading for comprehension. In A. P. Sweet and C. E. Snow (Eds.), *Rethinking reading comprehension* (pp. 1–11). New York: Guilford Press.

Taylor, D. (1993). *From the child's point of view.* Portsmouth, NH: Heinemann.

Terry, A. (1974). *Children's poetry preferences: A national survey of upper elementary grades* (NCTE Research Report No. 16). Urbana, IL: National Council of Teachers of English.

Tierney, R. J., & Readence, J. E. (2005). *Reading strategies and practices: A compendium* (6th ed.). Boston: Allyn & Bacon.

Tomlinson, C. A. (2001). *How to differentiate instruction in mixed-ability classrooms* (2nd ed.). Alexandria, VA: Association for Supervision and Curriculum Development.

Tompkins, G. E., & Collom, S. (Eds.). (2004). *Sharing the pen: Interactive writing with young children.* Upper Saddle River, NJ: Merrill/Prentice Hall.

Tompkins, G. E., & Yaden, D. B., Jr. (1986). *Answering students' questions about words.* Urbana, IL: National Council of Teachers of English.

Tovani, C. (2000). *I read it, but I don't get it: Comprehension strategies for adolescent readers.* York, ME: Stenhouse.

Trelease, J. (2001). *The read-aloud handbook* (5th ed.). New York: Penguin.

Valencia, R. R., & Villarreal, B. J. (2003). Improving students' reading performance via standards-based school reform: A critique. *The Reading Teacher, 56,* 612–621.

Valencia, S. W., Hiebert, E. H., & Afflerbach, P. P. (1994). *Authentic reading assessment: Practices and possibilities.* Newark, DE: International Reading Association.

Valentine, S. L. (1986). Beginning poets dig for poems. *Language Arts, 63,* 246–252.

Von Sprecken, D., & Krashen, S. (1998). Do students read during sustained silent reading? *California Reader, 32* (1), 11–13.

Vukelich, C., & Christie, J. (2004). *Building a foundation for preschool literacy: Effective instruction for children's reading and writing development.* Newark, DE: International Reading Association.

Vygotsky, L. S. (1978). *Mind in society.* Cambridge, MA: Harvard University Press.

Vygotsky, L. S. (1986). *Thought and language.* Cambridge, MA: MIT Press.

Wagner, B. J. (1999). *Dorothy Heathcote: Drama as a learning medium* (Rev. ed.). Portsmouth, NH: Heinemann.

Wagner, B. J. (2003). Imaginative expression. In J. Flood, D. Lapp, J. R. Squire, & J. M. Jensen (Eds.), *Handbook of research on teaching the English language arts* (2nd ed., pp. 1008–1025). Mahwah, NJ: Erlbaum.

Watson, K., & Young, B. (2003). Discourse for learning in the classroom. In S. Murphy, & C. Dudley-Marling (Eds.), *Literacy through language arts: Teaching and learning in context* (pp. 39–49). Urbana, IL: National Council of Teachers of English.

Weaver, C. (1994). *Reading process and practice: From sociopsycholinguistics to whole language* (2nd ed.). Portsmouth, NH: Heinemann.

Weaver, C. (1996). *Teaching grammar in context.* Portsmouth, NH: Heinemann.

Weaver, C., McNally, C., & Moerman, S. (2001). To grammar or not to grammar: That is not the question! *Voices From the Middle, 8*(3), 17–33.

Whitin, P. E. (1996). *Sketching stories, stretching minds.* Portsmouth, NH: Heinemann.

Wilde, S. (1993). *You kan red this! Spelling and punctuation for whole language classrooms, K–6.* Portsmouth, NH: Heinemann.

Wilkinson, L. C. (1984). Research currents: Peer group talk in elementary school. *Language Arts, 61,* 164–169.

Wilson, L. (1994). *Write me a poem: Reading, writing, and performing poetry.* Portsmouth, NH: Heinemann.

Wilson, P. , Martens, P. , & Arya, P. (2005). Accountability for reading and readers: What the numbers don't tell. *The Reading Teacher, 58,* 622–631.

Wink, J. (2000). *Critical pedagogy: Notes from the real world* (2nd ed.). New York: Longman.

Wittrock, M. C., & Alesandrini, K. (1990). Generation of summaries and analogies and analytic and holistic abilities. *American Research Journal, 27,* 489–502.

Wolvin, A. D., & Coakley, C. G. (1995). *Listening* (5th ed.). New York: McGraw-Hill.

Wong-Fillmore, L., & Snow, C. E. (2002). What teachers need to know about language. In C. T. Adger, C. E. Snow, & D. Christian (Eds.), *What teachers need to know about language* (pp. 7–54). Washington, DC: Center for Applied Linguistics.

Wright, J. W. (Ed.). (2004). *The New York Times 2005 almanac.* New York: Penguin.

Yaden, D. B., Jr. (1988). Understanding stories through repeated read-alouds: How many does it take? *The Reading Teacher, 41,* 556–560.

Yokota, J. (1993). Issues in selecting multicultural children's literature. *Language Arts, 70,* 156–167.

Yopp, H. K. (1992). Developing phonemic awareness in young children. *The Reading Teacher, 45,* 696–703.

Yopp, H. K., & Yopp, R. H. (2001). *Literature-based reading activities* (3rd ed.). Boston: Allyn & Bacon.

## Children's Book References

Agran, R. (2003). *Pumpkin shivaree.* Brooklyn, NY: Handprint Books.

Alarcón, F. X. (1998). *From the bellybutton of the moon and other summer poems/Del ombligo de la luna y otros poemas de verano.* San Francisco: Children's Book Press.

Allard, H. (1977). *Miss Nelson is missing!* Boston: Houghton Mifflin.

Avi. (2002). *Crispin: The cross of lead*. New York: Hyperion Books.

Aylesworth, J. (1992). *Old black fly*. New York: Henry Holt.

Babbitt, N. (1988). *Tuck everlasting*. New York: Farrar, Straus & Giroux.

Back, C., & Olesen, J. (1986). *Chicken and egg*. Morristown, NJ: Silver Burdett.

Bang, M. (2004). *My light*. New York: Scholastic.

Berenstain, S., & Berenstain, J. (2002). *Down a sunny dirt road*. New York: Random House.

Blume, J. (1972). *Tales of a fourth grade nothing*. New York: Dutton.

Brett, J. (1999). *The gingerbread baby*. New York: Putnam.

Brett, J. (2004). *The umbrella*. New York: Putnam.

Bunting, E. (1992). *Red fox running*. New York: Clarion Books.

Bunting, E. (1994). *Smoky night*. San Diego: Harcourt Brace.

Byrd, R. (2003). *Leonardo: Beautiful dreamer*. New York: Dutton.

Carle, E. (2004). *Mister seahorse*. New York: Philomel.

Carson, L. M. (1998). *Sol a sol: Bilingual poems*. New York: Henry Holt.

Cheney, L. (2002). *America: A patriotic primer*. New York: Simon & Schuster.

Choi, Y. (2001). *The name jar*. New York: Knopf.

Christensen, B. (2001). *Woody Guthrie: Poet of the people*. New York: Knopf.

Cleary, B. (1993). *Ralph the mouse*. New York: Morrow.

Cleary, B. P. (2000). *Hairy, scary, ordinary: What is an adjective?* Minneapolis: Carolrhoda.

Climo, S. (1999). *The Persian Cinderella*. New York: HarperCollins.

Cole, J. (1996). *The magic school bus inside a hurricane*. New York: Scholastic.

Cole, J. (2001). *The magic school bus explores the senses*. New York: Scholastic.

Cole, W. (1983). *Poem stew*. New York: HarperCollins.

Coman, C. (1995). *What Jamie saw*. Arden, NC: Front Street.

Cooney, C. (1990). *The face on the milk carton*. New York: Bantam.

Cormier, R. (1977). *I am the cheese*. New York: Knopf.

Coville, B. (1991). *Jeremy Thatcher, dragon hatcher*. San Diego: Harcourt Brace.

Cowcher, H. (1990). *Antarctica*. New York: Farrar, Straus & Giroux.

Creech, S. (2001). *Love that dog*. New York: HarperCollins.

Crew, G. (1998). *Troy Thompson's excellent peotry [sic] book*. Victoria, Australia: Lothian.

Cronin, D. (2000). *Click, clack, moo: Cows that type*. New York: Simon & Schuster.

Cushman, K. (1994). *Catherine, called Birdy*. New York: HarperCollins.

Cushman, K. (2003). *Rodzina*. New York: Clarion Books.

Dahl, R. (1964). *Charlie and the chocolate factory*. New York: Knopf.

Dahl, R. (1982). *The BFG*. New York: Knopf.

Dakos, K. (1995). *Mrs. Cole on an onion roll and other school poems*. New York: Aladdin Books.

Dakos, K. (2003). *Put your eyes up here: And other school poems*. New York: Simon & Schuster.

Danziger, P. (1994). *Amber Brown is not a crayon*. New York: Putnam.

Deedy, C. A. (2000). *The yellow star: The legend of King Christian X of Denmark*. Atlanta: Peachtree.

Demi. (1997). *One grain of rice: A mathematical folktale*. New York: Scholastic.

dePaola, T. (2002). *What a year*. New York: Putnam.

DiCamillo, K. (2003). *The tale of Despereaux, being the story of a mouse, a princess, some soup, and a spool of thread*. Cambridge, MA: Candlewick Press.

Dotlich, R. K. (2003). *In the spin of things: Poetry in motion*. Honesdale, PA: Boyds Mills Press.

Edwards, P. D. (1996). *Some smug slug*. New York: HarperCollins.

Edwards, P. D. (2001). *Clara caterpillar*. New York: HarperCollins.

Edwards, P. D. (2003a). *Rosie's roses*. New York: HarperCollins.

Edwards, P. D. (2003b). *The worrywarts*. New York: HarperCollins.

Egielski, R. (2000). *The gingerbread boy*. New York: HarperCollins.

Ellis, D. (2000). *The breadwinner*. Toronto, ON: Groundwood Books.

Fleischman, P. (1988). *Joyful noise: Poems for two voices*. New York: Harper & Row.

Fleischman, P. (1997). *Seedfolks*. New York: HarperCollins.

Fleischman, P. (2000). *Big talk: Poems for four voices*. Cambridge, MA: Candlewick Press.

Fletcher, R. (2002). *Poetry matters: Writing a poem from the inside out*. New York: HarperCollins.

Florian, D. (2003). *Bow wow meow meow: It's rhyming cats and dogs*. Orlando: Harcourt Brace.

Forman, M. H. (1997). *From wax to crayon: A photo essay*. New York: Children's Press.

Franco, B. (2003). *Mathematickles!* New York: McElderry.

Fritz, J. (1995). *You want women to vote, Lizzie Stanton?* New York: Putnam.

Fritz, J. (2004). *The lost colony of Roanoke*. New York: Putnam.

Galdone, P. (1972). *The three bears*. New York: Seabury.

Galdone, P. (1974). *Little Red Riding Hood*. New York: McGraw-Hill.

Galdone, P. (1975). *The gingerbread boy*. New York: Seabury.

Galdone, P. (1983). *The gingerbread boy*. New York: Clarion Books.

Galdone, P. (1985). *Little Red Hen*. New York: Clarion Books.

Gardiner, J. R. (1980). *Stone Fox*. New York: HarperCollins.

George, J. C. (1972). *Julie of the wolves*. New York: HarperCollins.

George, J. C. (1990). *One day in the tropical rain forest*. New York: HarperCollins.

Gibbons, G. (1994). *Nature's green umbrella: Tropical rain forests*. New York: Morrow.

Gordon, R. (Sel.). (1993). *Peeling the onion: An anthology of poems*. New York: HarperCollins.

Gregory, K. (1996). *The winter of red snow: The Revolutionary diary of Abigail Jane Stewart, Valley Forge, 1777*. New York: Scholastic.

Guiberson, B. Z. (1991). *Cactus hotel*. New York: Henry Holt.

Heller, R. (1991). *Up, up and away: A book about adverbs*. New York: Grosset & Dunlap.

Heller, R. (1997). *Mine, all mine: A book about pronouns*. New York: Grosset & Dunlap.

Henkes, K. (1991). *Chrysanthemum*. New York: Greenwillow.

Henkes, K. (2004). *Kitten's first full moon*. New York: Greenwillow.

Hermes, P. (2000). *Our strange new land: Elizabeth's diary, Jamestown, 1609*. New York: Scholastic.

Herrera, J. F. (1998). *Laughing out loud, I fly*. New York: HarperCollins.

Herrera, J. F. (2003). *Super cilantro girl*. San Francisco: Children's Book Press.

Hesse, K. (2001). *Witness*. New York: Scholastic.

Hiaasen, C. (2002). *Hoot*. New York: Knopf.

Hinton, S. E. (1967). *The outsiders*. New York: Viking.

Hong, L. T. (1993). *Two of everything: A Chinese folktale*. New York: Albert Whitman.

Howard, E. F. (1991). *Aunt Flossie's hats (and crab cakes later)*. New York: Clarion Books.

Howe, D., & Howe, J. (1979). *Bunnicula: A rabbit-tale of mystery*. New York: Atheneum.

Hurd, T. (2003). *Moo Cow kaboom!* New York: HarperCollins.

Hutchins, P. (1968). *Rosie's walk*. New York: Macmillan.

Janeczko, P. B. (1994). *Poetry from A to Z: A guide for young writers*. New York: Bradbury Press.

Kasza, K. (1987). *The wolf's chicken stew*. New York: Putnam.

Katz, A. (2001). *Take me out of the bathtub and other silly dilly songs*. New York: McElderry.

Keller, L. (1998). *The scrambled states of America*. New York: Henry Holt.

Kimmel, E. A. (2000). *The runaway tortilla*. Delray Beach, FL: Winslow Press.

King-Smith, D. (2002). *Chewing the cud*. New York: Knopf.

Klise, K. (1998). *Regarding the fountain: A tale, in letters, of liars and leaks*. New York: Avon.

Klise, K. (2004). *Regarding the sink: Where, oh where, did Waters go?*. San Diego: Harcourt Brace.

Kraft, B. H. (2003). *Theodore Roosevelt: Champion of the American spirit*. New York: Clarion Books.

Kuskin, K. (2003). *Moon, have you met my mother? The collected poems of Karla Kuskin*. New York: HarperCollins.

Lee, C. (2004). *Good dog, Paw!* Cambridge, MA: Candlewick Press.

Lee, H. (1960). *To kill a mockingbird*. Philadelphia: Lippincott.

Leedy, L. (1993). *Postcards from Pluto: A tour of the solar system*. New York: Holiday House.

L'Engle, M. (1962). *A wrinkle in time*. New York: Farrar, Straus & Giroux.

Levy, E. (1992). *. . . . If you were there when they signed the Constitution*. New York: Scholastic.

L'Hommedieu, A. J. (1997). *From plant to blue jeans: A photo essay*. New York: Children's Press.

Lobel, A. (1979a). *Frog and Toad are friends*. New York: Harper & Row.

Lobel, A. (1979b). *Frog and Toad together*. New York: Harper & Row.

Longfellow, H. W. (2001). *The midnight ride of Paul Revere*. Brooklyn, NY: Handprint Books.

Look, L. (2004). *Ruby Lu, brave and true*. New York: Atheneum.

Louie, A. (1982). *Yeh-Shen: A Cinderella story from China*. New York: Philomel.

Lowry, L. (1979). *Anastasia Krupnik*. Boston: Houghton Mifflin.

Lowry, L. (1989). *Number the stars*. Boston: Houghton Mifflin.

Lowry, L. (1993). *The giver*. Boston: Houghton Mifflin.

Macaulay, D. (1990). *Black and white*. Boston: Houghton Mifflin.

Macaulay, D. (2003). *Mosque*. Boston: Houghton Mifflin.

MacLachlan, P. (1985). *Sarah, plain and tall*. New York: HarperCollins.

Martin, B. Jr., & Archambault, J. (1989). *Chicka chicka boom boom*. New York: Simon & Schuster.

McElligott, M. (2004). *Absolutely not!* New York: Walker.

McKissack, P. C. (1986). *Flossie and the fox*. New York: Dial Books.

Meddaugh, S. (1995). *Martha speaks*. Boston: Houghton Mifflin.

Montenegro, L. N. (2003). *A bird about to sing*. Boston: Houghton Mifflin.

Morimoto, J. (1987). *My Hiroshima*. New York: Viking.

Morris, A. (1989). *Bread, bread, bread*. New York: HarperCollins.

Naylor, P. R. (1991). *Shiloh*. New York: Atheneum.

Naylor, P. R. (1996). *Shiloh season*. New York: Atheneum.

Naylor, P. R. (1997). *Saving Shiloh*. New York: Atheneum.

Numeroff, L. J. (1985). *If you give a mouse a cookie*. New York: Harper & Row.

Numeroff, L. J. (1993). *Dogs don't wear sneakers*. New York: Simon & Schuster.

Numeroff, L. J. (1995). *Chimps don't wear glasses*. New York: Simon & Schuster.

Numeroff, L. J. (2002). *If you take a mouse to school*. New York: HarperCollins.

Nye, N. S. (1995). *The tree is older than you are*. New York: Simon & Schuster.

Osborne, M. P. (1993). *The knight at dawn*. New York: Random House.

Osborne, W., & Osborne, M. (2000). *Knights and castles*. New York: Random House.

Paterson, K. (1977). *Bridge to Terabithia*. New York: HarperCollins.

Paterson, K. (1978). *The great Gilly Hopkins*. New York: Crowell.

Paulsen, G. (1987). *Hatchet*. New York: Viking.

Pfeffer, W. (2003). *Dolphin talk: Whistles, clicks, and clapping jaws.* New York: HarperCollins.

Pinkney, A. D. (1993). *Seven candles for Kwanzaa.* New York: Dial Books.

Polacco, P. (1990). *Thunder cake.* New York: Philomel.

Prelutsky, J. (1984). *The new kid on the block.* New York: Greenwillow.

Prelutsky, J. (1996). *A pizza the size of the sun: Poems.* New York: Greenwillow.

Prelutsky, J. (1999). *The 20th century children's poetry treasury.* New York: Knopf.

Prelutsky, J. (2000). *The Random House book of poetry for children.* New York: Random House.

Provensen, A. (1995). *My fellow Americans: A family album.* San Diego: Harcourt Brace.

Pulver, R. (2003). *Punctuation takes a vacation.* New York: Holiday House.

Rappaport, D. (2001). *Martin's big words: The life of Dr. Martin Luther King, Jr.* New York: Hyperion Books.

Rathmann, P. (1995). *Officer Buckle and Gloria.* New York: Putnam.

Reid, M. E. (1996). *Let's find out about ice cream.* New York: Scholastic.

Ride, S., & O'Shaughnessy, T. (2003). *Exploring our solar system.* New York: Crown.

Rodgers, M. (1972). *Freaky Friday.* New York: HarperCollins.

Rowling, J. K. (1998). *Harry Potter and the sorcerer's stone.* New York: Levine.

Rowling, J. K. (2002). *Harry Potter and the goblet of fire.* New York: Scholastic.

Rubin, S. G. (2003). *Searching for Anne Frank: Letters from Amsterdam to Iowa.* New York: Abrams.

Ryan, P. M. (2000). *Esperanza rising.* New York: Scholastic.

Rylant, C. (1992). *Missing May.* New York: Orchard Books.

Sachar, L. (1998). *Holes.* New York: Farrar, Straus & Giroux.

Scieszka, J. (1989). *The true story of the 3 little pigs!* New York: Viking.

Scieszka, J. (2004). *Science verse.* New York: Viking.

Sendak, M. (1988). *Where the wild things are.* New York: HarperCollins.

Shapiro, K. J. (2003). *Because I could not stop my bike: And other poems.* Watertown, MA: Charlesbridge.

Siebert, D. (1991). *Sierra.* New York: HarperCollins.

Silverstein, S. (1974). *Where the sidewalk ends.* New York: Harper & Row.

Silverstein, S. (1981). *A light in the attic.* New York: Harper & Row.

Simon, S. (2003). *Spiders.* New York: HarperCollins.

Singer, M. (2004). *Creature carnival.* New York: Hyperion Books.

Smith, C. R., Jr. (2003). *Hoop queens.* Cambridge, MA: Candlewick Press.

Smith, R. K. (1972). *Chocolate fever.* New York: Dell.

Soto, G. (1987). *The cat's meow.* New York: Scholastic.

Soto, G. (1992). *Neighborhood odes.* San Diego: Harcourt Brace.

Soto, G. (1993). *Too many tamales.* New York: Putnam.

Soto, G. (1995). *Canto familiar.* San Diego: Harcourt Brace.

Speare, E. G. (1983). *The sign of the beaver.* Boston: Houghton Mifflin.

Spinelli, J. (1990). *Maniac Magee.* Boston: Little, Brown.

Steig, W. (1988). *Sylvester and the magic pebble.* New York: Simon & Schuster.

Steptoe, J. (1987). *Mufaro's beautiful daughters: An African tale.* New York: Lothrop, Lee & Shepard.

Stevens, J., & Crummel, S. S. (1999). *Cook-a-doodle-doo!* San Diego: Harcourt Brace.

Stevens, J., & Crummel, S. S. (2003). *Jackalope.* San Diego: Harcourt Brace.

Stevenson, J. (1998). *Popcorn.* New York: Greenwillow.

Taylor, T. (1969). *The cay.* Garden City, NY: Doubleday.

Terban, M. (1996). *Scholastic dictionary of idioms: More than 600 phrases, sayings, & expressions.* New York: Scholastic.

Van Allsburg, C. (1981). *Jumanji.* Boston: Houghton Mifflin.

Van Allsburg, C. (1985). *The polar express.* Boston: Houghton Mifflin.

Viorst, J. (1981). *If I were in charge of the world and other worries: Poems for children and their parents.* New York: Atheneum.

Vyner, T. (1994). *The tree.* New York: Barron's.

Watts, B. (1990). *Honeybee.* Englewood Cliffs, NJ: Silver Burdett.

Whatley, B. (2001). *Wait! No paint!* New York: HarperCollins.

Wheeler, L. (2002). *Sailor Moo: Cow at sea.* New York: Atheneum.

Whelan, G. (2000). *Homeless bird.* New York: Scholastic.

White, E. B. (1980). *Charlotte's web.* New York: HarperCollins.

White, E. E. (2001). *Kaiulani: The people's princess, Hawaii, 1889.* New York: Scholastic.

Williams, V. B. (1982). *A chair for my mother.* New York: Greenwillow.

Wong, J. S. (2002). *You have to write.* New York: McElderry.

Woodson, J. (2003). *Locomotion.* New York: Putnam.

Yep, L. (2000). *The journal of Wong Ming-Ching: A Chinese miner, California, 1852.* New York: Scholastic.

Yolen, J. (1987). *Owl moon.* New York: Philomel.

Yolen, J. (1992). *Encounter.* Orlando: Harcourt Brace.

Yorinks, A. (1986). *Hey, Al.* New York: Farrar, Straus & Giroux.

Zemach, M. (1983). *The Little Red Hen: An old story.* New York: Farrar, Straus & Giroux.

# Index